INFLUENCE AND POWER

Law and Philosophy Library

VOLUME 68

INFLUENCE AND POWER

Variations on a Messy Theme

by

RUTH ZIMMERLING

Johannes-Gutenberg-Universität,
Mainz, Germany

Springer

A C.I.P. Catalogue record for this book is available from the Library of Congress.

ISBN-10 1-4020-2986-1 (HB)
ISBN-10 1-4020-2994-2 (e-book)
ISBN-13 978-1-4020-2986-8 (HB)
ISBN-13 978-1-4020-2994-3 (e-book)

Published by Springer,
P.O. Box 17, 3300 AA Dordrecht, The Netherlands.

www.springeronline.com

Printed on acid-free paper

Printed in the Netherlands.

To Charlotte W. and Robert S. Chadima,
and to Sue, Sarah, and David,
my exchange family from Cedar Rapids,
to whose influence I owe so much.

TABLE OF CONTENTS

ACKNOWLEDGMENTS

Without the support and cooperation of a great number of people, this book would have turned out much worse, if at all. Over the past decade or so, I have greatly benefited from discussions with participants and audiences of seminars, workshops, and conferences in Alicante, Bamberg, Barcelona, Bonn, Caracas, Darmstadt, Genoa, Mexico City, Tampere, and Vaquerías (Argentina), which bore upon the topics treated here, and I am most grateful to them all.

My colleagues, at the University of Bamberg first and at Darmstadt University of Technology later, contributed more than a fair share of support throughout the gestation period of this study: they listened repeatedly to my (often rather confused) attempts to formulate my thoughts, and paid some of the opportunity costs when I had to neglect my institutional obligations with them in order to get on with my project. In both conditions, they were extraordinarily benevolent and patient – a disposition of which I have always been gratefully aware. I am particularly indebted to Reinhard Zintl and Rainer Schmalz-Bruns who read a previous version of the manuscript and provided very helpful criticism and advice. I also profited from stimulating electronic discussions on freedom and power with Kristján Kristjánsson. Special thanks go to the Research Institute for Social Sciences at the University of Tampere, above all to its former director Aulis Aarnio, for a most generous invitation to a visiting scholarship at the Institute in the spring of 1999.

As usual, my greatest debt is with Ernesto Garzón Valdés. He has been the provider and the backbone of most of the international academic network I have been privileged to become a part of over the past years; but his most important assistance was his own: perspicacious questions, innumerable hours of discussion freely donated whenever my answers were not satisfactory (often), advice and encouragement when I got stuck in the details (no less often), and the permanent challenge of his example as a first-rate analytical philosopher with an altogether uncommon ability to take fresh looks at old topics, overcome sterile orthodoxies and provide surprising new insights. My debt with him is beyond cancellation.

To Francisco Laporta and all co-editors of the *Law and Philosophy Library*, I am extremely grateful for accepting this work in their prestigious series.

This is a book about influence and my first book in English, so it is, finally, a fitting work to dedicate to my wonderful 'second family', Charlotte W. and Robert S. Chadima, and Susan, Sarah and David. They had me as an exchange student in 1971/72 and ever since, gave me a New World in more than one sense, and have had a deeper, more lasting influence on this Old European than they will imagine – for which I can never thank them enough.

Mainz, December 2003 Ruth Zimmerling

INTRODUCTION

Some years ago, on request of the German Political Science Association (DVPW), an empirical investigation „On the state and the orientation of political science in the Federal Republic of Germany“ was conducted by Carl Böhret. Among other interesting information, in the paper that was subsequently published[1] the author presented the results of a survey among 254 political scientists in the Federal Republic on what they considered to be the *sine qua non* basic concepts of the discipline. In various respects, the data are remarkable.

On the one hand, the enormous diversity of the answers[2] corroborates statistically what has long been known from experience, i. e., the existence of an extremely wide variety of standpoints, perspectives, and approaches within the discipline. An interesting case in point is the concept of *power*. Somewhat surprisingly, 'power' was not *the* most frequently mentioned term. But, it did, of course, end up at the very top of the list, in third place behind 'conflict' and 'interest'. What is noteworthy is that it gained this position by being named only 81 times, that is, by less than a third of the respondents. This is no insignificant detail. Certainly, to that minority of scholars whose conceptions of politics do include 'power' as an indispensable basic concept, the approaches of the vast majority of their colleagues for whom, as their answers in the survey reveal, 'power' does not play an eminent role must appear, in an important sense, mistaken or perhaps even incomprehensible.[3]

On the other hand, even more remarkable for the present purpose is the fact that (only) about one in eight political scientists in the survey also considered *influence* to be among those *sine qua non* basic concepts (34 mentions). Although the percentage is not very high,[4] it still placed 'influence' in position 14 of the over-all frequency-ranking of all terms mentioned.[5]

[1] Böhret 1985.

[2] Ibid., 307: Out of a total of 639 different terms given by the 206 tenured professors of political science who returned the questionnaire, more than two thirds (414) were mentioned only once, and another 13,5% twice; hence, less than 20% of all terms were mentioned by more than just two of the respondents. The distribution for the 48 untenured scholars whose answers were recorded separately was almost exactly the same.

[3] This must be the case, to mention just one variant, of anyone who agrees with Lasswell's and Kaplan's assessment that „The concept of power is perhaps the most fundamental in the whole of political science: the political process is the shaping, distribution, and exercise of power [...] However broadly the scope of the subject may be defined, power is always included [...]“ (Lasswell/Kaplan 1950, 75).

[4] In exact numbers, while for 'power' the percentage was 32,0% for the tenured and 31,3% for the untenured scholars, for 'influence' it was 12,6% for the former and 16,7% for the latter. Ibid., 310.

[5] Ibid., 308; for the two groups separately, it was rank 14 for the senior, and rank 9,5 for the junior scholars.

Assuming that regarding the question of relevant concepts the German sample can be taken to be more or less representative of political scientists in general,[6] from these simple statistical data we can draw the equally simple conclusions that

> *(1)* 'influence' is thought to be an important concept (and therefore, it may be assumed, its empirical reference is considered to be an important political phenomenon) by a substantial percentage of political scientists, and
>
> *(2)* to many political scientists, 'influence' and 'power' apparently mean different things (if it were otherwise, the significantly different results for the two terms in the survey could hardly be explained).

Both conclusions are confirmed by leafing through any collection of political science scholarship: the term 'influence' is used profusely in the literature; and very frequently, authors speak of both 'power' *and* 'influence', often even using the conjunctive formula 'power and influence', thus implying that the terms designate different, though perhaps closely related things.[7]

At least on one conception, this prominent role of 'influence' in political science should not come as a surprise. According to this view, indeed, the term must be expected to be ubiquitous in *all* social science, since *whenever* we are dealing with people in situations of interaction, we would be dealing with influence phenomena. The following quotation exemplifies that perspective:

„Surely it is inappropriate to think of the chooser as a social isolate uninfluenced by others. Indeed, *both influencing and being influenced are part of every situation.*"[8]

A similarly broad conception also seems to be at the basis of Banfield's well-known view that politics as such consists mainly of influence relations. In his own words:

„*Any co-operative activity* [...] *may be viewed as a system of influence* [...] Government, from this standpoint, consists of acts of influence [...] To study the patterns of influence by which action is concerted in public matters is to study government."[9]

But one does not need to share this extremely broad conception to expect a strong presence of influence – understood in the vague sense of ordinary usage –, if not in all social situations, then at least in the realm of politics. Because one may just as well argue that it is due to a *substantial* peculiarity of that field (rather than to a *structural* feature of all situations of interaction or cooperation, including political ones) that „The study of politics is the study of influence and the influential", as Lasswell[10] categorically asserted, or,

[6] According to Böhret, „adequate representativity" with respect to the main subdisciplines was guaranteed. Ibid., 220 f.

[7] Unless, of course, one assumes that political scientists, and not only they, have a peculiar, widely shared predilection for using a hendiadys when speaking of power (or influence?).

[8] Wildavsky 1994, 155 (emphasis added).

[9] Banfield 1961, 3 f. (emphasis added).

[10] 1936, 13; quoted from Dunleavy/O'Leary 1987, 137.

somewhat less radically, that „Just as politics is a constant struggle for power, it is at the same time also a constant struggle for the more effective influence“.[11]

In any case, whether for structural or for substantial reasons, the view that, to a great extent, politics consists of, or involves, influence phenomena, is prominent in the discipline.

This is also the case with the other idea clearly expressed in the last quotation, i. e., the assumption that in politics power and influence go hand in hand. A few examples may suffice to support this claim:[12]

* In 1979, Kurt Meier published a doctoral thesis about *Interest, Power and Influence* – a study the purpose of which, in the author's own words, is to investigate „what constellation of circumstances determines whether an organization is able to impose its claims on government. [... T]he question at the center of this work [...] is: Can the concepts of interest, *power and influence* be elucidated and shown to be useful with respect to that problem?“[13]
* More recently, Herbert von Arnim has come to the conclusion that „in the Federal Republic of Germany, *the power and influence of political parties* are particularly broad and comprehensive“.[14]
* Sheldon Wolin has called attention to special opportunities in pluralistic political systems for „*exercising power and influence* incognito“.[15]
* Gabriel Almond once pointed out that Robert Dahl „seems to maintain [...] his long-standing view that causation is fundamental to understanding *power and influence relations*“.[16]
* Edward Laumann and David Knoke have claimed that „*The distribution of power and influence* in a given system of collective decision making becomes fully interpenetrated over time“.[17]
* Steven Lukes posed „The question of whether rational persuasion is *a form of power and influence*“.[18]
* Russell Hanson has recalled the times when „'the people' sought and gained *power and influence* in the name of democracy“.[19]

[11] Schütt-Wetschky 1990, 33: „So wie Politik ein ständiger Kampf um Macht ist, so ist sie zugleich auch ein ständiger Kampf um den wirksameren Einfluß.“

[12] Here and in what follows, the examples are taken more or less randomly from political science literature; the list could easily be prolonged.

[13] Meier 1979, 2 (emphasis added): „[U]ntersucht werden soll, von welcher Konstellation von Umständen es abhängt, ob eine Organisation Forderungen gegenüber einer Regierung durchzusetzen in der Lage ist. [...] die im Zentrum dieser Arbeit stehende Frage [...] lautet: Lassen sich die Konzepte Interesse, Macht und Einfluß im Hinblick auf dieses Bezugs-Problem erläutern und als nützlich erweisen?“

[14] Von Arnim 1993, 13 (emphasis added): „Macht und Einfluß der politischen Parteien sind in der Bundesrepublik Deutschland besonders weitgehend und umfassend.“

[15] Wolin 1993, 468 f. (emphasis added).

[16] Almond 1990, 44 (emphasis added).

[17] Laumann/Knoke 1987, 162 (emphasis added).

[18] Lukes 1991, 31 f. (emphasis added).

[19] Hanson 1989, 69 (emphasis added).

* Anne Phillips argues that advocates of deliberative democracy expect that in the process of deliberation „Those who had previously monopolized positions of *power and influence* might be [...] encouraged to recognize their partiality and bias“.[20]

* Ursula Hoffmann-Lange has examined the „assumption of the institutional consolidation of *power and influence opportunities*“.[21]

* And Gerald Dworkin, known as a very analytically-minded moral and political philosopher, tells us that in the infamous Abscam scandal, the main charge against Senator Harrison Williams was that he had promised a business partner to „use his *power and influence* to obtain government contracts“.[22]

In view of this prominent role of 'influence' in the opinions and writings of scholars, one should expect that the conceptual question has long been solved satisfactorily, either in general – in the sense that by now we would have an explicit common understanding of the term – or at least by each author in particular – in the sense of a consistent use within each scholar's work, ideally based on an explicit definition. In fact, however, there still seems to be anything but clarity, not to speak of a consensus, with respect to the concept of 'influence' in general, or 'political influence' in particular.[23]

Although the unproblematic use of the term 'influence' in ordinary language suggests that there must be some shared understanding of its meaning, this common core is hard to pin down with any degree of precision. And as for specific social-scientific definitions, opinions range from the extreme view that the concept of 'influence' is „one of the most complex of concepts in social analysis“[24] to the other extreme of defining it in a very casual way – as when Habermas, for example, in the context of his critique of Parsons's concepts of power and influence,[25] matter-of-factly notes that „We can translate influence approximately with 'prestige' or 'reputation'“.[26]

Even a superficial screening of the pertinent literature readily reveals what is probably the greatest, and most widely diffused problem with 'influence' in political science, namely, the insufficient delimitation of this concept from that of 'power'.[27]

[20] Phillips 1995, 152 (emphasis added).

[21] Hoffmann-Lange 1992, 86 (emphasis added): „[... die] Annahme der institutionellen Verfestigung von Macht- und Einflußchancen“.

[22] G. Dworkin 1988c, 146 (emphasis added).

[23] It was surely not by arbitrary choice that Judith Gillespie illustrated her point that conceptual precision is one of the most important „missing elements in political inquiry“ with references to the use of 'influence' and 'power': „The missing element in a great deal of political inquiry is precision. [...] One need only look at most of the studies of power and influence [...] The words 'heart attack' are a lot like the word influence; both can mean a great many things“ (Gillespie 1982, 16 f.).

[24] Verba et al. 1987, 159.

[25] Habermas 1988/2, 385–419.

[26] Ibid., 410: „Einfluß können wir ungefähr mit 'Prestige' oder 'Reputation' [...] übersetzen.“ This is not only a very casual, but also a very unsatisfactory approach to the concept of influence. At least in common usage, while influence may (often) be linked with prestige or reputation, the words obviously do not mean the same. This can easily be seen by trying to use them interchangeably.

[27] Again, the following examples are taken randomly from the literature; they are intended to illustrate common conceptual deficits, not to point out particular flaws in the writings of particular individual authors. The sources are given here only in order to comply with scientific standards. – For a similar diagnosis concerning sociology, cf., e. g., Lenski 1986, 252, n 7: „In many sociological writings the relationship between power

i) Some authors do not distinguish between the two terms at all.[28] This practice poses no problem, of course, as long as it is explicitly acknowledged and argued for, as in the case of Robert Dahl who, in his classical analysis of „The Concept of Power", explains that for his purpose in that particular essay there is no need to distinguish between the terms:

„There is a long and honorable history attached to such words as power, influence, control, and authority. For a great many purposes, it is highly important that a distinction should be made among them [...] In this essay I am seeking to explicate the primitive notion that seems to lie behind all of these concepts. Some of my readers would doubtless prefer the term 'influence,' while others may insist that I am talking about control. I should like to be permitted to use these terms interchangeably when it is convenient to do so, without denying or seeming to deny that for many other purposes distinctions are necessary and useful."[29]

Similarly, Herbert Simon in his early essay on the measurement of power announces that „It is not necessary, for present purposes, to distinguish between influence and power, and I shall continue to use the two words as synonyms".[30] And more recently, John Rothgeb, with explicit reference to the example of Dahl, begins his study of „Influence and Force in the Contemporary International System" with the admonition that „throughout this work the terms *power, control*, and *influence* are used interchangeably".[31]

But much more common are cases where the terms are apparently used as synonyms without any manifest awareness on the part of the authors that this may be problematic and is, in any case, not self-evident.

Kerbo's and McKinstry's study on economic and political *power* in Japan, for example,[32] is a work in which, although – as the title of the book suggests – 'power' is one of the main topics, not only is the meaning of this term never spelled out explicitly; it is also used interchangeably with the (equally unexplained) term 'influence'.[33] In this

and influence is extremely confusing. Sometimes they are treated as synonymous, other times as two distinct phenomena with no area of overlap."

28 Terence Ball (1992, 16) has noted „the tendency of behavioral political scientists to treat 'power', 'influence,' and 'authority' as synonyms"; in his view, this is a consequence of their often mechanistic conception of power, equating it with causation. As the following examples will show, however, the tendency is much more widespread and often seems to derive simply from a lack of conceptual reflection.

29 Dahl 1957, 202 (1969, 80).

30 Simon 1953 (1969), n. 3. It is interesting to note, however, that in the same essay Simon then adopts Lasswell/Kaplan's definition of 'exercise of influence', without ever mentioning that these two authors *do* distinguish between 'power' and 'influence' – indeed, they devote entire chapters to each one of these terms – and that they explicitly state that „Power is a special case of the exercise of influence"; cf. Lasswell/Kaplan 1950, 76.

31 Rothgeb 1992, 18.

32 Kerbo/McKinstry 1995; the authors are sociologists, but their study can be regarded as falling inside the range of 'political-science' literature as it is mainly concerned with political phenomena.

33 At least, that is what *seems* to be the case. Since the concepts as such are not discussed at all, it is, of course, impossible to know definitely what the authors mean by them. Still, when they ask „For example, does one gain more *power* and rewards from being a prime minister, a top government minister, the head of a major corporation, or a senior military official? *In other words*, is Hirose Gen more *influential* in Japanese society because he is chairman of Nippon Life than is, say, Ozaki Mamoru as Vice-Minister of the Ministry of Finance [...]?" (op. cit., 5; emphasis added), or when they combine phrases such as „the extent to which some Diet members are gaining more *influence* in relation to the bureaucratic elite", „the argument for expanded Diet *power*", „The loss of *power* by the LDP in 1993", „how future politicians may or may not gain

aspect, the book is rather typical for many descriptive works which, while offering a wealth of information and data on their subjects, suffer from a conspicuous lack of conceptual stringency which, in my view, unnecessarily reduces their scientific value.[34]

Similar cases can be found concerning empirical studies of *influence*. Two recent examples are those of Diana Mutz (1998) and Noah Friedkin (1998). Mutz presents a book-length investigation of what she calls „impersonal influence“: basically, this is an empirical study of how the perceptions people gain, mainly through the media, of other people and their opinions 'influences' the formers' opinions and attitudes. Her's is one of those books which are explicitly about 'influence', only that the author never bothers to define what this term refers to.[35] In addition, in this book 'power' and 'influence' are sometimes used as if they were synonyms and sometimes as if they had different meanings.[36] Friedkin's book, in turn, offers an explication and an empirical test of his own 'structural theory of social influence'. In the course of it, he at least firmly sticks to the treatment of influence, without mentioning power, and thus does not add to the confusion between the two. But his book too is an example of those studies about social influence which lack any hint of a definition of their central concept. Although we learn something about the general nature of influence[37] and its functioning,[38] and we are offered a mathematically-looking, highly formalized „social influence network theory“ (ch. 2.1) as well as an equally impressive „structural parameterization“ including formalized measures of 'interpersonal influence' (ch. 4), we are never told exactly *what kind* of „causal effect“ the term denotes or *in what way* that effect „affects [...] attitudes and opinions“.

But, of course, deficient definitions of influence or the indiscriminate use of the terms 'power' and 'influence' are not the exclusive domain of authors interested mainly in empirical work and rich description. They can also be found in more theoretically oriented works. In „The Structure of Influence Relationships in the International System“, for instance, Steven Brams is consistent insofar as he himself uses only the term 'influence'; but he supports his assertions with quotations from other authors which refer expressly to 'power' – and he doesn't seem to think that this requires an explanation.[39] And still more confusing is the case of Salamon and Siegfried (1977) whose purpose is to formulate and test hypotheses about causal relationships between „Economic Power and Political Influence“, suggesting that power and influence belong to two different domains; but throughout their essay they speak indiscriminately of „political power“ too:

more *power*“, „the sources of *bureaucratic elite influence*“, and „Japanese *bureaucratic power*“ (ibid., 88 f.; emphasis added), there can hardly be any doubt that they regard 'power' and 'influence' as synonymous.

[34] Another example in case is Schäfer's (1994) comparative study of bureaucratic power which suffers from a very unsatisfactory account of the key concepts of power and control (cf. esp. ch. 3). In this respect, I tend to agree with Greve's complaint that „empirical science to a great extent ignores conceptual discussion – to its own disadvantage (that of empirical science, I mean)“ (Greve 1998, 39, n. 1).

[35] Gais 1996 is another example of such works: this book on *Improper Influence* offers neither a definition of influence nor does it say what makes influence – whatever it may be – „improper“.

[36] Specifically, as if influence were something that *has* or *gives* power (cf., e. g., Preface, 53, 217, 271).

[37] „Interpersonal influence is a causal effect (direct and unmediated) of one actor on another“ (56).

[38] „Interpersonal influence affects actors' attitudes and opinions“ (4).

[39] Brams 1969 a, 584 f. And in his „Measuring the Concentration of Power“ (1969 b), Brams uses 'power', 'influence' and 'control' without distinguishing between them.

they are interested in „the successful exercise of political influence" or „the successful exercise of political power"; and yet they apparently see no logical problem in assertions such as

„The key to policy-making power [...] is access [...] to [...] well-insulated and highly structured subsystems. [...] Effective access to the subsystems, however, is typically confined to those with the expertise, resources, and influence to provide stable sources of support to key subsystem actors over extended periods of time."

In other words (in view of the use of 'power' and 'influence' as synonyms in the rest of the paper): the key to political power (or is it influence?) is access; but the key to access is, among other things, political influence (or power?).[40]

ii) But even scholars who do give explicit and separate definitions of the two terms sometimes fail to stick to them consistently. An example of such a case seems to be Hoffmann-Lange (1992) who acknowledges that „At the beginning of any investigation there must be [...] a theoretical as well as an operational definition of the concepts of power and influence, which are often used interchangeably"[41] and then goes on to distinguish between the two concepts, depending on the type of resources an agent possesses, that is, according to whether or not an agent is able to impose sanctions on others.[42] Elsewhere in the same study, however, the author seems to be using the terms in a way that is not consistent with those definitions, as when she states:

„Obviously, [when attention is focused on *power* structures and political decision processes] besides elected politicians and the administrations they command we must also take into account a multitude of other orga-

[40] Salamon/Siegfried 1977, 1030. In fact, this is a stunning example of a paper that goes through all the formal motions of a scholarly work of theory construction without fulfilling any real function because of its severe conceptual flaws. These concern not only the lack of a distinction between power and influence. Also, the *successful exercise* of political influence (power) is measured simply by looking at the degree to which certain political outcomes are thought to benefit the actor under consideration; this measure is then correlated with certain structural features of an economic actor (taken to indicate economic power) to test the hypothesis that economic power generates political influence. That for conceptual reasons 'successful exercise', having an intentional and a practical dimension, *cannot* adequately be measured by 'outcomes' alone should, however, be obvious. The mere fact that certain policy outcomes happen to benefit a particular actor carries no information whatsoever about what this actor may have intended or done. – For similar conceptual flaws cf. also Becker 1983: a theoretical paper on 'political influence' generated by 'political pressure' without any explication of these terms, in which 'influence' and 'power' seem to be used as synonyms and whose lack of conceptual rigour raises doubts about the possible fruitfulness of the firework of formalization (differential equations, matrix notation, equilibria discussion, ...) offered to the reader – as long as it remains a mystery *what* is being aggregated, maximized or differentiated, the display of mathematical skills seems pointless.

[41] Hoffmann-Lange 1992, 354: „Am Beginn jeder Untersuchung muß [...] eine theoretische wie auch eine operationale Definition der oft austauschbar gebrauchten Begriffe Macht und Einfluß stehen."

[42] Ibid., 355. More precisely, Hoffmann-Lange refers to Lasswell's and Kaplan's definition in this sense as being „almost unanimously accepted in the literature"; she then asserts that, „therefore", the difference between an agent who has power and an agent who has influence is whether or not he is able to elicit desired outcomes without the use of sanctions (which implies that, with respect to the same outcome, an agent cannot at the same time have power *and* influence). Although she does not say so expressly, the reader must assume that Hoffmann-Lange adopts Lasswell's and Kaplan's definitions and distinction. In fact, however, whether someone *has command* over some means of sanction or whether he *needs to threaten* with sanctions in order to get what he wants are two quite different things, and from her formulation it is not entirely clear which one of the two ideas she regards as the decisive conceptual difference.

nizations. The *influence* of these organizations is based on their social *power* resources and as a rule is not legitimized through democratic elections [...]"[43]

If, as Hoffmann-Lange appears to accept, it is precisely the resources which are the criterion that marks the difference between power and influence phenomena, then it is difficult to see how an agent's „influence" could be grounded on her „power resources".

iii) Still more astonishing are cases such as that of David Baldwin. In an otherwise extraordinarily detailed and careful conceptual analysis of 'power' and 'interdependence', Baldwin remarks only in passing: „It should be noted that in this essay I am using the terms 'influence' and 'power' interchangeably".[44]

The problem with this is not so much that, for reasons of transparency, perhaps such synonyms should better be avoided – at least within a conceptual analysis and concerning one of the analysed concepts – or that, if they *are* used, this should perhaps better be announced at the beginning of the paper rather than at its end, and the announcement should be accompanied by an account of the reason why that use is thought to be unavoidable or desirable. The real problem is that Baldwin actually *does not* consistently use the two terms interchangeably. True, sometimes he does. But some passages in his essay make sense only if one interchanges 'influence' not with 'power', but with 'exercise of power' (which, though undeniably related to, is clearly different from power itself).[45] More importantly, there is Baldwin's general argument, which is that 'dependence' is commonly understood to mean what he calls „dependence as power". This is a kind of relationship implying vulnerability because of high opportunity costs and which, in his view, must be distinguished from „mere sensitivity or influence". In fact, the difference „between influence in general and dependence as a special type of influence" is Baldwin's main reason for objecting against the retention of the concept of 'interdependence' in its two versions of 'sensitivity interdependence' and 'vulnerability interdependence', as it has been widely accepted in the international relations literature. Thus, by taking Baldwin – *qua* author of n. 129 of his paper – seriously and „using the terms 'influence' and 'power' interchangeably", as he himself claims to be doing, one would wipe out precisely the distinction which the 'other Baldwin', the author of the main body of the paper, so assiduously explicates.[46]

[43] Ibid., 37 (emphasis added): „Es liegt auf der Hand, daß [sobald das Interesse sich auf *Macht*strukturen und politische Entscheidungsprozesse richtet] neben den gewählten Politikern und der ihnen unterstellten öffentlichen Verwaltung noch eine Vielzahl anderer Organisationen berücksichtigt werden muß. Der *Einfluß* dieser Organisationen beruht auf ihren gesellschaftlichen *Macht*ressourcen und ist im Regelfall nicht durch demokratische Wahlen legitimiert."

[44] Indeed, had the author intended to hide this statement, he could hardly have chosen a better place: it appears close to the end of the paper in a parenthesis within a footnote: Baldwin 1980, 502, n. 129.

[45] Ibid., 489 f. To add to the conceptual confusion, other writers stipulate exactly the opposite relationship: While for Baldwin 'influence' seems to stand for 'exercise of power', for others 'power' is what one has when one has the ability to exercise 'influence' (cf. Pettit 1996, 603; 1997, 79).

[46] For further examples of an indiscriminate use of 'power' and 'influence' precisely in the context of a conceptual analysis of power see, e. g., Russell Hardin (1996) in his critique of Bertrand Russell's conception of 'power' (esp. 323, 339), or Mario Stoppino (1990) who, in the prestigious Italian „Dictionary of Politics", edited by Norberto Bobbio et al., explicitly argues against the distinction between power and influence in the terms advocated, among others, by Lasswell and Kaplan or by Hoffmann-Lange, i. e., in terms of the presence

iv) And then, there are also those who use the terms 'power' and 'influence' in ways which imply *several different* kinds of relationships between the concepts.

Peter Bernholz and Friedrich Breyer, for instance, have dedicated two entire chapters of their – in my view, otherwise excellent – *Economic Theory of Politics*[47] to the analysis of 'influence': in one of them (ch. 15), they treat 'The influence of the bureaucracy on the process of political decision-making', in the next, 'The influence of interest groups on the process of political decision-making'. To begin with, it is interesting to note that although there are two chapters on influence and no chapter (not even a section) on power, the index to the book contains an entry for 'power' with a substantial number of references, but no entry for 'influence'.[48] Moreover, despite the prominence of both terms in the book, there is no definition of either 'power' or 'influence'. And the reader eager to discover the meaning given to those terms by the authors can find a number of different relationships between the two concepts, or phenomena, implied in the text. Thus, sometimes the terms are clearly used as synonyms:

„In this chapter we want to look at three different ways of how interest groups may exert *influence* in politics [...] However, the amount of *power* different groups of the population can exercise, through associations and organizations, must be analyzed carefully. Because it could very well be that the interest groups' possibilities to exert *influence* are neutralized, e. g., by their mutual competition."[49]

Elsewhere in their book, however, influence seems to be something one can (or must?) have power to, as when Bernholz and Breyer speak of „the *power* of interest associations to *influence* governmental measures".[50] But then, again, power is also taken to be something like a potential „cause" of influence:

„[A second] cause of the *influence* of interest associations that changes the political process [is the] exploitation of *power* positions as suppliers or buyers."[51]

or absence of (means of) coercion, on the grounds that the term 'power' is actually used in a great variety of meanings, including the denotation of non-coercive relationships (p. 843); Stoppino seems to think that the inappropriateness of one particular distinction is reason enough for not making any distinction at all (841, 844).

47 Bernholz/Breyer 1994, vol. 2.

48 Practically the opposite phenomenon can be found in French/Snyder 1959, or in Kohler-Koch 1996: there, the titles of the papers speak of 'power', while the texts speak primarily of 'influence'.

49 Bernholz/Breyer 1994, 166 (emphasis added): „Wir wollen uns in diesem Kapitel mit drei verschiedenen Wegen beschäftigen, auf denen Interessengruppen einen *Einfluß* auf die Politik geltend machten können [...] Allerdings muß sorgfältig untersucht werden, wie groß die *Macht* ist, die mit Hilfe von Verbänden und Organisationen von verschiedenen Bevölkerungsgruppen ausgeübt wird. Denn es wäre ja durchaus möglich, daß die *Einfluß*möglichkeiten der Interessengruppen z. B. durch den Wettbewerb miteinander [...] aufgehoben werden."

50 Bernholz/Breyer 1994, 169 (emphasis added): „Eine erste Ursache für die *Macht* der Interessenverbände, staatliche Maßnahmen zu *beeinflussen* [...]" Another prominent author who seems to think that „power" is what is used in order to exert (political) „influence" is Mancur Olson (cf. 1982, 69, 124, 126, 167).

51 Bernholz/Breyer 1994, 170 (emphasis added): „[Eine zweite] Ursache des den politischen Prozeß ändernden *Einflusses* der Interessenverbände [ist die] Ausnutzung einer *Macht*stellung als Lieferanten oder Abnehmer." Note that the first cause mentioned by the authors is not a cause of influence, but a cause of a special kind of power, namely, a „cause of the power [...] to influence"; cf. the quote at n. 34. The expression „the power to influence" appears repeatedly in the text, for example on pp. 172, 175.

On the other hand, influence also seems to be regarded as a means for enhancing power:

„Once *influence* on the political process has been established in that way, it can [...] also be used for broadening *power*.“[52]

But after the authors have listed what they hold to be the main „causes“ of influence („As a third, better-known cause of the *influence* of associations on the political process we can mention party financing [...]“), it turns out that they actually meant to be speaking of power all along: „So much for the primary causes of the *power* of interest organizations.“[53]

And, again, in yet another variant, they seem to locate power at the executive level, influence at the legislative and constituent level:

„As the tasks [performed by the state] expand, the *influence* of voters and legislature diminishes, and the *power* of the government and bureaucracy increases [...]“[54]

v) Finally, for a clarification of the concepts of 'power' and 'influence', it is also not very helpful to lament the confusion provoked by others only to come up with a not very clear and not very well-founded alternative oneself. In my view, this is the case, for example, when Laumann and Knoke first assert – with good reason, I think – that the work of Parsons „nicely exemplifies the complex and often contradictory ways in which the terms 'influence' and 'power' have been employed in sociological analysis“ and, more generally, deplore „the highly confused state of the scattered and noncumulative empirical literature devoted to the study of influence and control“,[55] and then offer as their own account of 'influence' only the following:

„As we have come to use the term in this chapter, influence has been treated as the emergent crystallization of the summary perceptual judgments of multiple actors engaged in a collective enterprise.“[56]

The preceding collection of examples of different problems in the conceptualization of 'influence' in political science and related social science scholarship should be evidence enough to support the claim that political science today is still in need of an extensive discussion of that important politico-scientific concept.

This is, of course, not meant to imply that nothing useful has been written on the subject as yet. On the contrary: all the authors mentioned above, and many more, have

52 Bernholz/Breyer 1994, 171 (emphasis added): „Besteht auf diese Weise erst einmal ein *Einfluß* auf den politischen Prozeß, so kann derselbe [...] auch zur Erweiterung der *Macht* verwendet werden.“

53 Bernholz/Breyer 1994, 171 (emphasis added): „Als dritte, bekanntere Ursache für den *Einfluß* der Verbände auf den politischen Prozeß kommt die Finanzierung der Parteien in Frage [...] Soviel zu den primären Ursachen der *Macht* von Interessenorganisationen.“

54 Bernholz/Breyer 1994, 234 (emphasis added): „Je umfangreicher die Aufgaben sind, desto geringer ist der *Einfluß* von Wählern und Parlament und desto größer ist die *Macht* von Regierung und Behörden [...]“; on the same page, however, the authors also comment on the case where „the power of government and bureaucracy is greater than that of parliament and voters“; another instance of the distinction between the 'power' of government and bureaucracy and the 'influence' of voters and parliament can be found on p. 244.

55 Laumann/Knoke 1987, 156.

56 Ibid., 188.

made interesting and valuable contributions. What I intended to show with the examples quoted is merely that, despite a voluminous literature on conceptual and empirical questions in the context of what is commonly called social or political 'influence', under the surface of an apparently well-known and unproblematic concept confusion still abounds. And since confusion is an obstacle to insight, it seems well worth the effort to try to dispel it, by careful analysis.

Because of the way in which political science has developed in the past decades, especially with regard to its conceptual heritage, this is a complicated and not always pleasant task. Precisely because of the many explicit and implicit conceptions already existing in the literature for the notions under scrutiny here, it cannot be approached simply with a view towards constructing yet another proposal for a definition of the concept of influence. My impression is, rather, that we have reached a stage where a lot of checking, of discussing advantages and disadvantages of existing definitions and usages, and probably also some *destructive* work is necessary in order to clear the terrain for new constructive efforts. The following reflections are intended as a contribution to that end.

My *ultimate* interest is to arrive at a concept of social, and specifically political, influence that may be able to do some useful work in political theory (of the positive, empirical as well as the normative, philosophical kind). My *proximate* interest in the present study is to prepare the ground for that. In pursuing this latter interest, I also hope to show that this is not as easy as it may seem, and to heighten awareness that serious conceptual problems are still waiting to be solved.

The critical and possibly destructive steps with which, as I have just argued, this kind of work must begin also make it necessary that in much of the present study, not influence, but power is discussed – a fact acknowledged in the title of this book. The reader should keep in mind, however, that the analysis of power is undertaken here not as an end in itself, but only as a means, serving the subject I am actually interested in: political influence.

To the naked, unbiased eye, at a glance, many existing conceptualizations of social power and influence look more or less plausible. Therefore, the purposes of this study will require aiming a kind of microscopic, penetrating view at them. Only careful attention to detail can be hoped to reveal their respective merits and shortcomings.

Such a detailed view risks to provoke a loss of orientation. This risk is counterbalanced here, I hope, by a general line of argument that is straightforward and simple. The first two chapters will be dedicated to a review and analysis of the state of the art concerning the conceptualization of social power (Chapter 1) and of influence (Chapter 2). The second chapter will conclude with a first, rough tentative proposal of my own for a concept of influence, as distinguished from a concept of power, in the light of the preceding considerations. The next two chapters then pursue two particular conceptual features of power which will have to be taken into account for any more elaborate distinction of the two concepts, with a view, above all, towards their normative implications, to wit: its relation to freedom (Chapter 3), and the distinction between factual and normative power (Chapter 4). In a brief final chapter (Chapter 5), I will present some considerations about the direction into which further work, especially about normative implications, will have to go.

PART I
CONCEPTS TAKEN APART

Vague and insignificant forms of speech, and abuse of language, have so long passed for mysteries of science; and hard and misapplied words, with little or no meaning, have, by prescription, such a right to be mistaken for deep learning and height of speculation, that it will not be easy to persuade either those who speak or those who hear them, that they are but the covers of ignorance, and hindrance to true knowledge.

John Locke, Essay Concerncing Human
Understanding, Epistle to the Reader

Ignorance of the significance of words; which is, want of understanding, disposeth men to take on trust, not only the truth they know not; but also the errors; and which is more, the non-sense of them they trust: For neither Error, nor non-sense, can without a perfect understanding of words, be detected.

Thomas Hobbes, Leviathan, ch. XI

[A] man that seeketh precise truth, had need to remember what every name he uses stands for; and to place it accordingly; or else he will find himselfe entangled in words, as a bird in lime-twiggs; the more he struggles, the more belimed. ...
By this it appears how necessary it is for any man that aspires to true Knowledge, to examine the Definitions of former Authors; and either to correct them, where they are negligently set down; or to make them himselfe. For the errours of Definitions multiply themselves, according as the reckoning proceeds; and lead men into absurdities ...

Thomas Hobbes, Leviathan, ch. IV

1. THE CONCEPT OF POWER

'Power' is now the most abused word in our language of politics.
Michael J. Oakeshott[1]

The concept of power has long been known to be „a peculiarly problematic concept" (Ball 1993, 548) for the social sciences.[2] It belongs to that large class of notions which one typically has no problem in applying, until the moment one begins to reflect about their meaning. In this sense, we could perhaps speak of a 'bicycle concept' – the bicycle being the proverbial prototype of an object the use of which is unproblematic as long as one does not stop to think about how exactly it works. Just as with bicycles, reflection about the exact functioning of 'bicycle concepts' is likely to trigger confusion, loss of balance, and sometimes even a fall flat on one's face.

Many, if not all, our theoretical concepts are of this kind. In everyday usage, where conscious and detailed reflection about concepts is unnecessary as long as communication functions reasonably well, this rarely creates problems. In scientific use, however, we must do better than just understand each other reasonably well. The reason for this is, above all, that unless terms are defined with sufficient precision, we will not be able to assess the truth or falsity or, more generally, the correctness or incorrectness,[3] of propositions, hypotheses or theories. This is so, of course, because their truth or validity depends on what objects or phenomena they are taken to refer to; and that, in turn, is determined precisely by the definition of the terms, i. e., by the concepts used in those theoretical statements. Hence, as long as there is a lack of conceptual reflection, and no certainty about what the terms someone uses are meant to designate, agreement or disagreement about theory must necessarily remain meaningless: agreement may be only apparent[4] if it results from different definitions of the relevant terms, or from the all too casual handling of the question of conceptual boundaries;[5] and the same is true for disagreement about the truth or validity of statements.[6] Far from being an intellectual glass-

[1] 1991, 447.

[2] As opposed to the natural sciences, or mathematics, where the term 'power' is used to designate sets of precisely and clearly defined properties.

[3] Where 'correctness' and 'incorrectness' are meant to include not only the criteria of truth or falsity in the case of descriptive statements, but also the corresponding criteria – 'validity', 'reasonableness', or whatever they may be called – for the tenability or untenability of normative statements.

[4] It may, of course, also be genuine; but only conceptual analysis can reveal whether or not it is.

[5] Elsewhere, I have tried to show that there are problems of this kind, e. g., with respect to the theory of so-called 'international regimes'; cf. Zimmerling 1997.

[6] The importance of the relationship between conceptual clarity and the possibility of causal generalizations has been emphasized especially by MacIntyre (1973); although I disagree with much of what he says about the alleged 'essential contestability' of social concepts, I think he is right on this point. In the same vein, cf., e. g., Care (1973, 15 f.); Robinson (1962, 70). MacIntyre also argues that the corresponding problems cannot

bead game, thorough conceptual analysis is therefore a necessary prerequisite for successful empirical science.[7]

But even the reader who accepts this may raise at least two objections against an analysis of the concept of power at this juncture.

(1) The first is that if influence, not power, is to be the main subject of the present study an extended consideration of the latter leads us away from the real topic. Plausible as this objection may sound, it can easily be dismissed: As already mentioned in the introduction, the concepts of influence and of power are generally regarded to be so closely related that they have regularly been treated almost like Siamese twins.[8] In fact, I know of no analysis of the concept of influence that would not define it by trying some-

be solved simply by way of an operational definition (for a similar argument specifically concerning operational definitions of power, cf. Connolly 1983b, 129). This assertion may seem wrong: Surely, operational definitions can generate clarity about what objects or phenomena a theoretical generalization is meant to apply to; thus, it is obviously operational definitions which make it possible to test empirical hypotheses in the first place. But what MacIntyre rather seems to be pointing at is the doubtful *validity* of many operational definitions with respect to the abstract concepts they claim to capture; and invalid operational definitions indeed cannot help us in testing causal generalizations. But whether or not an operational definition *is* valid can be assessed only if there already is a sufficiently clear and precise notion of the respective abstract concept. In that sense, MacIntyre's assertion seems to be correct: if an operational definition is to amount to more than the mere stipulation of a completely new, empirically measurable concept, i. e., if it is to 'translate' the abstract characteristics of a concept *already defined* into empirically perceptible indicators, it cannot itself generate, but rather *presupposes* conceptual clarity.

[7] Many readers will think that this is obvious, and so it seems to me. The reason why nevertheless I think it necessary to make the point is that in the past I have met with considerable resistance against efforts to elucidate concepts, from more than one political scientist who seemed to deny the need for, and the usefulness of, such an undertaking; not all of them have expressed this as openly as one colleague who frankly told me that he cannot see what purpose such „nominalistic trifles" could possibly serve. Experiences of this kind sometimes make one wonder whether the gulf between, e. g., theoretical and applied physics is as wide as that between theoretically and empirically oriented political science. In any case, as for the importance of conceptual clarification, I side with, and find support in, Robinson who in his marvelously transparent book-length study of *Definition* holds „the improvement of concepts and the creation of new concepts" to be „the key to one of the two or three locks on the door of successful science" (Robinson 1962, 68) and reminds us that „John Locke [already] observed that it is a frequent mistake to believe that 'the significations of common words are certainly established, and the precise ideas they stand for certainly known [...]'. He was once present, he tells us, at a meeting of physicians arguing whether a liquor flows along the nerves. To him the argument appeared to arise from the ambiguities of the word 'liquor'; but his fellow practitioners found it an odd suggestion that they should stop to consider what they meant by this word" (ibid., 69). Robinson's comment on this anecdote is that „Such resistance of our common instinct to the first requisite of science never dies. The scientist is still saying 'it depends what you mean by [...]', and the layman is still resenting the answer" (ibid.). As far as contemporary political science is concerned, I think it would sometimes already constitute considerable progress if the distinction between scientists and 'laymen' would indeed conform to Robinson's observation.

A fortiori, I do not share the view that striving for conceptual clarity in science can be detrimental, as seems to be the position, for instance, of Wolfgang Kersting (1991, 135; my translation) who, specifically referring to the concept of power, has argued that the „strategy of seeking greater analytical precision" has „considerable disadvantages" because it „robs the concept of power of its variety of meanings and destroys its differentiated historical semantics [...]". I fail to understand what the disadvantage is when „the tensions between antagonistic interpretations and irreconcilable value orientations which tear at and wear out [the concept of power] disappear with usage-oriented conceptual analysis" (ibid.).

[8] For a few examples, cf., e. g., Lasswell/Kaplan 1950, Mokken/Stokman 1975, Oppenheim 1981, Koller 1991.

how to contrast it with 'power'. Whether or not that is adequate or even necessary is one of the questions to be answered in the course of the following analysis. But until that answer is given, the only point of reference we have is actual common usage, which seems to regard the concepts as intimately related.[9] Nor would we be able to understand and discuss most of the existing literature on political influence without a prior understanding of the respective underlying conception of 'power'. This, I think, makes it necessary, at least for the time being, to approach the concept of influence by way of a close look at the concept of power.

(2) The second objection to be expected is that the concept of power in the social sense has already been analysed so often that it is a waste of time, energy, and the reader's patience to take it up once again; therefore, if the notion of power is a necessary prerequisite for a definition of the concept of influence, it should simply be taken, without much further ado, from the existing literature. The obvious counter-argument to this is that, even though – or perhaps precisely because – the concept of power has been the subject of numerous books and essays, the issue is by no means settled.[10] There are even those who argue that it must necessarily remain contested forever – a claim I will presently examine more closely. However that may be: because of the many different conceptualizations of 'power' proposed in the literature, the concept cannot simply be taken for granted. Rather, any choice of a particular conception of power from which influence is then to be distinguished needs to be argued for in terms of some criteria of adequacy. This does not require an exhaustive presentation of *all* existing versions; and therefore, such a presentation will not be forthcoming here. The idea is to offer an overview of some of the main perspectives to be found in the social sciences and in philosophy, focusing only on those parts and aspects that may be useful for the subsequent analysis of the concept of influence.

In any case, the kind of investigation envisaged here will require a somewhat uneasy maneuvering between the *stipulation* of a definition of 'influence' (for which a prior analysis of the concept of power would, of course, not be absolutely necessary), and a mere *interpretation* of common uses of that term. The purpose is to arrive at a *reconstruction* or *revision* of the concept of influence,[11] including its relationship to some of

[9] In this respect, conceptual analysis differs from other kinds of examinations in that here, in a certain sense, an 'ought' can very well be derived from an 'is' without committing a naturalistic fallacy: the bottom line for conceptual analysis and critique 'ought' to be the 'is' of actual linguistic usage.

[10] According to Dennis Wrong (1988, 2), „there are hundreds, perhaps thousands, of more recent definitions of social power", not even counting the older ones. Oskar Morgenstern once complained at a conference on 'Power and economic laws': „I have [...] heard many speeches about power. But I still don't know what power is [...] Power is still as undefined for political science as the concept of utility was for economics. I assume we know somewhat more about utility or value than about power. Of course, we have an intuition about it. But that is not enough [...] Often, the word 'power' is substituted by saying: A group has 'influence' on another group. But one does not know what influence is. And so it goes on and on. One undefined term is replaced by another." (Morgenstern 1973, 388; my translation) And almost thirty years later, Mancur Olson still felt compelled to say: „A theory of power has long been the Holy Grail for political science, but the Grail has not been found." (Olson 2000, 2)

[11] Oppenheim 1981, ch. 9, and Kristjánsson 1996, ch. 7, are two useful discussions of methodological issues in conceptual studies in political science; the former advocates 'reconstruction', the latter 'revision'.

the other members of what is sometimes called the 'family' of 'power terms',[12] that may be of use for the clarification of certain questions in – positive and/or normative – political theory.[13]

In order for such an undertaking to be meaningful, one does not need to believe that conceptual questions can ever, or must, be definitely settled. Actually, this mistaken belief is probably at least in part responsible for the still unsatisfactory state of conceptual clarity about such important notions as power and influence in the social sciences: The 'contestedness' of the concept of power, for instance, often seems to be regarded as a fact that makes further attempts to clarify the concept unnecessary ('As the concept is contested anyway, why bother to discuss the different conceptualizations?'), if not entirely futile ('As the concept is contested, what could conceptual analysis possibly accomplish?'). Unless this fundamental objection of unavoidable, 'essential' contestedness can be dismissed, it would make no sense to go on with the study of the concepts I am interested in.[14] And since this is a charge which is often repeated, but rarely discussed in depth in the pertinent literature,[15] it does, I think, deserve a more detailed treatment here.

1. The 'Essential Contestedness' Issue

'Power' has repeatedly been observed to be one of those terms the „meaning and criteria of application [of which] are forever open to dispute and disagreement". And at least on Terence Ball's reading this means that the concept of power is not simply 'contested', but 'essentially contested', since „According to W. B. Gallie [...] a concept is 'essentially contested' if its meaning and criteria of application are forever open to dispute and disagreement" (Ball 1993, 553).

Of course, the fact that there is no definite, final word on what the intension or the extension of a concept consists in is by no means an unusual and, therefore, particularly noteworthy feature. On the contrary, it is a very common characteristic shared by practically all our concepts, and certainly all theoretical or abstract ones. With most concepts, this is the case simply because definition is a matter of convention, and ordinary, non-formalized language inevitably is, to some degree, both *vague* and *ambiguous*.

[12] Cf., e. g., Koller (1991, 108) who speaks of a „network of related and connected concepts" which together constitute a „family of concepts"; Clegg (1989, xv) sees „a set of family relationships" and distinguishes „at least three family groupings"; Dahl (1968, 39) and Jack Nagel (1975, 8) speak of „power terms" (but Dahl 1970, ch. 3, calls them „influence terms"), Kristjánsson (1996, 144) speaks of „power concepts".

[13] That there are interesting, hitherto neglected questions about influence in normative political theory will be argued in Chapter 4, where I will treat some aspects of the question whether and, if so, in what way political influence phenomena may affect the legitimacy of a political system.

[14] Steven Lukes (1986a, 4), for instance, thinks it „likely that the very search for [...] a [generally satisfying] definition is a mistake".

[15] Useful discussions of 'essential contestedness' which mention, but do not specifically focus on, the concept of power, are Oppenheim 1981, 181 ff.; Connolly 1983a; Swanton 1985, 1992; Mason 1990, 1993; and Kristjánsson 1996, 180 ff. Cf. also Norman Barry who, starting with the 2nd ed. of his *Introduction to Political Theory*, has added a general discussion of the idea in ch. 1.2 and also mentions it specifically in the context of his discussion of the concept of power (N. Barry 1989, 13 ff., 82 f.)

1.1. CONCEPTUAL VAGUENESS AND AMBIGUITY

Disagreements and misunderstandings about what conceptual conventions really amount to or what exactly a term is thought to mean in a particular instance of use are therefore to be expected; and if this were meant by 'essential contestedness', then it would not be surprising at all that such contestedness is endemic. The question in this case would only be what attitude to adopt with respect to it, i. e., what conclusions to draw from it for our treatment of concepts, at least for scientific purposes.

As Felix Oppenheim (1981, 182–185) has explained in all desirable detail, particularly with respect to 'political concepts' (among them explicitly those of power and influence), the proper implication certainly is not one of a conceptual 'anything goes':[16]

(a) Vagueness, i. e., the existence of an area of penumbra which it is not clear whether or not a given term can properly be applied to, is, as Oppenheim observes, a property shared by most, if not all words of ordinary language. But vagueness is not simply to be accepted in resignation. It comes in degrees, and what degree of vagueness is acceptable depends on the context in, and the purpose for, which a concept is to be used. Certainly, the threshold of acceptability in this respect must be much lower for scientific purposes than in the ordinary use of language. And whenever vagueness is excessive, relative to the respective purpose in a particular instance, something should and can be done about it. The remedy against unacceptably high degrees of vagueness is an effort to reach greater precision precisely through conceptual explication.[17]

[16] Cf. also Hospers 1990, 119–126; Carrió 1990, 28–35, 47 f. Hart (1994, 124–136) has identified vagueness with the 'open texture' of language, a term coined by Waisman (1951) who uses it with a somewhat different meaning; cf. also Margalit (1981) and Schauer (1991, 34–37). Robinson (1962, 66 ff.) counts the elimination or reduction of vagueness and ambiguity among the advantages of stipulative definitions. Copi (1982, 151 f.) calls the kind of definitions called for in case of vagueness „precising definitions". – This is not the place to enter more profoundly into the age-old topic of conceptual vagueness and ambiguity. The interested reader may consult, among others, Max Black, Vagueness: An Exercise in Logical Analysis, in: Philosophy of Science 4 (1937) 427–455; Carl G. Hempel, Vagueness and Logic, in: Philosophy of Science 6 (1939) 163–180; Irving M. Copi(lowish), Border-Line Cases: Vagueness and Ambiguity, in: Philosophy of Science 6 (1939) 181–195; Bertrand Russell, Vagueness, in: Australasian Journal of Psychology and Philosophy 1 (1923) 84–92; I. Scheffler, *Beyond the Letter: A Philosophical Inquiry into Ambiguity, Vagueness and Metaphor in Language*, London: Routledge & Kegan Paul 1979; H. J. Skala, S. Termini and E. Trillas (eds.), *Aspects of Vagueness*, Dordrecht: Reidel 1984; Norbert Fries, *Ambiguität und Vagheit. Einführung und kommentierte Bibliographie*, Tübingen: Niemeyer 1980; and the article 'Vaguedad', in: José Ferrater Mora, *Diccionario de Filosofía*, 4 vols., Barcelona: Ariel 1994, vol. IV, 3625–3627, from which most of these references are taken. More references and other documents on 'vagueness', including a „test to help distinguish vagueness from ambiguity", could once (and perhaps still can) be found at: www.jneedle.demon.co.uk/vague.

[17] However, even some epistemologists express doubts about the usefulness of exercises in conceptual precision. One representative of this position is Max Albert who in a critical discussion of conceptions of voting power asserts that „Scientific progress is not made by substituting precisely defined concepts for vague concepts [...] The aim of achieving precision is elusive anyway because any chain of precise definitions necessarily ends with primitive terms that are not defined and are, therefore, more or less vague. And, last but not least, explicit definitions achieve nothing because the *definiendum* just stands for the *definiens*" (Albert 2003, 359). Albert expresses particular skepticism about the usefulness of further efforts to rescue a concept of power: „The definition of voting power [...] is disconnected from any positive theory and, therefore, useless for purposes of political science. A definition might of course inspire a successful theory, at least conceivably; however, previous definitions of power, like, for instance, Max Weber's, failed to do so." (Albert 2003, 359 f.). I agree with Albert that conceptual analysis and precisation make sense as a scientific undertaking only if they are ultimately pursued in the service of theoretical progress; but I would disagree with him

(b) Secondly, there is *ambiguity*, that is, the use of one single term for the expression of several different concepts – a „multiplicity of senses", in Hospers's (1990, 121) words. This too is a source of disagreement and an impediment for communication that can be reduced only by careful conceptual (re)construction. The decisive point is, in any case, that different meanings ought to be expressed by different terms. *What* the particular term is in each case is only of secondary importance – provided it does not unnecessarily depart from ordinary usage.[18]

As these two kinds of problems arising from a lack of conceptual precision can thus be solved through proper analysis in every particular case, I think one must conclude with Oppenheim (1981, 185) that they cannot be the source of 'essential contestedness' in any interesting, relevant sense.

1.2. VALUE-DEPENDENCE

This is a conclusion even Steven Lukes, probably the most prominent and ardent advocate of the idea that power is an 'essentially contested' concept, would probably agree with. In fact, on his account, what makes the contestedness of power 'essential' is neither vagueness nor ambiguity, but another, more significant and less common characteristic. In order to explain what he means by that, a first step is to recall his distinction of the *concept* of power from what he calls *views* of power:

> „Now, the *concept* of power [...], when interpreted and put to work, yields one or more *views* of power – that is, ways of identifying cases of power in the real world [...] alternative interpretations and applications of one and the same underlying concept of power [...]"[19]

The problem with the notion of power, Lukes goes on to explain, is that the concept as well as the different views of it are „ineradicably value-dependent",[20] „both [the con-

if he meant to say that a mere reduction in vagueness – as opposed to the (unattainable) elimination of vagueness – never serves this purpose or that the deficiencies of „previous definitions of power" imply that a theoretically useful concept of power is inconceivable; and I definitely disagree with him about the alleged failure of definitions to „achieve" anything: definitions can serve more than one purpose, and not the least important is the reconstruction of the *definiens*, so to speak, implied in the usage of a given much-used *definiendum*.

[18] Oppenheim 1981, 184. Oppenheim distinguishes yet another possible source of contestedness, related to vagueness, which he calls „open-endedness" and defines as „the impossibility of defining a concept by a set of necessary and sufficient conditions of their application". This, Oppenheim argues, is not as endemic as vagueness; above all, it is not a problem that arises with respect to any of the political concepts he analyses (Oppenheim 1981, 183 f.). In contrast, that „[t]here is no set of conditions each of which is necessary and which are together sufficient, for the application of the word to the world" is for Hospers (1990, 121) just another form of vagueness.

[19] Lukes 1974, 26 f. Cf. the explicit reference to John Rawls's distinction between (one) 'concept' and (several) 'conceptions' of justice, ibid., 27, n. 1. It should be noted that although this distinction is commonly attributed to Rawls, it goes back to an idea of H. L. A. Hart, as Rawls himself acknowledges in a footnote (cf. Rawls 1971, 5, note).

[20] John Gray (1977) argues against conceptions of 'essential contestedness' both in the sense of Lukes (i. e., emphasizing value- or norm-dependency) and in the sense of mere vagueness or open-endedness; he advocates yet another conception of „essential contestability" which, in his view, is helpful for social analysis. Gray especially discusses Lukes's contentions about the 'essential contestedness' of the concept of power to show the problems connected with that view.

cept's] very definition and any given use of it, once defined, are inextricably tied to a given set of (probably unacknowledged) value-assumptions" (Lukes 1974, 26). And it is „in consequence" of this, and not because of any other feature, that „the concept of power is [...] what has been called an 'essentially contested concept' – one of those concepts which 'inevitably involve endless disputes about their proper uses on the part of their users'".[21]

Thus, in Lukes's view, at the root of the contestedness of the concept of power lies the fact that, although there is (only) one „absolutely basic common core to, or primitive notion lying behind, all talk of power" (Lukes 1974, 26), that „primitive notion" must be further specified if it is to be of any use „in the analysis of social relationships". Only such a specification renders what he would call a 'concept' of the term, and there are, of course, all kinds of alternative possibilities for this. The specification favoured by Lukes himself, for example, leads to a concept of power in which „interests" play a central role. But – as he demonstrates with the examples of Parsons's and Arendt's definitions – there are also „conceptualisations of power" in which interests play no role at all and which, nevertheless, are „rationally defensible" (ibid., 30).

However that may be, what we have so far is still at most 'simple' contestedness. What makes this contestedness 'essential' is the alleged fact that the competing concepts and views are „value-dependent". Concerning the interest-based concept of power favoured by Lukes himself, this is so, he argues, because „the notion of 'interests' is an irreducibly evaluative notion".[22] And with respect to the alternative concepts proposed by Parsons and Arendt, he declares without further argument that their purpose is „to lend persuasive support to the general theoretical frameworks of their authors" (ibid., 29); thus, although he does not expressly say so, he must assume that those „frameworks" rest on specific „value-assumptions".

So much for the *concept*. On the other hand, with respect to *views* of power, Lukes likewise observes:

> „One feature which these three [previously examined] views of power share is their evaluative character: each arises out of and operates within a particular moral and political perspective." (ibid., 26)

And he even goes on to say that „I would maintain that any view of power rests on some normatively specific conception of interests".[23]

[21] Lukes 1974, 26; the quotes within the citation are from Gallie 1956, 169. For the view that the concept of power is essentially contested (or contestable) because of its value-dependence, cf. also D'Agostino 1992, 480.

[22] Ibid., 34. It is explicitly *this* Lukes means when he speaks of the 'ineradicable value-dependency' of the concept of power, and not, as Kersting (1991, 135; my translation) speculates, the fact that „the concept of power [...] is [...] a concept of guidance and orientation [...] which [...] possesses a great normative challenging force *(Herausforderungswert)* that urges cultural self-comprehension, and the scientific and philosophical theories reflectively promoting it, to take a stand." In Kersting's view, this is what explains why the concept of power is an essentially contested concept.

[23] Ibid., 35. Taken literally, this statement is, of course, false according to Lukes's own standards: it obviously does not hold for views of power based on some *concept* of power other than the interest-oriented one favoured by Lukes himself. And on a more benevolent reading, restricted only to views based on that specific concept, it is only a repetition of what has already been said: If interests *are* a central part of the underlying concept of power, if the notion of interest *is* „irreducibly evaluative", and if views of power differ precisely in

But if that is the case, then Lukes must regard views of power to be 'essentially contested' too.[24] And this is precisely what he asserts, at the very beginning of his analysis, about his own view of power: „The view I shall defend is, I shall suggest, ineradicably evaluative and 'essentially contested'" (ibid., 9).

In a way, then, according to Lukes, views of power are *doubly* 'essentially contested': On the one hand, if the concept of power is 'essentially contested' – i. e., if there are several „rationally defensible" concepts of power – and if views of power are nothing but different interpretations of such a concept, then all views of power are necessarily 'essentially contested' in a *derivative* way: they *inherit*, so to speak, the 'essential contestedness' of the corresponding concept; but, at the same time, they are also 'essentially contested' *in their own right*, in the sense that each (*per se* contestable) concept, in turn, allows for several „rationally defensible" interpretations.[25]

So much for Lukes's argument in support of the 'essential contestedness' of the concept of power as well as of the different views one can have of it.[26] Although often uncritically adopted by other scholars, this argument has drawn its share of criticism, so let us have a look at the different objections that have been brought forward against it.

1.3. A PRAGMATIC OBJECTION

One counter-argument put forward against this idea is of a rather pragmatic kind. Terence Ball has argued – not specifically against Lukes, but in general – that power simply *cannot* be an 'essentially contested concept' because that would mean that all communication and, with it, all life in community would be impossible:

> „[I]f the concepts constitutive of political discourse, and therefore of political life, are indeed *essentially* contested, then of course there can be no common moral language or civic lexicon; hence no communication; hence no community." (Ball 1993, 555)

their „interpretations of what are to count as interests", then that *means* that any view of power is characterized by its „specific conception of interests". This is precisely what B. Barry (1991c, 304) has identified – correctly, I think – as Lukes's „crucial thesis".

[24] Consequently, Lukes objects against Rawls's belief that one can defend one of the several possible conceptions (i. e., sets of principles) of justice as „ultimately [...] rational"; cf. Lukes 1974, 27, n. 1; 1979, 264.

[25] For instance, Lukes's own view of power would be 'essentially contested' as such, because it depends on one *specific* conception of 'interests' rather than on another, and it would be derivatively 'essentially contested', because it is grounded in an *interest*-based rather than in another concept of 'power'; in other words, his *concept* of power is contested with respect to the role interests play in it, and his *view* of power is contested with respect to the underlying particular interpretation of interests.

[26] For a fundamental critique of Lukes's approach to the definition of 'power', cf. McLachlan 1981/1994. He argues that Lukes's account is based on several confusions: „a confusion over the nature of a 'concept'" (1994, 308), „a confusion [...] between defining and classifying: between using a concept and using a word" (ibid., 317), „a confusion [...] between suggesting some empirical means in terms of which power can be identified and offering different concepts of 'power'" (ibid., 319). Both the idea of the value-dependence of power and of its essential contestedness, he says, result from these confusions. On a very strict reading of Lukes, I find McLachlan's objections convincing. Indeed, the following arguments against moral concepts and essential contestedness broadly coincide with his. Concerning Lukes's general account of different conceptualizations of social power, however, I have opted for a more benevolent reading, since in my view Lukes draws attention to a number of relevant aspects – even though he may sometimes get their relation to the concept of power not quite right.

That, however, is certainly not a cogent argument against the 'essential contestedness' of power. As long as a concept is 'essentially contested' it must also be a matter of ineradicable disagreement whether or not it is a concept „constitutive of political discourse". In that sense, Ball's argument begs the question since he can only assume that power is such a 'constitutive' concept if he presupposes that it is not 'essentially contested'. Nor is it at all self-evident that the 'essential contestedness' of a concept necessarily has the alleged detrimental consequences for communication and community.

1.4. AN EPISTEMOLOGICAL OBJECTION

But Ball has still another argument against the 'essential contestedness' thesis, and that is an epistemological one: That there *has* been disagreement over the concept of power in the past, he correctly notes, is not sufficient evidence – not even if, as Clegg (1989, xv) thinks, power is the „most 'contested' of concepts" – for supporting the claim that there also *must* necessarily be such disagreement in the future; hence, the claim that the concept of power is 'essentially contested' is unfounded: „At most, all that can be concluded is that 'power' is a *contingently contested* concept" (Ball 1993, 556).

This argument, reminiscent of the well-known argument against the rationality of inductive inference, is really a strange kind of argument to be used in a *conceptual* controversy. Ball seems to think that we are dealing here with an *empirical* matter: the concept of power is 'contingently contested', in his view, because it remains an open question, impossible to answer once and for all, whether or not it will *in fact* be an object of controversy in the future. This contention may be correct, but is beside the point:

On the one hand, it would certainly be a misreading – although an understandable one, because the term is indeed somewhat misleading – of the notion of 'essential contestedness' coined by Gallie and subsequently adopted by Lukes and others to understand it as implying that a concept thus qualified *must* necessarily be contested, *de facto*, at all times. Undoubtedly, it is an empirically contingent matter whether or not a concept with the properties specified by Gallie as making up 'essential contestedness' – among them most prominently that of having an „appraisive" nature, or, in Lukes's terms, of being „value-dependent" – is *de facto* contested at any point in time. Rather, what Gallie, Lukes and others seem to have in mind is that 'essentially contested' concepts are especially contest-prone, that the *likelihood* of their being contested at any particular time is particularly high, and that, above all, contest about them *can never be excluded* since there are no arguments that could settle such disagreement once and for all. In that sense, it would perhaps be more appropriate to speak not of 'contestedness', but of *'contestability'*, not of 'essentially contested', but of 'essentially *contestable*' concepts.[27] And that is, indeed, the term used by some of the participants in this debate.[28]

[27] For a similar argument cf. Mason 1993, 58 f.

[28] Cf. MacIntyre 1973, Gray 1977, and Oppenheim 1981, all of whom quite naturally treat Gallie's concept in the context of reflections about the „contestability" of social concepts. For yet another twist of the discussion, cf. Susan Hurley who distinguishes 'conceivably contestable' from 'essentially contested' concepts by saying that the former „do not normally, but might conceivably, admit of [...] substantive disagreement", whereas the latter „characteristically admit of substantive disagreement" (Hurley 1989, 45, 46), thus implying that the difference between the two concepts is only one of degree. Generally, cf. ibid., ch. 3, for a detailed analysis of the kinds of 'disagreements' („conceptual disagreement", „substantive disagreement", or „dis-

On the other hand, for the question of whether or not the concept of power really is such an 'essentially *contestable'* concept, the extent to which it is *de facto* contested is, if at all, of minor importance. What is at issue, instead, is the contention that the concept of power is „ineradicably evaluative".

This opens up two possible strategies for denying the essential contestedness[29] of power: one is to argue that the predicate of 'essential contestedness' is not (in a particular case), or cannot be (generally), consistently ascribed; the other is to deny that power is necessarily conceptually linked to a value-judgment. Both strategies have been employed in the literature, and I will now take them up in turn.

1.5. THE SIMPLE INCONSISTENCY OBJECTION

One rather obvious objection against Lukes's conception has been forcefully formulated by several authors. It holds that Lukes's account is *internally inconsistent* because his own treatment of the concept of power belies his contention of its 'essential contestedness': Although he insists that the concept and all views of power are 'essentially contested', Lukes himself does not hesitate to argue for the superiority both of his own favorite *concept* over the other concepts discussed, and of his own favorite *view* of that concept over the other views he presents. Such reasoning, however, would be pointless if the concept, in all its possible interpretations, were indeed 'essentially contested'. This is the argument put forward, for instance, by Brian Barry who, in an acidly critical early review of Lukes's book, clearly points out the inconsistency:

> „[I]t appears that he wants to hold two positions simultaneously. The first is that the concept of power is 'essentially contested' [...] The second position is that the third ('three-dimensional') conception is *superior* to the others [...] I do not see how, if the first proposition (irreducible value-conflict) is true, there can be any room for rational arguments of the second kind." (B. Barry 1991c, 304 f.)

In the same vein, Terence Ball (1993, 556) has observed that Lukes has contradicted his own alleged belief that power is an 'essentially contested' concept, since if he really held that belief, it would make no sense for him to advance arguments for or against any one particular concept or view of power.[30] On the contrary, Ball adds (ibid., 551), instead of having shown „that the conceptions of power he criticizes were mistaken *simpliciter*", Lukes even succeeded in plausibly arguing „that they are too narrow"; and

> „Far from supporting the thesis of essential contestability, these considerations suggest that disagreements about the meaning(s) of power are rationally debatable and, at least potentially and in principle, resolvable".

agreement in form of life") „uncontestable", „conceivably contestable", and „essentially contested" concepts may trigger, and the difficulties of distinguishing between them empirically.

[29] Or contestability; in the following, I will use the two terms indiscriminately.

[30] Cf. also Clarke 1979, 125, quoted from Oppenheim 1981, 185: „The claim that a concept is 'essentially contestable' commits the claimant to a radical relativism about essentially contested concepts in general". Also, Mason 1993, 50, who observes that if one holds that „disputes over essentially contested concepts are rationally unresolvable", then „there is an apparent inconsistency in claiming that some concept is (a) essentially contested *and* (b) has an interpretation that can be justifiably regarded as superior to others".

Christine Swanton (1985; 1992, ch. 1), in an extensive discussion, has attempted to refute this objection – which I will call the *simple inconsistency objection.* In her interpretation of the concept, 'essential contestedness' means that there are several competing *conceptions* of one and the same *concept.* She thus identifies the idea of different conceptions with Gallie's idea of different 'uses' of a concept (1985, 811; 1992, 1). The problem of essential contestedness arises when a concept has a 'core' meaning which, as such, is commonly accepted, but can be interpreted in different ways (1985, 813; 1992, 3). What makes this contestability 'essential', according to Swanton (1985, 813; 1992, 4), is the alleged fact that the inevitability and unresolvability of contests arise because of certain features of a concept itself (rather than because of any contingent – e. g., psychological – facts). The features at issue here come in two versions:

(a) a „relativist" or „ontological" version, basically grounded on the understanding that some concepts involve moral judgments, and since such judgments are relative there cannot be one best (or true) conception (Swanton attributes this version to Lukes); and

(b) a „skeptical" or „epistemological" version which holds that, even if there is a best conception, we can never know whether our belief about which conception that is is true (this version, according to Swanton, is the one adopted by Gallie) (1985, 814; 1992, 4 f.).

The objections usually raised against the essential-contestedness view (in either one of the two versions), she observes, are those of inconsistency or of a lack of justification (1985, 815). *One* example of the former is the *simple inconsistency objection* (Swanton here expressly refers to Brian Barry's critique of Lukes): that for someone who really holds the essential-contestedness view, it cannot make sense to engage in any contest about an essentially contested concept. As Swanton sees it, this charge is easily brushed aside, because to say that there is *no best* conception of some concept (or at least that we have no way of knowing which is the best conception) does not mean that one cannot have a criterion of *better* or *worse* (1985, 815; 1992, 9). Hence,

„there may be no tension, let alone incoherence, in Lukes's view: he may favor one conception of power because it is superior to certain other salient conceptions, while denying that there is a single best conception of power; for he denies any notion of moral truth or verisimilitude against the background of which the notion of 'single best conception' makes sense." (Swanton 1992, 9)

Swanton seems to think that with this she has refuted the simple inconsistency thesis. But at least as far as Lukes's account of the essential contestedness of evaluative concepts is concerned, her argument does not stand up to scrutiny. Although it is generally correct to say that the existence of a criterion for comparative judgments ('better') does not necessarily depend on the existence of a criterion for judgments of superlativity ('best'), „Swanton's solution to the problem is not available to Lukes", as Andrew Mason has plausibly argued, because on Lukes's account of the different views of power, „there is no objective or even shared standpoint from which one of these views is, or can be justifiably regarded as, superior to the others".[31]

[31] Mason 1993, 51. Mason also explains why Lukes's view, likewise, cannot be salvaged by Mason's own modified understanding of essentially contested concepts, which turns on „the (admittedly weaker) idea that an argument may establish a conclusion but permit reasonable disagreement" (Mason 1993, 56). The problem

1.6. THE SOPHISTICATED INCONSISTENCY OBJECTION

But even if Swanton were right on the last point, this would not mean much for Lukes's account. Swanton herself argues that besides the simple inconsistency objection, there is another, weightier and more *sophisticated inconsistency objection* which Lukes (and all those who share his view about essential contestedness) must deal with.[32] It concerns the question of whether or not the 'common core' of an essentially contested concept is itself essentially contested. That question gives rise to a dilemma: If the common core of a concept is *not* essentially contested, then it is difficult to see why there would not also be truth-conditions or assertibility-conditions with respect to some specification of that core concept, and thus essential contestedness would simply disappear. And if it *is* essentially contested, then, as Lukes himself acknowledges, one cannot even say that there is a contested concept,[33] because there is then no way to determine whether there really is disagreement about *one and the same* thing. In Swanton's view, the dilemma can be resolved, but only at the price of giving up the idea that essential contestedness involves interpretations of the 'common core' of a concept, i. e., by giving up the distinction between concepts and conceptions and stating the problem, instead, in terms of a common 'ideal' and different possible conceptions of it (1985, 818 f.; 1992, 6 f.).

For Kristján Kristjánsson (1996, 179), however, this conclusion is just another example of Swanton's „unreasonable charity" with certain views. He points out – correctly, I think – that while one must fully agree with her as far as the diagnosis of the dilemma is concerned, the remedy she proposes does not work, because „once the common-core assumption has been dropped, little remains of the *ECT [essential contestability thesis]* as a specific thesis" (ibid., 185). This means that, since the dilemma cannot be resolved without giving up an essential ingredient of essential contestedness itself, the sophisticated inconsistency objection against that concept is valid.

1.7. THE UNFOUNDEDNESS OBJECTION

But again, even if Swanton's claim that the dilemma can be resolved without distorting the account of essential contestedness were correct and both inconsistency objections had thus been refuted, she herself delivers yet another blow to that concept in admitting that her proposed strategy for countering the sophisticated charge of incoherence does have a great inconvenience: the resulting view of essential contestedness cannot withstand the second kind of objection, i. e., that it is unfounded. Three arguments support

with Mason's view is that on this weak understanding, it is difficult to see how 'essential contestedness' could still apply to *concepts*. Since concepts, or definitions of terms, imply neither a claim of truth nor a claim of correctness, there seems nothing left one could conclusively argue about. True, there is always the possibility of (potentially reasonable) disagreement about the appropriateness of different definitions for certain purposes, but that is something which does not allow of conclusive argument and which, besides, applies to *all* concepts *all* the time and thus cannot be singled out as a noteworthy property, called 'essential contestedness', of just some concepts.

[32] It is therefore not entirely correct to say that Swanton's „strategy is meant to save a writer like Lukes from accusations of inconsistency" (Kristjánsson 1996, 185).

[33] Swanton 1985, 816; 1992, 5 f. Cf. Kristjánsson 1996, 183 ff., for another very clear presentation of the same dilemma.

this contention. The first is that from the fact that „many political concepts are multiple and evaluative, and stand in no settled relation of priority with one another" it does not necessarily follow that there cannot be a best conception, or that at least it cannot be known; moral intuitionism, for instance, holds exactly the opposite view (1985, 820 f.). The second argument is that from the fact that political ideals are embedded in political theories or perspectives it does not follow that there is no best (knowable) conception of such an ideal; particularly, the incommensurability thesis about political theories does not yield that result (ibid., 821–823). And the last argument is that from the (alleged) fact that there is no 'Archimedian point' external to all moral or political theories or perspectives from which to judge the quality of conceptions of political ideals it does not necessarily follow that there can be no well-grounded belief in a particular conception as being the best (ibid., 823–827). Since, according to Swanton (ibid., 827), these three arguments are the only ones ever brought forward in support of the essential-contestedness view about evaluative concepts, that view has, at least so far, not been shown to be well-founded. Although, as she is careful to note (1992, 9), this stops short of the claim that the essential-contestedness view is wrong, she has shown that on the basis of presently available arguments belief in its truth does not seem warranted.

In summary, we have a kind of cascading argument against the tenability of predicates of essential contestedness: *(i)* On the first level, either one accepts – with Barry, Ball, and Mason – the simple inconsistency objection, and that is the end of essential contestedness, or one accepts Swanton's solution for it. *(ii)* In that case, the second level becomes relevant. Here, either one accepts – with Kristjánsson – the sophisticated inconsistency objection and the argument ends, or again one accepts Swanton's solution. *(iii)* But by then, at the very latest, the idea of essential contestedness has been watered down to such a degree that now – according to Swanton – the unfoundedness objection applies.

1.8. VALUE-DEPENDENCE EXAMINED

The second strategy mentioned above for denying the 'essential contestability' of power is to argue that the basic concern underlying the ideas of Gallie and Lukes, namely that it is the appraisiveness or value-dependence of the concept which gives rise to especially stubborn conceptual disagreements, is unfounded. It is the strategy chosen perhaps most prominently by Felix Oppenheim. His starting point is the observation that terms referring to political phenomena are, indeed, among those most often alleged to be 'essentially contestable', where

> „This means that speakers and writers committed to different political outlooks are bound to use them in different senses, and that there is no justification for singling out one or the other" (Oppenheim 1981, 182).

If true, this would obviously present a serious challenge to political science as such, and Oppenheim dedicates an entire chapter (ch. 8) of his investigations of political concepts to the examination of the contention that „political concepts are contestable [...] also – and perhaps primarily – because of their valuational dimension" (ibid., 195). His assessment of the matter is based on the understanding that the fundamental standard of adequacy for the *scientific* use of terms and concepts is whether or not they foster communication. One of the most important aspects of scientific communication certainly is that the basis of agreements and disagreements should be as clear as possible; and that is a point on which empirical concepts containing normative elements – „moral notions“, as Oppenheim calls them – are notoriously weak: when there is disagreement about the proper application of such a concept, we cannot know whether the disagreement concerns the empirical aspects or whether what the disagreement really is about is, e. g., a moral judgment. This weakness, moreover, is unnecessary. As long as we are not dealing with purely normative concepts (such as 'good', 'just', 'appropriate'), it is very well possible to separate the descriptive from the evaluative elements of an idea and thus construct purely descriptive concepts. The advantage of doing this is that it allows communication about empirical matters among people with different standards of evaluation (e. g., different moral outlooks), without preventing anyone who wishes to do so from expressing, *in addition*, an evaluation of the corresponding empirical instances. Clearly, it is one thing to *identify* something as an instance of some descriptive concept, and quite another to *evaluate* it.

In this context, it may be useful to recall the difference between 'defining characteristics' and 'accompanying characteristics', as explicated by John Hospers (1990, 117–119) with the help of the famous swan example: For a long time, no non-white swans were known; but then, one day, an animal was discovered in Australia that had all the characteristics of swans, except that it was black. The question then was, obviously, whether that bird should be called a 'swan' too, or whether the term 'swan' should be reserved to the white class of birds, and the newly discovered black one should be given another name. At first sight, this may seem a trivial and unimportant matter that could be decided, for instance, by the toss of a coin. But, might there not be good reasons for one or the other decision? In the case of the example, the question boils down to whether whiteness is to be regarded as a *defining characteristic* of swans – i. e., as a necessary or 'essential' property that „tells us how to identify something as being“ a swan –, in which case the black bird would have to get another name denoting another concept; or whether whiteness is to be regarded merely as a property which happened to *accompany* all swans until the black variety was discovered, and still applies to most (though not all) swans found ever since, and which therefore „tells us something about the *thing* already defined“.[34] What may have been a plausible reason for the authorities of biological taxonomy to opt for the second alternative? The main reason, as explained by Hospers, was that variation in colour is a very common phenomenon in the universe of living creatures, and that concerning other species there already existed a well-established convention to regard colour merely as an accompanying, and not as a defining characteristic.[35] Our concept of 'dog', for instance, does not include a particular colour as a neces-

[34] Hospers 1990, 118. Another famous example of the problem to classify objects which fit under the intension of an accepted concept, except that they also have an *additional* characteristic is J. L. Austin's 'exploding goldfinch'; cf., e. g., Schauer 1991, 36 f. On the problem of telling *definitions* of the 'All p are F' kind from *empirical hypotheses* (synthetic generalizations) of the same form, on the fact that sometimes what previously used to be an empirical hypothesis becomes a definition and *vice versa*, and on the implications of such shifts for our knowledge of the world, cf. Ayer 1946, ch. 5; von Wright 1957, ch. III.

[35] Recall that there are even animal species whose members adapt their colour to their surroundings and situation. For most purposes, it would certainly not be convenient if their species classification changed with their colour.

sary characteristic. Therefore, in the case of the black swan-like bird, in the absence of any special reason to the contrary, there was, indeed, good reason to stick to the practice of regarding a uniform colour at best as an accompanying characteristic of certain species and, therefore, to adopt a concept of swans that allows for them to be of different colours.

What can these considerations contribute to the question of whether or not politically relevant concepts such as power or influence should include normative properties as defining characteristics? Can we perhaps construct an argument analogous to the one used in the case of the black swans? I think, indeed, that we can. For instance, when it comes to forging political concepts involving actions, we can think of action concepts in general: Although, undoubtedly, some kinds of actions carry a negative connotation for most, if not all, people, whether a particular instance of such an action ultimately is to be condemned or praised will depend on a careful analysis of the respective circumstances and is not implied in the identification of the action as 'such-and-such an action'. For instance, 'shoving someone out of the way' may evoke a *suspicion* of meanness and, therefore, a *disposition* to reproach; but until we know whether someone was 'shoved out of the way', e. g., in order to make room for the shover or to prevent the shoved from being run over by an approaching car, we do not know how to evaluate that particular instance of 'shoving someone away' morally, whether to reject it or approve of it. This means that the concept of 'shoving someone out of the way' does not include the evaluation of its being mean as a defining characteristic (even if perhaps it is a kind of action that in most instances actually turns out to deserve that adjective). Similarly, most of our general action concepts are descriptive concepts that do not carry a 'moral tag' or some other normative label as a defining characteristic; instead, for expressing our value-judgments we have a great variety of adjectives and other linguistic devices at our disposal. This constitutes a sort of 'precedent' for the construction of political concepts about action too, in the sense that it seems advisable to conceive of normative aspects not as defining, but at best as accompanying characteristics.

But then, someone might question whether the established practice that the colour of an animal or the normative quality of an action is not considered a defining characteristic has anything to recommend it in the first place. This challenge, however, can easily be met. After all, as has been remarked earlier, definitions are not a matter of truth or falsity, but of expedience.[36] They always involve decisions about an adequate degree of abstraction, the extension of the phenomena to be referred to, and the kind of information to be conveyed with the use of a term. Therefore, the appropriateness of the decisions implied in a definition is always *relative to some purpose*. One plausible and uncontroversial criterion for the appropriateness of *scientific* concepts seems to be that of conceptual parsimony: let concepts be as specific as necessary, but no more. The reason for this rule is obviously that, by generating an unnecessary inflation[37] of terms, exces-

[36] So-called 'lexical definitions' can, of course, be true or false, but that is only because, strictly speaking, they are not really definitions at all, but rather descriptive statements: 'reports' *about* definitions, i. e., about an established linguistic usage.

[37] 'Inflation' can be taken rather literally here: with too fine a maze of concepts, there is an 'excessive supply' of terms, with the consequence that the use of each one of them can 'buy' very little in terms of informational content.

sive specificity of concepts hinders communication. Not only is it cumbersome to have to refer to larger classes of things by a conjunctive use of a plurality of more specific terms – it can also bring confusion and error and thus operate against the purpose of science, as it may lead one wrongly to believe that things designated by different terms actually differ in *relevant* aspects, and it may prevent one from seeing the full extension of the class of things that are relevant for a given purpose, thus causing a loss of possible insights (what in German is proverbially known as 'failing to recognize the forest behind all the trees').

For scientific purposes, it therefore seems adequate (and also possible) to start with descriptive concepts, constructing normative concepts on the basis of those descriptive ones only in case of particular need, in the context of the treatment of specific subject matters.[38] With respect to the concept of power, this means that if 'power' were indeed, by well-established usage, a normative term (that is, a term containing a value-judgment among its defining characteristics), for the purposes of political science we would need to 'invent' another term for denoting the more encompassing class of phenomena which share merely the descriptive characteristics of the corresponding normative concept.

This is not to deny that with 'power', as the term is commonly used, it is as with the example given above of 'shoving someone out of the way': it seems to be burdened with a moral presumption against it. But again, as with the example, one can easily think of instances where instead of a negative evaluation, its existence or exercise is praised, or its absence deplored – the 'power' to keep a villain from carrying out his criminal schemings is one ready example. With the normative status of power it seems to be as with the colour of swans: Perhaps many, but certainly not all instances of it deserve a negative evaluation, just as many, but not all swans happen to be white. In both cases we are dealing with a characteristic that *accompanies* a great number of cases, but which there is no need to regard as a *defining* characteristic.

With this conclusion, nothing has been said as yet that could help us to end the controversies and disagreements about the *descriptive* characteristics involved in the concept of power. In that direction, almost everything remains to be done. As Brian Barry

[38] Of course, for some purposes we may wish to have a special term for referring to a class of actions, or relationships, or states of affairs, which, besides sharing certain empirical characteristics, are also evaluated in the same way; but such concepts are necessarily parasitic on descriptive ones, because what is evaluated are, after all, certain empirical facts. An example in point is the distinction of 'murder' as a specific subclass of 'killing'; even if we had the concept of murder *only* for the purpose of referring to that class of killings which have no (moral or legal) justification or excuse, it is a concept that is parasitic on a broader, purely descriptive concept of killing. Descriptive concepts of kinds of actions are, in that sense, logically prior to evaluative concepts of kinds of actions. And, of course, even if the *intensional* definition of 'murder' were a purely evaluative formula, such as „'Murder' means 'evil killing'", in order to be able to identify the members of its *extension* we would need a list of empirical features and circumstances which (are thought to) make a killing evil (on the difficulties of sorting out the empirical features which, for moral or for legal purposes, distinguish cases of murder from other cases of killing, cf., e. g., Uniacke 1994). To avoid misunderstandings, let me clarify that with this I do not mean to say that the meaning of evaluative terms, such as 'evil', can themselves be completely reduced to descriptive factors; all I mean to say is that it is possible – at least theoretically, although it may often be difficult in practice – to separate the descriptive content of a concept from its evaluative content; whether or not the respective descriptive features then actually do, in a given social context, uniformly give rise to a certain evaluation is entirely contingent. Cf. Hare 1981, ch. 4, for a clear account of the difference between this position and 'moral descriptivism'.

(1991b, 298) concisely stated: „Power is not an essentially contested concept but it is an essentially messy concept.“[39]

Therefore, if a useful concept of influence is to be based on the concept of power, an effort must first be made to clear up that 'mess'. The remaining part of this chapter will be dedicated to this task.

2. Conceptions of Power

In political science scholarship, the concept of power certainly is among those most often analysed. The literature on this topic is abundant, and very heterogeneous. Contributions stretch widely over centuries[40] and paradigms[41]. To call to mind only a few fundamental facts and keywords: On the one hand, we have Hobbes's early, clear and concise, though in the last instance not very satisfactory definition, in the tenth chapter of *Leviathan*: „THE POWER of a Man [...] is his present means, to obtain some future apparent Good“, or Weber's much later, but nevertheless already classical, often (mis)-quoted characterization of power as „any chance to impose one's own will in a social relationship, even against resistance, regardless of what that chance is based on“.[42] On

[39] For a lucid and witty presentation of the many issues involved in *de facto* contests about the concept of power in the past, cf. A. O. Rorty 1992. What Brian Barry means with his *dictum* about the 'essential messiness' of the concept of power will be considered in detail below, in Section 2.3.

[40] On the development of the concept from antiquity to modern times, cf. esp.: Faber/Ilting/Meier 1982; for a history of the concept of power from Aristotle to the present, cf. Röttgers 1990, part I; Clegg 1989 provides a readable, though somewhat idiosyncratic and not always well-structured presentation of the main points in the long debate on the concept of power, treating among others the conceptions of Hobbes and Machiavelli (ch. 2), Dahl and the 'community power' group (ch. 3), the 'intentionalists' Bachrach/Baratz, Russell, Weber, Wrong (ch. 4), Lukes (ch. 5; cf. Figure 5.1 for a useful summary of the main ingredients of the 'faces of power' debate), Parsons and Giddens (ch. 6), and Foucault (ch. 7). A collection of many of the most important social-scientific essays on the concept and the phenomenon of power in this century is contained in the three volumes on *Power* in Routledge's 'Critical Concepts' series (Scott 1994). Other collections of relevant 'classical' contributions are, e. g., Bell/Edwards/Wagner 1969; Lukes 1986; Olson/Marger 1993.

[41] Cf., for instance, Hradil 1980; Weiß 1995, 1998. – My own, certainly incomplete bibliography on the concept of social 'power' currently contains more than 200 titles. In shaping my thoughts on power and influence, I have tried to take into account as much of this immense literature as I could; but Galbraith's (1984, xv) disclaimer applies: „I must not seem to suggest, even remotely, that I have read all that has been written on it. No life is that long; there are some books that simply cannot be read; and there is much, I am sure, that I have missed. Everyone should be very cautious in his claims where the literature on power is concerned.“

[42] Weber 1922, 28 (my translation): „[...] jede Chance, innerhalb einer sozialen Beziehung den eigenen Willen auch gegen Widerstreben durchzusetzen, gleichviel worauf diese Chance beruht“. It is less well known that in a later chapter of the same work (1922, 631), Weber reformulated the definition: „Unter 'Macht' wollen wir dabei hier ganz allgemein die Chance eines Menschen oder einer Mehrzahl solcher verstehen, den eigenen Willen in einem Gemeinschaftshandeln auch gegen den Widerstand anderer daran Beteiligten durchzusetzen.“ [„Here, by 'power' we shall understand, very generally, a person's or a plurality of persons' chance to impose their own will in the context of a social activity, even against the resistance of other participants“; my translation.]

It is remarkable that Weber's very famous definition is frequently misquoted in translations, by omitting the word 'even' („auch“). Weber has therefore often been misinterpreted as an author who holds that power situations *necessarily* involve resistance and that where such resistance is absent one cannot speak of power. This view is untenable if Weber's definition is read correctly. Rather, he must be classified among those who hold that for power to exist (and even to be exercised) the actual presence of resistance is *not* necessary; all that is

the other hand, more recently and from very different perspectives, there is Luhmann's conception of power as a *medium* of communication, a code,[43] or Foucault's productive, identity-producing power networks.[44] And in between, there is a wealth of other conceptions and variants – among them the two, three, four or even „many" 'faces' of power that have been distinguished by different authors in the past decades.[45]

For social-scientific work on power in the second half of the 20th century, John Scott's (1994) collection of dozens of articles serves well for a rough overview over the main currents of investigation during that period.[46] The *Chronological Table* included at the beginning of the first volume, which lists the articles in the order of their original publication, reveals that the number of reprinted essays increases for every decade: 9 are from the 1950s, 16 from the 1960s, 23 from the 1970s, and 26 from the 1980s. Of course, from this fact it cannot be inferred that total output on the subject has likewise steadily increased; but at least it proves that after the heyday of power studies in the 1960s and 1970s, when most of the famous works now regarded as 'standard' were published, power has by no means been abandoned as a subject worthy of consideration. However, to the extent that the collection can be taken as a more or less representative sample of the literature, it shows that in the 1950s and 1960s conceptual and communi-

needed is that the power-holder *could* impose his will *if* he met resistance. Hence, on Weber's view, ascriptions of power do entail arguments about the truth of counterfactual conditionals (statements about what *could* happen *if* resistance were to arise); but that is a very different matter, and has nothing to do with the inclusion of resistance among the defining characteristics of power situations. Cf. Baumann 1993, 14 f., and Wrong 1988, 23, for similar arguments.

Dennis Wrong (1988, 262 f., n. 1) reports that Anthony Giddens *(New Rules of Sociological Method*, New York: Basic Books 1976, 173, n. 26) already made the same point. In his attempt to dismiss Giddens's implicit reproach of sloppiness, Wrong throws some light on the genesis of the mistake: apparently, the second definition has been translated correctly ever since the first English translation of that part of Weber's work was presented in 1946 by H. H. Gerth and C. Wright Mills. Unfortunately, however, that definition is hardly ever mentioned. The one that has been used instead by almost everyone in the English-speaking world is the first, which appeared in English for the first time in 1947 in a translation by A. M. Henderson and Talcott Parsons (Weber 1947). It seems to have been the small, but significant inaccuracy of these translators that has been carried down through generations of scholars who have relied on their translation as authoritative. The latest reproduction of it I am aware of can be found in Olson/Marger 1993, 37. [Another, later translation of the passage as „the probability that an actor in a social relationship will be in a position to carry out his own will despite resistance [...]" provides no substantial improvement; Weber 1978, 53, quoted from Caporaso/Levine 1992, 161.]

A correctly translated, though unacknowledged, paraphrase can be found in Habermas 1997, 175 [1992, 215]: „I use the term 'social power' as a measure for the possibilities an actor has in social relationships to assert his own will and interests, even against the opposition of others." When Habermas is classified as an advocate of a 'communicative' concept of power, it is often forgotten that he distinguishes several different kinds of power, and that as a concept of 'social power' he adopts the Weberian proposal without any modification.

[43] Luhmann 1975, 2000.

[44] Foucault 1978; but cf. also Foucault 1994 for a (relatively clear and accessible) presentation of a rather different, more 'behaviouralist' conception of power. An informative critical analysis of Foucault's conception of power can be found in Honneth 1991, esp. ch. 5.

[45] The „second face" by Bachrach/Baratz (1962, 1970), the „third face" by Steven Lukes (1974) (another set of „three faces" has been proposed by Kenneth Boulding [1989]), the „fourth face" by Peter Digeser (1992), and „many faces" by Dahl (1970, ch. 3), Abell (1977) and Thomas (1978).

[46] From the first half of the century, the collection contains only one contribution (Goldhamer/Shils 1939).

ty-power studies clearly dominated the field; in the 1970s, while conceptual controversy continued, networks came up as a new topic that fascinated political and other social scientists;[47] and in the 1980s, although 'power' was still a prominent subject, with only a few exceptions contributors seem to have grown tired of conceptual (and related theoretical) questions and, despite building on an unsure foundation, have moved on to empirical matters. It is surely not entirely unreasonable to think that this near-demise of conceptual studies on social power was to a large extent a consequence of the publication of Steven Lukes's book in 1974 and the ensuing discussion about the alleged essential contestedness of the concept, which left many convinced that there is really no point in further pursuing an impossible quest.

At the same time, however, towards the end of the period covered by Scott's collection, Kenneth Boulding – eminent economist and peace researcher, and „a fairly unrepentant thinker" (his own words) who is not afraid of bold statements – has passed a harsh judgment on the 'state of the art', finding most previous work in philosophy, sociology and political science about the concept and phenomena of power, with only a few noted exceptions,[48] „surprisingly meager", useful perhaps as a source for „a great many good little quotes", but not for profound and systematic insights (Boulding 1989, 12 f.). Although in its excessive generality this verdict undoubtedly does not do justice to many individual contributions to the subject, there is a grain of truth in it: even if one looks only at the concept and theory of *social* or, still more restricted, of *political* power, important basic questions remain open.[49]

In order to come to terms with this „messy" concept of power in a way that will allow me to build on it for the analysis of the concept of influence, I will begin with a presentation and discussion of one representative example each of three kinds of conceptions – sociological, philosophical, and economic – to be found in the literature, which either have been of special importance in scholarly debate or, in my view, contribute especially interesting aspects to it. This will be followed by a discussion of some of the main points of contention.

2.1. SOCIOLOGICAL CONCEPTIONS: FROM MAX WEBER TO STEVEN LUKES

The trajectory of what has come to be known as the sociological view or conception of power is well-known and does not need to be recalled here in much detail. I will make

[47] Possibly the most forceful advocate of the view of „societies as organized power networks" to date has been sociologist Michael Mann with his sweeping history of social power (Mann 1986 and 1993). It is probably no mere coincidence that he began work on this project in the 1970s when the idea of power networks was 'in the air'. Since the theoretical fruits of this author's historical investigation are projected to be reaped in the final volume of a series of four (of which at the time of my writing, only two – vol. I on agrarian societies from „the beginning" to the first industrial revolution, and vol. II on the „long century" between the first and the second industrial revolution – have appeared; vol. III is projected to cover the rest of the 20th century), it is to be expected that, if all goes as planned, the theoretical work on the 'networking' qualities of power will reach a new peak sometime early in the 21st century.

[48] He mentions Thomas Hobbes in philosophy and Dennis Wrong in political sociology.

[49] Boulding's own contribution, although it contains some interesting insights, is itself much too narrowly focused to qualify as the „systematic treatise" he clamours for.

do with a brief sketch, merely to call to mind some of its most relevant (and contested) aspects.

As with so many other subjects in contemporary social science too, once again it is Max Weber who must be credited with having laid the foundation. Although, of course, neither a concept of power nor this particular conception of it was totally unknown before his writing, Weber gave it a concise formulation[50] that has served practically as an obligatory point of reference for all those interested in a social concept of power ever since – whether they simply adopt it, use it as a starting point for improvement on the same line or, on the contrary, as a model of how power should not be conceived. Taking Weber as a point of departure, one can then draw a fairly straight line (abstracting from some detours and bifurcations) all the way down to Steven Lukes who has become, so to speak, the next 'compulsory stop' for any voyage on the path of the development of a social conception of power in this century.[51]

Lukes's contribution to the field is twofold since he has not only added his own proposal to those already existing, but has also offered excellent summaries of the different conceptions developed by others before him.[52]

As explained above, in Section 1, Lukes starts from the idea that there is one single concept underlying all the different existing views or conceptions of (social) power:

„The absolutely basic common core to, or primitive notion lying behind, all talk of power is the notion that *A* in some way affects *B*.“ (26)

But since there are myriads of ways in which agents may 'affect' each other, most of which do not involve that which we (however vaguely) have in mind when ordinarily speaking of power, „something further is needed“, some other criterion for distinguishing power situations from non-power situations: the way how an agent with power affects another must be, in a particular sense, „non-trivial or significant“ (ibid.). Lukes explains that different conceptions of power part company on what the appropriate criterion should be and how it is to be interpreted. He classifies existing views into two main groups: those that do and those that do not take interests – more precisely: a *negative* impact of one agent on the interests of another – to be the basic criterion for the identification of power situations.

This, the interest-oriented view, is the one Lukes himself favours. It is a view that has been given many names, but is perhaps best known as the 'sociological' or 'behavior(al)ist' conception of power. Lukes defends the idea that a negative impact on one of the parties' interests, and therefore conflict (if only latent) should be a defining

[50] See above, at n. 42.

[51] Of course, there are also a great many 'facultative stops' on the way between Weber and Lukes which should certainly not be passed by in any more detailed account, but which we do not need to go into for our present purpose. Besides, Lukes is not the end point of that line, as the not very numerous, but important later contributions show (e. g., Oppenheim 1981, Morriss 1987, Koller 1991, Isaac 1992, to name but a few); but I think it would not be wrong to interpret the conceptual controversy about power in the social sciences as significantly divided into a 'pre-Lukes' and a 'post-Lukes' era.

[52] In the rest of this sub-section, I will follow the exposition in Lukes 1974 (unless otherwise indicated, page numbers in brackets will refer to this work) complementing it with my own observations every now and then.

characteristic of power, against the rival views of Parsons and Arendt whose conceptions emphasize consensus and the pursuit of collective goals (27–31). Theirs, he argues, is not really a *social* conception of power, involving a relationship between agents, at all; what they are talking about is not 'power over' but 'power to'; they thus miss one of the main reasons for holding power to be socially relevant, to wit, that it has to do with „the [...] securing of people's compliance by overcoming or averting their opposition"; furthermore, by sticking to the interest-oriented conception of power and using other, well-established terms[53] for the situations they are interested in, „All that Parsons and Arendt wish to say about consensual behaviour remains sayable, but so does all that they wish to remove from the language of power" (31).

But the interest-based conception itself is not without problems, in the first place because it comes in several versions, depending on each author's view of what it means to affect someone's interests negatively. Different answers to this question give rise to different, though always interest-oriented, conceptions of power. Lukes identifies three such answers, constituting what he calls a 'liberal', a 'reformist', and a 'radical' conception of interests (34 f.) which, in turn, have led to three different conceptions of social or, more specifically, political power – each focusing on a different one of the famous three 'faces' of power:[54]

(1) The „one-dimensional view" (of which Robert Dahl and other early students of community-power are the most prominent representatives)[55] looks only at a 'first face'. It is the face which can most easily be identified empirically, as it refers to situations exhibiting a manifest conflict of interests where, with the help of certain resources, in open contest one side succeeds in imposing its will on the other(s), e. g. – in the political realm – by managing in some manner to control the content of political decisions:[56]

> „[T]his first, one-dimensional, view of power involves a focus on *behaviour* in the making of *decisions* on *issues* over which there is an observable *conflict* of (subjective) *interests*, seen as express policy preferences, revealed by political participation." (15)

One of the most important points in his exposition of this approach to the concept of power is Lukes's observation about the discrepancy between Dahl's well-known definition of power as one agent's *ability* to make another change his 'normal' course of ac-

[53] Lukes specifically mentions 'influence'. I will come back to that in the next chapter.

[54] Cf. pp. 11–25 for the presentation of the one-, two-, and three-dimensional view, pp. 36–45 for their comparison, and p. 25 for a useful schematic representation of their main features.

[55] Rothgeb (1992, ch. 2) is one recent author who still defines power following exclusively the work of these 'classical' behaviourists (Dahl, Simon, Deutsch, Baldwin, Keohane/Nye, Lasswell/Kaplan, Singer, Russett/Starr ...) without considering any later writings.

[56] The idea that power involves, above all, participation in decision-making had already been presented by Lasswell/Kaplan (1950, 75): „*Power* is participation in the making of decisions: G has power over H with respect to the values K if G participates in the making of decisions affecting the K-policies of H." But note that for these authors a 'decision' exists only when a policy is effectively implemented, and decision-making thus involves the entire process, from making a policy choice to implementing that choice (ibid., 74 f.). How, by which means the „effective control over policy" power consists in is actually obtained does not matter for them (ibid., 76); what does matter, however, is that there must be the *possibility* of imposing „severe deprivations for nonconformity" (ibid., 76). Lasswell/Kaplan's definition thus comes very close to that of Max Weber. Lasswell/Kaplan's conception will be treated in more detail in the next chapter.

tion[57] and his subsequent almost exclusive preoccupation with situations in which there is, in fact, a successful attempt to impose one's will, i. e., a successful *exercise* of power. This is one of the most often criticized points of the 'one-dimensional' conception.[58] In order to facilitate an operational definition that would make social power a readily observable and perhaps even measurable magnitude, the concept was tailored in such a way that a great many situations which would fit under the 'ability' definition were simply excluded from consideration. Thus, the strength of this conception – it's usefulness for empirical studies – was bought at the high price of linking power relations only to past or present *actual* and *active* performances, thus disregarding both the possibility that someone may be 'under' the power of another even if no 'exercise' of that power has as yet taken place (and that such a situation in itself, even if an exercise would never occur, is worthy of the attention of anyone seriously interested in the study of social power) and that power may also be exercised in non-obvious ways which do not involve overt decision-making (36 f.). At best, Lukes concludes (14), there is a substantial degree of inconsistency in this respect between some of the conceptual and the empirical work of Dahl and others in his footsteps.[59]

(2) The recognition of some of these shortcomings led to the elaboration of the „two-dimensional view" which besides the one just presented also takes into account a 'second face' of power. This 'second face', inseparably linked to the names of Peter Bachrach and Morton S. Baratz, is perhaps the most widely known of them all.[60] Two aspects in their account constitute major improvements over the previous conceptions:

The first of these has nothing to do with the issue of the two dimensions or faces of power. Rather, it involves conceptual precision: Bachrach/Baratz do not follow the practice of Dahl and others of using the different 'power terms' as synonymous. Instead, they elaborate a typology, distinguishing 'power', 'authority', 'influence', 'manipulation', and 'coercion' (1963, sects. I–V; 1970, ch. 2). The distinction between these terms is not at issue here, so I will not comment on it at this point.

What is of interest in the present context, however, is the definition of power they arrive at: The first point Bachrach/Baratz strongly emphasize is the *relational* nature of (social) power. Power, they observe, is not a property or „possession" of an agent, independently of the desires of other agents. An important corollary of this view is that no amount or constellation of resources *automatically* assures anyone power over anybody else. Whether or not there is a power relation between two agents always depends, in the

[57] Dahl 1957, 202 f.: „*A* has power over *B* to the extent that he *can* get *B* to do something that *B* would not otherwise do" (emphasis added).

[58] For a devastating critique of Dahl's application of his own concept of power in his *Who Governs?*, cf. Morriss 1972.

[59] Surprisingly, one of those walking – at least some of the time – in Dahl's footsteps is Foucault (1994) who, in his 1982 reflections on why power is studied and how power is exercised, explains that „'power' designates relationships between partners" (226), but that „Power exists only when it is put into action" (227), when „certain persons exercise power over others" (225), and that „in order to understand what power relations are about, perhaps we should investigate the forms of resistance" (220) to it.

[60] With their 1962 article about 'The Two Faces of Power', Bachrach and Baratz coined the metaphor of the 'faces' of power; for their contribution, cf. also Bachrach/Baratz 1963, as well as Part I of Bachrach/Baratz 1970 (the first two thirds of the theoretical part of their book contain an almost unmodified reprint of the 1962 and 1963 essays, the former in ch. 1, the latter in ch. 2 and the beginning of ch. 3).

last instance, on the 'receiving end' of it: „the successful exercise of power is dependent upon the relative importance of conflicting values *in the mind of the recipient* in the power relationship".[61] For such a relationship, the authors specify three *necessary* conditions:

(i) „there must be a conflict of interests or values",
(ii) the interests of one side must in the end actually prevail,
(iii) for one side (supposedly, the prevailing side) there must be an „availability of sanctions" (ibid., 97).

Immediately afterwards, however, Bachrach and Baratz explain that „availability" alone is *not sufficient*: there must, in fact, actually be a *credible threat* of a sanction which is recognized by the threatened party as a *deprivation* constituting a *greater disvalue* than that avoided by complying with the *demand* which must also be (recognizably) connected to the sanction.[62] All these different elements they finally bring together in their definition of power:

> „A power relationship exists when (a) there is a conflict over values or courses of action between A and B; (b) B complies with A's wishes; and (c) he does so because he is fearful that A will deprive him of a value or values which he, B, regards more highly than those which would have been achieved by noncompliance."[63]

So far, this definition is perhaps more precise, but does not seem to add much to the combined definitions of Dahl and Lasswell/Kaplan. The second improvement of the two-dimensional view, however, is, as the authors subsequently explain, an extension of

[61] Bachrach/Baratz 1963 (Scott 1994/II, 98); the upshot of this argument is that not always the guy with the gun is the guy who has the power; whether or not he does depends on the other side's preferences and dispositions; the authors illustrate this with the standard example of the would-be suicide who 'takes advantage' of a sentry's 'Halt or I'll shoot!' and, by walking on, 'forces' the sentry – whom he knows to be under a credible threat of severe sanctions from his superiors were he to neglect his soldierly duties – to shoot him, thus saving him the trouble of having to kill himself (ibid., 97). It may be questioned whether in that hypothetical case the suicide can be said to exercise power over the sentry; but what is uncontroversial is that, despite the gun, the sentry does *not* have power over the suicide. Similar cases can be made of other agents with 'unusual' preference orders, such as heroes, fanatics, or martyrs. The importance of what has come to be called a power subject's 'motive base' is also emphasized by Lasswell/ Kaplan 1950, 77; Cartwright 1969, 151 f.; Blalock 1989, ch. 2; N. Barry 1989, ch. 4; or Stoppino 1990, 383 and 341; Oakeshott 1991, 445, among others. As early as 1937, Carl J. Friedrich noted that „To convert [resources] into power, the power-seeker must find human beings who value the things sufficiently to obey his orders in return [...] It is, therefore, impossible to study politics as the process of acquiring, distributing, and losing power without taking into consideration the major objectives of the human beings involved in the situations studied" (quoted from Lasswell/Kaplan 1950, 77); very similarly, despite of his different approach and terminology, Luhmann 1975, 22, 27; 2000, 27.

[62] Bachrach/Baratz 1963 (Scott 1994/II, 97 f.) In a later paper, they declare to have modified their conception in the sense that they now think that power can also be exercised *indirectly*; in the extreme case, neither of the two sides needs to be aware of the other's existence; hence, there must also not necessarily be a communication of a demand; cf. Bachrach/Baratz 1975 (Scott 1994/II, 202).

[63] Bachrach/Baratz 1963 (Scott 1994/II, 98). Strangely, while the authors otherwise consistently speak of the sanctions involved in power-relationships in terms of „deprivations" and „threats", just once (ibid., 97) and without any explanation they remark that by 'sanctions' they mean „any promised reward or penalty by which an actor can maintain effective control over policy". It is, of course, a considerable difference for a conception of power whether it postulates that power can be exercised only by way of threatening with deprivation, or also by way of offering rewards. Bachrach and Baratz seem not to be aware of it. (The issue of the systematic difference between threats and offers will later, in Chapter 3, play some role in the discussion of the relationship between power and freedom.)

the conception of power, as compared with the earlier ones. Because they argue that agents may be negatively affected in the possibility to pursue their interests concerning certain issues not only by policy-decisions with an unfavourable content, but also by being prevented from demanding that an issue is discussed (and subsequently decided on) at all. If persons dissatisfied with the *status quo* of some matter are denied the chance to argue and mobilize for a change, those who successfully arrange such „nondecisions" certainly exercise power over them. This idea has received even the blessing of Brian Barry who in his otherwise critical review of Lukes's book nevertheless concedes that „the superiority of the two-dimensional over the one-dimensional view is patent in that ability to control the agenda is obviously power".[64]

Of course, strictly speaking, it is a misnomer to call it 'nondecisions' when issues are prevented from being decided on by blocking their entrance into a political forum, and Bachrach/Baratz have consequently not failed to remark that, in a way, even here decisions are involved (albeit on another decision-making level, concerning matters – primarily procedural questions – which precede the final decision-making on substantial issues). But two things must be noted here.

The first is that there is a relevant difference between the decisions considered in the one- and in the two-dimensional view: according to the former, only decisions taken in an open contest of interests qualify as potentially involving exercises of power, hence those who exercise power *can hardly fail to be aware* of it. On the latter account, in contrast, exercises of power must *not necessarily* be performed „consciously":[65] an agenda-setter may be unaware of the fact that with her arrangement of the agenda she is „effectively prevent[ing] certain grievances from developing into full-fledged issues which call for decisions";[66] she may even be unaware of the fact that she *could* use her position to do so (although in today's highly professionalized political environment, such naïvité would surely not last long). This is so because exercises of power along the second dimension are always at least one step removed, so to speak, from the conflict of interests about the respective issue, and that conflict must therefore not necessarily be at the center of the attention of those who are responsible for a 'nondecision'.

[64] Barry 1991c, 305. 'Agenda-setting' (or, more generally, 'gatekeeping') power has meanwhile become a specialized subject, with a large, often highly formalized literature of its own; cf., e. g., several articles published in the *Journal of Theoretical Politics* in the past few years (Eavey/Miller 1995, Young 1996, Boockmann 1998) and the many works cited there. William Riker has ingeniously illustrated how agenda control (in various ways, not only in the manner envisaged by Bachrach/Baratz) is one of the main pillars of what he calls „heresthetic", i. e., the art of „structuring the world so you can win" (Riker 1986, ix). However, cf. Holmes who, against such „[c]onspiracy theorists", emphasizes that „agenda-narrowing" or the „politics of omission", far from being merely „a technique by which sinister elites exert power over their hapless victims" (Holmes 1988, 21), can also have an important „disencumbering or agenda-uncluttering function" (ibid. 23), especially in deeply divided societies; nevertheless, Holmes acknowledges that this is a double-edged sword because „gag rules, although often presented as impartial measures serving the cause of communal peace, can easily be turned into weapons in a partisan struggle" (ibid., 52).
The question of barriers to 'political entry' also belongs under the heading of the 'second face' of power; cf. the special issue of the above-mentioned journal on this subject (Holler 1991). According to Cartwright (1969, 140), the theory of gatekeeping was first developed by Lewin (1951, ch. 8).
[65] 1962 (Scott 1994/II, 88).
[66] 1963 (Scott 1994/II, 107).

The second observation, which reinforces the first, is that, *pace* Barry, agenda-setting as such is, in fact, not the main aspect of the second face of power. Bachrach and Baratz admonish their readers that 'nondecision-making' is not to be confused with „the negative aspects of decision-making (deciding not to act or deciding not to decide)".[67] Rather, agendas reflect 'nondecision-making' only to the extent that the fact that certain issues do not appear on them – i. e., do not come up for debate and decision – is due to what, following Schattschneider, the authors have called the 'mobilization of bias' rather than to an authoritative decision by some agenda-setter. In other words: an agent who 'makes a nondecision' is not someone who makes (and imposes) the decision not to decide on some issue, but someone who makes *others* refrain from even demanding that a certain issue be put on the agenda, and/or third parties from supporting such demands, by invoking „the dominant values, the accepted rules of the game, the existing power relations among groups, and the instruments of force, singly or in combination" (ibid. 106 f.). Unfortunately, however, the authors subsequently muddle up their own account by not sticking consistently to what they said before. The previous citation is taken from the final section of their 1963 paper – precisely the section that was later omitted in the book. Instead, in the book[68] they stress that a 'nondecision' is a decision, after all – a decision precisely of those whose interests would be jeopardized should the issue in question be accepted as a matter to be decided on: „a decision that results in suppression or thwarting of a latent or manifest challenge to the values or interests of the decision-maker".[69] What produces this result, however, is *not* this decision itself (as would be the decision of an agenda-setter to ignore some issue), but an entire *process* of nondecision-making; and only nondecisions secured in *one* of several possible manners, namely: by a threat with negative or a promise of positive sanctions, constitute exercises of *power*.[70]

Besides such questions about internal consistency, the two-dimensional conception proposed by Bachrach and Baratz has met primarily with two kinds of criticism which have, so to speak, put the screws on it from two opposing ends.

On the one hand, it has been argued, especially from defenders of the one-dimensional view, that „[t]he core of the problem is the difficulty of identifying nondecisions",[71] in other words, that this conception converts power into an unobservable and hence, for the purposes of an empirical science, a useless property. This objection had to

[67] Ibid. Thus, it is not correct to interpret the novelty introduced into the debate by Bachrach/ Baratz as merely an emphasis on the importance of 'omissions' as opposed to 'actions'. The above-quoted passage clarifies that they are concerned with omissions at best secondarily. It is, therefore, not a cogent argument against the originality of their account if it is pointed out – correctly, I think – that from a systematic point of view the idea of 'omission' does not add anything to that of 'action'.

[68] Ch. 3.III; the relevant citations can also be found in Lukes 1974, 18 f.

[69] 1970, 44 (quoted from Lukes 1974, 18).

[70] Just how much Bachrach/Baratz, despite all their criticism, still stand in the tradition of Lasswell/Kaplan becomes evident in their idea that it also constitutes a 'nondecision' when „demands for change [...] can be [...] maimed or destroyed in the decision-implementing stage of the policy process" (ibid.). Only if 'decision' is understood in the sense of Lasswell/Kaplan, as including the entire implementation process of a policy (cf. above, n. 56), does this make sense. On the ordinary understanding that what is implemented already *is* a decision, we would have the strange case that one and the same thing would be a decision *and* a nondecision.

[71] Wolfinger 1971 (Scott 1994/II, 129). In the same direction, cf. also Frey 1971 and Debnam 1975, reprinted likewise in Section 3 of Scott 1994.

some extent been anticipated by the authors when they argue in the book[72] that, although a nondecision as such cannot be *observed*, its existence can be *inferred* from the observation of the typical 'ingredients' of a nondecision-making process, that is, above all, processes of the 'mobilization of bias', and the existence of either openly voiced, but neglected or (at least politically) hidden „grievances" specifically on the part of those who are disadvantaged by existing 'biases'. Whether the validation and the observation of these indicators is, indeed, as unproblematic as Bachrach and Baratz seem to have assumed is controversial. But to their credit, it must be said that in the elaboration of concepts easy observability is certainly not the only, and not even necessarily the primary, scientifically valid criterion for the quality of a definition.[73]

On the other hand, it has been Steven Lukes himself (37 f.) who has formulated a critique from exactly the opposite perspective. In his view, Bachrach and Baratz do not go far enough in their attempt to overcome the shortcomings of the one-dimensional view: there is still too much individual decision-making and too much visible conflict in their account. He thus holds it against them that their two-dimensional view „confines itself to studying situations where the mobilisation of bias can be attributed to individuals' decisions that have the effect of preventing currently observable grievances (overt or covert) from becoming issues within the political process", because in this manner it defines away „the complex and subtle ways in which the *inactivity* of leaders and the sheer weight of institutions" may prevent the introduction, or even the struggle for the introduction, of certain grievances into the political process. His summary of what the second face of power involves clearly reflects that opinion:

„So I conclude that the two-dimensional view of power involves a *qualified critique* of the *behavioural focus* of the first view (I say qualified because it is still assumed that nondecision-making is a form of decision-making) and it allows for consideration of the ways in which *decisions* are prevented from being taken on *potential issues* over which there is an observable *conflict* of (subjective) *interests*, seen as embodied in express policy preferences and sub-political grievances." (20)

(3) With his presentation of the „three-dimensional view", Lukes expressly proposes to break with the Weberian tradition and to dissociate the concept of power, in a much more „radical" way than Bachrach and Baratz, from the idea of individual decisions and observable conflict (22 f.). If power consists, as Dahl defined it, in one agent's

72 Cf. ch. 3.IV which deals explicitly with the question of the empirical identification of nondecisions.

73 Cf. their reply in this sense to the critique of Geoffrey Debnam: Bachrach/Baratz 1975 (in Scott 1994/II, esp. 203). Generally, empiricists seem to think that theorists should say something like 'My grand theory about <power> in the sense of <A and B and C> is actually nothing but a lot of hot air. I admit that it makes no sense to say that <power> is <A and B and C> if, as my empiricist colleagues have authoritatively established, all that can be empirically researched is A; therefore, the concept of power should be restricted to denote A, and I should elaborate a more modest theory', whereas theorists, in turn, think that empiricists should say 'I agree that it makes sense to conceive <power> as meaning <A and B and C>, but unfortunately my research instruments are limited; hence, when I say that I've been investigating power I am just bragging; I ought to be more modest and admit that it is not power I have been investigating, but only aspect A; but the other aspects are certainly just as important and I'll do my best to find ways how to investigate them too'. Being a theorist myself, I am more inclined to adopt the latter position, although this is not the place to argue for it. In any case, this part of the controversy about an adequate concept of power is only one example of the eternal contest between theoretically and empirically oriented political scientists. For a lucid and elegant attempt to reconcile the two interests, cf. Kliemt 1981, treated in the next subsection.

ability to get another to do „something that [he] would not otherwise do", all depends, after all, on what 'otherwise' is understood to mean. On the one-dimensional view, it means something like 'if he weren't prevented by another's intentional action from doing what is actually in his (perceived) interest to do'; on the two-dimensional view, it may also mean something like 'if he weren't prevented by another's nondecision-making from doing what is actually in his (perceived) interest to do'. But, Lukes insists, this does not exhaust the possibilities. Because 'otherwise' may also be interpreted to mean something like 'if he weren't prevented, by existing social circumstances, from *perceiving* what his (objective) interest actually is':

„Indeed, is it not the supreme exercise of power to get another or others to have the desires you want them to have – that is, to secure their compliance by controlling their thoughts and desires? [...] is it not the supreme and most insidious exercise of power to prevent people, to whatever degree, from having grievances by shaping their perceptions, cognitions and preferences in such a way that they accept their role in the existing order of things [...]?" (23, 24)

This, then, is the third possible 'face' of power, which must be incorporated into a definition in order to complete the first two dimensions identified by Lukes's predecessors. The resulting conception of power, Lukes describes as follows (24 f.):

„In summary, the three-dimensional view of power involves a *thoroughgoing critique* of the *behavioural focus* of the first two views as too individualistic and allows for the consideration of the many ways in which *potential issues* are kept out of politics, whether through the operation of social forces and institutional practices or through individuals' decisions. This, moreover, can occur in the absence of actual, observable conflict, which may have been successfully averted – though there remains here an implicit reference to potential conflict. This potential, however, may never in fact be actualised. What one may have here is a *latent conflict*, which consists in a contradiction between the interests of those exercising power and the *real interests* of those they exclude." (Where that a conflict is 'latent' means that „it is assumed that there *would be* a conflict of wants or preferences between those exercising power and those subject to it, were the latter to become aware of their interests"; 25, n. 5)

Again, we see that the core concept of power for Lukes is not different from that of the previous accounts: it is all a matter of one agent or group of agents negatively affecting another's interests. But while, as we have seen, the difference between the one- and the two-dimensional conception basically concerned only the ways in which (subjective) interests may be expressed and, consequently, the controversy between these two views was almost exclusively about the question of empirical researchability, the basic difference between the former two and Lukes's view is substantial, turning on the difference between subjective and objective interests.

Nevertheless, just as the second 'face', Lukes's third 'face' of power has also been criticized on the grounds of unobservability. And just as in the former case, Lukes too had anticipated that critique and argued, much on the same line as Bachrach/Baratz, that it may be difficult, but is not impossible to find empirical indicators for the existence of power-relationships of the third kind (in fact, the last third of his book is almost exclusively dedicated to that question).[74] Furthermore, he also points out that if one

[74] Besides, it cannot plausibly be expected that power relationships (in any of the above senses) are always easily observable: In view of their negative impacts on the interests of others, it must rather be expected that

takes the 'would not otherwise do' clause of Dahl's definition seriously, then observability even of the first 'face' of power is no easy matter. The observation of an overt conflict provides *one* possible ground for *assuming* that someone would have acted otherwise under different circumstances and that, therefore, one is witnessing an exercise of social power; in the absence of such conflict, one must look for „other, indirect grounds" for it; but in all cases, concerning all 'faces' of power, what matters is the identification of „a relevant counterfactual" (41); hence, the differences in the empirical observability of the three conceptions are not as great as they are sometimes made to appear.[75]

But this controversy about the adequacy of Lukes's conception for empirical purposes is of secondary importance. The real issue, of course, is Lukes's contention that there is such a thing as objective or 'real' interests, that people's subjective interests – interpreted as their actual 'wants' – may not always coincide with the former, and that precisely such a situation may be the result of an exercise of power:

> „The radical [...] maintains that men's wants may themselves be a product of a system which works against their interests, and, in such cases, relates the latter to what they would want and prefer, were they able to make the choice." (34)

As Lukes himself must certainly have expected, the introduction into the debate of 'real' interests as opposed to actual 'wants' has provoked much criticism.

One objection made by several authors is that Lukes failed to support his proposal with sufficient argument.[76] This may be true, but is, of course, not ultimately decisive against Lukes's view. It is also certainly not a hard blow against Lukes's conception when one author complains about his „employing a Marxian notion in a very non-Marxist way".[77] One does not need to adopt a Marxist approach to be able to make sense of the idea Lukes – whatever the defects of his presentation in 1974 – clearly was concerned with: that there is no reason to think that the only reasonable way of defining

power-exercisers, at least when acting intentionally, will try to conceal or camouflage what they're up to. This seems to be precisely the „self-concealing tendency" Lukes (1979, 270) has attributed to power.

75 In his famous empirical study, based explicitly on Lukes's conception of power, of how power relationships of the 'third dimension' produced „quiescence" with existing social arrangements in a specific social setting in the United States, John Gaventa (1982) has made a valiant effort to overcome the problems of observability.

76 Thus, Boulding (1989, 12) calls the book „a charming little essay" which, however, is „not very profound"; B. Barry (1991c, 304) complains that „there is no space for the proper articulation of arguments"; and Bradshaw (1976, quoted from Scott 1994/II, 271 f.) is unsatisfied with Lukes's reliance on a mere „illustrative methodology".

In this context, it is perhaps fair to note that the brevity of the book has not prevented some readers from getting lost in the complexity of the issues: in his review essay, Brian Barry, after having professed his agreement with the superiority of the two-dimensional over the one-dimensional view (cf. above, at n. 64) likewise admits that „one aspect of the three-dimensional view is also patently superior to either. It is simply obvious that a power-relation may be exhibited (and in an extreme form) when the inferior does not raise an issue that he would like to, either because he knows it is hopeless and does not want to waste effort or because he fears that he will suffer a sanction even for raising it." (1991c, 305) What Barry describes here is, of course, not an aspect of the three-dimensional, but of the two-dimensional view.

77 Bradshaw, op. cit., 271.

'interest' is by reference to a person's *de facto* preferences, wants, or desires as expressed in her manifest behaviour.[78]

Certainly, the concept of interest is just as contested and 'messy' an issue as that of power, and I cannot pursue it here in any depth. I will offer only a few remarks, to support my opinion that Lukes must be credited with having contributed an important aspect to the debate of the concept of power. To begin with, it is by no means uncommon in ordinary language to say of someone that 'He acted without realizing that he was hurting his own interests'. Sometimes this happens when one lacks relevant information, sometimes because our rationality and even more our will-power is limited (after all, Hume already observed that human beings have an almost universal tendency to hurt their own long-term interests by excessively discounting the future – 'excessively', that is, on their own terms, not on anyone else's standards). And from there it is only a short step to the ideas of moral philosophers and welfare economists who argue that the most plausible foundation for an approach to assessments of social arrangements is the assumption that generally, under 'normal' circumstances, what is common to all human beings is the desire to survive and to avoid suffering and humiliation, that these most basic and universal ends define a basket of 'basic needs' and that the satisfaction of these basic needs can, in turn, be regarded as constituting a person's 'objective interest'.[79] One consequence of such an approach is, of course, that the satisfaction of a person's interests in that sense and her *perception* of that satisfaction (her *subjectively perceived* interests) may diverge.[80] And such divergence may (though it must not necessarily) be induced by the – intended or unintended – conduct of other people, individual agents or groups, directly or indirectly, through certain consequences of the social arrangements established and/or maintained by them.

When, for instance, Amartya Sen says:

„Consider a very deprived person who is poor, exploited, overworked and ill, but who has been made satisfied with his lot by social conditioning (through, say, religion, or political propaganda, or cultural pressure). Can we possibly believe that he is doing well just because he is happy and satisfied?" (1988, 8),

or, more drastically,

[78] On this idea, Lukes can meanwhile muster support from a perhaps unexpected quarter: As is well known, in past decades economists and social scientists using a so-called 'economic' approach – certainly under no suspicion of Marxian, not to speak of Marxist, leanings – have insisted that when social interaction settings possess certain structural features, it cannot be expected that behaviour will indeed always 'reveal' preferences. Specifically, „Akerlof (1984) has built models to show how the power of social custom (or that of the ruler over the ruled) may persist as a result of a mutually sustaining network of social sanctions when each (rational) individual conforms out of fear of loss of reputation (with third parties) from disobedience [...] Kuran (1987) has a related model of collective conservatism (securing the power of the established ruler or custom) which is reinforced by the influence on an individual's *private* preference formation of the justifications others give for their *public* preferences for the status quo" (Bardhan 1991, 273). Both authors seem to refer to the 'mobilization of bias', Akerlof in the sense of the second, and Kuran in the sense of the third 'face' of power. Cf. also Kuran 1995, chs. 10 and 11.

[79] In the Introduction to the collection of essays on power he has edited, Lukes himself (1986, 5–7 and 10) has explained his idea of 'real' interests precisely in the sense of 'welfare interests' or 'focal aims'.

[80] Without the possibility of such a divergence, it would, for instance, be impossible, at least from a liberal perspective, to argue for the moral justification of paternalistic acts. Cf. Garzón Valdés 1990.

„If a starving wreck, ravished by famine, buffeted by disease, is made happy through some mental conditioning (say, via the 'opium' of religion), the person will be seen as doing well on [the] mental-state perspective, but that would be quite scandalous" (1985, 188),

he is, I think, referring exactly to what Lukes was driving at: the possible divergence between 'happiness' or satisfaction with one's existing circumstances (subjective interest) and 'well-being' or satisfaction of values (objective interests) induced, in these cases, by social circumstances. Partha Dasgupta has presented an example case that can be taken as prototypical:

„Mothers in impoverished circumstances routinely *sacrifice their own interests* for the sake of their families. There is *little or no complaint*, others' interests having been internalized via her *perception* that the family's welfare is her own well-being [...] It doesn't quite do to insist that women are forced to behave thus. In one sense, of course they are, but this would be to miss the point. Nor would it do to suggest that they dislike fulfilling these obligations, for this is a sort of situation where a person's *sense of duty* may direct her to comply, and to comply in a way that is welfare-enhancing for her, because she is *resigned to it*. But they are a far cry from activities that would promote her own well-being. That a mother or daughter *gladly offers or allows herself to be used* does not obliterate the fact that she *is* used. The rupture between utility and advantage is complete here, as is the *breach between desire-fulfilment and well-being*." (Dasgupta 1993, 58 f.; emphasis added)[81]

On the face of it – on the *first* and *second* face of power, that is –, given that no 'grievances' are observable here, the situation described by Dasgupta would not be seen as offering any reason for thinking that a power-relationship may be involved. But then, what is it that brings about this peculiar behaviour-*cum*-attitude of those women? It does not merely seem to be some humanly common psychological mechanism, since not all persons, and not even all persons living in the same conditions, but only a certain group of people living under certain circumstances, specifically in certain *socially, not naturally* determined relationships with others, manifests it. This is certainly not enough evidence yet to allow one definitely to draw „the line [...] between structural determination, on the one hand, and an exercise of power, on the other" (Lukes 1974, 52); but it is a first, necessary step towards the awareness of the very possibility that power, in that very general core meaning of agents negatively affecting the interests of others in a „non-trivial or significant" way, may have something to do with it after all. Now, the reason why it may be interesting to inquire into that possibility is that we may want to know whether and how the situation, e. g. of the women described by Dasgupta, *could be changed*. For that purpose, it is obviously of fundamental importance to distinguish between 'natural' consequences and 'man-made', socially conditioned situations. The latter is what the idea of the third face of power is apparently thought to capture. Because, as Lukes observes, there is at least one necessary condition for postulating the existence of a power-relationship in such cases:

[81] For an impressive literary presentation of the same argument, cf. Peter Handke's *Wunschlos unglücklich* (literally: 'unhappy with no desires'), a description of his mother's life as one of resigned unhappiness in which all aspirations and desires have been cut back to fit within the narrow frame of (perceived) given possibilities. The title plays on the German expression '*wunschlos glücklich*' – 'happy beyond desires, so happy that one does not wish for anything else'.

„[T]o identify a given process as an 'exercise of power', rather than as a case of structural determination, is to assume that it is *in the exerciser's or exercisers' power* to act differently." (55)[82]

Whether or not this is the case is of immense importance, not only for assessing possibilities of change, but also for another purpose: the normative evaluation of social arrangements. Lukes has made this very clear:

„[A]n attribution of power is at the same time an attribution of (partial or total) responsibility for certain consequences. The point [...] of locating power is to fix responsibility for consequences held to flow from the action, or inaction, of certain specifiable agents."[83]

But, having said this, Lukes must be careful not to run into a difficulty concerning his earlier insistence that, on the third face of power, an agent or group of agents may exercise power even without being aware of it. Lukes examines several possible interpretations of what 'unawareness' can mean and concludes that the relevant case is that in which a power-exercising agent does so without the intention of producing the *consequences* his action has on the other side.[84] If he wants to uphold the idea that power can be exercised unintentionally in this sense and, at the same time, that ascriptions of power always imply an ascription of responsibility, he must, if his position is not to become inconsistent, restrict the possible unintentional exercise of power to cases where ignorance does not prevent the ascription of responsibility. This is, in fact, precisely what he does when he says:

„[W]here power is held to be exercised unconsciously in this sense (i. e. in unawareness of its consequences), the assumption is being made that the exerciser or exercisers could, in the context, have ascertained those consequences." (52)

Although Lukes has thus avoided falling into the trap of inconsistency between responsible and unintended action, his idea that power can be exercised „unconsciously" has another noteworthy – and, in my view, undesirable – consequence: Having severed the necessary relationship with 'wants' not only on the side of power-subjects, but also on that of power-exercisers, Lukes is forced to introduce a rather awkward distinction, be-

[82] Here, 'power' is obviously not used in the social sense, but merely in the sense of 'ability' or 'power to'.
[83] 56. Some years later, in a reply to a critique by Bloch/Heading/Lawrence (1979), Lukes (1979) has treated the controversy between those who insist that even power is 'structurally determined' and those who, like himself, link the concept of power to contingent human actions, under the heading of 'Contest 1' (ibid., 265–268; 'Contest 2', in contrast, is the controversy about the question how many 'faces' power has and takes place *within* the interest-oriented 'actionist' approach, 'Contest 3' concerns Lukes's polemic against Parsons's conception of power). There, he reiterated his position that power is an 'action concept', that he is „committed to the idea that the power of human agency involves the power to act otherwise" and that „the point of identifying the power links in the chain or structure of causation is to identify, within (variably) structural limits, which (individual or collective) actors are responsible for which outcomes" (ibid, 266 f.). His arguments – which in this respect are, in my view, plausible – have not convinced entrenched structuralists such as, e. g., Jeffrie Isaac (1992), who continue to voice the same objection against Lukes which Lukes had raised against Bachrach/Baratz: that his break with the 'behaviouralist' or 'empiricist' current has not been 'radical' enough.
[84] 51; in fact, Lukes considers only the case of agents who are *ignorant* of those consequences; but his argument can easily be adapted to include that of agents who, knowing about the consequences, simply disregard them, or accept them as unavoidable side-effects of the action they 'really' intend to perform.

tween what he calls merely „effective" and „successful" exercises of power (40). On that account, an 'effective' exercise of power takes place *whenever* some (individual or collective) agent *A* significantly (and negatively) affects some other agent *B*'s interests, by „changing *B*'s course" *in any way*, regardless of whether or not the change conforms to his own 'wishes': he simply may not have any wish to that effect, or he may have a wish that is not realized. This means that, in the extreme, it would even have to be considered an 'effective exercise of power' if a change induced in the behaviour of a power-subject goes entirely *counter* to the power-exerciser's wishes. Think of a father and a son: Unknown to the father, the son has decided to become a lawyer. Imagine also that, in view of the son's talents, this is actually in his 'welfare interest'. The father, who himself dearly wishes his son to become a lawyer, implores him to do just that. *Therefore*, the son who, stupidly, thinks it is a sign of independence to spite one's old man, changes his mind and decides to become a doctor instead. The father, who is very unhappy about this development, has (unconsciously: he neither intended it nor is he aware of it afterwards) affected his son's (subjective and objective) interests negatively. On Lukes's account, this would have to be regarded as an 'effective' exercise of power by the father over the son – an assessment which seems, to say the least, totally contrary to the ordinary usage of the term 'power'. In contrast, „in the case where *B*'s change of course corresponds to *A*'s wishes, that is, where *A* secures *B*'s compliance" (40 f.) an exercise of power is not only 'effective', but also 'successful'.[85]

However this may be: With the preceding considerations about the relationship between power and responsibility, it becomes clear that we have come a long way from the early students of community power, primordially occupied with finding methodologically adequate empirical measures for a very specific, rather narrowly defined relation between the behaviour of different actors, to Lukes who is above all interested in identifying situations where people are negatively affected in their 'interests' (actions, choices, life-chances, or whatever you prefer to call them) by *man-made* processes for which responsibility can be attributed to (if not always easily) identifiable agents:

> „To use the vocabulary of power in the context of social relationships is to speak of human agents, separately or together, in groups or organisations, through action or inaction, significantly affecting the thoughts or actions of others (specifically, in a manner contrary to their interests). In speaking thus, one assumes that, although the agents operate within structurally determined limits, they none the less have a certain relative autonomy and could have acted differently." (54)

This concludes the brief overview over some of the most prominent (most controversial but also most frequently quoted and used) sociological conceptions of power. Before I present some conclusions on the subject, I will have a look at two other, perhaps less well known, but no less valuable conceptions which, focusing on some other aspects, complement the panorama. The first of these will be a conception from a philosophical point of view, the second an economic conception of power.

[85] In view of the possibility of overdetermination, Lukes also distinguishes exercises of power which, though not effective, are „operative". But this distinction does not concern me here.

2.2. A PHILOSOPHICAL CONCEPTION: HARTMUT KLIEMT

When Kenneth Boulding[86] declared that since Thomas Hobbes nothing systematic has been written on the concept of power from a philosophical point of view, not least of all he overlooked the contribution published just a few years earlier by Hartmut Kliemt[87] – only a short essay, but very rich in content, which offers a number of original systematic insights. The author's declared purpose is a „purely conceptual analysis [...] to substitute a very vague concept with a more precise one", i. e., an exercise in conceptual explication, where the *explicandum* is an „intuitive notion" of power and the *explicatum* a „theoretical substitute" for that notion (56). The explicit subject of this exercise is power „in its social sense" (52), and the theoretical concept to be constructed is „an 'all-including' concept of power" which „may function as a map for purposes of theoretical orientation, showing how unique 'partial' approaches are connected both to each other and to the problem of a valid measurement of power in general" (53).

With respect to the intuitive notion to be explicated, Kliemt joins the ranks of the multiplicity of authors who hold that social power consists in an ability to trigger some kind of *causal* process:

> „To modern scientists [...] 'power' – in its social sense – is a kind of ability to exert purposefully a causal influence on social results or on other people. In short, 'power' is the ability to influence social outcomes [...] according to one's wants."[88]

At first sight, this definition looks almost identical with the one proposed already by Goldhamer and Shils (1939, quoted from Scott 1994/I, 103): „A person is said to have power if he influences the behavior of others in accordance with his own intentions". In two important respects, however, the two conceptions differ:

(1) While Goldhamer and Shils do not distinguish between 'having' and 'exercising' power,[89] Kliemt makes it clear from the beginning that he holds the basic notion

[86] 1989, 12 f.; cf. above. p. 33.
[87] 1981; page numbers in brackets in this sub-section refer to this article, unless otherwise indicated.
[88] Kliemt 1981, 52; elsewhere, he reiterates this definition with similar formulations: power is „an ability or potential to get what one wants" (56), „the ability to influence social outcomes according to one's preferences" (60, 63), „an ability to get what one wants regardless of the specific techniques that can be applied to that purpose" (63). As these definitions show, Kliemt is one of those who understand 'influence' in the sense of 'that which one is able to do with power'. I will accept this for the time being as a way of speaking we have no problem to understand, and will comment on it in the next chapter.
[89] If one took their definition literally, one would have to think that power is something a person 'has' always and only during the time she 'influences' others, something she 'loses' the moment she stops doing so, but that somehow reemerges when she makes another successful attempt at it. Obviously, that makes no sense, so their definition *cannot* be taken literally; it is ambiguous and, in the last instance, inconsistent. To make it comprehensible, one must substitute either 'exercise' for 'have' ('... is said to exercise power ...'), or 'can influence' for 'influences' ('... if he can influence ...'). This ambiguity, far from being a particular property of Goldhamer/Shils's definition, is rather common. We have already seen that Lukes, with some reason, has attributed it to Dahl (whose definition is unambiguous, but whose application of it is not). Those who base their considerations on such an ambiguous definition frequently do rely on a substitution in one of the two indicated senses, though often only implicitly, without any notification, and sometimes even using *both* substitutions in one work, as if they were interchangeable. Needless to say, this practice does nothing to reduce the confusion about the concept of power.

of power to refer to an *ability*. As we will see presently, this is by no means an irrelevant distinction; it has important theoretical consequences.

(2) The second difference refers to the object of the potential effects of power: Like most authors from the social sciences, Goldhamer and Shils regard it as unquestionable that the object of power in a *social* sense can only be „the behaviour of others". Kliemt too is interested exclusively in power in the social sense, but his conception of the universe of the possible objects of such power, as reflected in the above definition, looks much broader: besides „other people", it includes „social results" or „social outcomes" in general (52). Such outcomes, he explains – somewhat cryptically – include „the state of the world as well as the mind-state of other people". What receives no special mention and thus remains unclear is whether *actions* are thought to be 'social outcomes', i. e., to belong to the „state of the world" too. But it would be strange if they weren't, given that actions can be such decisive (co-)determinants of „social results"; besides, it would be difficult to understand why anyone should have a 'want' or preference with regard to the „mind-states of other people", i. e., why it should be relevant to include *them* into the universe of objects of power, if not for the fact that mind-states are believed to have some bearing on how people *behave*. Kliemt does not explicitly say anything more about what exactly he means. In any case, an outcome concerning the 'state of the world' which does not *directly* refer to a mind-state or behaviour of another agent will certainly deserve the attribute 'social' only if it depends not exclusively on a power-holder's own behaviour (plus certain natural conditions), but also on the behaviour of other agents. Thus, although social power in Kliemt's sense is a 'power over outcomes' rather than a 'power over someone', *indirectly* the relationship with the behaviour of other agents must be maintained.[90]

There is another relevant aspect, however, on which Kliemt agrees with Goldhamer/Shils, Dahl, and others, against Lukes,[91] and that is the necessary (conceptual) relation between a power-holder's „purposes", „wants" or „preferences" and his power. In other words, power is regarded as an ability in a strong sense: It is not only an 'ability' in the sense that it can exist in a latent form, i. e., that it can 'be there' without being 'actualized' through its exercise; and it is not an ability in the sense of a mere empirical possibility, like the 'ability', e. g., of a car to go at a certain speed. It is an ability in the specifically 'human' sense of a 'know-how' to produce intentionally – or „purposefully", as Kliemt says – a certain kind of effect on the world. Power, then, consists basically in the ability, in the sense just explained, of agents to get some 'state of the world' to conform to their respective preferences or wants. For such a conception, obviously, the question of whether or not an agent, in exercising power, may be *unaware* of it does not arise. He may, of course, be unaware of the fact that it can be *called* an 'exercise of power', but one surely cannot be unaware of the 'thing itself', since exercising power on

[90] J. Nagel (1975, 29), who proposes an almost identical definition of power, is more specific on the kinds of outcomes the definition refers to: „*A power relation, actual or potential, is an actual or potential causal relation between the preferences of an actor regarding an outcome and the outcome itself*", where for power in the social sense the respective outcome must be a *social* outcome, i. e., „a variable indicating the state of another social entity – the behavior, beliefs, attitudes, or policies of a second actor".

[91] And possibly against Bachrach/Baratz, though, as we have seen, their record on this question is not entirely clear.

that account *means* successfully completing a „purposeful" exercise. By way of the purpose, awareness is, so to speak, built into the concept.

Kliemt's „intuitive notion" of power, thus, amounts to an agent's 'know-how'[92] to make certain „social outcomes" conform to his preferences. This focus on outcomes instead of other agents as the objects of someone's (social) power has, on the face of it, at least two conceptual advantages:

(i) On the one hand, it resolves the classical controversy about whether or not social power is conceptually linked to conflict, resistance, and coercion. All these terms apply only to relationships between agents, especially between one agent's wishes and another's actions; they simply make no sense when what we are looking at are relationships between someone's preferences and 'states of the world'. On a 'power over outcomes' account, therefore, the ability to prevail, if necessary, even over resistance – as definitions in the footsteps of Weber have it – does not seem to belong to an 'all-including' basic core concept of power. Of course, *one* possible way how an agent may manage to get the outcomes he wants is by exerting 'power over someone', ultimately perhaps even through the use of coercion in order to overcome resistance. However, Kliemt argues, that is not power as such, in its broadest sense, but only one of a number of different possible „techniques" of power:

> „Thinking of power as something intrinsically coercive leads either to an overly broad usage of 'coercion', sometimes subsuming even propaganda and advertising under this term, or some techniques of influencing social outcomes, which in some contexts may be equivalent to coercive techniques of influence, are excluded from the outset [...] The ability to influence social outcomes has many 'aspects' and can make use of different 'techniques'. From a purely theoretical point of view it is worthwhile to develop a conceptual framework of the minimal concept of power that does not exclude any of these aspects and techniques." (53)

> „Undoubtedly there are some important problems about kinds of influence on social outcomes that are somehow coercive. However, it seems inadequate to regard power as something intrinsically coercive [...] Power over social outcomes may include techniques of exerting 'power over someone' or coercion. But if we ascribe a coercive character to power itself and restrict 'power' to 'power over someone' we seem to regard power to be in itself a technique." (63)

I think this is a point that can be conceded to Kliemt, even though his own remarks on it are somewhat misleading, in that they sound as if he believed that 'power over someone' is always basically a coercive affair. If that were indeed the case, then, considering that power over social outcomes, in the last instance, invariably involves securing 'compliant' behaviour (or, as he might prefer to say, the corresponding 'mind-state' that will bring about such behaviour) from others, his argument would fail. Because, one could ask, what can the ability to „get what one 'wants'" (52) in a social setting ultimately mean other than that of, somehow, eliciting a desired outcome even when it is not readily forthcoming, e. g. when the mere expression of one's want by itself is not enough to produce the necessary behaviour of others? Of course, someone's power may partly reside in his ability to *prevent* resistance from arising in the first place.[93] But the inclusion

[92] Not only in the theoretical, but in the practical sense of 'knowing how' successfully to employ available resources.
[93] Obviously, that concerns Lukes's 'third face' of power which (except for the issue of 'awareness') very well fits under Kliemt's basic notion.

of the formula „even against resistance“ in Weber's definition of power allows for that; the only thing it entails is that one cannot speak of power, in the above sense of 'an ability to get what one wants', if *in case* resistance arises (e. g. because the 'mind-state' of another is set on something else) one *cannot* get what one wants. Only when one allows that 'power over someone' also includes at least one kind of relationship in which *possible* resistance has no role to play does Kliemt's argument hold. And, indeed, I think that such a kind of power can be imagined: *'de facto' authority* is commonly regarded as that very special sub-type of 'power over someone' which rests on a subject's *willingness to accept* certain utterances of 'an authority' as exclusionary reasons for action.[94] Thus, with respect to this variant of authority it makes no sense to say that it is an ability to get what one wants „even against resistance“, because for *conceptual* reasons 'de facto' authority and resistance are incompatible: where resistance could arise, there is *per definitionem* no such authority. Hence, *if* authority is understood to be a kind of power, then it is power *without* an ability to get what one wants „even against resistance“, from which it follows that the ability to overcome resistance cannot then be a defining characteristic of the basic concept of power.[95]

(ii) On the other hand, the 'power over outcomes' approach also has the advantage that, incidentally, it averts, at least superficially, a problem all conceptions of power as 'power over someone' which at the same time regard power as a *causal* concept face: namely, the question whether one can really say that actions can be 'caused' and whether, therefore, a causal relationship between one agent's actions or wants and another agent's actions is conceptually possible. To the extent that actions are based on an agent's *reasons*, the causal conception does not seem to be entirely appropriate.[96] But as long as power is conceived as involving a relationship merely between one agent's wants and some kind of 'outcomes', that question does not – at least, not on the face of it – arise.[97]

Furthermore, when the basic concept of power is understood in the broad sense advocated by Kliemt,[98] it becomes immediately clear why power is such an extremely important subject: The ability to control one's environment, not only as far as its natural, but also as far as its social component is concerned, is of fundamental importance for all human agents:

94 Cf. Raz 1990a; Raz distinguishes 'de facto' from 'legitimate' authority. The latter arises from normative power and is not conceptually linked to compliance. For a discussion of normative power, see Chapter 4.

95 The only alternative, if one wants to hold on to the 'resistance' formula in the definition of power, would be to give up the idea that authority is a special kind of power.

96 Unless one would be willing to accept that reasons are themselves caused and that they, in turn, cause actions.

97 It does, however, come to the fore when one looks more closely into the already mentioned 'techniques' of exerting power, specifically those which do involve 'power over someone'. I will come back to that issue in the last section of this chapter. Kliemt, who elsewhere has defended the Humean conception of causation, would perhaps deny that there is such a problem at all. But at least he is careful (as most other authors are not) to note that although power is a *causal concept*, it is neither the same as *causation* nor is it a *cause* itself: „'power' should not be regarded as a 'cause' in the ordinary sense of that concept. A cause is one thing and an *ability* to exert a causal influence on social outcomes is quite another“ (56).

98 It is, in fact, sufficiently broad for Kliemt to think, not implausibly, that even „Hobbes could easily have accepted“ it (61).

„Within [the process of social interaction], above all, we want to have clearance for certain activities of our own choice. In other words, we want to have control over at least a certain 'part' of the social outcome. Therefore, the ability to influence social outcomes according to one's preferences becomes a primary good for everyone [...] power may even be regarded as the most fundamental resource that individuals, or coalitions of individuals, can possess." (60)

For this same reason, it is also of utmost importance from an *ethical* point of view – and especially from the perspective of a *liberal* social or political theory – to know something about the *distribution* of power, thus understood, in a society, because it is undoubtedly one of the most relevant criteria for the moral evaluation of existing social and political arrangements:

„Whether a society, from a moral point of view, may be called a 'good society' depends on the distribution of power among its members [...] 'the' fundamental problems of distributional justice are problems of the just distribution of power over social outcomes." (60)

Specifically,

„we demand from a 'good' moral and legal order that it ascribes rights to us in a manner that allows for the greatest possible clearance and thus for the greatest individual ability to exert influence on social outcomes [...] it is the power they confer on individuals that makes rights attractive" (62).[99]

An important implication of these considerations is that, far from being something merely to keep empirically-oriented political scientists happily occupied, but of no practical relevance of its own, the elaboration of a theoretically adequate and empirically useful measure of power should be of no small interest to anyone seriously interested in normative political theory.

On the other hand, in view of the reasonable principle that 'ought implies can', with theoretical insights into possible distributions of social power (and this means, above all, into possible limits to its redistributibility under given circumstances in a society[100]), we may also gain an important criterion for assessing different moral theories and the prescriptions they make about how power *ought* to be distributed (62).

These philosophical reasons give strong support to the desirability of a measure of social power. Consequently, the explication Kliemt offers of the core notion of power is an attempt to develop a „theoretical framework" specifically with an eye to the possibility of constructing such a measure (53 ff.). His basic idea to this end is that if power is defined as the ability to make social outcomes conform to one's preferences, then the *magnitude* of someone's power must be related to the 'degree' of conformity the agent *can* succeed in securing between social outcomes and his own preferences. And from this it follows that an adequate measure of power must, in turn, rely on „a measure of similarity between preferences and social outcomes".[101]

[99] Of course, this is true at best for some, but not for all kinds of rights. The 'empowering' view of rights has been contested, e. g., in Kramer/Simmonds/Steiner 1998 and McConnell 2000.
[100] Insights for which having a measure of power may be helpful, since „the analysis of the factual distribution of power may yield information about the feasibility of social institutions" (62).
[101] 53. This has been a very rough description of the intricate explication given by Kliemt. But although the details of his idea of a measure (for instance, his distinction between a 'local' and a 'global' version of it; cf.

This may sound unproblematic. But it involves the difficult question of knowing which preferences and which outcomes must be taken into account for such a measure. Since power was defined as an agent's *ability* to get the social outcomes he 'wants', to say that someone has 'great' power with respect to some specific issue means that, whatever the preferences of other agents may be, this agent's own preference – again: whatever it may be – can 'make a great difference' for the outcome; and, analogously, to say that he has 'little' power over it amounts to asserting that, *ceteris paribus*, the constellation of his preference can at best 'make a small difference' for the outcome. In the limit, that someone has absolute power (i. e., full control) over an issue accordingly means that if his preference concerning the issue is *a*, then he can make the outcome be *a*, but should his preference change to *b*, he could also make the outcome be *b*.

Systematically, this means that if power is conceived as an ability, attributions of power always involve *counterfactual conditionals* – an idea we already encountered in Lukes's attempt to argue that the difficulty of supporting attributions of power with empirical data is not all that much greater in the three-dimensional than in the one-dimensional view because in the end all depends on the plausibility of a „relevant counterfactual".[102] Now, from a very different perspective, Kliemt argues the same point:

> „The concept of a counterfactual proposition seems to be necessary to an understanding of power [...] Dispositional concepts like 'power' necessarily involve considerations of merely possible events, considerations about 'what would happen if [...]'."[103]

One extremely important consequence of this, which, to my knowledge, Kliemt is the first and only one to have noted explicitly, is that, because it must take into account *all* those counterfactuals – that is, a great number of „merely possible events" which will in fact never occur (55) –, a measure of power cannot do any work for the *prediction* or *explanation* of specific social outcomes (56). The reason for this is of the strongest possible kind – it is a *logical* reason:

> „In measuring power we must already know 'what would happen if ...', and therefore we cannot foresee or explain specific social outcomes on [the] basis of a power measure [...] A valid measure of power requires all the nomological knowledge that can be used for the purposes of forecasting and explaining. It cannot be part of this knowledge." (56)

In this sense, „'power' has no 'explanatory power' as far as specific outcomes are concerned". However, a measure of power may in some cases be able to tell us something about the „patterns of social processes" to be expected – for instance in the case of an

p. 55), and of the theoretical problems in constructing it, are interesting in their own right, this is not the occasion to go into them; here, I am interested only in those aspects which may inform us about the underlying conception of power.

[102] Cf. above, p. 42.

[103] 55. For a similar presentation of the role of counterfactual – or, as he calls them, „subjunctive" – conditionals and dispositions for the analysis of power, cf. Goldman (1986, 158 f., 163 ff.). I will have to say more about the alleged dispositional nature of social power as an ability in Chapter 3. At this point, let me observe only that if it is a disposition at all, it is, in any case, different from the dispositions found in nature, which are based on 'natural laws' (more precisely, on sufficient conditions), because, on the present account, the ability that constitutes power is conceptually linked to a power-holder's *purposes* or *wants* or *preferences*.

agent who, as illustrated above, has 'absolute power' *and* has decided to use it: in that case, the measure of his power, being based on a measure of the distance between the outcomes preferred by that agent and 'actual' outcomes (a distance which in this case would be zero), would tell us that social outcomes in this case will reflect *this agent's* preferences and not anybody else's – but, of course, it cannot tell us *what* those preferences will be.[104]

And these considerations also show another important feature of all possible measures of power (at least, all those based on similar premises): The construction of such a measure, if it is to be well-founded and to reflect faithfully the conceptual content of the core notion, requires an enormous amount of knowledge about facts as well as about natural and, still more problematic, social 'laws' – knowledge we actually possess only to a very small extent. Hence, we must expect that existing measures of power are either 'realistic', in the sense that they are made to take into account only the knowledge we actually possess, which makes them in practice well-founded, but only very rough estimates of what they are supposed to measure; or they are 'ideal', in that they are made to require all the pertinent information, which makes them in principle 'good' (valid) measures but insufficiently founded in their practical application (because the values of many of the parameters can be filled-in only by way of – more or less educated – guesses instead of on the basis of empirically corroborated data and laws).

As it might be felt that all these problems throw some doubt on the usefulness of the entire enterprise, Kliemt himself gives ample room to the discussion of the adequacy of his explication of the core notion of power and the conception that results from it (56 ff.). He identifies four „standard requirements" for the adequacy of conceptual explications in general: the *similarity* between the explicated notion and the resulting conception, and the *precision*, *simplicity* and *fruitfulness* of that result. How does his own explication fare on those standards?

- The easiest matter to assess is that of *precision*: Since the result of his explication is a measure which is expressed as a sum of the (in principle, quantifiable) distances between all the relevant pairs of preferences and outcomes, the degree of precision which is conceptually guaranteed is about as high as it can possibly be.
- As for *simplicity*, the record is more ambivalent: We have seen that the ideas on which the measure is based are simple enough. What is not simple at all, however, is the calculation of the value of the measure for any particular case. After all, the measure constructed by Kliemt belongs to the class of 'ideal' measures and as such, as has been explained above, presupposes knowledge about very complicated matters which it is extremely difficult, if not outright impossible, to come by.

[104] 56. Because of this last point, one might think that, in any case, if we had both a measure of power *and* information about an agent's preference concerning a specific issue, the combination of these two elements would make prediction (or explanation) possible. Kliemt's argument is precisely that this idea is wrong: the information we need in order to calculate the measure of someone's power already *includes* the 'prediction' of which outcomes (are likely to) correspond to which preferences; therefore, if we know the agent's preference, we don't *need* the measure of his power for predicting the outcome; it's rather the other way round: we need the prediction of the outcome in order to get the measure. – Most of the 'actual' outcomes as well as most of the 'preferences' of the agent in question that go into the calculation of the measure are, of course, only *counterfactually hypothesized* 'actual' outcomes.

- On the other hand, the way how that measure is constructed is precisely by explicating the core notion of power as faithfully as possible and without taking into account other considerations, such as operationalizability. The advantage of that measure as the result of the explication is, therefore, the great *similarity* between *explicandum* and *explicatum*.
- The major challenge with respect to the *fruitfulness* of that explication thus is to improve the record on simplicity without, at the same time, paying too high a price in terms of the similarity criterion. Kliemt's proposal in this direction is, roughly, the following (58 f.):

The basic notion from which the explication started was an 'all-including' concept, and therefore the complex measure derived from it is also all-including, i. e., very general. For most practical purposes, however, we are only interested in power of a special kind, in some specific social context. Our limited interests in such cases make it possible to simplify the measure of power accordingly. In other words, considerations of fruitfulness allow us to gain in simplicity by relaxing the requirement of generality rather than that of similarity,. For instance, for some purposes we might be interested only in the power of agents who participate in „specific institutional or organizational settings“: „within 'families', 'markets', 'firms', 'government institutions', 'parliaments', 'clubs' etc.“, and only with respect to the social outcomes produced in those settings. This means that we are then not concerned with *the* power of those agents overall, but only with a specific „aspect“ of it, as Kliemt calls it.[105] On the other hand, there are different methods or „techniques“ of how power can be exercised, and for some purposes it is sufficient to restrict considerations to only one or, at most, a few of these. For such specific research purposes, restricted to only some aspects and/or some techniques of power, simpler measures of power can often be taylor-made. And if the corresponding measures are still too complex to permit computation in particular cases, there is yet another option: Researchers may content themselves with investigating only the *necessary* conditions for an agent to have some degree of power, in the sense of being able to make a notable impact on outcomes, in specific social settings, e. g. under particular institutions (such as, for instance, voting rules).

This last point is of special importance to political scientists. Following Kliemt's reflections, we see that the field of political institutions is particularly amenable to the empirical study of power distributions, because

> „Often a scrutiny of the official rules of an institution will be so simple that it allows for the actual computation of numerical values of a power measure. Such numerical values will induce an order between individuals or coalitions of individuals with respect to their 'official' power“.[106]

[105] 58. The nearest example is, of course, the very collection in which Kliemt's essay appeared (Holler 1981), with its special interest in 'voting power'.

[106] 59; as an example of such „customary power indices“, Kliemt mentions that of Shapley-Shubik. The upshot of Kliemt's considerations is – as should be clear, but sometimes seems to be forgotten – that such indices, though usually called 'power indices' without any qualification, are in fact only very partial indices of specific aspects, linked to particular techniques, of power. For discussions of the Shapley-Shubik index and other indices of power, cf., e. g., Brams 1975, Holler 1998, the Symposium on 'Power Indices and the European Union' in the *Journal of Theoretical Politics* 11:3 (July 1999), or most recently Albert 2003. For a very critical discussion of the way in which Shapley/Shubik and others (prominently among them, Steven Brams) have interpreted the Shapley-Shubik index as being a measure of power, cf. B. Barry (1991b) who argues that

To conclude this exposition of a philosopher's view of power,[107] it may be helpful to summarize the aspects Kliemt has contributed to the debate.

1) His basic, core notion of power compares with some of the others we have seen as follows:

* it is *like* Hobbes's, *except* for its restriction to social situations;
* it is *like* Weber's, *except* for the aspect of resistance;
* it is *like* Dahl's, *except* for not referring exclusively to behaviour; and
* it is *like* Lukes's, *except* for requiring awareness in exercises of power.

2) The explication he offers of this core concept is guided by the objective to derive a *measure* of power.

In these first two points, Kliemt's philosophical approach thus differs only in some specific aspects and nuances, but not yet fundamentally from the sociological approaches to the concept of power reviewed before.

3) On the other hand, the importance of power and its distribution for *ethical questions* is explicitly underlined. This is the point that can perhaps be regarded as distinctive of a *philosophical* approach to the conceptual question about power: the concept is analysed in the light of what it is that makes the phenomena we mean to refer to in using the term important for the agents involved or affected.[108] At the same time, Kliemt thus provides a bridge, so to speak, between the early 'behavioralist' interest in the measurement of power, on the one hand, and the 'radical' concern for responsibility and the potential moral illegitimacy of power, on the other.

„the whole approach embodied in the Shapley-Shubik index is inappropriate" (277) precisely because it does not measure what it pretends to measure – i. e., in Kliemt's terms, because there is no sufficient 'similarity' between 'power' and that which is in fact measured by this index – since the index merely measures the *a priori* probability of being the pivot in a winning coalition, but pivots actually do not „in the relevant sense change the state of affairs" (276). For the history as well as the 'state of the art' specifically of 'voting power' indices, cf. Felsenthal/Machover 1998. A program that calculates Shapley-Shubik, Banzhaf and other 'voting power' indices for simple voting games in single-chamber or multi-chamber systems was released in 1997 by Thomas Bräuninger and Thomas König (and could at the time of writing be downloaded from www.uni-konstanz.de/ FuF/Verwiss/koenig/IOP.htm).

107 For other modern philosophical approaches to the concept of power, cf., e. g., Russell (1938, 1986) whose conception is marred by his overly broad core concept of power as „the production of intended effects" (for critical assessments of Russell's work, cf., e. g., Knight 1939; Wrong 1988, 2; Hardin 1996); Morriss (1987) who treats a number of aspects in a similar way as Kliemt (above all, the idea of the importance of knowledge about power for the ethical assessment of the actions of individuals or the properties of institutions; for a critical, but on the whole positive critique of Morriss, cf. B. Barry 1991d); or Hösle (1995) whose attempt to grapple with the question of the compatibility of „Power and Morality" is, as I have tried to show elsewhere (Zimmerling 1995), neither plausible nor consistent.

108 In his book-length philosophical analysis of power, Morriss (1987) likewise emphasizes that the evaluation of power structures in a society and the attribution of responsibility to agents are two primary reasons why the study of power phenomena is important. Another philosopher, in the context of a conceptual analysis not yet of power but of freedom, has stated this most clearly: „in a good conceptual study [... it] must be shown why the point of the given concept *is* or *should be* of interest to people, given their human nature, and how the term designating the concept must be defined so as to correspond to this point" (Kristjánsson 1996, 193). On this criterion, Lukes would arguably have to be included among those who have approached the concept of power from a philosophical rather than from a sociological point of view.

4) Another perhaps specifically philosophical characteristic, which besides indicates Kliemt's analytic leanings, is his careful reflection about *necessary requirements* for, as well as about *necessary consequences* of, particular conceptual decisions. The former is shown in his argument that in order to be qualified as 'social' it is *not* necessary for an object of power to be an action (contrary to the idea implicit in most conceptions of social power that the object of power is either an action or not 'social'); the latter in his argument that if power is conceived as an ability then measures of power, for logical reasons, are incapable of being used for specific explanations or predictions.

5) Finally, in the same vein one can also mention his *systematic* (rather than merely pragmatic) argument for the desirability and necessity of breaking down the *general concept* and the derived general measure of power, into *partial aspects* of power which are conceptually and empirically more manageable.

6) The only unresolved points of his conception, in my view, remain the question of what precisely '*social outcomes'* are thought to include, the question of the *causal* nature of power processes which is related to the former, and the question of the conceptual relationship between power and *influence*. I will have to say more about these issues in the next section as well as in the next chapter.

2.3. An economic conception: Brian Barry

If the characteristic of philosophical approaches to the concept of power is, as the example of Kliemt's contribution has illustrated, above all an underlying concern with those aspects which are related to a possible *moral evaluation* of the corresponding phenomena, economic approaches must be expected to give special attention to another question involving evaluation, namely the evaluation of a situation – whether by participating agents or external observers – from a *cost-benefit* or *incentives* point of view. Concerning this perspective, I will use as the main point of reference the considerations presented by Brian Barry, and complement them with ideas – sometimes concurring, sometimes dissenting – contributed by such economists as Pranab Bardhan, Jack Hirshleifer, John K. Galbraith, and others, in order to extract from these 'economic' views some aspects which may complement the list of ingredients of social power derived so far.[109]

With the purpose of 'de-mystifying' the 'mystery of power',[110] Brian Barry has contributed what he himself has called „An Economic Analysis“ of power;[111] and his reason for using this label is precisely his focus on *incentives* (226). Incentives are, of

[109] For a survey of recent literature 'On the concept of power in economics', cf. Bardhan 1991. Note that Michel Foucault (1994, 219 and 220) also asserted the need for „a new economy of power relations“, but he of course uses the term 'economy' with a different meaning.

[110] For a really mysterious work on 'The Mystery of Power', cf. Herrmann 1896.

[111] Barry 1991a; page numbers given in brackets in this subsection refer to this essay unless otherwise indicated; cf. pp. 254 f. for Barry's remark on the desirability of a „de-mystification“ of the concept of power. Barry 1991a is, of course, only an essay, albeit a relatively long one; so de-mystification is possible only up to a certain point, since in such reduced space not all imaginable aspects of power can be treated. It is to Barry's credit that, in contrast to many other authors, he explicitly acknowledges and reflects on the limitations of his work: the final three sections of it contain considerations about limitations concerning the scope of his analysis, the operationalizability of his 'paradigm of power', and the practical relevance of the kind of power based on sanctions (264–269).

course, conceptually linked to actions. Hence, if power is conceived as something involving the operation of incentives, it must be understood, not in Kliemt's apparently more general sense of 'power over social outcomes', but in the more narrow sense of power as exclusively involving effects on actions.

And indeed, closely following Dahl's definition,[112] Barry specifies that the core concept of power he is interested in is that of „the ability to cause things to happen when the object is actions by other people".[113] Although thus restricted to actions, this is still a very general concept, and Barry's approach is similar to Kliemt's insofar as he suggests that it may be helpful to classify *different kinds* of power, according to how, by what *method*, other people's actions are 'caused to happen'. However, the reason he gives for this approach is different from Kliemt's: whereas Kliemt proposed conducting partial analyses, restricted to particular techniques (and/or aspects) of power, in order to reduce the complexity of the respective measure (and because most of the time this is all we are interested in), Barry argues that it is necessary to break down the general notion of social power into several different objects of analysis according to the different methods that can be used to affect other people's actions, because the resulting different types of power each require their own *method of analysis*. In any case, just as with Kliemt, Barry's purpose is not a discussion of the core concept of power itself, but a systematic explication of one specific version of it, with special attention to the different techniques how power can be exercised (in Barry's case, above all to those involving incentives). Thus, he starts with a distinction of different methods, then defines the corresponding kinds of power, and finally indicates what analytic instruments the study of each of these kinds of power requires.

His classification of the relevant methods is a slightly changed version of Parsons's (1963) proposal of four different modes of intervening in others' decisions:[114]

[112] In fact, economics seems to be the discipline where most followers of the early definitions of power proposed by Dahl (1957) and Simon (1953) are found today. Cf. Bardhan 1991. One of the – at the time of writing – latest economic approaches based on a conception of power that is very closely related to that of Dahl, March (1957), Simon, Harsanyi (1962a), or French/Raven (1959) is that of Bowles/Gintis 1999 (esp. 24; also 1992). Their purpose is to show that even in situations of voluntary exchange in a market setting, power may be involved, provided the market is non-clearing in equilibrium and 'contingent renewal' (of contract) is involved: „When contingent renewal is operative, the principle of *short-side power* holds: agents on the short side of the market have power over agents on the long side with whom they transact" (1999, 22). Implicitly, it becomes clear that for these authors exercises of power necessarily involve 'compulsion' or 'coercion', where „the asymmetrical capacity to invoke sanctions is sufficient" for regarding a choice as 'coerced' (1999, 14 and n. 6).

[113] 223. He argues against a 'power over outcomes' view exactly in the terms I have already alluded to in the previous subsection, when I presented Kliemt's 'power over social outcomes' conception: the only alternative to restricting the possible objects of power exclusively to actions which he seems to see is expanding it to include „things" in general (223; he specifically quotes Bertrand Russell [1938] who, indeed, advocated such a broad conception; cf. p. 25 of the 1988 reprint of Russell's book).

[114] 223. Cf. Parsons 1963 (p. 105 of the 1986 reprint; also 1967, 363 and 364); in contrast to Barry, for Parsons only coercion ('deterrence') and physical constraints ('compulsion') involve power. Barry groups together Parsons's third and fourth modes to one single method, and instead adds a fourth of his own. For a list that is very similar to Barry's, cf. already Harsanyi (1962a, 168) who mentions reliance on „legitimate *authority*", „supply [of] *information* (or misinformation)", „*rewards* and *punishments*", and „*new* advantages or disadvantages [...] subject to no condition". Also Galbraith (1984, 4 ff. and chs. II and III), whose categories of 'condign' and 'compensatory' power correspond to 'coercion' and 'inducement' (inducing „submission by inflicting or threatening appropriately adverse consequences" or „submission by the offer of affirma-

* 'activation of commitments',
* 'persuasion',
* 'inducement' (promise of positive sanctions, offer) *or* 'coercion' (threat with negative sanctions, punishment), and
* 'physical constraints'.

The last category is of a special kind, different from the other three, so let's consider it first. What Barry means with 'physical constraints' is the method of forcing another person to do certain things by modifying her physical environment, i. e., by changing some of the *factual* components which constitute the other's background or framework of action – for instance by eliminating a *necessary* condition for a particular action and thus causing the other's „incapacitation“ for it (224 f.). The particular kind of power connected with this method is simply „the capacity physically to restrain or constrain the actions of others“ (226). Note that Barry, expressly following Lewis (1898), takes only the negative side of shaping another's environment, that is, the ability to „reduce the range of actions“, as constituting a method of power.[115] He departs from Lewis, however, in acknowledging that 'physical constraints' which make it effectively impossible for another to perform a certain action may be produced not only by way of 'force'. This category of power methods is, as Barry notes, linked to one of the others, through a kind of 'side effect' it can produce: by constraining an agent's set of feasible actions, one may not only prevent him from performing a specific action at a particular occasion, but also affect his entire situation in such a way as to change his bargaining position relative to some other agent (whether the power-holder himself or a third party), which in turn may have substantial consequences for the relative power positions of all sides involved concerning the ability to 'induce' or 'coerce'. What Barry does not mention, but what is important is that, for logical reasons, this method functions only for getting someone *not* to do something, i. e., for making a certain action impossible for him, not for eliciting the performance of a specific action: It is, of course, possible to destroy a necessary condition for an action, thus eliminating it from another's set of feasible actions; and it is even possible that someone may be in a position to do this for a great number of single actions. But it is logically impossible to destroy necessary conditions for *each and every* possible action *except* a desired one, in order to 'force' the performance of precisely that action through the method of 'physical constraints'; in other words, it is logically impossible to create *sufficient* conditions for a desired action, i. e., to make one single action „causally necessary“.[116]

tive reward“; Galbraith 1984, 5), while his 'conditioned' power, submission to which „reflects the preferred course; the fact of submission is not recognized“ (Galbraith 1984, 6), covers both Barry's categories of 'persuasion' and 'activation of commitments'.

115 Cf. Mokken/Stokman 1975, 35, for the objection that most conceptions of power are thus biased towards the negative side, instead of understanding both the ability to *restrict* as well as to *expand* another's options as constituting power.

116 It is logically impossible to destroy *necessary* conditions for *all but one* action because for something to be a feasible action, the agent must have *at least two options*: performing the action or omitting it; and the 'physical facts' constituting the background situation in which an agent chooses an action can never by themselves be *sufficient* conditions for his performing a certain action, since there is no direct *causal* relation between external states of the world and actions: they are always 'mediated' through the agent's will (cf. von

If we now come to the other three methods of exercising power over another's actions, the first thing to note is that all of them differ from the 'physical constraints' method in one significant aspect: they do *not* operate on any *facts* in a power subject's environment, but on the subject's *own mind* or *will*, and in the last instance, if successful, on his *choice* of action. All three of them are, therefore, methods which may work equally well in favour of the *commission* or the *omission* of an action.

The *first* of the three, the method called 'activation of commitments', functions, as Barry formulates it, by „cashing in on some norm“: it gives rise to the kind of power over others that is based on their *de facto* acceptance of a normative authority[117] and which can be defined as „the capacity at one's own discretion to get people to do what they would not otherwise do by invoking some standing commitments to obey some source of instructions“ (226). This is an especially interesting kind of power, not the least because the key to it is, obviously, in the power-subject's rather than the power-holder's hands: the subject can, so to speak, switch it on or off, by agreeing or denying to accept another's (claim to) normative authority.[118]

The *second* of the methods working on a subject's will, identified by Parsons as 'persuasion', and adopted by Barry under the label 'change of mind' (224), is the method of changing merely the subject's *own* ideas about what he ought to do, leaving everything else equal.[119] Barry observes that it can come in two versions: *(a)* either by modifying a person's beliefs about the adequacy of certain *means* to her (given) ends, e. g. her *technological* beliefs; *(b)* or by working directly on her preferences for certain *ends*. The kind of power involved in this method therefore is „the capacity at one's own discretion to change people's perceptions or goals by some means or other so that they want to do something they would not otherwise do“ (226).

Finally, the *third* of the methods affecting others' mind-states is that of working on their incentives for or against the performance of certain actions. Here, again, two versions can be distinguished, since incentives may be positive or negative, i. e., consist in an offer or promise of a benefit as a *reward* for a desired behaviour, or, on the contrary, in a threat with some cost or harm as a *punishment* for the failure of behaving in the desired way.[120]

Although all three of these methods work on an agent's will, the mechanisms they rely on are obviously very different: Appeals to an 'authoritative' norm prevent an agent

Wright 1963, 54; 1984, 133 ff.; 1998) Therefore, Foucault, for instance, is wrong when he maintains that „what defines a relationship of power is that it is a mode of action which does not act directly and immediately on others. Instead *it acts upon their actions: an action upon an action*“ (Foucault 1994, 228; emphasis added) – unless this is somehow meant in a metaphorical way. Strictly speaking, actions simply *cannot* act upon other actions. One could, of course, imagine a situation in which physical constraints are such that an agent cannot avoid to make certain bodily movements; in such a case, the conditions are, indeed, *sufficient* for him to make those movements – but they do then not constitute an *action* of his (cf. von Wright; similarly, Mackie 1990, 206).

117 „If *B* accepts a norm giving authority to *A*, then *A* has the ability to 'activate commitments' for *B*.“ (223).

118 I will have more to say on this kind of power in Chapter 4, where normative power will be analysed.

119 The *locus classicus* for a discussion of persuasion as a method of power is, of course, Platon's *Gorgias*.

120 225. Whether 'coercion' is an appropriate term for the method of eliciting compliance by a threat with negative sanctions is a question we may leave open at this point. Cf. Chapter 3.1 for Felix Oppenheim's explication of what it means for a threat to be 'coercive'.

who *de facto* accepts the authority from deliberating himself on how to act and, in this sense, from taking 'a decision of his own'. Persuasion – whether in the technical or in the teleological sense – leaves the deliberation with the agent, but changes his perceptions of the adequacy of certain actions. And with the change of incentives, the deliberation and final decision also rests with the agent, who rather than experiencing a change of his technological or teleological *beliefs*,[121] must in this case make his decision under external conditions which have changed, in the sense that the consequences he can or must expect from certain actions have been modified. This modification, however, is not brought about by a change in the 'physical world' (as in the very first method considered), but merely by an *act of will* on the part of the other to perform certain conditional reactions.

These different methods and the corresponding kinds of power, Barry holds, ought to be distinguished because they require *different methods of analysis*. He does not specify any such method of analysis for the 'physical constraints' variant, presumably because it is too broad a category and, in any case, involves the *natural* rather than the social sciences. But with respect to the three methods operating on a person's will, he explicitly makes that distinction:

(1) The activation of commitments is the proper subject of *sociology*, more specifically, of the sociology of „legitimate authority" or the sociology of law; that is where the appropriate methods for its treatment must be found;[122]

(2) the „analytic tools" for the study of the method of changing another's mind can be found in *psychology* and in different sub-disciplines of sociology (such as the sociology of attitude change or of knowledge);[123] and

(3) the working of incentive changes „falls within the province of ordinary economic theory" and some of its special theoretical developments, such as bargaining theory and game theory.[124]

True to the announcement made in the title of the paper that it will contain an 'economic analysis', in the remainder of it Barry is primarily interested in that last method of getting others to do certain things, and in the corresponding kind of power, i. e., the ability of getting another to do something he would not otherwise have done, by making threats or promises. In fact, nearly half of the essay is dedicated to a careful investigation of the question what exactly this method of exercising power by changing another's incentives

121 Above all, this method „does not alter the attractiveness of the action in question in the eyes of *B*" (225).

122 224. For some very perspicacious considerations on what kind of questions the sociologist must ask if he wants to account for the social phenomenon of (esp. legal) authority, cf. Baurmann 1999.

123 224. Social psychologists have traditionally treated this method under the heading of 'influence', not 'power'. I will therefore say more on it in the next chapter.

124 226. One must assume that by 'ordinary economic theory' Barry means something like 'a theory using an approach hitherto known primarily from economics', rather than 'the theory *of* economics'. After all, he is a political philosopher himself, rather than an economist; and it is not a source from the field of economics, but from psychology that must be accredited with one of the earliest attempts to account for power in game-theoretic terms: as early as 1959, J. W. Thibaut and H. H. Kelley illustrated the structures of different kinds of power relations with the help of payoff matrices; cf. Cartwright 1969, 130.

involves. With the help of analytic tools first developed primarily in economics,[125] Barry analyses the different structures of the situations in which a power-holder and a power subject may find themselves with respect to their possible gains or losses, in attempting to exercise power, on the one side, or in complying with such attempts, thus converting them into successful exercises, on the other.[126] Although especially his detailed analysis of the respective differences in threat and promise situations, as well as of the relationship between the credibility of a threat, the potential costs of carrying it out and the probability that it will be complied with (242–253) are models of analytical clarity, they are of no immediate relevance for the present purpose.[127] In addition, however, Barry also treats a number of issues which are of more general interest for any consideration of the concept of power. To these alone the following presentation will be limited.

(a) A first point worth noting is that, although with respect to the first three methods Barry defines each corresponding kind of power in terms of an 'ability' or 'capacity', the kind of power linked to changes of incentives is defined, rather clumsily, as „the possession by one actor *(A)* of the means of modifying the conduct of another actor *(B)* by means of an expectation in *B* that one or more of the alternative actions available to him will (with some probability) result in reward or punishment brought about by *A*" (226). However, immediately afterwards Barry explains that in fact possession of the means of conferring a benefit or inflicting a harm on another is never in itself sufficient to consti-

[125] Tools which, of course, have nothing 'essentially economic' to them. Cf. Baurmann (2001, Introduction) for an illuminating explanation of how the use of these tools and the underlying approach in the social sciences is not an 'imperialist' encroachment of economics upon 'foreign' territory but, quite to the contrary, the restitution to the social sciences of what belonged to them in the first place: „[C]uriously enough it was the work of Adam Smith that initiated the decline of the liberal vision of an interest-oriented society of enlightened and free citizens. Smith was already much more skeptical than his predecessors about the political and moral consequences of self-interested behaviour. In his view, the advantages of the pursuit of self-interest accrued only to the economic sector [...] With this restriction, of course, Smith laid the foundations of economics as an independent discipline. But together with the advantages of specialization this also meant a narrowing down of the field of investigation. The approach of analysing *social* phenomena in general from the perspective of interest-oriented behaviour was thus reduced to the study of *economic* phenomena and interests. It was to take more than two-hundred years until that approach with its more encompassing original claim reappeared – and then, ironically, it was labeled the 'economic' approach, although the attempt to explain the ordering of human society and the individual behaviour of its members on the basis of individual interests is older than economics itself."

[126] Lest there be any doubt about it, note that 'gains' and 'costs', of course, are here not limited to tangible assets: „it should be borne in mind that among the costs of *A*'s carrying out threats is the repugnance that *A* may feel about it" – for instance if the threatened sanction is the death penalty (252). Barry concludes, among other things, that the credibility of threats decreases with an increase in their repulsiveness (to the threatener himself).

[127] For an earlier economic analysis of threats and offers involving only two sides, cf. Harsanyi 1962a, who among other things presents a clear account of the 'blackmailer's fallacy'; Harsanyi 1962b for an extension to *n*-person situations. Cf. Zagare 1987 for a study in the area of international relations which uses similar 'economic' tools (specifically, the variant of game theory known as the 'theory of moves') to analyse threats – particularly how they function in situations of inter-state deterrence – with interesting theoretical results not only for international-relations theory; cf. Wagner 1988 for an analysis of different aspects, among them the 'blackmailer's fallacy', to be taken into account in assessing the limited political fungibility of economic power.

tute power, and that there are at least two other prerequisites: threats and promises require *communication*, and they also require the possibility of *monitoring* behaviour.[128] Thus, Barry's formulation of the definition of this kind of power is, to say the least, not a very happy one,[129] because it leads almost automatically to the confusion of two different kinds of 'means': the 'means' one must in fact 'possess' in order to create in another an *expectation* of positive or negative sanctions that will make him change his behaviour are not necessarily „the means of making someone better off or worse off" (227), i. e., the means of actually *imposing* a negative or positive sanction, as Barry – who here seems to have fallen into his own trap – believes.[130] My ability to change another's incentives does not rest on my possessing certain means in the latter sense, but on my ability (based perhaps merely on rhetorical 'means') to create in the other certain *expectations* about my conditional reactions to certain events.[131] As long as another, for whatever reason, *believes* that I possess the means for sanctioning him as well as for monitoring his behaviour, I do not actually need to possess either of them in order to make a credible threat. My having such means are *not the only possible grounds* for such a belief. This seems to me to be an important point, and I will discuss it in more detail in the next section.

[128] Barry does not elaborate on it, but note that these requirements are of two very different kinds: The first is a *conceptual* requirement: threats and promises are *constituted* through communicative acts (when Boulding 1989, 110, remarks that „Threats are useless unless they can be communicated to the threatened party", he seems to forget that where there is no communication, threats are not useless, but inexistent). The second condition, in contrast, is a *practical* requirement, assumed to be necessary in order to make a threat or promise effective because an agent can credibly commit himself to a *conditional* reaction only if he can be expected to know when the conditions for one or the other reaction obtain. On monitoring ability, cf. also Cartwright 1969, 137, who refers to the work of Thibaut/Kelley (1959).

[129] A fact he doesn't seem to notice, however, since the idea that „Power is the possession by *A* of the means of modifying the conduct of *B*" is later repeated on p. 229, and similarly on p. 253.

[130] Cf. esp. p. 255, where the ability actually to impose negative or positive sanctions is, in fact, included as one of the conditions of Barry's „paradigm of power". [In this context, cf. Münch 1976, 91, for the idea to distinguish the *definition* of power as the disposition over certain resources or „means of motivation" (political support, means of coercion) from its *characterization* – whatever that may mean – as an ability in Max Weber's sense. This is not very plausible, I think, because it does not give us a *social* concept of power; more precisely, the 'point' of speaking about power, which should be reflected in the definition itself, seems to be not the consideration of what someone possesses, but of what he *can do*, in a very special sense, with what he possesses, i. e., what consequences his possession may have for the actions of others.)

[131] Cf., e. g., Harsanyi (1962a, 168 f.) who underlines that the strength of a power-holder's power depends on the *perceptions* of the respective subject rather than on objective facts.

What *does* rest on my possession of certain means, however, is my ability actually to improve or worsen another's situation, i. e., actually to reward or punish him. When in possession of such means, one can, of course, employ them conditionally or unconditionally. But only their *conditional* use is conceptually linked to exercises of power, Barry notes: „if *A* makes *B* worse off unconditionally this is not an exercise of power, because it is not associated with any attempt to modify *B*'s behaviour" (259). In that sense, a sadist who tortures another merely because he enjoys to see him suffer does not exercise power, but rather inflicts 'naked' violence, whereas a 'special forces' agent who threatens to torture the terrorist who knows where the bomb is hidden, and actually tortures him when he keeps silent, but makes it understood that he will stop doing so *on the condition* that the other speak, attempts – in applying violence – to exercise power. For an economic approach to power which does *not* make this distinction and rather defines power – extremely broadly – as „any form of impact of one human on another" (quoted in Bardhan 1991, 266, n. 1), cf. Bartlett (1989).

Another doubt about his 'change of incentives' category of power methods concerns the appropriateness of Barry's decision to fuse Parsons's two categories of 'inducement' and 'coercion' together into one single method of power. Barry is aware of the differences between threats and promises, but he thinks that they are not relevant for his analysis and that „for analytical purposes we can assimilate threats and promises into one theory" (225). He seems to believe that only by regarding them as one and the same kind of method we „can handle" cases where a certain action is elicited by a combination of a threat and a promise (that is, a 'throffer', as Michael Taylor has called it). But the controversial issue here is, of course, whether an offer, i. e., the promise of a benefit in return for a desired behaviour, should be considered an exercise of power (or at least the attempt of such an exercise) at all, or whether promises and offers should not be subsumed instead under the category of 'exchange'. The question is important enough for Barry to dedicate an entire section of his essay to it.[132] In his view it does not have one single right answer; instead, what matters is awareness of the consequences of each possible answer (257):

(i) If the answer is that effective promises are to be regarded invariably as exercises of power, the implication is that „*A* can exercise power over *B* even if *B* actually gains in comparison with the *status quo ante* [...] *B* need suffer no net loss from compliance." The simple argument in favour of this answer is that „compliance is compliance whether it is induced or coerced".[133]

[132] Sect. XII. Note, however, that even the question itself is controversial: According to Viktor Vanberg, for example, it is a wrong question since power and exchange are not alternatives exclusive of each other: „Power is a phenomenon that is *inherent* to social exchange, it plays [...] a role in *all* exchange relations [...], because all exchange relations are based on an *interest* in certain performances of the respective other side [...] Power is a *reciprocal* relationship: *both* sides of an exchange relation have power over the other, although of course that power is not necessarily *distributed equally*. The question of the distribution of power in exchange relations is a question of the relative urgency of each participating side's interest in the realization of the exchange transaction [...] In most cases, when one speaks of 'power' in social relationships what is meant is the case of an unequal distribution of power, that is, of one side 'overpowering' the other." (Vanberg 1982, 59 and n. 49; my translation)
Bardhan (1991, 270) distinguishes three different kinds of possible power relations *within* exchange relations: *(a)* „monopoly power", *(b)* „power of extortion or blackmail", and *(c)* „power of robbing someone with threat of violence". One may be obliged by circumstances (urgency and lack of alternatives) to enter into an exchange relation with a monopolist, but that doesn't mean that the monopolist himself 'forces' one to it, i. e., ignoring a monopolist produces the same result as if the monopolist (together with the good he offers) simply did not exist – that result may be very unpleasant, but it is not a harm inflicted on one by the other side. In contrast, ignoring the threat of an extortionist or a robber, refusing to 'do business' with him, may result in such a harm, the difference between the extortionist and the robber being that the latter infringes on one's „well-defined property rights", whereas the former „abuses" a positional advantage.
For the controversy about the relationship between power and exchange, cf. besides Barry and Vanberg, e. g., Blau 1964; Baldwin 1971, 1978; Birnbaum 1975; Lively 1975; Stolte/Emerson 1977; Oppenheim 1981, ch. 3.4; N. Barry 1989, 86 f.; Kersting 1991; Bowles/Gintis 1992, 1999; except for Kersting, who, without proposing or endorsing any criterion for distinguishing exchange from power relations, merely *postulates* that the conception of power current in exchange-theoretic approaches is inadequate and that power phenomena cannot be understood as exchange phenomena, all these authors discuss various criteria for the distinction.

[133] Cf. Oppenheim 1981, 41, for a consenting reference to this passage; cf. also, e. g., Baldwin 1971 for a defence of this view. For Oakeshott (1991, 445), only „fear of injury or want elevated into need are the conditions of a power relationship", and therefore „the promise of a satisfaction" establishes such a relationship

(ii) If, instead, the answer is that promises are not to be regarded as a method of exercising power, this seems to imply the idea that „To be in someone's power is something we would prefer to avoid: people seek to escape from the power of others. But the possibility of exchange is never something that we would prefer to avoid because it enlarges our freedom of choice".[134]

(iii) Finally, if one thinks that there is no simple answer to that question, i. e., that promises sometimes are and sometimes are not exercises of power, then obviously what is needed is a criterion for deciding when they are and when they are not. Barry himself thinks that this is, indeed, the most appropriate way of answering the question.

Regarding the necessary criterion, after identifying „two false trails" in the literature,[135] he suggests that there exists a power relationship if, and only if, „one party stands to gain more out of the relationship than the other, because it is in a position to exploit the weakness or necessity or vulnerability of the other" (258). One advantage of this *criterion of asymmetric gain* is that since many asymmetric relationships are held to be unfair it confers plausibility to the impression that power is very frequently an object of disapproval. A second advantage, Barry thinks, is that it supports the idea that „threats are *always* an exercise of power, rewards only sometimes" (258): When there is a successful threat, the relationship between the two sides is always asymmetric in that the threatener gains while the threatened loses something (since the threatened bears the 'cost' of compliance while the threatener can enjoy the 'gains' from it without having to 'give' anything in return). In contrast, in the case of an offer or promise, whether or not there is an asymmetry depends on the relative bargaining positions of the agents involved (258 f.): if they are such that *B*'s 'compliance costs' are fairly compensated by his 'gains' through the rewards offered by *A*, no power is involved; but if „*A* can obtain a large amount of compliance of high value at low cost" (259) while *B*'s high 'cost' of compliance (i. e., compliance despite great reluctance) is rewarded with only a small 'gain', then there is an asymmetry of the indicated kind and, therefore, a power relationship. Surprisingly for an otherwise so scrupulous and critical analyst, Barry does not bother to comment on the problems of such a view. After all, the ideas of 'exploitation' and 'fairness' in a compliance-against-reward situation are far from obvious and would need to be argued for by specifying and justifying the respective baselines – not to speak of the problem of the intersubjective comparison of the gains and losses in order to say whether or not they are symmetric.[136]

only when the „respondent [...] is so far unwilling to forgo it that he regards it as an otherwise unobtainable necessity".

134 This is reminiscent of Gerald Dworkin's and Harry Frankfurt's 'identification view' of freedom, i. e., roughly, the idea of taking into account a person's second-order rather than her first-order preferences; cf. Kristjánsson 1996, 44 f. and 131 f.

135 „One of these misguided suggestions is that we use 'power' only to refer to cases where someone can obtain a large amount of compliance with a high degree of probability" (257); „The other misguided suggestion is that we use 'power' for relationships of which we disapprove" (258). These suggestions are 'misguided', Barry argues, because they do not conform to ordinary usage.

136 These problems should be obvious, and since they are not germane to the present purpose, I will not pursue the issue here.

Besides, Barry's conclusion at this point that threats always, but offers only sometimes constitute exercises of power, does not seem to square well with his earlier insistence that threats and promises should be 'assimilated into one theory', nor with his initial acceptance of the core concept of power in the sense of the ability of „getting other people to do things" (223). If changing incentives by way of threats is the same method as doing it by way of offers, if both ways succeed in „eliciting desired behaviour from other people" (266), and if the latter is the general core definition of social power, then successful offers should constitute exercises of power just like successful threats. If that is denied, it seems to indicate that either there is another, not explicitly mentioned condition in the underlying concept of power, or threats and offers are in a relevant respect not the same kinds of methods after all.[137]

And there is still another point in this context which makes Barry's position appear inconsistent: After having declared that the criterion for distinguishing exchange from power is asymmetry in the sense just explained, he goes on to say something entirely different, namely that whether there is power or exchange depends, in the last instance, not only on the *existence* of an asymmetry in the bargaining positions of the agents involved, but rather on *how* those bargaining positions came about:

> „[S]uppose that after *A* has made *B* worse off he then comes along and, taking advantage of *B*'s distressed situation, is able to obtain compliance in return for an offer that *B* would have turned down before. Even more, suppose that *A*'s reduction of *B*'s well-being was deliberately designed to bring about a state of dependence. I think that in such a case we would be inclined to say that *A* was exercising power over *B* through offering rewards for compliance, even if we might not say the same if the relative positions of *A* and *B* had come about without the intervention of *A*."[138]

Barry cannot have it both ways: either he sticks to the 'asymmetry criterion', in which case it does not matter *how* an asymmetry comes about (with the consequence that the situation he uses for illustration would constitute a power relationship regardless of who is responsible for it); or he must discard asymmetry as a criterion for the distinction between power and exchange and define something like a 'responsibility criterion' or 'blameworthiness criterion' instead.

[137] One argument in that direction refers to the relationship between power and freedom, on the one hand, and between threats or offers and freedom, on the other. I will have more to say about this in Chapter 3, when the conceptual relation between power and freedom will be considered.

[138] 259. Barry reminds us of the relevance of these considerations when he adds: „This has an obvious bearing on the question of whether the countries of the 'Third World' are subject to the power of the developed [...] countries. Those who argue that they are not will point to the existing pattern of trade relations and say that these relations are mutually beneficial. But if what has just been said is true, the 'dependency' theorists are right to say that we have to ask how these patterns of trade came about in the first place." (259) I think Barry (*unlike* most dependency theorists) here confuses attributions of *power in* a relationship with attributions of *responsibility* or *blame for* a relationship of certain characteristics: it is one thing to say that someone *now* profits unfairly from an exchange relation which is extremely skewed because that same someone has *previously* made it so through an exercise of power; and quite another to say that, for instance, a trade relationship *now* is not one of exchange, but of power by one side over the other. Bardhan (1991, 267), who otherwise very closely follows Barry's account, seems to see this problem too, since he deviates from Barry, precisely in the sense I just mentioned.

On the whole, concerning the similarities and differences between threats and offers, on the one hand, and between power and exchange, on the other, Barry's account leaves something to be desired.

(b) Second, Barry also considers the relationship between 'having' and 'exercising' power. To begin with, he insists that power is something an agent 'has', 'possesses',[139] and that, obviously, such a possession of power *may*, but must *not necessarily*, be manifested or actualized in any particular instance through its exercise.[140] Now, it would seem that if someone has power over another, that is, the ability to get the other to do (or omit) certain things, then any 'exercise' of that power would be an instance of actually getting the other to do precisely those things. Not so for Barry, who argues that someone who has power „may of course be either successful in achieving its object or unsuccessful" in any particular exercise of it; because of a „lack of skill", there is always a „possibility of slippage" (227 f.). Barry gives a strange reason for this opinion. In his view, it is only because of this possibility that „we have a framework for causal explanation":

> „To say that *A* got *B* to do something that *B* would not otherwise have done because *A* had power over *B* becomes as vacuous as saying that someone became angry on a given occasion because he had an irascible temperament, or that opium makes people sleepy because it has the *virtus dormitiva*." (228)

Here, Barry seems to confuse two different questions:

On one possible reading of the sentence, it is indeed 'vacuous' as a *causal* explanation, and that is if we take it to express *analytic* statements about power, anger, and soporificity, which as such certainly cannot say anything about causal relationships.[141] Having the *virtus dormitiva* and having the disposition to make people sleepy are indeed *conceptually* equivalent in this sense. However, the above assertion about power becomes analogous to that about opium only if it is changed, in either one of two possible ways: '*A* got *B* to do something that *B* would not otherwise have done' *means* (conforming to Barry's own accepted definition) that '*A* has *exercised* power over *B*', and '*A* had power over *B*' *means* that '*A was able* to get *B* to do something that *B* would not otherwise have done'; therefore, what is 'vacuous' in the same way as the assertion about the soporificity of opium are the assertions '*A* got *B* to do something that *B* would

[139] In contrast to Bachrach/Baratz and Lukes who emphasize that power is not a possession, but a relationship.

[140] Therefore, Barry argues in an aside, it is not at all 'awkward', as Dahl complained, that – in contrast to 'influence' or 'control', which are substantive as well as verb forms – there is no verb to go with power: Since it is something one 'has', we do not need a specific verb for referring to it, because „everything that can be said logically, given the meaning of the word, can be said with auxiliary verbs" (228). Cf. Cassinelli 1996, 44, n. 1, for the suggestion that although „There is no English verb 'to power'" one should perhaps think of stipulating it. The suggestion may be worthy of consideration; but it is surprising that it should come from Cassinelli for whom 'power' means *only* a potential or ability and what is exercised is either control or influence, not power. Cf. also Wrong (1988, 6) for the argument that the inexistence of 'power' as a verb is „unfortunate" because it may foster the common, but mistaken idea „that power is a property rather than a relation".

[141] Note that all three concepts mentioned here by Barry involve a *disposition* – an aspect to which I will come back in the next section.

not otherwise have done because *A* exercised power over *B*' and '*A* was able to get *B* to do something that *B* would not otherwise have done because *A* had power over *B*'.

But on another reading – which, however, has no application to the opium case – , to say 'that *A* got *B* to do something that *B* would not otherwise have done because *A* had power over *B*' may very well serve as an explanation, if only a very elliptical one;[142] less elliptically, it would amount to something like '... because *A* had power over *B* concerning *x*, *and A* wanted *B* to do *x*, *and A* exercised his power over *B* to that avail'.[143] This is, of course, not a complete explanation of *B*'s *x*-ing, because it does not inform us about what the basis of *A*'s power is or why *A* wanted *B* to *x*. But it is, in any case, a partial explanation of why *B* did *x* instead of something else, and it has nothing to do with a „possibility of slippage" on the part of *A* in his exercises of power.[144]

An entirely different question is whether in a *mutual*, but *asymmetric* power relationship between two agents *A* and *B*, where each has some power over the other, but *A* presumedly has more power over *B* than *B* has over *A* because *A* possesses more resources he could potentially use for an exercise of power over *B* than *B* commands for exercising power over *A*, there may not be a 'possibility of slippage' in the sense that *A* may sometimes 'lose' against *B* even in contests in which the employment of resources is decisive. Empirically, there are many situations where the apparently 'weaker', commanding less power resources, nevertheless 'win' over the apparently 'stronger'. Barry does not consider this kind of situations, because his analysis is limited to one-sided power relationships.[145] But, also using an economic approach and a conception of power in the sense of an ability to overcome resistance, Jack Hirshleifer (1991) has analysed this apparent „Paradox of Power" and argued – in my view, convincingly – that there is nothing paradoxical about it. After all, everything depends on who is willing to employ *which* and *how many* of the resources available to him *for what* purpose;[146] and one can show that under certain conditions, taking opportunity costs into account, it may at least be perfectly rational on both sides that the agent possessing more resources

[142] And whether it can properly be called a 'causal' explanation I will leave open at this point.

[143] Similarly, with respect to the case of anger, the proposition could be read to assert something in the sense that a person's anger was triggered because she has an irascible temper *and* the corresponding dispositional conditions were satisfied. Only in the opium case, 'makes people sleepy' and 'has the *virtus dormitiva*' are irremediably linked conceptually, not causally – a fact Molière apparently trusted his audience to capture at once (even though at the time of his writing the tautological character of such 'explanations' was still a brandnew insight, as Thomas S. Kuhn notes in *The Structure of Scientific Revolutions*, 3rd ed. Chicago and London: University of Chicago Press 1996, 104) when, in the 3rd Intermezzo of *Le malade imaginaire*, he made fun of medical 'science' by having a medical candidate say in examination: *Mihi a docto doctore / Demandatur causam et rationem quare / Opium facit dormire. / A quoi respondeo, / Quia est in eo / Vertus dormitiva, / Cujus est natura / Sensus assoupire*. Barry is very fond of this example of the explanatory incapacity of analytical statements: he already refers to it at least twice in Barry 1970 (pp. 90, 96), but only traces it back to Barrington Moore for whom, in turn, it seems to be „famous" enough not to warrant a reference.

[144] There is, however, a 'possibility of slippage' that may easily be confused with unsuccessful exercises of power: It is, of course, possible and perhaps not uncommon that agents make mistakes in their assessment of the power they have, and therefore *attempt* to exercise a power they don't have; in such a case, unless an agent is lucky, success will not be forthcoming. On the potentially disastrous consequences of such „illusions of power", cf. esp. Boulding 1989, 66 ff.

[145] This is one of the deliberate „technical limitations" of his essay; cf. sect. XIV.

[146] For a similar point, cf. also Coleman 1990, 783; less systematically, Wolfers 1962, 111 ff.

spends less of them on an exercise of power over the other than *vice versa*, even if this has the consequence that the side which *has less* power (resources) seems to *exercise more* power and thus succeeds in obtaining compliance from the other side for an outcome that is relatively more beneficial for the 'weaker' than for the 'stronger' side.[147] This is, of course, another argument in support of the assertion that the mere *possession* of the means to change another's incentives is not sufficient to determine actual social outcomes, and it underlines once again the importance of a careful theoretical distinction between 'having' power and 'exercising' it.

(c) Third, Barry presents some ideas concerning the question of measurement. Here, again, he takes an unusual road. The criterion for deciding whether someone has great or small power is often regarded to be related mainly with 'how much' an agent can get another to comply with his wishes, i. e., with the side of the alleged power-*holder*.[148] Instead, Barry argues that a measure of power should be linked to the other side of the power relationship – that of the *subject* of power. The underlying idea is that an agent's power over another must be considered the greater, the stronger the subject's *resistance* or reluctance which the power-holder is *able* to overcome, that is, the more the subject can be made „to give up by obeying", „the more it costs him, taking as the baseline what he would have preferred to do in the absence of" the other's exercise of power.[149] According to this idea, in order to measure someone's power over another, what is needed is a scale on which different actions can be located,[150] ranging from those performed with 'no reluctance' at all, on one end (the point of „zero compliance", i. e., of what the agent would 'otherwise' do anyway), to the highest degree of reluctance the respective agent may summon up. Such a scale Barry calls a power subject's „compliance line" (230). The measure of a power-holder's power over another is then given by that point on the respective compliance line which denotes the highest degree of reluctance he could potentially overcome; all actions located below this point the power-holder is able to elicit at will, all those above it are literally 'beyond' his power.

Perhaps the most important insight Barry offers in this context concerns a significant difference between the various power methods. The idea of measuring power along an agent's compliance line makes sense only in the cases of *authority* and *change of incentives*, but not in the other two cases: When *factual constraints* impeding some action

147 On the theoretical limits of Hirshleifer's approach, cf. Bardhan 1991, 275, n. 9. For an interesting historical case study in an international relations context supporting Hirshleifer's argument, cf. Paul 1994.

148 In the case of Kliemt, for instance, the measure of power was directly linked to the 'distance' between an outcome desired by a power-holder and the outcome he can succeed in securing (in all hypothetically possible situations). – For a critique and further development of early sociological attempts to design a measure of social power from an economic point of view, including above all a consideration of opportunity costs, cf. the seminal work of Harsanyi (1962a, 1962b).

149 232. Remember that this road was not open to Kliemt since his concept of power was not restricted to 'power over someone' and, therefore, the ability to overcome resistance was not a necessary characteristic of power for him.

150 Barry correctly points out that actions as well as 'inactions' can be located on such a scale. The behaviouralist objection that 'inaction' cannot be observed he calls „an absurd piece of [...] metaphysics". The only thing that cannot be observed but must *always* (for actions as well as inactions) be theoretically constructed is the counterfactual conditional involved in all statements about someone's having or exercising power (232).

are created, the consequence is not that the power subject more or less reluctantly *chooses* to do one thing rather than another; it is that a certain choice option simply ceases to exist for him. This does not involve pushing him upwards on his compliance line; rather, it means that the new external circumstances relocate the omission of the action in question at the subject's point of 'zero compliance'. Similarly, when an agent succeeds in *changing another's preferences* for certain ends, *or his beliefs* about the adequacy of certain means to his ends, this is not a matter of making the latter move up on his compliance line, away from the 'zero compliance' point; instead, what changes is the alignment of actions on that line, i. e., their relative positions to the point of 'zero compliance', with the possible consequence that what the subject *now* wants to do out of his own choice coincides with, or is at least 'closer' to, what the power-holder wants him to do (232). This seems to be an idea worth remembering for the discussion in subsequent chapters of the difference between power and influence.

With the help of Barry's conception of a measure of power, we can also expand some more on Hirshleifer's analysis of the 'paradox of power'. One thing that analysis has shown was that from individual cases of *de facto* compliance with another's wants alone one cannot draw valid conclusions about who 'has' (more) power over whom. This is a point Barry himself has treated, in another one of his several essays on the concept of power (1991d, 309 ff.). There, he has taken up Peter Morriss's idea (Morriss 1987) to distinguish between 'power as ability' and 'power as ableness', in order to refer to yet another conceptual nuance which makes *attributions* of power even more complicated. Power-as-ability is defined in the familiar counterfactual terms, by reference to the *highest* degree of reluctance in another an agent *could* overcome *if* he were to be confronted with it. Being based on counterfactual considerations, it has the advantage of being independent of *actual* preferences and of the reluctance an agent in fact faces.[151] But, of course, in 'real life', where others' preferences are given, what degree of such power-as-ability an agent has relative to another may not be decisive for his *factual* ability, *under given circumstances*, to get the other to do what he wants him to do. This *actual* ability is what Morriss has called an agent's 'power as ableness'. Thus, an agent with little power-as-ability may in some circumstances have considerable power-as-ableness, simply because he does not meet much resistance (at least, no more than what his little power-as-ability allows him to overcome); and *vice versa*, an agent with great power-as-ability may find himself in a situation where the resistance he confronts is so strong that his considerable power-as-ability is not enough to give him any power-as-ableness.[152] In these terms, Hirshleifer's case of the will of a 'weak' prevailing over that

[151] In other words, using Barry's idea of measuring a power-holder's power on a power subject's compliance line, a measure of power-as-ability merely indicates one single point on a compliance line, no matter where on that line different actions may be located in terms of the resistance the subject in question is in fact willing and able to oppose to them. In usual power-theoretic parlance, that means that a measure of someone's power-as-ability does not tell us anything about the actual *scope* of that power.

[152] In order to know which of these cases obtains, we need information not only about where on the respective compliance line a power-holder's power registers, but also where on that line, in view of the subject's preferences and dispositions, different relevant actions are located. Those actions actually located on *lower* levels of resistance than the power-holder's measure of power-as-ability constitute the set of actions with respect to which the power-holder, for the time being, has power-as-ableness, i. e., the actual *scope* of her power.

of a 'strong' agent is equivalent to a situation where the 'strong' has the greater power-as-ability, while the 'weak', due to the actual preferences of the 'strong', has – at least temporarily – sufficient power-as-ableness to prevail.

The problem with power-as-ableness, Barry observes, is that it depends more on „good fortune" than on anything else, and as such is a „fragile" and „evanescent" thing. Moreover, whenever there is no resistance at all, it is not even applicable.[153] This makes it „a very tricky concept" which is responsible for „a good deal [of] the confusion rampant in the literature on power" (1991d, 311). Still, it is a concept of considerable relevance for a number of questions, not least when what we are interested in is the possible moral (co-)responsibility for another's action (e. g. when the question is whether or not someone is guilty of a negligent omission because on a given occasion he could have intervened successfully with another's harmful action, but did not do so) (ibid., 321).

(d) Finally, Barry draws attention to yet another aspect of general interest for the study of the concept of power, namely that the adequacy of conceptual decisions depends on the uses a concept is intended to serve. He considers three different purposes investiga-

[153] Barry 1991d, 312 f.; cf. also Dowding 1990. When an agent „commonly" gets what he wants from others because, without any need for him to exercise or even to have power, what they do anyway happens to coincide with his wishes, he is, Barry says, plain 'lucky'. Hence, success can be based on luck *or* on the decisiveness that derives from power, and it is *logically* impossible to make an inference from someone's success to his power. That is true. I think, however, that Barry here fails to distinguish two different kinds of situations: One is the situation where no intervention whatsoever is needed to get what one wants because others *do it anyway*, for whatever reasons; in that case, power-as-ableness does not apply; in Dahl's terms, the *amount* of power is then necessarily zero (i. e., no intervention can increase the probability that the action in question is performed, since this probability is already 1). But quite another situation is that of an apathetic, indifferent person who on her own account would *not* do what I want her to do, but who, when I tell her to do it, simply does it, *without any reluctance* or resistance (and who, had I told her to do something else, would have done *that* just as readily). In the latter case, I think it makes perfect sense to speak of a power situation even in Barry's terms (the *amount* of power in this case is positive since the probability that the action in question is performed was less than 1 and has risen to 1); hence, that there is no resistance does not necessarily imply that the notion of power-as-ableness does not apply. Of course, over such a person who always does what she is told because she doesn't want, or doesn't feel to have the strength, to make an effort of resistance, *anyone* would have power-as-ableness, and therefore it may not be a very useful and interesting kind of power – but it is power-as-ableness, as defined above, after all.
The relationships between luck, power and success for the special case of voting in political committees have been analysed in detail by Barry himself in the context of his critique of the Shapley-Shubik and the Banzhaf power indices (Barry 1991b; cf. also Dowding 1991, 1996, whose books are partly based on a development of Barry's distinction between power and luck). On that analysis, Kersting (1991, 138; my translation) has remarked that „what Barry tells us here about 'luck' and 'power', about the challenge value *(Herausforderungswert)* of chance and the action-impeding *(handlungserschwerende)* significance of the cognitive inaccessibility of the future for a reflective and rational individual interested in pleasant and intended outcomes, only narrates once again what we can already draw from the famous power analyses of the history of ideas. Machiavelli's struggle between de-moralized and power-skilled virtù and capricious fortune clearly shines through Barry's comparative discussion of the unequal reliability of 'power' and 'luck'. In both cases, the same message is transmitted [...]" Kersting does not seem to have noticed that his interpretation has little, if anything, to do with the definitions Barry himself has given of his terms. Nevertheless, he is certainly right in that there is a relevant similarity between Machiavelli and Barry. As far as I understand it, the similarity is that both deal with *technical* questions and hence transmit a *technical* 'message' which, as such, has nothing normative; but I wonder whether that is the similarity Kersting had in mind.

tions of power relations may have and points out some implications of the respective interests for an adequate conception:

(i) Prediction of exercises of power. One important issue about power relationships is certainly that of knowing under what circumstances it is to be expected that a power-holder actually *exercises* his power over another. It does not seem farfetched to assume that this is probable only when a power-holder (believes that he) stands to gain something from such an effort. On this assumption and if one is interested in events rather than in latent structures, one may prefer a definition of power which „concentrates on *A*'s net advantage".[154] Two aspects must be taken into account here: First, to say that someone *has* power if he can get another to do what he wants only at prohibitively high costs to himself would not be adequate from that perspective, because the *exercise* of such 'power' would be highly unlikely. This would speak for a concept of power where the ability to secure compliance *at low cost* – what Barry calls the 'opportunity' to exercise power – is written into the defining characteristics.[155] And secondly, that someone *has the ability* to secure compliance from another at low cost would be irrelevant for the former's actions if there were nothing he might actually want the latter to do. Thus, Barry thinks that when the focus is on the prediction of exercises of power, only a concept of (having) power which contains among its defining characteristics the existence of some *motive* for intervention (some desire of *A* concerning *B*'s behaviour) as well as an *opportunity* for it will be adequate:

> „The resulting definition would be on the following lines: *A* has power over *B* if and only if *A* can profitably get *B* to do something *A* wants or, more formally, if and only if there is some level of compliance by *B* such that *A*'s net gain from it would be positive." (260)

(ii) Prediction of (changes in) patterns of distribution. The basic notion of what social power is all about may also give rise to questions about the distribution of costs and benefits within such a relationship. This, Barry says, would suggest a definition of power based on the very criterion of asymmetric gain he himself favours: that an agent has power over another if, and to the extent that, he can make him do things which are more profitable to the former than to the latter:

> „Formally, then, the definition of power on this conception would be on the following lines: *A* has power over *B* if and only if the maximum net gain for *A* from compliance by *B* entails either a net loss by *B* or a smaller net gain by *B* than that enjoyed by *A*." (261)

[154] In all this, Barry writes as if what mattered were *actual* and not *perceived* possibilities. Earlier we have seen a similar problem in his account of effective threats. His disregard for the distinction between *facts* and *perceptions* is, in my view, one of the most serious shortcomings of the essay under scrutiny.

[155] The idea that a measure of power must take into consideration the costs for a power-holder of exercising his power was already developed by Harsanyi (1962a), though he didn't go so far as to make 'low costs' a conceptually necessary condition. Instead, Harsanyi developed his 'schedule sense' of power, arguing that the scope, extension, amount and strength of an agent's power all depend on „the costs of power he is prepared to bear" (ibid., 171). Still earlier, Thibaut/Kelley (1959) observed that for power to be 'usable' its exercise must yield a net gain; cf. Cartwright 1969, 130. For the concept of power, this seems to imply that it should not be based on what someone *could*, but on what someone *would* maximally be willing to 'invest' in getting others to do what he wants. This idea, of course, makes power-as-ability just as 'fragile' and 'evanescent' a thing as power-as-ableness.

Just as in the previous case an ascription of power to someone was designed to imply a prediction of certain kinds of actions by the power-holder, according to this conception, Barry thinks, the attribution of power to someone over another implies the prediction that over time there will be a growing difference in their relative positions: „Unlike the first definition, this would enable us to predict changes in the pattern of distribution" (261). However, since the definition contains no condition for the absolute amount of *A*'s net gain – to which his motive to exercise his power is thought to be linked – „it does not predict behaviour as well as the first definition does" (ibid.). Thus, for example, according to the second definition *A* would have great power over *B* even if she could secure for herself only a maximum net gain close to zero, provided she can do it by imposing a great net loss on *B*. What Barry omits to say is that this definition of power 'predicts' shifts in the patterns of distribution only *on the condition* that the power-holder actually does exercise his power, at least once in a while. But since the definition contains no element directly connected to a power-holder's motive for exercising power, whether or not this will happen is entirely contingent. Therefore, I fail to see how an attribution of power to some *A* over some *B* according to Barry's second definition can serve to 'predict' anything at all about changing patterns of distribution. After all, the *ability* to reap asymmetric gains by eliciting compliance at low cost is *neither a necessary nor a sufficient condition* for a change in some pattern of distribution actually to occur.

(iii) Assertion of dependence. The third concern with power Barry mentions is directed not towards the conditions under which some *A* is able to profit from a social relationship, but towards sufficient conditions for *B* to be *secure* from demands of compliance. If *A* has no motive *now* to command compliance from *B*, she may have one tomorrow. Therefore, as long as *A* has the ability and *opportunity* to elicit compliance, *B* is under a perpetual risk: at any moment, *A*'s desires or preferences might change and there might then be something she wants *B* to do badly enough to demand compliance. Such a relationship between *A* and *B*, which may be a cause of constant concern for *B* even at times when *A* does not give it any importance,[156] could also be the basis for a conception of a relation of power by *A* over *B*. In that case, „*A*'s power would [...] consist simply of the ability to obtain low-cost compliance".[157] The 'point' of such a conception is to bring attention to the *situation of B*, regardless of whether *A* acts on it, rather than to *what A actually does* (or may be expected to do):

[156] Cf. Cartwright 1969, 155: „People with power in organizations are often reluctant to recognize that the very possession of power poses a threat to those in its domain. The subordinate knows, however, that even a benevolent boss has the potential to cause him harm, discomfort, or inconvenience." Cf. also the discussion of Pettit's views in Chapter 3.2.

[157] 262; ibid.: „If *A* has power over *B* in the sense that *A* can at a low cost to himself obtain compliance from *B*, then *A* has *B* in his power. *B* may not be subject to demands from *A* at the moment but he cannot count on that happy state of affairs continuing. *B*'s freedom depends on *A*'s not choosing to exercise his power." Barry argues that such a situation may create a dilemma for *B*: the 'poorer' *B* is, the less 'attractions' he offers to *A*, the more secure he will be from demands for compliance by *A*, which implies that his options are either to stay 'poor' or to become liable to exercises of power from *A*'s side. This applies to relationships between individuals as well as between collective actors. Barry refers to international relations, contending that the historical 'independence' of countries like Montenegro, Switzerland or Ethiopia has at least been helped by „the fact that their poverty has made them unattractive acquisitions" (263).

„The argument in favor of the conception of power as the ability to secure compliance at relatively low cost is that it focuses on the realities of dependence. Even if a state is independent it is surely a relevant fact about it that its independence is contingent on the apathy of those states with power.“[158]

This is the relevant *substantial* difference between *(iii)* and *(i)*. The *formal* difference between them, in turn, is that while both definitions contain the opportunity condition, definition *(iii)* lacks the motive condition included in definition *(i)*. The third definition is therefore the broader of the two, subsuming under the label 'power' many more relationships than the first, i. e., the extension of the first is a genuine subset of the extension of the third.

The relation between definitions *(iii)* and *(ii)*, in turn, is not entirely obvious; it depends on how *(ii)* is interpreted. If it is taken to include nothing but the asymmetric-gain condition, the extensions of *(iii)* and *(ii)* overlap only partly. But perhaps the more plausible interpretation is to say that the asymmetric-gain condition implies the satisfaction of the opportunity condition. After all, at the root of the asymmetric-gain condition is the idea that there must be a possibility of a *net* gain, however small, for the power-holder, and that means that 'costs' are 'low' relative to the total benefit.

From a systematic point of view, then, Barry has mentioned three different defining characteristics – opportunity, motive, and asymmetric gain –, and his definitions differ with respect to the combination of these features that is stipulated in each case. Now, there is a total of seven logically possible combinations of one, two or all three of these features. But note that one of the three characteristics – namely: opportunity – seems to be a *sine qua non*, rather than an optional feature, for any definition of power that is to make some sense. Based on Barry's three conditions, we thus do not get seven, but only four different logically feasible definitions, as shown in the following table:

LOGICALLY POSSIBLE DEFINITIONS OF POWER, USING BARRY'S THREE CONDITIONS

Barry's definitions	**Opportunity**	**Motive**	**Asymm. Gain**
iii	x		
i	x	x	
ii	x	x	x
–	x		x
–		x	
–			x
–		x	x

(If 'opportunity' is considered a necessary feature, only the first four cases apply.)

[158] 264. Cf. Baldwin 1980 for an illuminating analysis of the conceptual relations between power and (inter) dependence; also Keohane/Nye 1977, 1987.

Definitions *(i)* and *(iii)* have already been explained. Barry's definition *(ii)* is the version combining opportunity with asymmetric gain, which has the consequence of filtering out cases considered to represent exchange rather than power relations. But where there is an asymmetric gain, there is, *a fortiori*, a gain and that means a motive. Hence, definition *(ii)* implies the satisfaction of all three conditions, and the formally possible fourth case, where only the opportunity and asymmetric gain conditions obtain, is impossible because of the conceptual interdependence of asymmetric gain and motive.

As we have seen before, all these definitions are problematic: the 'asymmetric gain' condition is plagued by the considerable problems connected with that concept; the inclusion of the 'motive' condition converts power into something other than a mere ability; and if nothing but the 'opportunity' condition is stipulated, then power and exchange situations become indistinguishable. Thus, Barry's proposals do not constitute a ready kit from which one would onely need to select the appropriate 'tool' for each respective purpose.

3. Conclusions

What I have offered so far is a – far from complete – view of the jungle into which power analyses in the social sciences have grown over the past decades. I have picked out three *vistas* of that jungle – the three that seem to me most comprehensible and useful for the purposes of political theory – and attempted to describe them as systematically and benevolently as I could, here and there also pointing out some traps and stumbling blocks hidden along the way. What are we to make of all this now?

As the presentation has shown, it has been a general strategy for reducing the confusion about the concept of power to introduce all sorts of classifications, in order to facilitate a comparison of different conceptions of power or of different sub-types within one and the same broader conception. The distinction of different 'faces' of power has been one such attempt. For the following conclusions too, it seems advisable to begin with the definition of a – necessarily, very general – conceptual grid that can then serve as an instrument of orientation in cutting a path through the thicket of some of the aspects and ideas about power which the preceding analysis has brought up.

3.1. A CLASSIFICATORY FRAMEWORK

The most elaborate and systematic general classificatory framework of this kind I am aware of has been proposed by Rainer Künsken (1976).[159] It is intended to permit the classification of the most diverse definitions of power, depending on which from among

[159] Künsken's game-theoretical study of power has remained unknown to most political scientists interested in power. Not even Balzer (1992), although he writes on the same subject, seems to be aware of its existence. This neglect, though undeserved, is understandable since the book is not easily accessible to a wider audience: it is a doctoral thesis for which the author, an economist by training, received his Ph. D. from the Technical University of Berlin in 1976; written in German, it has, to my knowledge, been published only in the mimeographed version I have seen. The study compares theoretically (and for one exemplary political case, empirically) the different methods and indexes available at the time of writing in the theory of power with game-theoretic methods for computing the amount of an actor's power.

a list of a dozen variables are taken to be relevant features of power, and what values they are given.

Table 1.1 Künsken's Categories

1. *power-holder*	(kind of agent: individual, collective, ...?)
2. *power subject*	(kind of agent: individual, collective, ...?)
3. *relationship*	(between power-holder and power subject: direct, indirect, none; between all or some elements, in case of collective agents?)
4. *transitivity*	(necessary, unnecessary, excluded?)
5. *awareness*	(necessary, unnecessary, excluded; on one or both sides?)
6. *costs*	(on both sides, one, or no side?)
7. *resistance*	(of power subject: necessary, possible, excluded; if not excluded: how, against what?)
8. *impact*	(on opinions, attitudes, decisions, behaviour, utility, outcomes, ...?)
9. *base*	(physical, legal, epistemic, ...?)
10. *means*	(methods, strategies: force, threat, promise, persuasion, manipulation, ...?)
11. *realization*	(exercise, ability, ...?)
12. *amount*	(what measure?)

For easy reference, Künsken's categories are here collected in a table.[160]

[160] Cf. Künsken 1976, 10–17, for the list and more detailed explanations. I have translated his categories somewhat freely. All are to be understood as *variables* which, as such, can assume different values; in each case, I have briefly sketched in brackets, with no claim to completeness, the kind of values to be considered in case a variable is regarded as relevant. In Künsken's view, the existing confusion about the concept of power could be substantially reduced if anyone using the term 'power' in a social-scientific context began by stating which of these variables, and having what values, the respective conception includes as defining characteristics (ibid., 9 f.). He acknowledges (ibid., 9) that his schema is based on the work of Terry Clark (1967) and Josef Zelger (1971, 1972; cf. also 1975).
It is not my purpose here to discuss the possibility or convenience of refining, enlarging or reducing Künsken's list. I think that it is useful, as it is, for structuring the following discussion. Note that a few years after Künsken's publication, a strikingly similar list has been presented by Steven Lukes, in the form of a 'questionnaire' (1979, 263 f.; also 1991, 83 f.): „Consider the following questions about power: Is power a property or a relationship? Is it potential or actual, a capacity or the exercise of a capacity? By whom or what is it possessed or exercised: by agents (individual or collective?) or by structures or systems? Over whom, or upon

3.2. THE QUESTION OF CAUSATION

Künsken's list has one inconvenience: it contains no reference to one fundamental issue of contention that plays a major role when it comes to the definition of power. That is the question whether social power can, should, or must be conceived as being of a *causal* nature. Since it will be helpful to have a few considerations about that issue already in mind when going over the different categories of Künsken's catalogue, I will treat the question of causation first, and then conclude the section with the exercise of spelling down the list.

As the presentation of the different positions in Section 2 of this chapter has shown, many authors assert the causal nature of power without paying much further attention to the matter. But this is, obviously, a question that concerns the very foundations of the social sciences and the study of human action in general, and therefore deserves careful consideration. In the following, I will, of course, not even attempt to go all the way back to that general foundational question. Instead, I will present in condensed form the terms of the controversy about the causal nature of social power and indicate some implications.

Causal definitions of power

From the beginning of the modern institutionalization of the discipline and its consolidation as an empirical science, the causal conception of power has been very prominent in political-science circles.[161] One of its earlier formulations, which was to have a lasting impact on political science scholarship, has been contributed by Herbert Simon:

> „[F]or the assertion, 'A has power over B,' we can substitute the assertion, 'A's behavior causes B's behavior.' If we can define the causal relation, we can define influence, power, or authority, and vice-versa."[162]

what is it exercised: agents (individual or collective?) or structures or systems? Is it, by definition, intentional, or can its exercise by partly intended or unintended? Must it be (wholly or partly) effective? What kinds of outcomes does it produce? Does it modify interests, opinions, policies, preferences or behaviour? If a relation, is it reflexive or irreflexive, transitive or intransitive, complete or incomplete? Is it asymmetrical? Does exercising power by some reduce the power of others (is it a zero-sum concept?)? Or can it maintain or increase the total of power? Is it demonic or benign? Must it rest upon or employ force or coercion, or the threat of sanctions or deprivations – and, if so, what balance of costs and rewards must there be between the parties for power to exist, and how is this to be measured? Does the concept only apply where there is conflict of some kind? If so, what is the conflict between, and must it be manifest or may it be latent: must it be between revealed (how revealed?) preferences or can it involve real interests (and how are these to be defined?)? Is it a behavioural concept, and, if so, in what sense? Is it a causal concept?"

161 Sarah Joseph (1988, 8) suspects that this may have been due to disciplinary interests rather than epistemological insights: „It was felt that power could play a role analogous to that of cause in the natural sciences. Power, like cause, could be used to describe the connections between empirical phenomena [...] The analogy between power and cause was considered to be particularly important because it could help increase the practical importance of political science and make it a more effective policy science".

162 Simon 1957, 5; quoted from Ball 1992, 16. Ball himself belongs to the minority of authors who have reservations about such a view; he observes that Simon was „Apparently unaware that this solution was already three centuries old by the time he proposed it" and notes that in the years following Simon's publication, other authors, such as Dahl, March, or Oppenheim, also embraced such a „mechanistic" concept. Another reservation is voiced by Blalock who also quotes Simon approvingly, but remarks that „Given the difficulties in

Two authors who defend such a causal view of power – Joseph Oppenheim and Jack Nagel – have provided somewhat more than the usually found sparing remarks and almost obligatory references to Simon, Dahl, or March. The following considerations will therefore in great part be based on what they have to say about it.

Oppenheim (1981, ch. 3.2) treats 'Power and Causation' in some detail, and asserts that neither do they coincide nor is power a subset of causal relations:

„[T]here can be causation without power. There can also be power without causation [...] Power and causation are overlapping categories." (ibid., 32 and 33)

The dividing line, in his view, runs between having and exercising power. When someone *has* power over another, but does not exercise it, surely no causation is involved.[163] But whenever power is *exercised*, according to Oppenheim, a causal relation is established: „Exercising power is the area where power and causation overlap" (ibid., 33).

A somewhat different view is advocated by Jack Nagel. For him too, the only satisfactory approach is the „causal conception of power" which he attributes particularly to Simon, March, and Dahl.[164] And just like Oppenheim, Nagel does not think that this amounts simply to equating causation and power. But in his view, 'power' rather denotes only a subclass – it is a special kind of *ability to cause*.[165] And the problem he then diagnoses is that

„theorists have not yet identified *which proper subset of causal relations should be identified with the power relation* [...] Power relations have been placed within the *genus* 'causal relation', but a suitable *differentia* is missing" (ibid., 11 and n. 22).[166]

On the other hand, although the causal view is clearly the most widely adopted, once in a while one also encounters the rare scholar who argues against it.

Keith Dowding does not leave any room for doubt about his position on this issue when he flatly declares:

„The simple problem with the causal definition is that it is false." (Dowding 1991, 4)

pinning down causation (and thus power) in reasonably complex conflict situations" (1989, 29), such a general definition may often not be very helpful.

[163] Oppenheim does not consider the possibility, that the mere *fact* that someone has power over another may have any kind of effect (of which it would then, obviously, be the cause). But see Pettit's account of the relationship between power and freedom, presented in Chapter 3.2, for just such a claim.

[164] Nagel 1975, 9; also ibid., 10, n. 21: „Van Doorn, Etzioni, and others who define power as a capability do so in essentially causal terms, though they avoid the word 'cause'." Three chapters of Nagel's book (chs. 2–4) are dedicated to different aspects of the notion of causation and its relation to the concept of power. Nagel not only endorses Simon's causal conception of *power*, but also his conception of *causation* (in ch. 4).

[165] On the relationship between cause, causation, and power as an ability, cf. also above, the quotation of Kliemt in n. 97 of this chapter.

[166] In a footnote, Nagel (1975, 9, n. 15) points out that, besides advocating the well-known „resource version of power" in the *Leviathan*, Hobbes elsewhere *(De Corpore)* says that „The power of the agent and the efficient cause are the same thing [...] cause respects the past, power the future time", thereby obviously adopting a causal conception of power. But while Hobbes's conception, no doubt, is a causal view, it is questionable whether it is also a *social* view.

Dowding – who, of course, does not fail to mention the usual suspects (Dahl, Simon, and Nagel) as the most eminent advocates of causal definitions of power – puts his finger on the fundamental problem of all such „behaviouralist“ approaches: what they lack is an adequate theory of action. In his view, that is the fundamental reason why they fail to understand that the more plausible alternative to the causal view of power is a dispositional account (ibid., 4 f.).[167]

Another prominent political scientist who has argued, though for reasons that are very different from Dowding's, that, contrary to what most authors believe, relations of power should *not* be understood as causal relations is Gabriel Almond:

„Herbert Simon has stated that 'for the assertion '*C* has power over *R*', we can substitute the assertion, '*C*'s behavior causes *R*'s behavior'. If we can define the causal relation, we can define influence, power or authority, and *vice versa.*' Andrew McFarland asserts that 'definitions of power or influence based on such concepts as force, incentives or utilities, and minimum winning coalitions are [...] reducible to causal terms.' [...] And Robert Dahl [...] seems to maintain (although with some caveats) his long-standing view that causation is fundamental to understanding power and influence relations: 'When we single out influence from all other aspects of human interaction in order to give it special attention, what interests us [...] is that one or more of the persons in this interaction get what they want, or at least get closer to what they want, by causing other people to act in some particular way. We want to call attention to a *causal relationship* between what *A* wants and what *B* does.'" (Almond 1990, 44)[168]

Against these views, Almond (ibid.) objects that, in fact, rather than *causal necessity*, mere *constraints on options* are at issue:

„There is no 'necessity' inherent in the outcome of an attempt to assert power over another person [...] The target of the power attempt may, for any number of reasons, act differently than the power wielder would have him act. This is because a power relationship [...] is an interaction of two choosing and mutually constrained individuals, each with his own resources, goals, purposes, interests, and strategies. The intentions and resources of the first certainly constrain the choices and actions of the second, but they do not determine those choices and actions in any sort of cast-iron sense. This 'looseness of fit' between the behavior and intentions of actors involved in an attempt to exercise power means that their relationship is not readily generalizable; neither is it particularly amenable to strict covering-law explanation.“[169]

[167] Dowding himself is, consequently, committed to such a dispositional conception. He specifically argues (ibid., ch. 2.2 and p. 29) that a rational-choice approach based on a Davidsonian theory of action is the most suitable way to a plausible concept of social power. It would exceed the limits of the present investigation to discuss this specific proposal here. In any case, one need not accept it in order to agree with his critique. For a discussion of some of the problems connected with a theory of action that grounds reasons for action on the desires and beliefs of agents, cf., e. g., the monothematic issue of *Analyse & Kritik* 21:1 (August 1999) on 'Practical Reason and Understanding', esp. the contributions by Heuer, Schaber and Iorio. For instructive new insights in the theory of action, cf. González Lagier 2002, esp. ch. VII on the question of causation and the role of reasons for action.

[168] Some of the authors mentioned in this quote obviously do not see any relevant differences between power and influence, concerning this issue of causality. I will not comment on this here, since the concept of influence will specifically be treated in the next chapter.

[169] In this context, Almond also quotes from H. L. A. Hart and A. M. Honoré's *Causation in the Law* (Oxford: Clarendon 1959, p. 52): „The statement that one person did something because [...] another threatened him, carries no implication or covert assertion that if the circumstances were repeated, the same action would follow; nor does such a statement require for its defense, as ordinary causal statements do, a generalization.“

Necessary and sufficient conditions

From Almond's objection we can infer that he understands the notion of cause in terms of conditions *making* a certain effect *necessary*, and that means, in terms of conditions which are *sufficient* for that effect to come about. Sufficient conditions do indeed have 'cast-iron control' over their effects; and since such control does not exist in human interaction, such interaction cannot constitute causal relationships.

That objection can be backed by another consideration. As we have seen in Section 2, it is a central element of most conceptions of social power that the effect of an exercise of power (whether it consists in an action, a state of affairs or something else) is thought to be an effect in the strict sense of the word, i. e., something which *would not otherwise* have occurred. But this 'would not otherwise' clause, rather than to a sufficient condition, points to the exercise of power only as a *necessary* condition for the respective result.

Interestingly, most authors never bother to reflect on this kind of fundamental implications of their conceptual decisions, nor on objections such as Almond's or Dowding's. However, at least one of our stern defenders of a causal view of power, Joseph Oppenheim, approaches the topic precisely by looking at necessary and/or sufficient conditions. Moreover, like Almond, he understands causation in terms of necessary conditions. So he is forced to deal with the above objection. Contrary to common assumptions, Oppenheim (1981, 34 f.) therefore explicitly argues against interpreting power relations as involving *necessary* conditions for an agent's action, in the sense just explained. Take a situation in which an agent *P* performs an action *x*, and another agent *R* performs an action *y*. In Oppenheim's view, it does not matter whether *R* would or would not do *x* in the absence of *P*'s doing *y*: regardless of what he might do under different circumstances, as long as *if P* does *x* it becomes „highly probable" that *R* subsequently does *y*, *P* exercises power over *R* by doing *x*.

Now, although with this conception he has taken care of the second part of the objection, his stipulation that an exercise of power needs to make the intended reaction of the power subject merely 'highly probable' still seems to fall short of the needed *sufficient* condition. But, a sufficient condition is what Oppenheim actually means to argue for. Only that he is well aware of the fact that this creates a problem when human action is involved (and that it may therefore give rise to objections of the kind formulated by Almond).

So what are his options? For once, he could try to square the circle and argue that 'highly probable' is equivalent to a sufficient condition after all. And this is precisely what he does. In his view, all we need to do is change the deterministic account to a probabilistic account, i. e., understand causation not in terms of sufficient conditions proper, but in terms of „probabilistically sufficient" conditions (ibid., 34), where such conditions are precisely conditions that make certain events 'highly probable'. Hence, he suggests, the notion of causation „should be taken in the sense of a probabilistically sufficient condition in the defining expressions of the various power concepts" (ibid., 192).

As an argument for saving the causal conception of power, this is not very convincing.[170] But what seems valuable in Oppenheim's account despite this flaw is his having underlined that it does, in any case, not make much sense to speak already of an exercise of power when the *only* thing someone does with his action is provide a *necessary* condition for another's action, i. e., when all he does is to make that action *possible* (ibid. 1981, 36).

Intention and reasons for action

Of course, the big nuisance for all causal conceptions of social power is the fact that intentions are involved – not only on one, but on both sides of the relationship. When Russell (1988, 25) said that „Power may be defined as the production of intended effects", this was – besides its other shortcomings as a definition of power – already misleading in that it suggested that intention is involved only on one side, and that the rest is an ordinary relationship of cause and effect.

Curiously, Oppenheim, despite his strong advocacy of a causal conception of social power, in the last instance does not want to commit himself either to a „causalist" or to an „intentionalist" position. He acknowledges that intention does play a role for the actions of both agents involved in exercises of power.

„However, a power concept like exercising influence refers to R's intention or choice not only in relation to his *own* subsequent behavior (and this relation may or may not be causal), but also in relation to some *other*, antecedent action y of P. There can be no doubt that such relationships of *interaction* are causal." (Oppenheim 1981, 192)

In other words, what Oppenheim is saying is that an exercise of power by *P* over *R* means that *P*'s action *y* causes *R* to respond in a certain way, by way of choosing a certain action, because it *causes R* to have the corresponding *intention*. But he can say that only because his idea of causation is unorthodox: he sees cause at work „even in the absence of causal laws", a view for which he argues as follows:

„[W]e do say, quite correctly, that the dropping of the atomic bomb on Hiroshima was a cause [...] of Japan's decision to capitulate, even though *we can hardly refer to any generalization* from which this particular statement could be derived. Given this causal relation and given the definition of influencing in terms of causing others to choose to act in certain ways, it follows that the United States exercised influence and hence had power over Japan in this respect." (Oppenheim 1981, 193; emphasis added)

[170] If I am not mistaken, Oppenheim confuses two different things in his probabilistic account (1981, ch. 3.2): the *nature of the relationship* between the actions of two agents when we speak of an exercise of power; and our *possibility of making assertions* about such events. It is one thing to say that 'exercise of power' *means* that *P*'s action *x* was a necessary and/or sufficient condition for *R*'s action *y*, and quite another to *know* whether such an exercise has taken place. If the causal view of power is to be upheld, then probabilities may be involved in *explanations* of events as instances of exercises of power, but not in exercises of power themselves. As Oppenheim himself holds elsewhere, exercises of power are by definition always „successful" (1981, 13) – there are no probabilities involved.

But whether this is as correct as Oppenheim wants us to believe is questionable. Specifically, the question is what 'cause' could *mean* if it is to be conceived without any reference to regularity.[171]

In fact, it seems that it is not even true that 'we' invariably say that Hiroshima was the 'cause' of the Japanese *decision* to capitulate. When it comes to decisions, it seems much more appropriate to speak of *reasons* – and 'we' often do so, if only by intuition. In contrast, the failure of a good number of political theorists to distinguish between reasons and causes seems to be responsible for much confusion in accounts of the alleged causal nature of social power.

Another case in point is precisely the second of the two authors mentioned earlier as holding an argued-for causal view of power: Jack Nagel. Nagel (1975) directly understands „Power as Causation by Preferences" (thus the title of his ch. 3). In his view, it is the power-holder's preference which, being the proximate *cause* of his action, is the remote *cause* of the subject's reaction; hence, an exercise of power is a causal relationship between one agent's preference, as cause, and the outcome of another agent's reaction, as effect (1975, 28 f.). And, unlike Oppenheim, Nagel even thinks that this is perfectly compatible with a purely Humean conception of causal relations:

> „According to the convincing argument of Gasking (1955), the notion of causality originated in observation of effects produced by human manipulation. As science advances, however, this 'recipe' notion of causality gives way to causation as an 'inference license', in which 'cause' comprises the cluster of conditions from which occurrence of the effect can be deduced [...] Quite possibly, many behaviorists employed the primitive idea of causation in defining power. Thus, it may have seemed inconceivable that one actor could exercise power over another – cause the other's behavior – without *doing* something." (Nagel 1975, 17)[172]

Clearly, the 'inference license' Nagel is speaking of refers to the possibility at least of *prediction* – or retrodiction, for that matter –, in the strong sense of postulating a regularity or law, if not to *explanation*.

However, in the light of the objections to the causal account presented above, it is no surprise that even that has been contested. Thus, for example, Connolly (1983b,

[171] Cf., e. g., von Wright 1984, ch. 3, for a particularly clear account of the received notion of causality. Whatever else one may demand of a causal relation, the Humean idea of regularity seems to be the smallest common denominator; if that is given up, nothing is left. An explanation which, though couched in a causal vocabulary, does not refer to any law, is what von Wright calls a 'quasi-causal' explanation. Analogously, one could perhaps say that Oppenheim's conception of power is not really causal, but 'quasi-causal'.

[172] Nagel here fails to see that linking the concept of causality to the idea of the possibility of manipulation has nothing to do with a „manipulative matter-in-motion concept of causation" (ibid.). Moreover, the Humean notion of mere regularity of joint occurrence cannot fully account for what we mean when we speak of causation (cf. von Wright 1984, esp. ch. II), and the idea that assertions of causal relations entail assertions about what one would have to do if one would intentionally want to bring about a certain event is far from being „primitive". Now, as Nagel's definition of power, which he holds to be a causal one, shows, he subscribes entirely to the Humean conception of causation, in the sense that a regular sequential occurrence of a certain preference of one agent *A* and a certain outcome brought about by another agent *B* means that an instance of the „subset of causal relations" called 'power' has occurred. However, I tend to find von Wright's view more plausible, according to which it would be strange to speak of *A*'s preference having caused *B*'s outcome unless one had some idea about the kind of connection between the two factors, and that means about the 'mechanism' by which *A*'s preference brings about the effect on the outcome on *B*'s side. This 'mechanism' must not necessarily be an action, of course; but some idea of mechanism seems to be necessary, if only because otherwise it would be impossible to distinguish between causal and coincidental sequences of events.

101) has pointed out that the usefulness of the concept of power lies in that it „enables participants and investigators to locate responsibility for the imposition of limiting conditions“, and *not* in its *predictive qualities*: Situations in which power is exercised, he argues, are by no means situations in which action is predetermined and, hence, predictable:

„If I exercise power over another, I impose obstacles to his ability to act in support of his wishes, interests, or obligations, but I do not thereby ensure that I [...] can closely predict his resulting behavior (or assign a probability to some act x). He could do any number of things [...] [H]is conduct could vary from my expectations, but as long as the element introduced did in fact increase the costs or risks in meeting his interests, wishes, or obligations, I would have exercised power over him. Thus he might accede to my wishes; he might accept suffering in the pursuit of higher objectives; he might misread the message and suffer heavily because of his ignorance; he might deflect costs to others, increasing the load of guilt he carries; he might refuse to comply and flee the country; or he might refuse and commit suicide. I exercise power over him in each of these cases, but because he is a creature of self-interpretation with a capacity for choice [...], I cannot predict with any certainty how he will respond [...] Power is a disappointing concept to predictivists [...]“ (ibid., 100 f.)

But even if one were to favour a causal conception, the considerable difference between Oppenheim's and Nagel's account of the way in which social power can be said to be of a causal nature is disturbing. The fact that such two very different interpretations exist, neither one of which provides a satisfactory answer to Almond's objection, not to speak of a convincing theory of action, as requested by Dowding, indicates that considerable need for clarification still exists. In the meantime, conceptions which merely stipulate the causal nature of social power – without further reflection on what that means and what it implies, referring at best to always the same handful of sources – and which, at the same time, define power as a relationship between two (or more) agents, can only be used with great caution.[173]

In the last instance, it is difficult to understand why so many authors insist on the causal view, despite its apparent problems. In my view, it would seem much more promising and plausible to give it up and replace it with another, based on careful considerations of reasons for action. Since in the context of social relations, the objects of the effects of what is called 'power' are human acts, it seems that a conception of power that refers exclusively to causality *cannot* be entirely appropriate. It is impossible to account for the different 'mechanisms' by which an agent can manipulate other people's acts exclusively in such causal terms. As Francisco Laporta, relying on von Wright's account, has observed – in my opinion, convincingly – in an essay about 'Power and Law':

„What is characteristic of actions or omissions elicited by others, and therefore of the phenomenon of power over others, is that between the eliciting action which is the alleged 'cause' and the elicited action which is the alleged 'effect' there is a mediation of deliberation, of practical reasoning on the part of the passive subject [...] And it is this mediation which [...] in thinking about power makes it advisable to abandon that alleged strong link between the idea of power and the notion of causality.“ (Laporta 1996, 450; my translation)

[173] And those which, in order to overcome the predicament, renounce the second condition, cease to be 'social' in any interesting sense.

3.3. CUTTING THROUGH THE JUNGLE

On the background of these considerations about the unsatisfactory state of reflection on the basic nature of power phenomena, I will now use Künsken's categories for an attempt at a brief systematic summary of some relevant similarities and differences between the positions analyzed in this chapter.

Power-holder and power subject (1, 2)

If the focus is to be on a concept of *social* power, there does not seem to be much room for dispute about the necessity that (at least) two parties of *agents* must be involved. It will be a matter of the underlying theory of agency to decide what qualities must obtain for an entity to be able to count as a power-holder or a subject of power, respectively.

The review of the different conceptions in the last section has shown that, in fact, these two categories do not constitute a major bone of contention; they have proven to be hardly controversial at all.

Power relationship (3)

Controversies begin, however, as soon as the kind of relationship between the agents involved are at issue. We have seen a number of different conceptions of what social power is a relation between.

To say simply that it is a relationship between 'agents' as such is not very informative; particularly, it does not permit any deep explanation of power phenomena. With few exceptions, most authors do not pay much attention to possible theoretical implications, and postulate all kinds of imaginable relations: for example, between one agent's preferences (wants) and another's actions, one agent's actions and another's interests, or both agents' actions (as, e. g., Dahl, Lukes, or Foucault and Bachrach/Baratz, respectively).

Moreover, in some cases, the 'receiving end' of a power relationship is considered to be directly a state of the world, an 'outcome'. In that case, it is conceived, variably, as a relationship between an agent's preferences, wants, intention, or action, on the one hand, and an outcome, on the other (examples of such views are Hobbes, Russell, Kliemt, or J. Nagel 1975). In such cases, we still move in the realm of *social* concepts of power only if the 'outcome' in question can, in the final analysis, be traced back to an action (or preference, want, intention, ...) of another agent, i. e., if they constitute some kind of a relationship between agents.

In that context, more specifically, one of the traditional controversies about 'power over' has been whether it operates exclusively and directly on other people's behaviour, as the 'behaviourist' view proposes, or rather on outcomes in general, although of a 'social' kind, as Kliemt says. An interesting difference between the two positions is that in the first case, one could say that power is an ability to make others *do* certain things, whereas in the second, it could only be the ability to make others *suffer* certain things – 'suffer' here in the neutral sense of making things (whether bad or good) happen to other people, of shaping the environment they move in.

As we have seen, Brian Barry has been among those who argue that the alternatives are only: that power operates on *actions*, or power is *not a social concept* (since it then operates on 'things' in general, and where those 'things' are not actions, it is not social, but 'natural' power – i. e., not 'power over', but 'power to').

Kliemt, in contrast, has pointed out that there is still a third possibility, to wit, that power operates on 'outcomes', but outcomes of a special kind – namely, 'social outcomes'. In his view, such outcomes are either states of the world or 'mind-states of people'. Look at the latter first. What happens when a person's mind-state changes? Why should anyone intend to bring such an outcome about? Although this is not a logical necessity, but a contingent, empirical matter, someone who wishes to change another's mind-state will want to do so, except for rare occasions, because of the impact it is expected to have on the other's actions.[174] Now, what about 'states of the world'? As I said before, a state of the world can be regarded as 'social' only if its *production* is a 'social' affair, i. e., if actions of a plurality of agents are involved. In that sense, then, affecting social outcomes by changing (or preventing the change of) social states of the world also seems to depend, ultimately, on affecting others' actions.

Seen in that light, Brian Barry and others seem to be on the side of greater plausibility in saying that with respect to 'social' power, what matters ultimately is the (potential) impact on the behaviour of others, and that power which does not operate on actions is not social power.

Only if power is conceived as a purely *causal* concept, it seems, it would make no difference whether the 'outcomes' it involves are somehow related to actions. But besides the fact that this would again raise the question in what sense such power could be called 'social', I have argued above that such a view should better be abandoned.

The 'realization' of power (11)

The mode in which power is thought to exist, i. e., whether it is defined as something that *is* exercised, or that *can be* exercised, or *both*, is of fundamental importance, not only in itself, but also because it has implications for the remaining categories. It is therefore convenient to advance its consideration, although it is only second to last in Künsken's list.

Common usage, at least for those languages I am familiar with, provides the possibility to distinguish 'having power' from 'exercising power'. So, whenever the concept of power is at issue, both these expressions must be taken into consideration. There are three possibilities to deal with this issue: one can opt for either one of the expressions and deny that the other one means anything, or at least: anything relevant, or one can give meaning to both of them and say something about how they are conceptually linked.

(1) Sometimes, it is stipulated that power exists only in the 'exercise' mode, i. e., that as long as no 'exercise of power' (by some agent over another) takes place, there is

[174] The exceptions seem to be limited to changing another's mind-state on the *emotional* dimension – I may want to make another happy, or angry, just because that's what I want him to *be*; where the change concerns beliefs or preferences, an intention to bring it about that would not be driven by any further purpose is hard to imagine. Cf. also Dowding 1991, 1996, who distinguishes 'outcome power' ('power to') as such from 'social power' ('power over'), defined as an agent's ability to affect outcomes *through* work on another's actions (specifically, through purposively changing the other's incentive structure).

no sense in which one could rightfully speak of an existence of power, or of a power relationship between agents.

Thus, for example, Bachrach/Baratz insist that, because it is relational, power cannot be 'possessed' ('had') by an agent. They therefore try to avoid speaking of someone 'having' power over another, and treat only cases of 'exercises' of power. Unfortunately, it turns out that they cannot consistently stick to that ideal. At some point, for instance, they say that „the availability of sanctions *endows* A with power over B" (1963, quoted from Scott 1994/II, 97; emphasis added). But when I am 'endowed' with something, what else does this mean if not that I then 'have' or 'possess' it? However, the authors quickly move away from that (for their professed conception) dangerous thought and point out that the 'availability' of sanctions 'endows' an agent with power only if that agent actually *threatens* another. This results in a conception of a 'power relationship' only in its actualized form, so to speak: In Bachrach's and Baratz's view, a power relationship never exists 'latently', during the time a power-holder does not choose to exercise his power. That, indeed, is a very counter-intuitive view: that the availability of sanctions (the possibility that I could sanction another) does absolutely nothing to my relationship with another in terms of power, but that as soon as, without any further external change of the situation, by an act of will, I set out to threaten the other with the imposition of those sanctions (which were available to me all the time), miraculously, the availability of the sanctions 'endows' me with power.

Note also that, since all Bachrach/Baratz acknowledge are 'exercises' of power (as well as of influence, etc.), they have difficulty to classify what happens when someone, e. g., *attempts* to exercise power (say, by threatening with a sanction), but his demand is complied with by the other side for a *different* reason – say, because the threatener is regarded as an authority by the addressee of the threat. The authors must then say that the former „sought to exercise power but in fact exercised authority" (1963, from Scott 1994/II, 104). If 'exercise' is understood in an intentional sense, that sounds strange, to say the least.[175]

(2) Now, let us take a look at the other 'monoscopic' possibility, i. e., an exclusive emphasis on power as something one can 'have', without relating it in any way to something that could be exercised. It seems that taken in *this* sense, the objection of Bachrach/Baratz mentioned above acquires plausibility: If power is conceived to be *only* a property of one agent that is not somehow, through an 'actualization', through making 'use' of it for some act, at least potentially related to another agent, then we are no longer dealing with power in a *social* sense. On this line, Oppenheim argues:

> „There are [...] several reasons why I think it inadvisable to use 'power' in the sense of 'ability to do something' in our technical language." (Oppenheim 1981, 29)

And one of his reasons is precisely that the simple identification of 'power' with 'ability' does not refer to 'power over' but to 'power to'. But if that is all it means, then to say 'can do' is much less complicated than to say 'has the power to'. Hence, Oppenheim

[175] For another example of the difficulties connected with the attempt to focus exclusively on the *exercise* of power and to deny any independently relevant sense to the *having* of power, cf. the discussion of Kristjánsson's view in Chapter 3.3.

thinks, it would be preferable to reserve the term 'power' generally for the social sense of 'power over'.

(3) Hence, it seems that common usage of language as well as the aim to arrive at a social concept of power recommend the third option, that is, that of constructing the concept in such a way that it will be possible without great problems to speak of 'having power' as well as of 'exercising' it. In fact, this seems so natural to most authors that they take it as self-evident that this is the way it must be.

What exactly 'having power' should be taken to mean is, however, controversial; one finds several answers to this question in the literature. But by far the most frequent is that 'power' is best understood as an *ability* one can *have* – specifically, an ability to trigger particular reactions (depending on what choices are made regarding the other categories of Künsken's list) from another agent. Such an ability, which exists over time in a latent state, can then, of course, be 'actualized' on certain occasions, i. e., the power one 'has' over another can occasionally be 'exercised' over her. In other words: '*A has* power over *B*' in that sense means, roughly, '*A* has the ability to trigger certain things in *B* (or certain outcomes through *B*)'; and '*A exercises* her power over *B*' therefore means '*A* in fact triggers some such thing in *B* (or outcome through *B*)'.[176]

Such a view has a number of important implications, which are not often reflected upon. So, at this point it is convenient to call to mind some aspects conceptually linked to 'abilities'.[177] When someone, by accident, happens to get a certain thing done once, but could not repeat the performance if he wanted to, that would not be an appropriate case for speaking of that agent's 'ability' to get the thing done. Ability requires more than just accidental success – it implies 'know how':

„The mere fact that by some haphazard movements of my hands and fingers I succeed in opening a door with a complicated lock-mechanism does not entitle me to say that I *can* open a door with this type of lock. But if normally, *i. e.* on most occasions, when I set myself to the task I succeed in opening the door without much trial and error, then I may be said to be able to do this sort of thing. I then *know how* to do it." (von Wright 1963, 48 f.)[178]

This has the further implication that one can speak of an ability only with respect to whole categories of acts, not with respect to individual acts:

[176] An idiosyncratic view is advocated by Oppenheim (1981, 29 f.) who argues that one should not confuse 'having power' with 'having the ability to exercise power', as is often done in definitions of power (he cites Riker, B. Barry and Held as cases in point). Oppenheim's underlying reason here is that for him 'having power' (or influence, for that matter) presupposes the performance of some action, by which an agent „avails himself" of the „means" constituting his power base. He thus wants to avoid that someone is said to 'have' power over another if all he actually 'has' are some means he could potentially, if he wanted to, convert into instruments for exercising power (ibid., 30). What is important in this argument of Oppenheim's is certainly his pointing out that possession of certain means is not sufficient for 'having' power.

[177] The most plausible account of the fundamental issues involved in the concept of ability I am aware of is that given by Georg Henrik von Wright in his seminal work *Norm and Action* (1963), on which the following observations are based. (I am indebted to Pablo Navarro for having reminded me of the relevance of that work to the present context.) Similarly also, more recently, von Wright 1998.

[178] Von Wright at this point introduces two other helpful concepts that should be distinguished from 'ability': that of 'skill', which refers to the mastering of techniques (whereas ability refers merely to 'know how': I may be *able* to do something, without being particularly *skilled* at it); and that of 'capacity', which refers to the possibility to *acquire* a certain ability, i. e., to a kind of „second-order ability".

„That I 'can do' something has a different meaning when it refers to an act-individual and when it refers to an act-category. That on some occasion a certain state of affairs [...] comes [...] into being as a *consequence* of some *activity* on my part [...] is a necessary and sufficient condition for saying that I can [...] do this thing [...] *on that occasion* [...] Of this 'can do' no 'know how' and no reasonable assurance of success before the attempt is required. These are requirements of that 'can do' which refers to act-categories and which alone amounts to ability." (von Wright 1963, 50)

The 'can do' we usually mean when we speak of someone 'having' power over another clearly is an ability in that sense. It does not refer to act-individuals, but to act-categories; therefore, it requires both some 'know how' and what von Wright calls „reasonable assurance of success".

And this connotation even carries over to the notion of 'exercising' power: What is implied in saying that an agent *A* has *exercised power* over another agent *B* is *more* than merely that on a specific occasion, just once, and perhaps even without knowing how he did it, *A* happened to produce the impact on *B* which the respective conception of power refers to – for instance, that *A* happened to get *B* to do (or refrain from doing) something *A* wanted her to do (or refrain from doing). Also, again using the same conception of power as an example, we would not say that *A has power* over *B* if there were no conduct of *B* that we think *A* can, if he puts his mind to it, elicit or suppress more or less *ad libitum*. To say that *A* has power over *B*, in that sense, *means* that *A* 'knows how' to control certain acts of *B*, and is, on the whole, successful when he sets out to exercise that power.[179]

Here, the question whether 'success' is or isn't a necessary condition – whether it is enough to be 'on the whole, successful' – comes up again. The advantage of von Wright's account is that he does not claim that these concepts are *causal* concepts;[180] hence, an account in terms of *sufficient* conditions (cf. subsection 3.2) is not necessarily warranted.

But however this may be, in any case, an *exercise* of power as such must always be successful. If unsuccessful, power simply was not exercised: there was merely a (failed) *attempt* at such an exercise; and a failed attempt may count as an indicator that the agent is *powerless*, i. e., that he does not have the corresponding ability, because it seems difficult to understand what it could mean that someone 'has' power (where 'having' denotes an ability), but is, nevertheless, unable to exercise it. It seems that if a failed attempt is *not* to count as an indicator of a *lack* of power, additional explanations for the failure are required. With von Wright's distinction between 'ability' and 'skill' in mind, this is how Brian Barry's view that there is a „possibility of slippage" in the exercise of power because of a potential „lack of skill"; (B. Barry 1991a, 228) might be made plausible, after all.

[179] Note that success, in turn, is not a concept that can in any way be referred to an act-category; it is always relative to particular, identifiable „opportunities", whereas abilities, referring to act-categories, are entirely independent of opportunities (ibid., 50 f.). – Another relevant aspect in this context is the relationship between the ability to do or to omit something: „An agent's abilities with regard to corresponding acts and forbearances [...] are reciprocal. That which an agent can effect as a result of his action he can also forbear to effect as a result of his action, and conversely" (ibid., 54).

[180] For his advocacy of an *intentionalist* approach to action, cf. esp. von Wright 1984, ch. III.

Finally, of special interest in the context of the analysis of power is the classification of those acts „which relate to an agent's ability to interfere with the ability of another agent to perform a certain act“ (von Wright 1963, 54):

„To *compel* an agent to do something is the same as to *prevent* him *from forbearing* this thing. And to *hinder* an agent from doing something is the same as to *force* him *to forbear* it.
To hinder an agent from doing something is to act in such a manner that it becomes *impossible* for that agent to do that thing. To hinder or prevent is to 'make impossible'. The result of the act of hindering an agent from doing a certain thing on a certain occasion is to change the world in such a way that the agent cannot do that thing on that occasion.“ (ibid., 55; emphasis added)

Thus, hindering or preventing refer to the ability to perform a certain act-individual on a particular occasion („can-do as success“), not to act-categories („can-do as ability“).[181] When someone is deprived of the ability to an entire category of acts, this is usually called 'disabling' instead (ibid., 55).

And one last remark on abilities: Note that if 'having' power is an ability, it is not always necessary to see it 'in exercise' in order to know that the ability exists. The existence of abilities in general can often be induced from knowledge of certain empirical data: one does not need to see a lion kill a man in order to know that he has the ability to do it, as Morriss has perspicaciously observed (cf. Bardhan 1991, 274 f.).

All these aspects, and more, would need to be taken properly into account for a conception of power as an ability which can be 'actualized' through exercise in order to be adequate from an action-theoretic point of view.

Another fundamental issue in the conceptual struggle with power that belongs in this same context is the question how, if at all, my ability to block your way and thus force you to deviate from it is related to my power over you; or, less metaphorically speaking, the question how conceptually to delimit social *power* from *mere ability* to affect another's environment in ways which, in turn, affect the other's behaviour.[182]

One solution is to say that any such ability, provided it can be used purposefully to get someone else to do what one wants them to do, should be regarded as falling under the concept of someone 'having' power over another. The inconvenience of this solution is that on this account practically everyone has power over everyone else who happens to cross their paths and that, therefore, it is contrary to the common understanding of what power relations are all about. It would be strange to say that anyone driving his automobile on the street has power over all other drivers present on the same street at the same time because, by stopping his car in the middle of the road, every driver *could* force all others either to stop too or to 'go out of their way' in order to circumvent the obstacle. If this were power, it would perhaps be a kind of power that would rarely be 'exercised', but one would 'have' it nevertheless. Still, when driving on a road one does not usually have the impression of being surrounded by big numbers of

[181] Also: „Compelling or preventing is an annihiliation of power to do or forbear. The power thus annihilated, however, is the 'can do' which refers to act-individuals, and not the 'can do' which refers to act-categories.“ (ibid., 111)
[182] Cf. on this Pettit's proposal to distinguish between 'conditioning' and 'compromising' another's freedom, in Chapter 3.2.

powerful people. A counter-objection to this would be to say that 'having power' does not necessarily mean 'having *a lot* of power'; and that our reluctance to identify drivers of cars on roads as 'socially powerful' stems from the mistake of equating 'having *little* power' with 'having *no* power'; one could argue that the power of driver *A* over driver *B* is 'small power'.[183]

Transitivity (4)
Another issue that is not explicitly treated by very many of the authors who have written about power is transitivity. It is, however, an extraordinarily important issue from a political point of view. In much of ideal political theory, for instance, it is one of the main conditions that the location of power can be fixed and circumscribed, assuring the stability of some distribution pattern of power. Whether power is or is not conceived as being of a transitive nature is of utmost importance to such ideas.

The question about the transitivity of power is one of those that need to be answered differently for having and for exercising power:

(1) If *A has* power over *B*, and *B has* power over *C*, does A necessarily *have* power over *C* too? Independently of the specific conception of power one holds, there is, I think, a logically necessary answer to the question: If, and only if, getting *B* to *exercise* the power he has over *C* is within the scope of the power *A has* over *B*, then the answer must be affirmative. If *A* can make *B* exercise power over *C*, that is just as good as if *A* had (the ability to exercise) power over *C* herself.

(2) If *A exercises* power over *B*, to the effect of *making B exercise* power over *C*, so that there is an *exercise* of power by *A* over *B*, and an *exercise* of power by *B* over *C*, is there at the same time also an *exercise* of power by *A* over *C*? The answer to that question seems to depend on the answer one gives concerning category (3): If an exercise of power requires a *direct* relationship between the two sides involved, then obviously *A* does *not* exercise power over *C* in such a case. Otherwise, one could say that *A does* exercise power over *C*. In that case, one has to deal with the further question of over-determination, since it would seem strange to say that *both A* and *B* then exercise power over *C*.[184]

Awareness (5)
A further interesting question, with considerable implications, is whether or not power is to be understood in a sense that makes awareness of its existence on either of the two or on both sides of a power relationship a necessary feature. And again, for this question too, the possible answers depend on a prior decision concerning category *(11)*.

If power is conceived, in the most common way, as an ability agents can *have*, it is an entirely contingent matter whether or not a power-holder and/or a power subject

183 Just as Hobbes thought that „The Sciences, are small Power" (*Leviathan*, ch. X, 151 [42]). If that thesis of Hobbes's is interpreted to refer to power in the *social* sense, which seems to be at least a *possible* interpretation, it does not contradict Francis Bacon's more famous *dictum* that „Scientia et potentia humana in idem coincidunt" (Novum Organum, lib. aph. 3, quoted from G. H. von Wright, *The Tree of Knowledge*, Leiden: Brill 1993, 127, n. 1).

184 Considering that exercises of power may raise questions of *responsibility*, this is no irrelevant matter.

are aware of that fact.[185] And *if* the concept of *exercise* is understood in a way that necessarily relates it to intentions and purposes, i. e., if accounts of events in terms of 'exercises' of power are to refer to *agents* and their *actions* in the strict sense, then awareness on the part of the power-holder is conceptually necessary. In contrast, it would seem to make the concept of power inadequately narrow for most purposes if it were restricted exclusively to situations in which the power-subject too is aware of the fact that power is exercised over him – whether or not subjects are aware of the nature of the thing that is happening to them does not seem to make a relevant difference to the nature of that thing itself.

But there is a further aspect to this, which complicates the matter: Even if an *exercise* of power presupposes a corresponding intention and 'success-orientation' – and that means awareness – on the part of a power-holder, while his *having* power does not necessarily presuppose any such thing on either side of the relationship, if a power subject *is* aware of the fact that another *has* power over him, this alone can have considerable consequences, even in the absence of any purposeful exercise of power by the power-holder (and even without his awareness). This is important, particularly for political theory. In the strict sense, not ability, but only *exercise* of power, i. e., its purposeful, intended 'use', and the subsequent change of the social situation, may be a question of *responsibility* and require *justification*.[186] But, especially in political contexts, it is to be expected, on the one hand, that power, once 'had', is *likely* to be exercised, and on the other, that the subjects of such power are, perhaps more than in other contexts, *likely* to be *aware* of the existence of latent power relations, with the consequences just indicated. Therefore, to the extent that the distribution of political power in the *ability* sense is 'man-made', through the establishment (or prevention of the establishment) of institutions, those who *create* such power conditions are responsible for certain effects, even *before any exercise* of power may ever have taken place.

Costs (6)

The aspect of costs, as we have seen in the previous section, plays a decisive role in some conceptions because they restrict the existence of power relationships to cases where either the (successful) *exercise* of power can be effected by a power-holder at *absolute costs* below a certain *threshold* (at 'reasonable costs' or 'low costs', as the

[185] Cf. on this the discussion of Philip Pettit's idea that one of the most significant consequences of the existence of latent power relations are the psychological effects induced by 'common knowledge' of that fact and its implications, in Chapter 3.2.

[186] That one is responsible only for one's actions or omissions, and their consequences, not for one's characteristics or position within a relational system, is emphasized, e. g., by Morriss and Brian Barry: „Morriss rightly scotches the claim, made especially be William Connolly, that ascribing power is also ascribing responsibility. As Morriss points out, people are held responsible for what they do actually do (or fail to do), not for what they could do: 'we are blamed for our acts (and omissions), not for having power' (p. 39). The question of power arises here only because powerlessness in some matter necessarily negates responsibility for the outcome, while power to have prevented an outcome entails responsibility for it." (B. Barry 1991d, 305). Isaiah Berlin (1969, xiv) has expressed the same idea in one of his superb examples: „I cannot see how one can say of Helen not only that hers was the face that launched a thousand ships but, in addition, that she was responsible for [...] the Trojan War, if the war was due solely to something that was the result not of a free choice – to elope with Paris – which Helen need not have made, but only of her irresistible beauty."

threshold is sometimes rather vaguely determined), or there is a certain *relation* between the costs respectively incurred by the power-holder and the power subject.

Especially when one rejects the *causal* conception of power and acknowledges that power phenomena involve *agents* and their *reasons* for action, the question of costs becomes highly important already on the *conceptual* level. But the corresponding 'cut off' decisions require careful consideration and reasoning if it is to be avoided that relevantly similar phenomena are separated by definitional *fiat*.

Resistance (7)

The question whether and in what sense 'resistance' may be a necessary feature of an adequate concept of social power is, as we have seen, mentioned in almost all accounts. It is another of those issues which require a distinction between *having* and *exercising* power. Concerning the former, there seems to be little controversy. Brian Barry's answer can be taken as representative for the great bulk of the literature on this aspect:

„We must, then, insist that there is more to (social) power than being able to do what you choose to do. Your having power entails that you have the ability to overcome resistance or opposition and by this means achieve an outcome different from the one that would have occurred in the absence of your intervention." (B. Barry 1991d, 308)

Concerning the latter, we have seen that opinions are divided on whether it should be conceived as a *conceptual* necessity that an exercise of power involves overcoming actual resistance. On this issue, it is useful to take into consideration some reflections from legal theory about the question how meaningful it could be to speak of the imposition of a prescriptive norm even in cases where the prescribed conduct would be forthcoming anyway, without the norm, for other reasons. In the present context, some observations of Frederick Schauer (1991, ch. 6.4) about normative authority – which, at least on some accounts, can be understood as a subclass of social power – are of particular interest:

The characteristic feature of normative authority, according to Schauer, is that it gives rise to a particular kind of *reasons for action*, namely, *source-dependent* reasons, as opposed to *content-dependent* reasons.[187] Now, when reasons for action do not depend on the *content* of a prescription, but only on its *source*, then disagreement with the content – i. e., a reason for 'resistance' – acquires a special relevance:

„Because authority is content-independent, its presence makes a difference only when the subject of the authority disagrees with the content of an authoritative directive [...] authority exerts its true decisional bite when the subject would not otherwise have conformed to the content of the directive." (Schauer 1991, 129)

„Given that the question of authority arises in an interesting way only when there is disagreement between authority and subject, the rational authority is led to attempt to require obedience just as the rational subject is led to disobey." (ibid., 131)

On this line, one could argue that an exercise of power, too, can plausibly be regarded as having been *successfully* performed only if it has 'made a difference'. This would speak

[187] „Existing analyses of authority start, correctly, from the premise that authority is, in the terminology of Hart and Raz, content-independent. Authority exists when and only when the source of a directive provides a reason for the addressee to follow it independent of the content of that directive." (Schauer 1991, 128 f.)

in favour of making 'resistance' in some sense a conceptually necessary condition. But *what* this sense could plausibly be would need to be carefully argued for.

Impact (8)

The question about the *kind(s) of impact* power is conceived to have is closely related to the question about the kind of relationship power is understood to be, i. e., with category *(3)*; perhaps one can distinguish the two categories by saying that where the latter refers to the basic entities that are connected by a power relationship, the aspect of 'impact' refers to the specific 'point of intrusion' on which power mechanisms operate. In that sense, it obviously concerns primarily the exercise dimension of power.

However, authors who emphasize (or exclusively see) the latent side of power relationships also have some idea of the 'difference' it makes whether or not such a relationship obtains, and consequently about the kind of impact, and the *locus* of impact such relationships may have.[188]

As for the exercise of power, much of the analysis in Section 2 concerned precisely the substantial disagreement, and the many different facets taken into account by different authors, with regard to the question of 'impact'. I can only repeat here that as long as the conception of power is not firmly based on a plausible theory of action, all such accounts, whether more or less plausible, can only be regarded as preliminary, tentative proposals.

Base (9)

The distinction of different kinds of 'bases' of power, depending on the particular kinds of relationships existing between the involved agents, on which the power relation is parasitic, or the general kinds of resources power is based on, obviously makes for very different kinds of concepts. Künsken himself, in explaining his list of categories, names what are probably the most important distinctions to be made in that respect: whether power is based on *physical*, *normative* ('legal'), or *epistemic* grounds.[189]

This is, however, a distinction to be made only *after* a more basic, general concept of social power is in place. In that sense, it directs us to a different level than the other categories so far considered. And even if for specific purposes only one of the corresponding subcategories of power will probably always be of interest, for conceptual reasons the connection to the other fields should never entirely get out of sight.

Means (10)

The question of which means, if any, are conceptually necessary for power is, together with that of impact *(8)*, the main playing field of the controversies about the concept of power. But, of course, means being something that is employed purposefully towards certain ends, it concerns only conceptions of power which give some importance to the *exercise* dimension.

[188] Cf. the reference to Pettit, in n. 185 above.

[189] In this context, cf. B. Barry's observations presented in the previous section, in the sense that different bases of power make power phenomena a subject of different disciplines; see also Chapter 4 for an analysis of the distinction between *factual* and *normative* power.

One issue concerning means, to which I have alluded earlier and which I think has not always received due attention particularly in sociological conceptions of power is the fact that what ultimately matters for power may not be the actual *existence* of certain means, but merely the *belief* in their existence. After all, as Hobbes already knew,

„the power of the mighty hath no foundation but in the opinion and belief of the people."[190]

Obviously, this plays an especially great role for those conceptions which focus on the availability of a *threat of sanctions* as one of the most important, if not the only, means for the exercise of social power.[191] Because if my threat is effective, i. e., if it induces another to comply with what I want, then he will never *know* wether my not inflicting the threatened harm on him is indeed my premeditated conditional reaction to his behaviour, or whether it is rather due to my lack of the means for inflicting the harm on him in case of non-compliance, or perhaps to my lack of a reason to do so simply because I am unable to monitor his behaviour. In other words, as long as a threat is effective, the threatened person will not be able to interpret the threatener's 'reaction' as a signal of his ability or inability to follow up on his threat. This is so because the reaction to compliance following an effective threat is, in principle, exactly the same as the 'reaction' to be expected, *whatever* the other does, from someone who has issued a threat *not* backed by the means or the ability to impose a conditional sanction: no sanction is inflicted. Hence, someone who, on whatever grounds, believes that the other does have those means and ability, and therefore complies on one occasion, will not have a reason to change that belief as a consequence of the other's reaction to his compliance on that occasion. The only way to find out for sure whether or not a threat is empty is by *not* complying with a respective request or order and see what happens – a strategy which, of course, implies some risk of suffering the sanction. This means that for a threat to be potentially effective, the only really *necessary* condition with respect to the threatener's means and monitoring ability is that the threatened party *must not know it* if one of the two does *not* exist. Obviously, this is quite different from stipulating that it is necessary that they *exist* or that he *knows* them to exist. On the other hand, it is, of course, also *not sufficient* that they *exist* nor that he *knows* them to exist. After all, the threatener might be *unwilling* to employ the means even if he does possess them.

[190] Hobbes 1668 (1990, 16); I am indebted to Johannes Schmidt for this reference.

[191] The stipulation that (the exercise of) power involves (the threat of) sanctions seems to square well with Lukes's view that power is necessarily linked to affecting others' interests negatively. Mokken/Stokman (1975) are among those who have taken issue with the 'bias' implicit in such definitions of power, in the sense that only negative consequences are taken into consideration. In this context, it is therefore not without interest to note that in the past decade or so, scholarship has emphasized the fact that many kinds of social interactions – most importantly perhaps the celebration of contracts with strangers – are *facilitated*, if not made *possible*, by the availability of sanctions (cf., e. g. Schauer 1991, 140). Thus, the enforcement of norms through (the effective threat of) sanctions is not only sought to be dodged by those who are tempted to break the norms; it is also sought to be implemented and ensured, perhaps even by the same persons, in order to make it possible to engage in the kind of action that would constitute norm-conforming behaviour in the first place (it is precisely the problem of establishing and ensuring such enforcement that is seen today by many social theorists as one of the greatest problems of social interactions; cf., among many others, Baurmann 2001; or the writings of Douglass North, e. g. 1986, 1990, 1993).

In the case of a positive sanction,[192] such as, for instance, a promise, the situation is slightly different: here, it is *non*-compliance which does not require a specific reaction, whereas compliance requires the fulfilment of the promise. Thus, a promise may be effective, in the sense of inducing compliance, at best a few times, or even only once, before the compliant party will know from the promiser's reactions whether or not the promise is credible. But, again, that someone does not make good on a promise on certain occasions does not necessarily imply that he does not have the necessary means, or the ability to monitor the other's actions; it may simply be the case that he does not have the will to do it. Hence, here too, it is *not sufficient* for making a promise credible that the means and monitoring ability exist, and it is not even sufficient that the other side *knows* this to be the case. However, for a promise to be effective over a longer series of occasions – and, thus, possibly provide a basis for power in the ability sense –, it is, indeed, *necessary* that the corresponding means and monitoring ability exist.

Amount (12)
Finally, the last aspect to be considered here concerns the question whether power is to be understood as something that is in any sense measurable, and if so, how such a measure could be constructed.

Since it seems natural to speak of someone's having or exercising power in terms of 'great' or 'little', 'more' or 'less' power, a conception of power without *any* quantitative orientation, however vague it may be, is difficult to conceive. More specifically, some sort of quantitative dimension is already implied in all those social-scientific conceptions in which the aspects of *scope* and *domain* play some role. At least in principle, the extension of the scope and domain of an agent's power over others can be taken as a foundation for a measure.

In the presentation and discussion particularly of Kliemt's and Brian Barry's conceptions of power, we have seen that the measures of power that are in fact most often quoted in social-science scholarship usually consider only one 'dimension' (each a different one) of this multi-dimensional concept, which goes a long way towards explaining why they are so different.

Kliemt and Brian Barry have also given special attention to the question to what extent these measures (most prominently that of Shapley/Shubik) are adequate and useful. The special problems related with the idea that power is an ability have already been treated and need not be taken up again at this point. Another question was what exactly a measure of power should focus on. Of course, how a measure of power is constructed depends on what are taken to be the main aspects of the 'difference' the existence or non-existence of more or less power makes for the respective outcomes. In this respect, Kliemt's own measure differed from that of Shapley/Shubik. In order to understand

[192] It is, of course, highly controversial whether positive sanctions can ever plausibly be seen as means for the exercise of power. For example, Bachrach/Baratz – much like Lasswell/Kaplan, whom they follow in many respects – are strict supporters of the view that power is necessarily linked to „sanctions" in the form of „deprivations". Note, however, that this does not easily square with their later (1970) contention that non-decisions through the exercise of power can be based on negative *or positive* sanctions. If positive sanctions are included in the forms of exercising power, then the definition of power given by the authors in 1963 must be modified. – For a more detailed discussion of the controversy about whether or not offers of reward can be employed in exercises of power, cf. Chapter 3.

exactly how these measures are different and why the difference matters, it is helpful to take up, again, an idea elaborated by Frederick Schauer in the context of his considerations about the 'normative force' of different reasons for action (Schauer 1991, 114 f.).

Schauer argues that 'normative force' is not an all-or-nothing affair; rather, it comes in degrees, which can be located along a continuum:

* At one extreme, there are those reasons which have the least possible 'normative force' – where 'least possible' means that if they had less, they would cease to be reasons at all and their normative force would drop to zero. Such reasons are what Schauer calls '*ceteris paribus* reasons': they „determine the result [...] when there are no other applicable reasons or when the other applicable reasons are so evenly opposed as to provide no reason for decision one way rather than another".

* At the other extreme, there are 'absolute reasons'. These are reasons which are „infinitely stringent", which „cannot be overridden" no matter what, and which, if applicable, are therefore „conclusive or action-determinative".

* And in between the two extremes, there are all those reasons which have some weight, other than counting merely *ceteris paribus*, but which can be overridden by some other, more weighty reasons.

In a certain sense, Schauer's idea of '*ceteris paribus* reasons' seems to share a similarity with the idea of a 'pivot' as it is captured in voting-power indices: just like a *ceteris paribus* reason, a pivot makes a difference for an outcome only if all other co-determinants of this outcome are in perfect equilibrium, thus leaving the issue undecided (or if there simply is no other co-determinator). And just as *ceteris paribus* reasons have *no* normative weight when these conditions do not obtain, a potential pivot also has no impact on an outcome when the conditions do not hold.

In this sense, measures concentrating on a *pivotal* role for deciding an outcome capture only a *minimal* idea of power: if an agent can make no difference for an outcome even when no-one else makes any difference, then that agent can hardly be said to have any power at all concerning that outcome. If the outcomes under consideration are actions, or choices of actions, by other agents, then the idea of having the power of a pivot even collapses entirely into the idea of being the source of a *ceteris paribus* reason.

On the other extreme, the idea of absolute reasons which, when applicable, are completely and exclusively action-determining, may be understood in analogy to that of 'absolute power', in the sense of the exclusive and complete control over an outcome. Just as the former is the maximal normative force a reason may have, the latter is also the maximal amount of control someone may have over an outcome. And again, if the outcomes in question are actions or choices of actions, having absolute power over such an outcome and being the source of absolute reasons for the other's action or decision seems to be one and the same thing.

Hence, where social power is concerned, Shapley/Shubik's measure amounts to an ascription of the normative force of a *ceteris paribus* reason, whereas Kliemt's proposal measures an agent's extent of absolute normative force. All other possible measures must, for logical reasons, lie somewhere in between these two extremes.

2. THE CONCEPT OF INFLUENCE

The heads of politicians are thin-walled ... and are therefore very easily influenced, even by currents of air.

Alvaro Cunqueiro

The American Chief executive is the most powerful person in the world, a man who can exercise huge influence for good or ill.

Tony Judt

Dear Jack: I have an abnormal accumulation of thoughts on dollars, Latin America, ... foreign aid and recessions which I would gladly share with you. Apart from the undoubted nourishment to my ego – nothing, I would gather, is so rampant these days as the desire to be known as a constructive force – perhaps it might be useful.

John K. Galbraith, Letter to the President-Elect, Dec. 5, 1960

The decision-making 'loop' depends on physical proximity to B – who's whispering into his ear most regularly, whose office is closest to the Oval, who's standing or sitting next to him when a key issue arises ... In this administration you're either in the loop or you're out of the loop, but more likely you don't know where the loop is, or you don't even know there is a loop ...
I'm losing confidence that my memos are getting to B ... I ask Hillary for advice. 'Send them to me,' she says. 'I'll make sure they get to him. ...' Now I have my own loop.

Robert B. Reich, US Secretary of Labor 1992–1996

Something must have happened to you, said father António. I met a couple, said Pereira, a boy and a girl, and perhaps I have changed through knowing them. That happens, said father António, people influence us, it happens. I don't know how they can influence me, said Pereira, they are two poor romantics with no future, if anything, I should be the one influencing them ...

Antonio Tabucchi[1]

[1] These quotes are taken from: CLAVES de Razón Práctica (Madrid) 40 (Marzo 1994) 80 (my translation); Judt 2000, 98 (Judt thought, however, that with Colin Powell as George W. Bush's Secretary of State there would be someone still more powerful and/or? influential than the President because Powell would be likely to become „an all-powerful secretary of state, exercising unimpeded influence over an uncertain newcomer"; ibid., 99); Galbraith 1998, 35 f.; Reich 1997, 179 f.; Tabucchi 1995, 120 (my translation).

No-one would probably deny that the distribution of 'influence' relationships is one of the key factors for understanding a polity's effective constitution. Moreover, it is a common belief that some people would be willing to do almost anything in order to gain or keep political 'influence', a fact which even in relatively respectable political systems every now and then makes for – somewhat morbidly – fascinating public scandals.[2]

But what exactly does Cunqueiro's metaphor about the 'thin-walled' heads of politicians mean? Does the 'influence' ascribed to the President of the United States by Tony Judt have anything to do with the 'power' he is also said to have? Are the two things perhaps the same, are they somehow related, or independent of each other? Is someone who, by 'sharing thoughts' with such a powerful agent, becomes politically 'useful' as a 'constructive force', such as Galbraith hoped to become for Kennedy, influential, or powerful, or both? Is having one's own 'loop' of access to the ear of 'B', like Robert Reich, a matter of influence or of power? Or, if it is 'Hillary' on whom the existence of that loop depends, is it rather *her* influence, or *her* power? Is influence something that just 'happens' to someone? Or can it, to some extent, be controlled? Does it depend on any identifiable set of resources or means, as Tabucchi's protagonist seems to believe? Is it perhaps precisely that set of resources which conceptually distinguishes influence from power?

To the extent that political influence is, indeed, regarded as a relevant phenomenon at all, these are questions political theory – and *a fortiori*, a normative theory of democracy – must provide answers to.

In fact, however, the fate of the notion of influence, and particularly political influence, has in several respects been similar to that of power. Just as the concept of power is often invoked in political science scholarship, so is the concept of influence.[3] On the one hand, the term 'influence' is frequently used in very unspecific ways, seemingly denoting not much more than some kind of adaptation to some external impact. In that sense, to the extent that, generally, „humans are adaptation-executers", and „human behavior [...] should be explained as the output of adaptations (using present circumstances as input)",[4] influence is omnipresent, the concept is not a *social* concept, and it cannot explain anything – in short, it is not an interesting category for the political theorist. On the other hand, the notion of influence must also frequently be used with a much more specific meaning. Because just like power phenomena, influence phenomena – or, more precisely, what are commonly *called* 'influence phenomena' – are often looked upon with suspicion, particularly in democratic contexts, as if there were an intuitive presumption against their legitimacy. And if the state of reflection on the concept of power has been found to be not entirely satisfactory, this applies even more to the concept of influence. In political science, publications about the *concept* of influence (as opposed to alleged influence *phenomena*) make up only a small fraction of the number of books and articles one can find about that of power. Moreover, as mentioned before,

[2] Of course, what to the public at large seems scandalous is often conceived by those involved merely as a perfectly normal, even necessary, „cultivation of the political landscape", as the German euphemism for the purchase of political 'access' (or more) calls it.

[3] As pointed out in the Introduction, the two frequently appear together, and many authors use them, more or less consistently, as synonyms.

[4] Tooby/Cosmides 1990, 420, quoted from Lal 1998, 199, n. 23.

not all publications claiming to treat the subject of influence regard it as something distinct from power. Explicit attempts to establish a clear and precise distinction between the two concepts are hard to come by. I have been able to find only a handful (Lasswell/Kaplan 1950; Cassinelli 1966; Parsons 1967; Mokken/Stokman 1975; Oppenheim 1981; Koller 1991), and certainly not for want of searching. Some other authors, though they mention the distinction, do little more than adopt some version of it without much analysis or argument.[5]

In this chapter, I will look at several proposals for a definition of influence as distinguished from power, and discuss their respective merits and shortcomings. Although the analysis cannot possibly pretend to be exhaustive, I hope to cover the most important conceptions, both from a systematic point of view and considering their degree of diffusion in political science scholarship. It should be clear from the start that, just as in the case of power, in what follows I will be interested only in influence in a *social sense*; particularly, I will not be concerned here with the conception of 'influencing' as something almost synonymous with 'causing' or 'affecting' in general.

The fact that influence is most commonly defined, if at all, by explicitly contrasting it from power makes the analysis of the concept in some sense easier and, at the same time, in another sense more difficult: easier, because it provides a basis from which to start; more difficult because, to the extent that the foundation itself is unsure and controversial, these inconveniences are, of course, passed on to the concept of influence. This must be kept in mind in what follows.

1. Distinguishing Influence from Power: General Remarks

There is, of course, the option of using 'influence' simply as a synonym for 'power'. As pointed out in the introductory chapter, it is an option which has been chosen explicitly by some authors (e. g., Baldwin 1980) and tacitly by others (e. g., Kerbo/McKinstry 1995). An obvious advantage of that choice is that, as a consequence, theories which say something about power, but nothing specifically about influence – such as most normative theories concerned with the justification of political systems – do nevertheless not suffer from an 'influence gap'. On the other hand, however, there are also substantial disadvantages to that option:

– Either it is simply *stipulated* that 'influence' is a synonym for 'power'. But then the question arises why we should need a second term at all. At least in scientific usage, in order to avoid confusion and misunderstandings it would surely be

[5] In the social sciences in general, conceptions of influence are divergent, and are rarely spelled out explicitly. In Coleman's *Foundations of Social Theory* (1990), to give one prominent example, influence plays no role at all (there is only one fleeting mention of influence processes in collective behaviour, where influence seems to be closely related to a kind of demonstration effect, as in „fads and fashions"; cf. pp. 237 ff.). And Koschnick's German-English *Standard Dictionary of the Social Sciences* (1992/93), curiously, has an entry for *Einfluß* referring to the English 'influence', but it *also* has several entries for terms deriving from the related German verb *beeinflussen* all of which refer only to 'persuasion' terms (thus, e. g., the German *Beeinflußbarkeit* – literally, 'influenceability' – refers the reader exclusively to the English 'persuasibility'). The implied reduction of influence to persuasion seems to be particularly widespread in social-psychological approaches.

preferable to drop one of the terms entirely. And in view of the existing amount of scholarship on 'power', that would probably have to be 'influence'.

- Or the assertion that 'influence' is synonymous with 'power' is to be understood as a *lexical* definition – that is, as an *empirical* statement about actual usage, or at least as an approximate reconstruction of it. In this case, the assertion is obviously false. It is simply not true that in ordinary usage the terms are understood as completely interchangeabe, i. e., that we would always be willing, for instance, to attribute power to anyone we consider influential.[6]

It therefore seems that assuming the synonymity of 'power' and 'influence' is not a tenable option. If talk about 'political influence' is not to remain vague and obscure, we simply cannot spare ourselves the effort to try to specify the defining elements of that notion. In view of what has been said before, the easiest way to approach this task is to inquire into how influence can be, and has been, conceived in distinction from power.

From a general, purely formal point of view, there are several ways how two concepts thought to be closely related may be distinguished. They are rather obvious, and practically all of them have, in some variation or other, found prominent supporters, concerning the distinction between influence and power. For a start, it may be useful to recall how on the most abstract level the two concepts can be thought to be related:

(1) The most general and perhaps most obvious approach is that of *conceptual subordination*, i. e., the definition of one concept as the more general, and the other one as referring to a special case, to some subclass of the former. In our case, this opens up two alternatives:

(a) influence conceived as a special case of power, or
(b) power conceived as a special case of influence.

With respect to each one of these alternatives, in turn, one can then imagine a number of different specific manners how the respective 'special case' can be delineated. Again, on an abstract level, one can say that wherever the more general concept leaves room for variations, any one of its defining characteristics may, in principle, be singled out as a criterion for defining a 'special case'.

6 Just think of social scientists: some (few) members of that species are sometimes said to have a certain political influence; but hardly anyone would be prepared to say that they also have political power. „Was Keynes powerful (rather than immensely influential) ...?", Steven Lukes asks (1986a, 16). More recently, when communitarianism was the latest political fad, the press repeatedly reported that Amitai Etzioni, political scientist and communitarian activist of some renown, had a certain 'influence' on members of the Clinton administration as well as on European social democrats such as Tony Blair or Rudolf Scharping; but as far as I remember it has never been asserted that therefore Etzioni had political 'power'. The same applies to social or legal philosophers with some degree of public visibility, such as Ronald Dworkin in the United States or Jürgen Habermas in Germany. (On the general incapacity of social scientists to produce social and especially political effects, cf. Gunnell 1998.) This is not to say, of course, that influence and power never coincide, or that the distinction between the two is always clear and uncontroversial. In the case of the infamous Rasputin, for instance, as long as the concepts remain fuzzy, one can probably dispute endlessly about whether he had political 'influence' or political 'power'.

(2) Alternatively, the same method of singling out a class of cases sharing some special feature can be used, not for establishing a conceptual sub- and superordination, but for defining instead mutually exclusive, *complementary concepts*, simply by taking some 'special case' as defining one of the two concepts, and then defining the other by explicit *exclusion* of that special case.

In this event, however, it is important to note that what is needed if the two concepts really are to be complementary and not entirely unconnected is a *third* concept which must provide the link between the two as well as the criteria for delimiting them from the 'rest of the world'. In other words: one must specify what the 'totality' is of which one of the concepts defines a special case and the other one the remaining cases.[7] Thus, for instance, if power and influence were to be distinguished by reference to the *means* involved in their exercise (say, by defining power as involving exclusively coercive and influence as involving exclusively non-coercive means),[8] then if they are not to be entirely unrelated they must also *share* some feature, or combination of features, which must be exclusive to them. This implies that there must be a third, more comprehensive concept which makes no reference to means and covers exactly the extensions of both power *and* influence.

Though it is often not made explicit, what social power and influence generally seem to be thought to have in common on the most abstract level is that both involve *one agent somehow affecting another's internal state of mind and/or external behaviour*. It certainly adds to the confusion about power and influence that in order to refer to that *more general, encompassing* notion, there seems to be no other word available in ordinary usage than that of 'influence' itself. Advocates of the definition of power and influence as complementary concepts thus find themselves in the uncomfortable situation that their distinction between 'power' and 'influence' implies a third concept which, if at all, is *also* usually referred to as 'influence'.

So far, three possible views of the basic conceptual relationship between power and influence have been distinguished: power as the more general concept; or influence as the more general concept; or power and influence as mutually exclusive, but in some way complementary concepts. As we will see presently, one can find examples for each of them in the literature.

But before looking at specific examples of such definitions, it may be useful also to systematize, at least roughly (and without any claim of being exhaustive), the different possibilities for locating the particular distinctive features. In order to do this, we must begin with an assumption concerning the basic similarity between power and influence. The difficulty of stating the exact conceptual *difference* between them could not even arise if the terms were not thought to refer to, in some sense, basically *similar* social

[7] This follows necessarily from the notion of complementariness: One thing 'complements' another if the conjunction of the two makes some third thing 'complete'. Thus, two sets are 'complementary' only relative to a third, encompassing set of which they must both be (disjunct) subsets and which must contain *all and only* the elements of these two subsets. Standard examples of complementariness are the concept of 'complementary colour' which implies the concept of whiteness, or the concept of 'complementary angle' which implies the concept of a right angle.

[8] See below for specific examples of such distinctions.

relationships. Therefore, I think we can safely start from the assumption that the conceptual skeleton of social influence is the same as that of social power, that is, that both, very generally, involve relationships between (at least two parties of) agents, one of which, in some way and by some means, affects the other(s). For simplicity's sake, let us denote that very primitive standard pattern of an influence or a power relationship by *ArB*, where *A* and *B* stand for the two parties and *r* stands for the specific relationship between them. If one accepts this fundamental idea, then a convenient way of systematizing the different possible conceptual differences is to look at these three core elements of power as well as influence relationships, and at the variations the concept of power as discussed in the previous chapter admits in their respective configuration:[9]

(i) Concerning the *A-element*, i. e., the side on which power is located, two fundamental 'states' were distinguished practically by all authors treated in the previous chapter, namely: power as something agents *have*, i. e., as an ability, and power as something they *exercise*. This provides one possible starting point for distinguishing our two concepts.

Now, of the logically possible alternatives of linking power and influence to ability or exercise in order to derive two either mutually exclusive or super- and subordinated concepts, to my knowledge only the one conceiving of power as an ability, and influence as the 'actualization' of that ability – i. e., power defined as 'the ability to exercise influence' – has in fact been proposed.[10]

(ii) Second, concerning the *r-element*, i. e., the link between the two sides of a power relationship, it has been generally uncontroversial that power, whether as ability or as exercise, must have a base in some kind of resources (not necessarily of a material, tangible type) in order to produce the corresponding specific relationship between the agents involved. This feature, obviously, gives rise to a multitude of possibilities for distinction. And, indeed, distinguishing between the two concepts with a view toward the *sources* on which the possession of power or influence is based, or toward the *means* employed in their exercise has been an especially prominent approach. To recall only some of the most common options taken on that line, we find conceptions of

(a) power as based on (negative) *sanctions*, influence as based (also or exclusively) on *other* means;

[9] For a somewhat similar approach in analysing the concept of (social) power, cf. Hradil 1980, ch. 2.

[10] One example of this position was mentioned in the previous chapter, with the conception of Hartmut Kliemt (1981). The conceptual relationship in his case is one of complementarity, arrived at by choosing one of the two possible pairs of mutually exclusive concepts that can be derived from the ability-exercise criterion. For clarity's sake, just this once I will spell out all the other logical possibilities too: The distinction along the lines of the ability-exercise criterion could also, in principle, give rise to a conception of *(2)* influence as the ability to exercise power (rendering the second mutually exclusive pair); *(3)* power as the general concept comprising ability as well as exercise, and influence as the sub-category which refers either *(a)* only to ability, or *(b)* only to exercise; or *(4)* influence as the general concept, in the same sense, and power as either one of the two possible sub-categories. Since given any criterion the logically possible cases follow straightforwardly, in what follows I will refrain from performing the tedious exercise of listing them all in each case, and will mention only the versions that have found some resonance in the literature.

(b) influence as based exclusively on *persuasion*, power as based (also or exclusively) on *other* means;

(c) power as based on *normative* authority, influence *not*; alternatively, this is sometimes also presented by saying that power as *institutionalized* (or institutionalizable), influence *not*.

(iii) Finally, on the side of the *B-element*, i. e., of the subject of power, as the 'receiving end' of a power relationship, there are variations in the conceptions of the kind of impact power (potentially) has, of *what* exactly it affects, and *in what way*, which can give rise, in turn, to a distinction between power and influence. Here, again, there are several possibilities, among them, for example,

(a) influence as inducing *whatever* kind of change in behaviour, power as inducing *specific* (e. g., 'desired') changes;

(b) power as affecting *factual* circumstances, influence as affecting *opinion*;

(c) power as *negatively* affecting the subject's *interests*, influence as *not (necessarily) negatively* affecting the subject's *interests*;

(d) power as determining an agent's set of *alternatives*, influence as determining which *action* he will choose from a given set;

(e) power as affecting the subject's *freedom*, influence as *not* affecting *freedom*.[11]

For easier reference, I have ordered these different possibilities in the table reproduced on the next page:

* The columns in the table contain the three general ways of distinguishing between the two concepts (those which were labeled above as *(1.a)*, *(1.b)*, and *(2)*, respectively).

* In the rows, we have the different criteria by which this can be done (corresponding to what I denoted as categories *(i)*, *(ii)*, *(iii)*, with their respective subcategories).

* In the cells, I give some indications – which are, of course, far from exhaustive, in order not to blow up the table to unmanageable proportions – of some of the more important and/or prominent publications in which the corresponding conception is advocated. Italicized entries indicate the proposals which are explicitely treated in the course of this chapter.

[11] Obviously, there are strong cross-relations between some of the categories listed in *(i)*, *(ii)*, and *(iii)* (e. g., between *(ii.b)* and *(iii.b)*: 'persuasion' as a means is conceptually linked to an effect 'on opinion'). Hence, the differences between some of these categories are more a matter of emphasis than of substance.

Table 2.1 Influence – Power: Types of Distinction

	1) subordination		**2) complementarity**
	a) power general, influence special	*b) influence general, power special*	
i) A-element ('mode' of power/influence):			
possession/ability vs. exercise			*Kliemt 1981* *Cartwright 1969* *Cassinelli 1966* *Katz/Lazarsfeld 1955* *French et al. 1959/60*
ii) r-element (type of means):			
a) sanctions	Luhmann 2000?	*Lasswell/ Kaplan 1950*	Habermas 1988*?* *Moscovici 1979?* Parsons 1963 Wolfers 1962
b) persuasion	Oppenheim 1981		Etzioni 1968, 1993 Connolly 1983b
c) normativity	*Pörn 1970* *Raz 1990b*		
iii) B-element (type of change induced):			
a) intended vs. unintended		*Wrong 1988* *Zimmerling 1991*	
b) on facts vs. on opinion			Etzioni 1968, 1993 Parsons 1967
c) effect on interests			*Lukes 1974*
d) on alternatives vs. on actions			*Mokken/Stokman 1975* Baumann 1993
e) effect on freedom		Hradil 1980?	Pettit 1996/7? Kristjánsson 1996?

2. The *Power*-as-Ability-to-*Influence* View

Let us begin the review of conceptions of the distinction between power and influence with a view that is often used implicitly, as a common way of speaking, though it is only rarely spelled out as an explicit conceptual distinction between the two concepts. I mean the idea that *influence* is simply what results when *power* is (successfully) exercised or, more generally, that power is something one 'has', and influence is something that 'happens' when power is somehow used. On such an account, the two concepts obviously have no overlap; they are located, so to speak, on two different conceptual levels, one denoting an ability or potential, the other one the use or 'actualization' of that ability or potential by a power-holder (category *2.i* of the table above).

In the previous chapter, it was already pointed out that Hartmut Kliemt seems to find it natural to use the term 'influence' in this sense when he defines power basically as the „ability to exert purposefully a causal influence [...] the ability to influence social outcomes [...] according to one's wants".[12] Here, I will present two authors who have explicitly argued in favour of such a distinction.

(i) The first of these two authors is C. W. Cassinelli (1966). In the work I here refer to, Cassinelli is mainly interested in analysing human freedom. But he finds it important in that context to disentangle the concepts of influence, power, authority and control, among others, and for this purpose he develops a somewhat idiosyncratic conception of power and influence. Power is, he says, „the final potential to influence or control" (45); more precisely, it is „one person's potential to influence or control another" (44). This means above all, as he is careful to note, that, unlike influence or control, power „does not actually take place" (44).

This is plausible: if power is conceived as an ability, it certainly is not something that can 'take place'. But Cassinelli goes one step further. In his view, not only does power not take place; it is also *not* something that can be *exercised*. Instead, what *can* be exercised, he says, is either influence or control (45). Power is nothing but the *ability* to do just that, and an ability, Cassinelli apparently thinks, can only be *possessed*.[13]

But if power is the ability to influence, what exactly does 'influence' mean in Cassinelli's conception? First of all, it must be noted that, as the citations show, influence in his view does not stand alone – it has, so to speak, a conceptual companion,

[12] Cf. Chapter 1.2, n. 88.

[13] Influence and control can, in Cassinelli's view, also be *possessed* – but 'possession' then means something entirely different from what it means in the case of power: The *exercise* of influence or control, he explains, establishes a causal relationship between the 'activities' of two agents (43 ff.). And someone *possesses* influence or control over another, in Cassinelli's view, to the extent that such a relationship between the agents' activities *would* exist, *if* the potential subject did not already perform the corresponding activity for some other reason: „Possessing influence and control is directly related to exercising influence and control in a contrary-to-fact way. An agent can possess control or influence without exercising it" (53). Now, since power is defined as the ability to influence and control, and influence and control can either be possessed or exercised, Cassinelli can consistently hold that the power to influence or control can itself be divided into the „power to exercise" and the „power to possess" influence or control. Hence, power is for him „the ability to perform the activity sufficient for the response in the concepts of the possession and exercise of influence and control" (55).

namely 'control'. Influence and control are said to stand in the same kind of relationship with power. But if they are to denote two different concepts, then there must, of course, be a difference between them, and Cassinelli therefore presents the nature of influence by contrasting it with the nature of control. In his view, both refer to „the effects that one man's activity can have on the activity of another", but they are „exclusive subtypes" of such effects (44). One important difference between them is that „In an exercise of influence, the influencer need have no special purposes or intentions" (47); in a case of control, in contrast, there must be „a conscious effort to elicit a certain response" (48). But that difference alone does not give us two mutually exclusive universes of cases yet, because while an influencer does not *need* to exercise his influence intentionally, he *may* do so, at least on Cassinelli's account. As for the other end of the relationship, concerning the subject of either influence or control, Cassinelli thinks that in either case it makes no relevant difference whether or not the subject is aware of the situation (47 f.). But then, how can one distinguish between a case of control and a case of intentionally exercised influence? The decisive difference between the two, Cassinelli holds, is that in influence the subject *chooses* his response,[14] whereas in control he has *no choice*. One consequence of this is that even when influence is exercised intentionally, the outcome may be very different from the one intended:

„In all types of intentional influence [...] distortions in communication, errors in judgment, and limitations to performance frequently result in discrepancies between what the influencer intends and what the respondent does." (49)

Still, as long as the influencer's 'activity' triggers any change at all, in whichever direction, in the respondent's action, this counts as a case of influence. On the other hand, even if a subject reacts exactly as intended by a power-holder, as long as this is so because of the subject's own choice, what has taken place is still influence, not control.[15] Only where this is no choice, control is involved: „[I]n an exercise of control the respondent acts more or less as the controller intended, and he is unable to avoid this response." (48)

Together with Cassinelli's concept of freedom, an implication of this account of the difference between influence and control is that „when an activity is influenced it is free and when it is controlled it is unfree" (49).

Obviously, this conception therefore has important consequences for any normative theory of social interaction, including theories about the justification of political procedures and practices. But let us put aside, the issue of freedom and Cassinelli's understanding of it,[16] and concentrate on his conception of power and influence, which raises several questions.

[14] For whatever reason: „In an exercise of influence, the respondent does not need to have a special motive for performing the influenced activity." (47)

[15] That is why it is perfectly consistent that for Cassinelli, contrary to most other authors, *de facto authority* is a subclass of influence rather than of power. After all, it remains a subject's choice whether to accept someone as an authority, i. e., whether to treat someone's (descriptive or prescriptive) utterances as authoritative.

[16] Cassinelli even contends that the mere *possession* of control produces unfreedom in the subject, even if it is not exercised, whereas the possession of unexercised influence has no effect whatsoever (54). This is not the

One problem with Cassinelli's conception concerns his main criterion for the distinction between influence and control, that is, whether the subject does or does not have a choice. As has been observed in the context of the previous chapter, it is difficult to imagine what it could mean for someone to be 'unable to avoid' an action, i. e., to have no choice about it at all – not even between doing and forbearing it. Strictly speaking, an agent *always* has a choice, unless he is physically compelled to perform certain movements, in which case there is good reason not even to speak of an action *of his* at all. In a broader sense, one could of course argue that there may be circumstances in which, because of an agent's psychological make-up, although on the face of it he has a choice, he may in fact be 'unable to avoid' choosing one option instead of another. But that position, in turn, raises tricky questions about the criteria for determining when a theoretically existing option is practically ineligible for an agent. However, I will not pursue this point here, since for Cassinelli himself the question of choice concerns the distinction between influence and control rather than that between influence and power, which is my present topic.[17]

A second problem with Cassinelli's account concerns his assertion that influence can be possessed as well as exercised. The problem with this is, very briefly, the following: As proposed by Cassinelli, when influence is *exercised* this can happen without any specific intention of the influencer, and even when such an intention exists, the result of the corresponding exercise of influence need not be an action that 'fits' to that intention; rather, it can be *any* action at all, as long as it is different from what the subject would have done without the exercise of influence. Thus, it is not part of the essential ingredients of an exercise of influence that there is, so to speak, a 'fixed target'; it rather resembles a shooting contest where *any* hit at all, no matter what you hit and how far it is of the mark, counts as a 'good' shot. That someone *possesses* influence, in turn, is defined by Cassinelli to mean that there is some action which the potential subject of the influence performs 'anyway' but which, if this were not the case, *could* also be provoked by the influencer through an exercise of influence. Hence, obviously, in the possession of influence there *is* a 'fixed target', and therefore the *exercise* of influence counterfactually involved in Cassinelli's notion of the *possession* of influence must be certain to be *successful* in the sense of 'hitting' not just anything, but precisely that 'target', i. e., triggering not just any, but a specific response. At the very least, this indicates an odd asymmetry between the possession and the exercise of influence in Cassinelli's conception. But I think it even contains an inconsistency: if the potential of a successful exercise implied in the possession of influence is understood not merely as the possibility of an accidental occurrence, but as something linking certain (hypothetical) exercises of influence *systematically* to a certain response, then it is difficult to see where there could still be room for the subject's *choice* which, by definition, must always exist for influence to take place. Inadvertently, Cassinelli seems to have linked the *possession of influence* to the *exercise of control*.

place to go into these questions. The relationship between power and freedom will be treated in more detail in Chapter 3.

[17] As Cassinelli correctly observes, the questions involved here are closely connected with the concept of freedom, and some of them will therefore be treated later in the chapter referred to in the previous note.

I do not wish to enter into a more detailed analysis of Cassinelli's conceptual problems at this point. What has been mentioned should suffice to establish that his proposal, as it stands, does not give us a readily usable concept of influence. But that may be due to its specific flaws, and does not yet definitely disqualify the kind of distinction between power and influence it is based on. So let us look at the second example of the power-as-ability-to-influence approach and see whether it fares any better.

(ii) Shortly before Cassinelli presented his conceptions, Dorwin Cartwright, then professor of psychology at the University of Michigan's Research Center for Group Dynamics, published an instructive article offering an overview over what was at that time the state of the art of influence studies (Cartwright 1969, first published 1965). As an organization theorist, in this paper Cartwright is mainly interested in accounting for the specific behavioural regularities often found within organizations, and particularly in the question how the conduct of the members of organizations is 'influenced' in such a way as to result in desired organizational outputs. Unlike some other authors, Cartwright does not think that „the study of influence is [...] a bottomless swamp“, but he concedes that „the terrain does have its soggy spots“ and intends with his article to provide a kind of „map“ that may help others cross that terrain without getting their feet muddy (125). In some respects, he succeeds admirably in laying out such a map: in an enviably clear and systematic way, in less than forty pages Cartwright manages to offer a review of a wealth of aspects and approaches – from game theory to psychology – that have been, or ought to be, taken into account in studying social influence, citing in the course of it almost two hundred scholarly contributions (most of them empirical studies), without making a mess of it. But there is a price to be paid for his approach, and this price is that Cartwright is forced to use a very broad concept of influence. Moreover, and surprisingly for an author of his qualities, he gives very little thought to its definition and delimitation from other, related concepts. Instead, he disposes of the matter in the briefest possible way:

„When an agent, *O*, performs an act resulting in some change in another agent, *P*, we say that *O influences P*. If *O* has the capability of influencing *P*, we say that *O* has *power over* P.“[18]

At least, this definition looks straightforward, and it is not plagued by the kind of problems encountered in Cassinelli's rather peculiar tripartite conception. But precisely because of its simplicity and clarity, it is also easy to see why it is inadequate. Although *some* people, even some scholars, *sometimes* do use the terms as defined by Cartwright, this does not seem to be the only nor, more importantly, the most interesting way of dis-

[18] Cartwright 1969, 125; somewhat later (ibid., 143) he asserts, in the same vein, that „When we wish to refer to potential, rather than actual, influence we shall speak of [...] *power*“. The kind of change Cartwright himself is thinking of when speaking of influence is „a change in the psychological forces on *P* brought about by an act of *O*“ (ibid., 151). He does not elaborate on how this view relates to the definition he subscribes to in his article, but he seems to think that his own view is more specific. However, it seems plausible to think that the definition quoted above refers to mental rather than physical changes; „some change in another agent“ can, in the last instance, *always* be brought about only by „a change in the psychological forces“ working on this agent, and that means that Cartwright's mention of „psychological forces“ does not really add anything to the degree of specificity of the definition.

tinguishing between them. We can perhaps see this most clearly if we consider the implications of Cartwright's definition for how we can talk about power and influence.

If we were to accept that influence is nothing but the actualization of an ability or potential called ‚power', then we would have to make up our minds about which of the two can be ‚exercized'. Generally, in ordinary language, an ‚exercise' is something one can do with an ability (or some other latent feature, such as a right), but not with a manifest process or state of affairs. Hence, according to Cartwright's definition, it would make sense to speak of an ‚exercise of power', but not of an ‚exercise of influence'. However, in his review article Cartwright himself repeatedly speaks of the ‚exercise of influence'.[19] He apparently does not realize that either ‚exercise' in this usage cannot have its usual meaning or 'influence' cannot mean what he himself has stipulated. Moreover, although he seems to try hard he does not succeed entirely in avoiding to speak *also* of the ‚exercise of power'.[20] How is this to be understood? To some readers, the argument I am trying to make here may seem hair-splitting: Certainly, Cartwright's article is clearly written, and no-one in his right mind should have a problem in understanding what he is talking about. I am not denying that. My point is, rather, that only if one does not take Cartwright's own distinction between power and influence too seriously can one make sense of the passages about their respective ‚exercise'. So we need to take a closer look at that distinction.

According to Cartwright, *any* response triggered in one agent by the action of another can be regarded as (a product) of the latter's influence on the former. And *any* agent who is able to influence another can be said to have power over him. This view has at least two notable inconveniences:

First, it is obviously an extremely broad notion of power and influence. For instance, one person's answer to another person's question falls under that definition, just as the situation in which two pedestrians walking towards each other on the same sidewalk from opposite directions swerve to avoid bumping into each other. In both cases, there is a change, or response, in one agent elicited by the action of another. But would we really be prepared to say that these are matters of power and influence? On such a broad conception, in any case, power and influence *as such* would not have any special significance for the political sphere. But what makes political power and political influence interesting and important does not seem to reside exclusively in their qualification as political – it seems to be something that has to do with power and influence themselves and which would therefore have to be reflected in the general concepts too.

Second, according to the power-as-ability-to-influence view, although there may be power without influence, there can, of course, be no influence without power. In other words: on that account, the influential necessarily are, *per definitionem*, also powerful. This conception leaves no room for the possibility that there may be agents who have *influence, but no power*; it implies that the set of agents with influence is a subset of agents with power. Moreover, it forces us to call the result of any *effective exercise* of power ‚influence'. Again, that seems to run counter to the way the term ‚in-

[19] Cf., e. g., pp. 127, 128, 129, 158, etc. – although, to be true, more often he says not that influence is ‚exercised', but that it is ‚exerted'.
[20] E. g., pp. 156, 159.

fluence' is ordinarily used. There are at least some ways of affecting another's action that we would probably be willing to call an ‚exercise of power', but would not therefore also call ‚influence'. And, *vice versa*, there are also some ways of generating a change of response in another that we would, without much thinking, be willing to qualify as (a product of) influence, but not therefore also as a manifestation of power.[21]

The power-as-ability-to-influence view, as expressed in Cartwright's definition, therefore does not seem adequate for capturing a great part of what is meant by ‚influence' – especially when the term is used specifically in distinction from power.

* * *

EXCURSUS:
THE CONCEPT OF INFLUENCE IN SOCIAL-PSYCHOLOGICAL SCHOLARSHIP

Since Dorwin Cartwright is himself a prominent social psychologist, this seems to be a convenient juncture to make a short detour through the field of social psychology. An investigation of social influence, even if its ultimate purpose is a contribution to the conceptual and theoretical arsenals of political science, may not, of course, pass over entirely unmentioned the work that has been carried out over the past half century in the one discipline regarded by many as the *inner sanctum* of influence studies.

Indeed, the work of social psychologists has made a notable impact far beyond the boundaries of their own discipline, in all the other social sciences where power and/or influence have been topics of interest. The reason why, nevertheless, I think it is not only justifiable, but convenient to relegate social-psychological conceptions of influence to an *excursus*, rather than taking them as the starting point for the present conceptual exploration is that, in my view, the social-psychological literature on influence is part of the problem, rather than of a solution to the reigning conceptual confusion about social influence in general and the relationship between power and influence in particular.[22] In what follows, I will try to support that claim. In doing so, it is not my purpose – nor would it be possible in the present context – to review exhaustively the history and state of social-psychological ideas on influence. Instead, I will again attempt to make my points with the help of the presentation and discussion of a few exemplary works which have either gained great prominence or stand out for other reasons.

[21] Most people would probably not think that if shopkeeper Jill does what mafioso Joe wants (for instance, pay a stiff monthly ‚fee' for the 'protection' of her shop) because otherwise Joe effectively threatens Jill with severe harm it would be an appropriate description of the situation to say that 'Joe is influencing Jill', although hardly anybody would hesitate to say that it is the power Joe has over Jill that is manifested in that situation. Inversely, if Jill talks the problem over with her friend Jackie, who spells out some reasons in favour of taking the case to the police, and in the end, on balance, Jill finds those reasons convincing and decides to act on them, it would be most natural to describe this as a case of influence, but – absent any further specifications of the relationship between Jackie and Jill – hardly as an exercise of power by Jackie over Jill.

[22] On this point, for once, I find myself in agreement with Luhmann (1975, 4 and n. 4) who complains that social psychologists tend to an „overburdening of the concept of power with characteristics of a very broadly and vaguely conceived process of influence". – For a more general critique, for methodological and philosophical reasons, of social psychology as such, cf. Bunge 1998, 44–47.

(1) One of those very prominent works is the early, pioneering study of Elihu Katz and Paul Lazarsfeld on *Personal Influence* (1955). The authors' main purpose with this book was to underscore, with the help of empirical findings, that even in the era of the mass media (which at that time was still in its infancy), individuals matter and can make an important impact on a larger public. But besides this purpose, they were also driven by a more general theoretical interest.[23] Consequently, they begin their book with an account of the state of social-psychological insights about the subject at the time of their writing.

Katz's and Lazarsfeld's study has many merits. With a view to the present context, not the least is that they do not contribute to the confusion between influence and power: they consistently stick to the terminology of 'influence', without mixing in any mentions of 'power'.

It is, therefore, all the more surprising that they apparently did not see any need to define the concept which, according to the title of their book, was their main subject.[24] Instead, they content themselves with the very meager remark that their considerations concern the „notion of personal influence, as implicitly defined by our procedure“ (ibid., 4). Hence, they leave it to the reader to distill from the text an interpretation of what they mean by 'influence'. To be sure, even without looking specifically at their „procedure“, it is not very difficult to get at least a vague idea of their conception. After all, there are indicators (such as the fact that „general influentials“ are also called „opinion-leaders“) that they conceive influence vaguely in the sense of something like 'impact on opinion'. And yet, it remains a remarkable fact that these two eminent scholars, with empirical *and* theoretical ambitions, have written an important book about personal influence that has quickly gained the status of a 'classic', but that contains not even a precise definition, not to speak of an analysis, of its central concept.[25]

(2) In the wake of Katz and Lazarsfeld, throughout the fifties and sixties influence studies mushroomed in social psychology. Dorwin Cartwright, whose power-as-ability-to-influence view I have already criticized above, was one of the leaders of the

[23] Thus, for instance, their ch. VI on 'Interpersonal Networks' is probably one of the earliest texts to be found on what in the meantime has come to be known as network theory.

[24] Here and elsewhere, when I say that there is no definition, I mean that there is not only no explicit stipulative definition: there is also not even a lexical definition (e. g., through reference to some other work).

[25] It is interesting to note that more than forty years later, their work has inspired political scientist Diana Mutz to publish a book on *Impersonal Influence* (Mutz 1998; cf. p. xvi for an explicit acknowledgment of the fact that the title of this book was chosen in direct reference to that of Katz's and Lazarsfeld's famous study). What Mutz's book has in common with their's is that, again, here we have a book-length study of 'influence' and not a trace anywhere of a definition of the concept (in Mutz's case, however, this defect is aggravated by the additional fact that, unlike Katz and Lazarsfeld, she also speaks of 'power', which – unsurprisingly – likewise remains undefined, but is used sometimes as if it were and sometimes as if it were not a synonym of 'influence'; cf., e. g., pp. xvi, xvii, 53, 217). And even today, Mutz does not stand alone with that curious omission: cf. Friedkin 1998 for another recent monograph on social influence with theoretical as well as empirical ambitions, but not a hint of a definition of its subject. In a way, Friedkin's work resembles that of Katz and Lazarsfeld more than Mutz's, for he consistently speaks of influence only, not also of power, and he seems to share their narrow conception of influence, more or less in the sense of 'impact on opinion' mainly by way of persuasion (i. e., in the sense of category 1.ii, b) of my classification).

field and the (co-)editor of two early collections of papers on the topic.[26] That body of work contains numerous aspects of interest for anyone working on social influence and/ or power. But what it typically does *not* offer is useful insights and clues for a conceptual distinction between the two. As can be seen at a glance merely by looking at the titles of the contributions, the terms 'power' and 'influence' are generally treated either as synonyms or at least as self-evidently related to each other.

For more substantial evidence of this, I will take as an example three articles (co-)authored by John French – another leading figure in the early social-psychological influence-research community – all three of which can be found in the two collective volumes just mentioned.[27] Let us look at them in turn.

The title of the earliest of these articles, first published in 1956 and written by French alone, announces, not too modestly, 'A Formal Theory of Social Power'. The text, however, suggests from the very beginning that its main topic is influence rather than power. In the very first footnote (n. 1, p. 727), for instance, the reader is told that the author sees his own work in the context of earlier attempts by several other scholars to develop „mathematical theories of social influence“[28]. As for the concepts, the nearest approximation to definitions of power and influence to be found in this paper are the following formulations:

> „Social influences are coordinated to force fields induced by person *A* on person *B*; and the strength of these forces is assumed to vary with the power of *A* over *B*“ (French 1960, 728),

and

> „the power of *A* over *B* (with respect to a given opinion) is equal to the maximum force which *A* can induce on *B* minus the maximum resisting force which *B* can mobilize in the opposite direction“ (ibid., 731).

With respect to a concept of influence and the clarification of its relationship to that of power, these remarks are not very illuminating. In fact, French himself does not seem to take them very seriously. What he is actually interested in throughout the paper is something far more simple, namely: a consideration of the main elements to be taken into account for an explanation of *opinion change* induced through social interaction. *That* is what, in a very common-sensical way, he seems to think the concept of social influence boils down to.

Somewhat more attention to conceptual questions is paid in another article, first published in 1959 and written by French together with Bertram Raven, on 'The Bases of

[26] Cartwright (ed.) 1959; Cartwright/Zander (eds.) 1960.

[27] French 1960, French/Snyder 1959, French/Raven 1960.

[28] In fact, this is a prototypical example of the times when (some) social scientists were very optimistic about the possibility of elaborating formal theories that would resemble those of the natural sciences. The article, thus, begins with a brief description of the „Model“, followed by „Postulates“ and „Theorems“. The mathematical theory everything is based on is „digraph theory“. However, the boldness of the form of this paper contrasts with the meekness of its content. Besides, there is reason to doubt that the author was aware of the epistemological foundations and requirements of his enterprise: he does not hesitate to claim that at least some of his (empirical!) theorems „have been proven“ by „formal proofs“ (p. 733).

Social Power'.[29] There, one finds at least some statements about the relationship between power and influence, as when the authors announce that „we shall define power in terms of influence, and influence in terms of psychological change",[30] as well as explicit definitions of influence and power:

„The influence of O on system *a* in the life span of P is defined as the resultant force on system *a* which has its source in an act of O. This resultant force induced by O consists of two components: a force to change the system in the direction induced by O and an opposing resistance set up by the same act of O." (French/Raven 1960, 608)

„[T]he power of O with respect to system *a* of P is equal to the maximum resultant force of two forces set up by any possible act of O: *(a)* the force which O can set up on the system *a* to change in the direction x, *(b)* the resisting force in the opposite direction." (ibid., 610)

According to these definitions, thus, power is clearly understood as an *ability* (the ability of an agent to produce, through his own acts, any kind of 'net' impact on another), and influence as the *actualization* of that ability – i. e., „power is potential influence" (French/Raven 1960, 609). This places the conception into category *2.i)* of my classification.[31] Much less clear is the authors' additional assertion (ibid.) that, *vice versa*, „influence is kinetic power". If, as defined, power is an ability or potential, while influence is not, then there simply is no way for influence to be (a subtype of) power. The question then is, once again, whether one should simply disregard such formulations which, if taken seriously, do not square well with the rest of what is said; or whether one should rather take them as an indicator of the fact that the authors unwittingly hold on to conceptions of power, influence, and the relationship between them that are not entirely captured by their own explicit definitions.

The third paper in the series, written by French and Richard Snyder around the same time as the second, once more prepares the reader for a lecture on power, only to turn out to be concerned with influence. And again, it contains only the barest minimum of a definition of its basic concepts, in announcing that leadership (the main topic of the paper) will be defined „in terms of power" and then actually defining that „Leadership is *the potential social influence of one part of the group over another*" (French/ Snyder 1959, 118). Although not many words are wasted by the authors to explain this, it seems

[29] Note that again the title of the paper refers to power whereas its content is to a large extent about influence.
[30] French/Raven 1960, 608. However, cf. also the odd remark on the preceding page: „We hope to define basic concepts of power which will be adequate to explain many of the phenomena of social influence" (French/Raven 1960, 607). Taken literally, this is incomprehensible: how could anyone ever hope to 'explain' a 'phenomenon' with a concept? Specifically, if power is *defined* „in terms of influence", then how could „concepts of power", i. e., in the last instance, concepts based on the *concept* of influence, contribute anything to the explanation of *phenomena* of influence?
[31] This also throws some light on what French in his earlier paper might have meant with the cryptical sentence about social influence, cited above. However, even in that light, it is not immediately plausible why in French's view influence, or rather the force exerted by it, „is assumed to vary with the power of *A* over *B*". It is precisely one of the characteristics of a 'potential' that its magnitude may never manifest itself in any actual occurrence. In other words, it is an entirely contingent matter whether someone who has a great ability to *x* will ever use that ability, i. e., will actually do *x*, to a greater extent than someone whose ability to *x* is, perhaps only slightly, lower.

to imply that they adopt the conception of the paper mentioned before, in the sense that 'power' is taken to mean simply 'potential influence'.

In summary, what one can learn from these three papers about the concept of influence hardly goes beyond what could already be found in Katz's and Lazarsfeld's book. Influence is conceived as having something to do with opinions and the way they can be changed. But there is no discussion about whether it is conceptually linked to *beliefs* or rather to *attitudes*, or to both of them, or perhaps even to the choice of *actions* or the *outcome* of actions. The only thing French and his collaborators add is a view about the *relationship* between power and influence: they advocate the well-known power-as-ability-to-influence view, the inconveniences of which I have already discussed.

(3) But, as elsewhere, in social psychology too there is no consensus about these conceptual matters. Take, as a third example, Serge Moscovici, yet another prominent social psychologist and long-time director of the Research Institute for Social Psychology at the *Ecole des Hautes Etudes en Sciences Sociales* in Paris. In 1976, Moscovici presented a monograph on *Social Influence and Social Change*[32] in which he suggested a markedly different conception of power, influence and the relationship between them from the one we have just seen. If power were nothing but potential influence for him, he could (or, in any case: should), for instance, not have written a sentence as the following:

„Just as society is a machine that produces, consumes and distributes wealth and power, society is also [...] a machine that creates, accumulates and processes influence."[33]

In fact, Moscovici himself expresses discontent with how the terms 'power' and 'influence' are being used in his own field. And his way of dealing with the matter shows just how confused – and confusing – it is. At one point, he sets out to investigate the question „Is it legitimate to go on using power and influence as interchangeable concepts?"[34]

32 In this book, Moscovici is primarily concerned with intended, purposeful influence as it may be exerted *by individuals on social groups*. More specifically, he is particularly interested in drawing attention to the important fact that for an understanding of social processes and developments, what matters is not only, or not always, how people can be directly induced to act in a certain way, but also how norms and institutions, which will then indirectly operate on people's choices of action, can be established, maintained or changed. He therefore opposes what he calls a 'genetic', change-oriented model of influence focused on what individuals do to collectivities in order to modify socially established norms, opinions, or practices (12 ff.) to what he claims is the traditional 'functionalist', control-oriented model which sees influence mainly as having the function of getting individuals to conform with social norms, i. e., as closely linked to the pressures exerted *on individuals by groups* (11 f.). Cf. also Moscovici 1985.

33 Moscovici 1979, 9 (the citations from this work here and in what follows are my own retranslations from the German translation of the book; the German version is therefore also given here): „Ebenso wie die Gesellschaft eine Maschine ist, die Reichtum und Macht produziert, verbraucht und verteilt, so ist die Gesellschaft [...] eine Maschine, die Einfluß schafft, sammelt und verarbeitet."

34 „Ist es legitim, Macht und Einfluß weiterhin als austauschbare Konzepte zu gebrauchen?" (Moscovici 1979, 73–78). That Moscovici frames a conceptual question as a matter of *legitimacy* is just one indicator of the problems the book raises. Here, as elsewhere, however, it is impossible to know whether the wording is ‚only' a problem of language – perhaps even only of the German translation?; unfortunately, I have been unable to consult the original version of the text – or of substance.

But his description of how those terms actually have been used indicates that they have *not* been regarded as interchangeable at all, but rather as different concepts:

„In this area, the more or less explicit assumption has always been that power is the only source of influence, and that influence is the consequence or the means of the exercise of power."[35]

Moscovici discards this view because he wants to propose a substantially different conception. He does not seem to notice that there is reason to discard it at least in part also for the still more cogent reason that it suffers from a problem of internal consistency: if power is a (or even the only) *source* of influence, then it is difficult to see how influence could at the same time be the *means* for exercising power – unless this is just another, clumsy formulation of the good old power-as-ability-to-influence view. In that case, however, the statement would not express an „assumption", in the sense of a hypothesis about an empirical relationship, but a conceptual choice. As so often in this context, once more we are at a loss about how seriously we should take the author's words: Is Moscovici's *description* of the view he wishes to criticize inadequate, or is that view *itself* as inconsistent as the description suggests?

In any case, Moscovici proposes another distinction between power and influence, making them complementaries, based on the means used in their respective exercise: in his view, there is, on the one hand, such a thing as „naked power based on coercion"; and then there is, on the other hand, the possibility to „propagate values, norms, and ideologies – in short, to exercise influence".[36] Moscovici's own conception thus seems to belong into category *2.ii)*.

A final point worth mentioning about Moscovici's conceptual discussion is the following 'argument': *Influence*, as defined by him, is responsible for the transmission of values; *authority* is based on the acceptance of certain values, and authority is a type of *power*. There is, thus, a type of power which depends on, and results from, influence. But, if power is, at least sometimes, an *effect* of influence, then, obviously, it cannot also be its *cause*. Hence, he concludes, it is wrong to say – as some authors do – that, generally, power is the cause, or 'source', of influence.[37] As an argument against the particular conception of power, influence and the relationship between them which Moscovici wants to discredit, this is obviously a non-starter, since it depends crucially on one's prior acceptance of Moscovici's own definition of influence. But if one accepts *that* (something authors who hold the incriminated view certainly do not), then one simply has no reason to hold also that power is the source of influence, i. e., to adopt the view the argument is intended to disprove. In other words: Moscovici's argument cannot convince anyone.

35 Moscovici 1979, 73: „In diesem Bereich ist die mehr oder weniger explizite Annahme immer gewesen, daß Macht die einzige Quelle von Einfluß ist, [sic] und daß Einfluß die Folge oder das Instrument der Ausübung von Macht ist."

36 Moscovici 1979, 77. Of course, these few words are not much to go by for an interpretation of the author's conception, but it is as close as one can get to a definition of his concepts in that book.

37 Ibid.: „That is why, if power presupposes influence and is in part a result of influence, we definitely cannot regard it as a *cause* of influence. It cannot at the same time be the cause and the effect." („Deshalb können wir, wenn Macht Einfluß voraussetzt und zum Teil das Ergebnis von Einfluß ist, sie unmöglich als *Ursache* von Einfluß betrachten. Sie kann nicht zugleich Ursache und Wirkung sein.")

Thus, Moscovici's book is another example of a social-psychological work which certainly treats many important (especially, empirical) aspects and questions, but which, unfortunately, has such a weak conceptual (and, therefore, generally, theoretical) foundation that, in the last instance, its scientific value remains doubtful.

(4) Whereas Moscovici's basic purpose was to offer an alternative to the focus of social-psychological influence studies on compliance, how to get others to comply with one's wishes has been, at least over the past two decades, the main interest underlying the influence studies of another, very popular social psychologist: Robert B. Cialdini. In 1984, Cialdini first published a book on *Influence* which since then has become a standard text, with several editions in English and translations in other languages.[38] In fact, Cialdini's is a rather special case, since while he has the academic credentials of serving as professor of psychology at Arizona State University and his book even today still appears on the reading lists of college-level psychology courses,[39] he is also possibly the influence scholar who has most skillfully marketed his product to a much wider, non-academic audience.[40] The basic components of what he calls the 'Science of Persuasion'[41] can also be found on his own large website.[42] His popular success is understandable, considering his claim that his writings explain what „social psychology" is said to have discovered: „the basic principles that govern getting to 'yes'" (2001, 62). Who would not want to profit from such insights?

But in fact, concerning the basic concepts, Cialdini offers no advance over other authors; he only produces a more trivialized version of the same conceptual confusions we have already seen. Thus, the 'definition page' of his website is replete with not only very basic, but also at best very sloppily formulated 'definitions':

> „Influence investigates the causes of human change – whether that change is a behavior, an attitude, or a belief. Inducing a change in behavior is called compliance. Inducing a change in attitude is called persuasion. Inducing a change in belief is called either education or propaganda – depending on your perspective [...] Beliefs are things known or believed to be true [...] [T]he dark side of social influence [...] combines compliance, persuasion, and propaganda tactics into a powerfully insidious form of coercive manipulation that robs an individual of his original identity [...]"[43]

[38] Note that between 1984 and 2001, this book, in its several slightly revised editions, has appeared with three different subtitles: *How and Why People Agree to Things*, *Science and Practice*, and *The Psychology of Persuasion*, in at least four different publishing houses (originally published by William Morrow, there have also been editions by HarperCollins, Quill, and Allyn & Bacon). It is not easy to keep track of which edition has appeared where under what title, since bibliographical references to the book are not entirely consistent. All these circumstances can provoke the impression that Cialdini has authored several books on influence, but as far as I have been able to find out, it is all basically the same book.

[39] As can easily be found out with the help of any of the more powerful search engines on the internet.

[40] One of the currently available editions of Cialdini's book has managed to collect as many as seventy online 'reviews' by readers at one of the major international online bookstores, most of them enthusiastic. The publisher of the, to date, latest edition of the book advertises it with the information, among others, that he is an „influential author [who] speaks frequently on 'The Power of Ethical Influence' to such organizations as IBM, the Mayo Clinic, and NATO".

[41] Cf. the title of one of his more recent articles in the *Scientific American* (February 2001).

[42] Cf. www.influenceatwork.com. It must be noted that the website is managed by his former student Kelton Rhoads who seems to be the author of much of the texts to be found in those pages; but since it is characterized as Cialdini's personal site, it can be assumed that these texts are approved by him.

[43] www.influenceatwork.com/definit.htm.

Influence, of course, „investigates" nothing; compliance is not „inducing" a change in behaviour, just as a belief is not „a thing [...] believed to be true"; and it is at least open to debate whether changes in attitude or belief can be induced in a „coercive" way.

That Cialdini makes no effort to distinguish influence from power can be seen, among other places, on the first of his two 'ethics pages'[44] where the main contention, unaccompanied by any argument that might support it, is that influence is „powerful" and that, therefore, influence infringes on people's freedom:

„I'd contend we only enjoy the limited amount of freedom that remains between the powerful influences that largely determine our everyday lives."

That Cialdini is not given to careful conceptual distinctions is also shown in his handling of the six human dispositions – „powerful motivators" (2001, 67) – he has identified as the main factors one may take advantage of for influencing others. These are: the tendencies to reciprocate, to be consistent, to emulate others, to please those one likes, to accept authority, and to value things according to their scarcity (ibid., 62 ff.). This is, of course, not a very original list – each one of the entries is well-known. But it is a list in which a very mixed bunch of mechanisms, dispositions, desires, principles, etc. is thrown together indiscriminately, under the unifying label of 'influence'. And different as they are, Cialdini does not even bother to distinguish very carefully between them.[45]

This author, then, is clearly not a social psychologist anyone interested in a careful analysis, satisfying basic scientific standards of rigour and consistency, can turn to for help.

(5) Someone might object that authors like Cialdini are not representative of the discipline; that the serious literature I have scrutinized so far is dated; and that the conceptual deficiencies from the infancy of the social-psychological investigation of influence have long been recognized and overcome. Unfortunately, however, the impression of persistent conceptual deficits in social-psychological scholarship about power and influence is confirmed by at least one recent and apparently very much 'mainstream' collective volume, published just in time for its consideration in these pages.[46] A surprising

44 www.influenceatwork.com/ethics.htm.

45 For example, he reports on an empirical study in which German subjects allegedly turned out to comply with requests primarily on the basis of *consistency*; but Cialdini's own description of their tendency is clearly one of compliance on the basis of normative *authority*. In contrast, the Chinese subjects of the study are said to have reacted primarily to *authority*, but the corresponding description rather points to compliance for *prudential* reasons, which is, however, not a category contained in the list (2001, 67).

46 Lee-Chai/Bargh 2001. It is the editors' professed purpose with this book „to bring power to the forefront, to make it a household name, at least in the social science circles", „to unmask the mystery of this enigmatic force" (Preface, xiii); in their view, power has been a much neglected topic in the social *sciences*, although they acknowledge the existence of *philosophical* studies on power. This indicates an extremely narrow disciplinary view. Indeed, it is surprising to see that with the exception of a few scattered references to Max Weber and Bertrand Russell, the psychologists who have contributed to this volume seem to be completely un-

lack of attention to conceptual questions is pervasive in that book too. If at all, conceptual issues are touched upon only in the briefest imaginable way. Judging from the content of this collection, one can hardly avoid the conclusion that the „recent conceptual advances made within social psychology" detected by contributors Michael A. Hogg and Scott A. Reid[47] have entirely passed by the area of power and influence studies. Thus, in this volume, the 'state of the art' in social psychology concerning the concepts of power and influence presents itself as follows:[48]

The late *David Kipnis*, „a legendary figure in power research" (editors' preface, p. xiv), opens the collection with a contribution in which 'power' and 'influence', although much used terms, remain undefined and are apparently used interchangeably.[49]

The latter also applies to the next essay, by *Bruce Barry*,[50] although there, at least an attempt to define influence is made. Under the heading 'Influence Defined', one finds this:

> „Social influence, in broad terms, describes processes by which individuals modify their cognitions, attitudes, and behaviors in response to socially constructed contexts. Dyadic social influence refers more narrowly to [... t]he processes involved when an individual (an influence agent) actively seeks to elicit attitudinal or behavioral compliance from a single, target other." (ibid., 20)

Of course, strictly speaking, neither terms nor concepts „describe" anything. Besides, the processes by which cognitions are changed are, it is to be assumed, rather different from those by which behaviour is modified; and the processes involved when someone „seeks" to elicit such changes are still of a more varied kind; thus, Barry's is, at best, an extremely vague and broad definition.

John A. Bargh and *Jeannette Alvarez*[51] then write about the abuse of „official", „officially licensed", „organizational", and „legitimate" power, i. e., about variants of power of a *normative* kind (on normative power, cf. below Chapter 4), and do not seem to notice that this does not – at least, not without further explanation – square well with their own express definition of power as the factual „ability to attain one's desired outcomes" (45).

Daphne Blunt Bugental and *Eta K. Lin*'s[52] contribution contains a section on 'Defining Power'; but in its two pages one actually finds only one single sentence about the concept of power (the remainder of the section is not about the concept, but mainly about the question how power is *perceived*), referring to Max Weber and Dorwin Cartwright and – unsurprisingly – following the power-as-ability-to-influence view without any amendments or improvements.

acquainted with the power literature written by philosophers, political scientists, sociologists and economists. Otherwise, one should expect to find at the very least some indication of the reasons for regarding it as irrelevant enough to flatly ignore it.

47 'Social Identity, Leadership, and Power', 159–180, 161.

48 I will refer only to ten of the fifteen contributions to the volume; the remaining five contain nothing about the topic worth mentioning at all.

49 'Using Power. Newton's Second Law', 3–17.

50 'Influence in Organizations from a Social Expectancy Perspective', 19–40.

51 'The Road to Hell. Good Intentions in the Face of Nonconscious Tendencies to Misuse Power', 41–55.

52 'The Many Faces of Power. The Strange Case of Dr. Jekyll and Mr. Hyde', 115–132.

Mark Snyder and *Marc T. Kiviniemi*[53] straightforwardly adopt French/Raven's (1959) proposal according to which „a person's social *power* is defined as the extent to which that person has the *potential ability to influence* another person in a given setting" (134; emphasis added). Whether there is a difference between an ability and a „potential ability" remains their secret. And they also do not say why they define power not simply as an agent's ability, but as „the extent to which" someone „has" such an ability, and what difference that makes.[54] But, however awkward their formulation, they actually seem to mean to follow French/Raven with their power-as-ability-to-influence concept and apparently see no problems with that which might need to be overcome.

Hogg and *Reid*, in the paper already cited above, in turn, must have another conception since for them „leaders do not need to exercise power [...] in order to have influence" (168; similarly, 175), whereas on the French/Raven conception, exercising power and being influential are the same thing. But although they tell us what they mean by 'exercising power' – to „persuade, gain compliance, coerce, or resort to force" (168) – they never explain their notion of 'having influence'.

Susan T. Fiske[55] contents herself with stating that „This approach defines power as control over resources" (182) – an extremely broad definition that is, besides, very much contrary to common usage. Having said this, it is strange that she later states that „Power is not simply carelessness" (184); with her definition in mind, one wonders how anyone could ever think that it could be 'carelessness' at all. She also does not explain why she thinks that „Power entails both absence of dependency and presence of entitlement" (186), since *(i)* controlling some set of resources does not entail that one controls *all* the resources one would ever need or want (which would seem to be a precondition for the absence of dependency), and *(ii)* it is also perfectly conceivable that someone might control a resource without being entitled to it.

Bertram H. Raven[56] reiterates the old power-as-ability-to-influence definitions of 1959, with social influence defined as „a change in the belief, attitude or behavior of a person" and social power as „the potential for such influence" (217). He mentions that the typology of six bases of power presented in his and French's 1959 article is „the most frequently utilized model of dyadic power in the social psychological and industrial/organizational literature".[57] Here too, then, we find no evidence that concerning the concepts of power and influence any progress has been made in social-psychological scholarship over the past four decades.

[53] 'Getting What They Came For. How Power Influences the Dynamics and Outcomes of Interpersonal Interaction', 133–155.

[54] Strictly speaking, it would seem that 'the extent to which' someone has the ability to influence another could – if one adopted French/Raven's conception – only be *the extent to which* that agent has power over the other, but *not* that power itself.

[55] 'Effects of Power on Bias. Power Explains and Maintains Individual, Group, and Societal Disparities', 181–193. The advantage of this paper is that, at least, Fiske does not mix influence into her considerations.

[56] 'Power/Interaction and Interpersonal Influence. Experimental Investigations and Case Studies', 217–240; this is based, among others, on Raven 1990, 1992, 1993, 1999.

[57] 218; similarly, Schwarzwald/Koslowsky (op. cit. in the next note), 196 f.

Joseph Schwarzwald and *Meni Koslowsky* also offer considerations on Raven's model.[58] One would therefore assume that they use the same definitions of power and influence. Instead, they have to say the following about these concepts: The term 'social power' „refers to the potential sources available to an individual for influencing another person to comply and do what he or she would not have done otherwise", whereas the term 'social influence' „describes the specific tactics explicitly exercised by the influencing agent in attempting to gain compliance" (196). Their reflections culminate in the explication that:

> „The actual exercise of power tactics is considered 'influence' whereas the potential to exercise power refers to 'power'." (ibid.)

Again, that is at best a very awkward way of putting it. Terms do not „describe" things; what is exercised is certainly not „power tactics", but power; on their own terms, in any case, „tactics" here can only concern influence, not power; whether „potential sources [...] for influencing" can be called „phenomena" seems questionable;[59] and that „influence [...] describes the [...] tactics [...] exercised by the influencing agent" is a formulation the meaning of which is up for guesses.

Finally, *Emmeline S. Chen* and *Tom R. Tyler*[60] never say what they mean by the term 'power', yet they „consider [it] a logical assumption" that „people who are advantaged – that is, those who are wealthy and privileged – hold the power in society", and they therefore announce that they will use the terms 'wealthy', 'privileged' and 'advantaged' as synonymous with 'powerful'. The reason they give for thinking that this is a „logical assumption" is that they hold 'advantaged' to mean „command[ing] a disproportionately large share of societal resources" (243). But how that relates to power, and whether what they are thinking of is actually a *logical truth* or merely a *plausible empirical assumption* their text does not reveal.

Hence, to the extent that this collective volume reflects the current state of social-psychological wisdom,[61] it shows that even today we cannot expect much help from these quarters when it comes to clarifying the concepts of social power and influence.

* * *

3. The Sanction-Based Distinction: Lasswell and Kaplan

Among those modern political theorists who have offered a systematic proposal for the distinction of influence and power by defining the former as the broader concept of

[58] 'The Power Interaction Model. Theory, Methodology, and Empirical Applications', 195–214. In fact, the close connection of these two authors with Bertram Raven is underscored by the fact that not long ago they published a paper on a similar topic together with him: cf. Raven/Schwarzwald/Koslowsky 1998.

[59] Do they perhaps not mean potential sources, but rather *actual* sources for a *potential* exercise of influence?

[60] 'Cloaking Power. Legitimizing Myths and the Psychology of the Advantaged', 241–261.

[61] And there is reason to think that it does, such as the uniformity of the references given in the different contributions, indicating that there is a body of work which is more or less consensually regarded as of obligatory reference, and from which nobody strays very much.

which the latter is a sub-category, probably the first and certainly the most prominent have been Harold Lasswell and Abraham Kaplan, with their famous study on *Power and Society*.[62] Even today, half a century after their book first appeared in print, it is often cited as authoritative on these concepts.[63] Acceptance of an authority, however, frequently precludes discussion and critical assessment, and this has also been the case of Lasswell/Kaplan's conceptions of influence and power. That is all the more unfortunate since not only are we dealing here with what in the authors' view are probably the most fundamental concepts of political science; their account of them is also not entirely clear and consistent. This makes it difficult to know what exactly it is that those other writers who profess to accept their definitions actually accept. To my knowledge, there is no established analysis of Lasswell/Kaplan's conceptions we could rely on, and we must therefore see for ourselves what they say, and what we can learn from it.[64]

First of all, it is important to realize that their conceptions of influence and power are not self-standing; they are, rather, themselves derived from the authors' more fundamental understanding of what kind of enterprise 'political science' must necessarily be. One can therefore understand and appreciate the former only if one takes into account the latter. Lasswell and Kaplan begin by explaining that to the extent that the social sciences are approached from what they call a „manipulative standpoint" – that is, with a view towards the formulation of technical norms[65] – they are „policy sciences", concerned with gaining knowledge about the workings of „the integration of values realized by and embodied in interpersonal relations". Different policy sciences are then distinguished according to their specific objects of inquiry; and the distinctive object identi-

[62] Lasswell/Kaplan 1950; references in the following will be to this work unless otherwise indicated. The book (finished in manuscript already in 1945; cf. Preface) is a model of what interdisciplinary teamwork – Lasswell being a political scientist, Kaplan a philosopher – can accomplish. At the same time, it is also a telling example of the optimistic conception of political science as an 'exact science' which can, and ought to, be conducted *more geometrico*, i. e., whose theoretical foundations are to be constructed in an analytical and deductive manner – the conception, that is, which was particularly widespread during the second third of the twentieth century when the academic treatment of political questions was moving away from being regarded as belonging exclusively to the realm of philosophy or the history of ideas (if it was not altogether dismissed as „a branch of literature" or mere „political doctrine"; cf. Lasswell/Kaplan 1950, x f.) and was slowly being recognized as an independent discipline within the social sciences. Lasswell/Kaplan's book stands out in that process because it is explicitly intended to provide the systematic conceptual and theoretical foundation that is needed if „Political science, as an empirical discipline" (xiv) is to be possible. Conforming to the authors' purpose „to formulate the basic concepts and hypotheses of political science" (xi), the book's organization in a sequence of definitions („DF.") and propositions („PROP.") at first sight makes it look more like a mathematical treatise than anything else. That impression disappears, however, when one realizes that there are no proofs. Thus, the work can perhaps best be described as a systematic inventory of the concepts the authors consider to be of fundamental relevance for the acquisition of empirical knowledge about 'political' phenomena, and of intuitively more or less plausible „regulative hypotheses" (xxiii) or „hypotheses-schema" (xxii), worthy of empirical investigation, about such phenomena.

[63] Cf., e. g., Hoffmann-Lange's observation (1992, 355; quoted above, in the Introduction, n. 42) that Lasswell's and Kaplan's definitions are „almost unanimously accepted in the literature".

[64] Lasswell and Kaplan would have been the first to object against the uncritical acceptance of their proposals. It was one of their main objectives to fight against „Semantic confusions" which, „in political theory as elsewhere, have markedly interfered with fruitful research", and they firmly believed that „obscurity, vagueness, and ambiguity [...] are inescapable only when no effort is made to escape them" (xix).

[65] For the concept of 'technical norm' and a discussion of the relations and differences between technical norms, anankastic propositions and hypothetical norms, cf. von Wright 1963, 9 ff.

fied by Lasswell and Kaplan of that particular policy science called 'political science' is none other than „influence and power as instruments of such integration" (xii).[66] That is the reason why, immediately after introducing the basic units involved in political processes in the first part of their book, they set out to analyse these two concepts, dedicating an entire chapter to each.[67]

Lasswell/Kaplan's conceptual framework constitutes an intricate web, and it is not easy to understand at first sight what their definitions of 'influence' and 'power' amount to, because their meaning depends, in turn, on a series of other concepts previously introduced by explicit definition.[68] One thing that can easily be seen, however, is how they view the *general* relationship between power and influence, as they specify it at more than one point in clear and unequivocal terms:

> „Power is a special case of the exercise of influence [...] power is comprised under influence [...] power is a type of influence [...]"[69]

And this 'special case' is distinguished according to the mechanisms or means through which influence operates:

> „It is the threat of sanctions which differentiates power from influence in general." (76)[70]

[66] See also p. 53: „The political interactions of various persons and groups are constituted by patterns of *influence* and *power* [...]". But cf. p. 82: „The [...] science of power (in the narrowest sense) is *political science* [...] For the theoretical analysis of the determinative conditions of power on the basis of disciplined procedures of observation, we speak of political science." Somewhere on the way, the role of influence seems to have gotten lost. That is, the specific object of political science seems to be not influence *and* power, but only that kind of influence which, in their view, *is* power. And this means that although they treat influence as a distinct concept, they do not seem to ascribe any independent relevance in political matters to it.
[67] Ch. IV to the concept of influence, ch. V to that of power.
[68] Therefore, it does not do justice to their conception when, as is often done, single catchphrases from their work are conveniently quoted in isolation. The reason why this is highly problematic is that Lasswell/Kaplan have a tendency to use familiar terms in a sometimes radically unfamiliar sense. But when quotations from their work are given without further explanation, an 'ordinary' reading is necessarily suggested. Such a reading then yields *a* conception of influence and power, but certainly not that of Lasswell and Kaplan. The meaning and the plausibility of *their* conceptual proposal can be assessed only by taking a closer look at all its relevant components.
[69] 76, 77, 84. Strictly speaking, there is already an inconsistency in this since it is not necessarily the same to say that power is a special case of the *exercise* of influence as to say that it is a special type of *influence* itself.
[70] By contrast, Almond/Verba (1989, 135) seem to make action based on a (perceived) threat of sanction the defining characteristic of influence: „We shall roughly define the political influence of a group or individual over governmental decision as equal to the degree to which governmental officials act to benefit that group or individual because the officials believe that they will risk some deprivation (they will risk their jobs, be criticized, lose votes) if they do not so act. Thus we define political influence as both the outcome of the decision and the motives of the decision makers." However, the inadequacy of this formulation is obvious: political influence is here defined at the same time as the *outcome* of a decision, the *motive* leading to the decision, and the *degree* to which the outcome of the decision benefits a group or individual. This confusion is perhaps understandable if one keeps in mind that the authors were actually interested in something other than an explication of the term 'political influence' when they wrote the quoted passage; but, in any case, for a clarification of the concept of influence this 'definition' is not very useful.

Hence, for Lasswell and Kaplan all cases of power are cases of influence, but only cases of influence involving a threat of sanctions are cases of power. Their proposal thus falls squarely into category *(1.b, ii.a)*.

Once this relationship is established, from a definition of one of the two concepts the other one can be derived. It should make no difference whether we define power by starting with a definition of influence and applying to it the indicated criterion, or whether, *vice versa*, we start with a definition of power and derive from it, by extending the concept beyond the indicated special case, the more general concept of influence. As it happens, Lasswell/Kaplan give explicit, self-standing definitions of *both* concepts. Their full conception thus consists of two definitions *plus* the statements about the features of the relationship between the concepts. This allows us to test the consistency of their conception, by investigating whether the two concepts actually do stand in the postulated relationship.

In order to do this, we must first recall what the authors have to say about the concept of power.[71] They define power as a *triadic* relation, between two agents and concerning some set of values:

„*Power* is participation in the making of decisions: G has power over H with respect to the values K if G participates in the making of decisions affecting the K-policies of H.“ (75)

At this point, the attentive reader may be surprised that what in the passage quoted earlier the authors had identified as the special characteristic of power – namely, the threat of sanctions – is not mentioned in this definition. But, indeed, it need not be, since it is already *implicitly* contained in it, by way of the authors' prior explicit definition of 'decision' according to which „A *decision* is a policy involving severe sanctions (deprivations)“ (74), where, in turn, a „*Policy* is a projected program of goal values and practices“ or a „course of action in relation to others“ (71).[72]

Hence, any would-be policy – or 'resolution', to call it somehow – that is not effectively and seriously implemented, that is, opposition against which is not confronted with a real threat of severe sanctions, simply is not a 'decision' in Lasswell/Kaplan's terms. Thus, if an agent *H* has a set of values *K* with regard to which he draws up certain policies, then concerning that set of values there 'is'[73] power of another agent *G* over *H*

[71] Cf. also above, Chapter 1.2.1, n. 56.

[72] The expression 'goal values' in this definition of 'policy' is probably an error and should read 'goal events' instead, since a 'value' is itself defined as a 'goal event'; cf. 16, 56. In any case, these intricacies of Lasswell's and Kaplan's conception of power illustrate my earlier point that one cannot understand their definitions without engaging in some conceptual genealogy.

[73] It is not quite clear what the specific 'mode of being' of power is in that case. When someone participates in a 'process' in which certain policies of one actor 'affect' policies of another, one would usually say that power is 'exercised'. But Lasswell/Kaplan at this point make no effort to distinguish between power as such, its possession, and its exercise; they say both that such a process 'is power', and that it is 'having power'. Taken literally, this obviously makes no sense: neither is possession ('having') a process, nor can one say that power itself 'is' a process if one also wishes to say, as Lasswell/Kaplan do, that power can be exercised (p. 75: „the political process is the [...] exercise of power“), since processes are not the kind of things one can exercise. I think it is fair to say that the usefulness of Lasswell/Kaplan's work, valiant and valuable as it may be, is impaired by their surprising linguistic sloppiness and lack of precision, and particularly by their failure consistently to distinguish between potentials and their actualizations.

if *G* actually participates in designing and/or implementing certain *other* policies which affect *H*'s policies regarding *K and* which, if necessary, are enforced with severe sanctions. This can also be expressed in a much less complicated way:

„Power [...] is the process of affecting policies of others with the help of (actual or threatened) severe deprivations for nonconformity with the policies intended." (76)[74]

If we now take this concept of *power*, and take into account how the relationship between power and influence has been described by them, we should expect Lasswell/ Kaplan's definition of *influence* to amount to a formulation equivalent to the following: ' ... the process of affecting policies of others – *with or without* the help of (actual or threatened) severe deprivations for nonconformity with the policies intended'; any other content of the definition would be inconsistent with what they say about power. In fact, however, it is far from obvious whether the explicit definition they give of the concept of influence actually satisfies that requirement. The definition, as well as the definitions of still other concepts involved in it, are formulated in very different – and, it seems to me, somewhat obscure – terms. According to them,

„*Influence* is value position and potential" (60),

where

„*Value position* is the place occupied in the value pattern" (57),[75]

[74] Cf. also p. 84: „A *form of power* is a form of influence in which the effect on policy is enforced or expected to be enforced by relatively severe sanctions." The authors emphasize, however, that it does not matter by which means the „effective control over policy" power consists in is actually gained in a particular case; all that matters is that sanctions are *available* (76). – Note that the authors apparently use the terms 'sanction' and 'deprivation' as synonymous. But 'deprivation' is explicitly defined to mean „decrease in influence" or „deterioration in value position and potential" (61). Hence, power in Lasswell/Kaplan's sense always involves the (actual or threatened) substantial reduction of another's influence. This is one of the details which suggests the inconvenience of prematurely accepting their definitions. It is, indeed, doubtful whether all writers who have paid lip service to their definition of power would really be willing to accept that power processes necessarily (for conceptual reasons) involve a reduction of the power subject's influence. Another noteworthy point in this context is that Lasswell/Kaplan explicitly acknowledge that whether in some particular case something is an exercise of 'mere' influence or an exercise of power is an entirely *subjective* question: it depends exclusively on the assessment of the respective subject (which, they conjecture, is *culturally* determined): „Any form of influence may be regarded as in fact a power relation if the deprivations imposed by the influential are important enough to those over whom influence is being exercised" (84). This makes it extremely difficult, if not directly impossible to formulate general assertions about what kinds of situations are likely to involve power – a result which, in view of many of the hypotheses advanced by the authors, is at least surprising. Take, for example, their assertion that „The king's mistress [...] has only influence, not power, over the king" (85): How do they know? Wouldn't that depend on what a particular king considered to be a severe deprivation? Would the case be different if we were talking about the wife instead of the mistress? Hans Kelsen, for example – who wrote his *General Theory of Law and State* at about the same time and who can also be classified as belonging into category *(1.b)* of those who conceive influence as the more general concept (for Kelsen, influence is socially ubiquitous; cf. Kelsen 1949, 193) and power (or rather, 'domination', as Kelsen calls it in the passage I have in mind) as a special case – at least considers the possibility that 'the king's mistress' may 'dominate' the king himself: „A study of actual social behavior would perhaps reveal that [the] ruler himself is ruled by other people, by an adviser, his mistress, or his chamberlain, and that the commands he issues are the result of influences that other individuals exercise upon him [...] these relations of domination in which the ruler himself holds the place of the ruled" (Kelsen 1949, 187).

[75] Value positions can be anything between „high" (or „favorable") and „low" (or „unfavorable) (57).

„The *value pattern* is the pattern of distribution of the values of a group among its members" (57),
„A value is a desired event – a goal event" (16),[76] and
„The *value potential* is the value position likely to be occupied as the outcome of conflict" [between actors competing for a favourable position regarding some 'competitive' value] (58).[77]

These are rather awkward formulations which, taken literally, give rise to serious problems. Since both 'value position' and 'value potential' are defined as 'places', the nature of influence on that account is that of *two* 'places', in two *different* 'patterns' – one actual, the other potential.[78] But the conception of influence as a 'place' (not to speak of two different places at a time) seems to be as contrary to the conception of power presented above as to ordinary usage: if power is a *process* and influence is a *place*, then it is clearly impossible for power to be a special case of influence. To understand what Lasswell and Kaplan really have in mind we need to revert to some of their explanatory remarks and some of the other concepts they define subsequently.

One helpful clue is their observation that „the number of party members in office" at any point in time is an „index of the influence of a political party", and that „the number of party members likely to be in office after the next election, or the next uprising, or some other probable conflict" is that party's „value potential (in terms of this index)" (59). Also, when a great percentage of a party's members refrain from voting in an election, they say that the party's „influence has not been fully actualized", that is, its actual value position is lower than its value potential (ibid.). All this seems to indicate that 'value position' and 'value potential' are meant to be *indicators* of influence, rather than influence itself.

Similarly, what they seem to be thinking of (at least at one point) is that influence may be *based on* an actual value position *or* on a value potential, not that it *is* always either one or both things at the same time:

„A group may be more and more influential even though its value position remains constant, if its potential is increasing (for instance, an increasingly popular and well-organized revolutionary party); and conversely a group may have little influence regardless of its value position, because of its low potential (as in the case of a ruling clique just before its overthrow)." (60)

The passage shows that Lasswell/Kaplan's idea is not really, or at least not consistently, that influence is a 'place' or rank in any pattern; here, they speak of it as a property, as

[76] The term 'value' is one of those „two or three terms used in this book" which the authors have „explicitly introduced as undefined" (3, n. 1). They do, however, give some indications of their conception of a 'value' which may serve as substitutes for a 'formal' definition. Cf. also p. 55: „Values are the goal-events of acts of valuation", and p. 16: „we speak of the object or situation desired as the 'value'".

[77] Note that Lasswell/Kaplan's remarks about the concepts of value, valuing, and valuation contain several inconsistencies whose exposure at this point would lead too far away from the present topic. For an overall assessment of their proposal, however, it must be kept in mind that the weaknesses of these concepts are, of course, passed on to all other concepts defined in reference to them, including those of influence and power.

[78] An instructive exercise is to replace each term used in the definition of influence with its respective *definiens* as given by Lasswell/Kaplan. The result is something like the following: 'Influence is the place occupied and the place likely to be occupied in the distribution of the desired events of a group among its members'.

something one can 'have'. Indeed, somewhat later, they explain that „To *have* influence is to occupy a high position (and potential) with respect to all the values important in the society" (71). This is perhaps more plausible than the above-quoted definition, but it is still not entirely clear how the 'is' in that formulation must be interpreted: whether 'to have influence' *means* 'to occupy a high position ...', i. e., whether the two phrases are conceptually equivalent, or whether there is some kind of *causal* relationship between them, in the sense that occupying a high position gives one influence or, *vice versa*, that having influence guarantees one a high position in some value pattern.[79]

Whatever the right answer to this question may be,[80] however, it will still not give us a concept of influence that fits to Lasswell/Kaplan's conception of power, namely, as a 'process of affecting policies of others'. Such a process comes into play only when the authors move on to the idea that influence can be *exercised*:

„The *exercise of influence* (influence process) consists in affecting policies of others than the self" (71), and

„Influence is *exercised* when its possession affects the interpersonal relations of those (other than the self) active in the shaping and enjoyment of the values [...] The exercise of influence consists in this effect on the policy of others",

where the effect „this" refers to is stated in the preceding sentence as being C. J. Friedrich's effect of 'anticipated reactions', that is, the effect

„that policies are determined by expectations of the resulting conduct of those having the influence" (71).

Here, now, we have a process, and the endpoint of this process is some effect on other agents' policies. The first of the two quotations even produces almost exactly the definition of influence one arrives at by derivation from that of power, namely as „the process of affecting policies of others". In this sense, the cause of confusion seems to have been 'only' that with respect to power the authors have given a definition concerning its *exercise*, whereas with respect to influence their definition concentrates on the potential involved in its *possession*. But note that according to the last quotation, there seems to be yet another important difference between influence and power (besides the fact that in the former, sanctions are not necessarily involved) in the conception of Lasswell and Kaplan:

An *exercise of power* always requires some intention or desire, leading to a decision (in the ordinary sense of the term) on the part of the power holder with respect to the other side's conduct, and subsequently to participation in a decision in Lasswell/

[79] Another element of this definition that is far from clear is the word 'all'; the authors cannot really mean that only someone occupying a high position concerning *all* important values has influence (that would, for instance, contradict what they have said about the influence of political parties).

[80] If there is such a right answer at all. The text supports both readings. When, for example, 'indulgence' is defined as „increase in influence" and it is then explained that 'indulgence' is a „general [term] for any improvement [...] in value position or potential" (61), this supports the conceptual equivalence of 'influence' and 'value position and potential'. On the other hand, the causal variant is backed by remarks such as: „Whenever X has influence over Y, there is some value with regard to which X enjoys a favorable position, and *because of which* he can exercise influence over Y." (83; emphasis added)

Kaplan's terms; in other words, there must be some sort of *demand*, with a severe sanction forthcoming as a response to nonconformity with that demand. All this implies that power is necessarily exercised through some *act* by the power holder.[81]

But no such act seems to be required in an *exercise of influence*. The exercise of influence, Lasswell/Kaplan say, „consists in" an „effect", *not* in an act. In an exercise of influence, the policies of others are affected *not* by anything the influential agent *does*, but merely by what he is *expected* to do. On this view, the *exercise* of influence, it seems, is, or at least can be, triggered somehow merely by „its possession". This means that when someone *has* influence (occupies a high value position or has a high value potential), then – sometimes, somehow (under what circumstances and how, Lasswell/ Kaplan do not specify) – the policies of others are affected *by this very fact* and its effect on those others' expectations *alone*. In particular, this does not seem to be anything the 'possessor' of influence must, or even could, always intentionally control. At least, in Lasswell/Kaplan's text the person who has influence does not necessarily play an active role in its exercise.

Obviously, this view of the exercise of influence is problematic, because speaking of an 'exercise' when in fact no act of the alleged 'exerciser' is involved unnecessarily blurs the distinction between having and exercising an ability and gives rise to serious misunderstandings since it flies in the face of the ordinary, common-sense notion of 'exercise'.[82] And it is even questionable whether this is really the view Lasswell/ Kaplan have in mind, because they themselves contradict these – their own – remarks on the exercise of influence immediately afterwards when in the accompanying footnote (71 f., n. 19) they observe that, alas, the exercise of influence „is itself a policy" – and as we have seen above, a policy is for them a „projected program" or „course of action".[83]

With all this, I have pointed out some of the questions concerning internal consistency to which Lasswell/Kaplan's conception of the relationship between power and influence gives rise. More remarks to the same effect could be made,[84] but those indicated should

[81] This also fits to the authors' earlier assertion that the concept of power „embodie[s]" the fact that „[t]he experiential data of political science are acts considered as affecting or determining other acts" (xiv).

[82] For example, one usually speaks of the *exercise* of a right only in the case of rights *to certain actions*, but *not* in the case of rights *to certain states of affairs*: I can exercise my right to vote, my right to free movement, or my right not to incriminate myself in court, etc.; but it would be very odd to say, for instance, that *I* am *exercising* my constitutional „right to life and physical integrity" (Art. 2 II of the German Basic Law) whenever in interaction with others *they* refrain from killing or hurting me.

[83] In the same footnote, they also make another dubious remark concerning the relationship between the actions of the agents involved in an exercise of influence, when they say that for influence to be exercised it is enough that there is a *correlation* between changes in the two sides' respective policies (i. e., between changes in the „influence-policy" on one side and changes in some policy on the other side). The statement as it stands obviously claims too much since a correlation can at best be a more or less reliable indicator, but never a sure proof of empirical relationships.

[84] To raise only one more point: On p. 203, they state „PROP. Influence varies with power [...]" and go on to explain „The hypothesis states, in other words, that the share of values received by an aggregate depends on its power [...]". Two things can be said to this. First, since for Lasswell/Kaplan power is a sub-category of influence, when there is an increase in power, there is *necessarily* an increase in influence; but this is an *analytically* true statement and therefore no candidate for a 'hypothesis'. Second, if what the authors mean to say is that, in addition to the conceptual relationship, variance in power is *causally* related with variance in some

suffice to support my point, namely that the account these authors give us does not warrant the assessment that they have provided us with a readily identifiable and applicable basis for the distinction between power and influence.

Another question is whether a distinction between influence and power conceiving of influence as the general concept and of power as comprising only those special cases where 'severe' sanctions are involved, if formulated in a precise and consistent way, may perhaps be adequate and useful. The answer to this question must have two different parts, since it involves two concepts. Whether power is adequately defined by reducing it exclusively to cases where sanctions, or 'deprivations', play an essential role has already been extensively discussed in the previous chapter. In the specific context of an attempt to distinguish power and influence, the main objection against such a definition has been reiterated by Dennis Wrong:

„[T]he ability to impose sanctions [...] is certainly an important form of power, but I see no good reason for excluding from an initial definition situations in which someone, whether willingly or even unknowingly, complies with someone else's intention, whether or not the latter is able, or is believed by the former to be able, to impose sanctions." (Wrong 1988, 21)

In fact, even Lasswell and Kaplan themselves, seemingly fierce advocates of a concept of power firmly linked to sanctions, deprivation and coercion,[85] are not entirely consistent on this point: They also define 'authority' as a type of power (1950, 133) – albeit „power of low weight" (ibid., 134). But authority, for them too, has *nothing* to do with coercion, that is, for authority to exist it is irrelevant whether or not means of coercion are available.[86] That such rigourous scholars as Lasswell and Kaplan, whose stated objective it was to avoid conceptual confusion, failed to avoid such an inconsistency in their own conception illustrates just how difficult it is consistently to defend the 'coercion view' of power. But even if one wished to stick to such a definition of power, this would still leave open the question of the definition of influence. In Lasswell/Kaplan, it was easy to see that influence is conceived as more general than power – the 'internal' delimitation *between* the two concepts was more or less clear-cut. But the same cannot be said for the concept of influence itself, i. e., its delimitation from the 'rest of the world'. It may therefore be of help to see whether we can gain more clarity or better criteria by looking at some other proposals.

4. The Intention-Based Distinction: Dennis Wrong

Dennis Wrong, author of a more recent, prominent book-length study of the concept and phenomenon of power and just quoted as opposed to the 'coercion view', has offered an

other kind of influence, this is certainly an empirical hypothesis; but in that case there is another problem with the above propositions. If 'Influence varies with power' can be reformulated („in other words") as 'the share of values received by an aggregate depends on its power', then 'influence' must mean 'share of values received' and 'power' (defined as 'participation in decisions') is, once again, not a sub-category of influence.

[85] Cf. Lasswell/Kaplan 1950, 97, where they practically identify 'coercion' with 'exercise of power'.

[86] On this, cf. my earlier discussion of Kliemt's view, in Chapter 1.2.2.

alternative distinction which, nevertheless, coincides with Lasswell/Kaplan's in that influence is understood as the more general concept and power as a special sub-category of influence.[87] But where Lasswell and Kaplan opted for a distinction in terms of *means*, Wrong instead emphasizes the *effect*, the kind of change induced in the subject of power, when he says:

„I accept [...] Lasswell and Kaplan's view that power is a special case of influence [...], namely, intended as opposed to unintended influence" (23).

„Power is identical with *intended* and effective influence. It is one of two subcategories of influence, the other empirically larger subcategory consisting of acts of *unintended* influence." (4)

With these definitions, Wrong's conception can be classified as belonging into category *(1.b, iii.a)* of *Table 2.1*.[88]

The distinction between unintended influence and intended influence (= power), is the *only* distinction Wrong makes concerning the two concepts. Particularly, it makes no difference for him whether an intended or unintended effect is induced on mental states (attitudes, preferences, desires ...) or actions:

„If A's intention is to affect or alter B's attitudes rather than his behaviour and he succeeds in doing so in the desired direction, then he clearly has power over B to this extent in the relevant scope to which the attitudes refer. If, however, his intention is to produce a particular act by B and he fails to do so, his attempt to exercise power eliciting only an inner disposition on the part of B to comply that is not acted on [...], then he has not exercised power over B but rather unintended influence." (13 f.)

Hence, three different kinds of relations between what an agent *A* does and what another agent *B* thinks or does can be distinguished, of which, according to Wrong, only one is a power situation:

(1) A intentionally attempts to affect something in *B* (a behaviour, an attitude, a preference, a desire ...) and *succeeds* in eliciting the desired reaction; in that case, *A* has exercised power over *B*.

(2) A intentionally attempts to affect something in *B* but *fails* to elicit the desired reaction; in that case, A has *not* exercised power over *B*; but if because of *A*'s intervention, although unintended by *A*, there is some *other* reaction in *B*'s attitudes or behaviour, then *A* has „exercised" influence over *B*.

(3) A has *no intention* to affect *B*, but there is nevertheless a reaction in *B*'s attitudes or behaviour to something *A* does; just as in the previous case, this is a situation

[87] Wrong 1988, to which pages numbers given in this paragraph will refer, unless otherwise indicated.
[88] This classification applies if the focus is on the kind of change induced in the 'influence-receiver'. Alternatively, one could argue that intention is a matter which concerns the *A-element* rather than the *B-element*. I think this is more a matter of perspective than of substance. In any case, Wrong himself, in speaking about intention, clearly emphasizes the aspect of the *effect* over that of the *source* of intentional interventions.

where *A* has an unintended effect on *B* which must therefore (although Wrong does not mention this case explicitly) count as a case of influence of *A* on *B*.[89]

Table 2.2 Wrong's distinction between power and influence

		Effect on B		
		as intended	*other*	*none*
Effect by A	*intended*	**power**	**influence**	(impotence)
	unintended	---	**influence**	---

Since in his study, Wrong is interested primarily in power rather than influence, he has little more to say about the latter. Two points, however, he explicitly makes.

First, he acknowledges that power relationships in his sense, that is, one agent's ability intentionally to affect another's actions or mental states, may often *also* have the (secondary) effect of generating influence that is *not* power. But that, Wrong correctly observes, is no reason to conflate the two very different kinds of phenomena:

„[R]ather than equate power with all forms of influence, unintended as well as intended, it seems preferable to stress the fact that the intentional control of others is likely to create a relationship in which the power holder exercises unintended influence over the power subject that goes far beyond what he may have wished or envisaged at the outset." (4)

The second point Wrong makes concerns the status of „anticipated but unintended by-products" of one agent's actions on another's actions or mental states. The question is whether these are to count as effects of power or of influence. Unfortunately, Wrong's position on this is not clear. According to his own proposal for the distinction between the two concepts, such effects should not count as manifestations of power, since his one and only distinguishing characteristic for an exercise of power is, after all, the existence of the corresponding intention, and an 'anticipated but unintended' effect is certainly no less unintended for being anticipated. Wrong himself seems to endorse this view when he insists that „there is a difference between acting in order to achieve a certain outcome and recognizing that other effects will unavoidably result from the action" and that „an adequate definition of power cannot ignore the difference between intended and unintended but foreseen effects". In the same paragraph, however, Wrong also observes that intentionality is sometimes conceived in a wider sense, comprising both effects that are sought and effects that are merely anticipated. And he then subscribes to this broader notion, saying that „so long as the effects were foreseen by the actor even if not aimed at

89 Note that the difference between power and influence in Wrong's terms is precisely what Lukes has presented (for situations which otherwise satisfy Lukes's additional defining characteristics of power relations) as the difference between 'successful' and merely 'effective' exercises of power (cf. Chapter 1.2.1, p. 45 f.).

as such, they constitute an exercise of power in contrast to unanticipated (and by definition unintended) effects" (5).

Wrong can consistently make this last assertion only if he either changes his criterion for the distinction between influence and power from intention to anticipation, or if he is willing to hold that whatever is anticipated is also necessarily intended. However, nothing in his text suggests that he would agree to either alternative. And in fact I think he has good reason to reject them both. But then an inconsistency remains, which is all the more unfortunate because there really is no need to muddle up the concepts in such a way, in order to accomodate the idea of 'anticipation'. The anticipation of the effects of one's actions, whether intended or unintended, is surely an important aspect, not only when what is at issue is the determination of *responsibility*; it is also relevant in the conceptualization of power relationships in Wrong's sense – but not, as Wrong mistakenly believes, with respect to his criterion for the distinction between power and influence. It seems much more appropriate to regard it, rather, as concerning the distinction between *having* and *exercising* power. Suppose I have power in Wrong's sense over a friend with respect to some attitude *a*; say, I am able successfully to trigger attitude *a* in my friend whenever I attempt to do so. Now suppose whenever that happens it has a 'by-product' *b*, for instance a certain change in another attitude of my friend. Finally, suppose that somehow I become *aware* of the fact that successful attempts of exercising power concerning *a* incidentally also trigger that particular effect of *b*. Once I am aware of this, I *anticipate b* in all my future exercises of power concerning *a*; and because of that anticipation I cannot only be regarded as responsible for bringing about *b* (incidentally) whenever I intentionally intervene on my friend's attitude *a*: I am then *also* able intentionally to trigger *b* as well. Generally, whenever I can *foresee* that some action of mine will inevitably have a certain effect on another, I have the *ability intentionally to bring about* that effect, i. e., I *have power* over the other, in Wrong's sense, with respect to effect *b* (provided, of course, I have the ability and opportunity to perform the corresponding action). Moreover, *unless* I can foresee that certain actions of mine will produce certain effects in another, I neither *have* power to that effect nor can I *exercise* it: I cannot even *attempt* to bring about an *intended* effect if I have no idea what it takes to produce it. This insight is all we need to link power in Wrong's terms to the anticipation of effects: as a *necessary* condition for *having* power. But from this it does not follow that anticipation must also be regarded as a *sufficient* defining characteristic for an *exercise* of power. Quite to the contrary: the relevance of the anticipation of certain effects for having power is an *implication* of defining power as involving *intention*.[90]

[90] The idea that one should speak of an *exercise* of power even in case of an *unintended* effect, as long as it is anticipated, is not only inconsistent with the rest of Wrong's account; it also has another unattractive consequence: it makes a mere change in awareness about an action's effects on others amount to a change in the 'power status' of all instances of that action. This means that with my emerging awareness of the fact that whenever I exercise power over my friend concerning attitude *a* I also trigger effect *b*, and therefore with my subsequent anticipation of effect *b*, my exercises of power become 'overdetermined': they are (and were) exercises of power because my action succeeds in bringing about *a*, but they are now *also* exercises of power because I *know* (which I did not before) that my action brings about effect *b* (which it always did). The 'power status' of effect *b* thus has changed not because of something I *do*, but merely because of my change of awareness. What was influence before has become power merely because I have *learned* something about it. Now, what happens if there is no attitude *a* which I can intentionally bring about and of which effect *b* is a

However, that one does not need to give up intentionality as a distinguishing criterion between power and influence in order to accomodate the idea of anticipation, says nothing about whether or not there are any good reasons to adopt it. What can be said in favour of the intentionality criterion? I think there are several aspects which make it look attractive, at least for anyone who shares the basic conception of influence as the more general concept and power as a subclass of it. The first is that it makes for a broad concept of power which does not *per definitionem* exclude any situations merely on account of the kind of resources such a relationship is based on.[91] Rather, it leaves room for the distinction of different subcategories within the broader field of power.[92] Second, it caters to all those views which, in one way or another, see power as intimately linked to (social) control, to the imposition of one's will in social interaction, to compliance and conformity, and/or which hold that the exercise of power is always a matter of the power-holder's *choice*, that it creates responsibility and requires justification.[93] Third, the intentionality criterion also takes care of the fact that in ordinary usage we intuitively make just that distinction and speak of influence, but not power in cases where one agent's actions unintentionally affect another's attitudes or actions: That millions of fans emulate the behaviour of a popstar is commonly attributed to the fact that the latter has *influenced* the former, and observed changes in fan behaviour seem to be regarded as sufficient evidence to support such a claim – no inference about the popstars likely intentions seems to be thought necessary.[94] In contrast, if someone were to maintain instead that the change in fan behaviour is a result of the popstar having *exercised power*

side effect? What if there is only effect *b*, which I learn to anticipate? It would not be plausible to reason that anticipation is a sufficient condition for linking an effect to an exercise of power only in case it is a 'by-product', since no effect is a 'by-product' as such. The existence of a 'by-product' *implies* the existence of an intended effect, and in that case, as we have just seen, anticipation is not needed as a criterion for the identification of exercises of power. Hence, whether anticipation is an adequate or plausible criterion becomes apparent only if we look at self-standing effects which are *not* by-products of any other, intended effect. If anticipation were *all* that is needed for an effect to be a manifestation of an exercise of power, then one would have to say that *before* I became aware of it, I never exercised power over my friend in bringing about effect *b* in him, but since I learned to anticipate effect *b*, I exercise power over him every time I perform the corresponding action and therefore effect *b* is produced. I may be indifferent about it, and I may even hate to bring about that effect – it would still have to count as an exercise of power. Moreover, it would *make no difference* whether it is my intention to bring it about or whether I hate it. I may sometimes find the effect undesirable and merely be unable to avoid it, and on other occasions find it desirable and successfully attempt to bring it about: *qua* exercises of power the two cases could not be distinguished. The redefinition of the distinction between *exercises* of power and of influence along the lines of anticipation instead of intention would thus result in a very odd conception of power which blurs important differences of social interactions.

91 As we have seen, narrowness was Wrong's main objection against Lasswell/Kaplan's proposal; and it was also a recurrent issue in the previous chapter.

92 Wrong, for example, distinguishes four „forms" of power. One of them is authority which Wrong, unlike Lasswell and Kaplan, has no problem to accomodate consistently as a subcategory of power. Cf. Wrong 1988, 24, for an instructive tree diagram depicting his conception of the relations between the different kinds of influence, the different forms of power, and the different subtypes of these forms.

93 Practically all the views about the concept of power treated so far, in this and the previous chapter, regard one or more of these conditions as necessary characteristics of exercises of power.

94 On this, cf. the literature on social learning, particularly recent works on fashion, fads, and 'informational cascades' for an (implicit) conception of influence as purely causal and not involving an intentional exercise by any agent: Bikhchandani/Hirshleifer/Welch 1992, 1998, Hirshleifer 1993.

over them, one would indeed expect that claim to be based on a different kind of evidence, namely, evidence to the effect that the change is something the popstar provoked intentionally. Finally, it is perhaps also an advantage of the intentionality criterion that concerning *both* power and influence it does not preclude any possible constellation of the subject's awareness of the situation. A subject may or may not realize that power is being exercised over her, and she may also realize or ignore that she is under someone's influence.

These are arguments which speak quite strongly in favour of the plausibility and usefulness of the intentionality criterion. Some time ago, I myself found them convincing enough to adopt this distinction in another work.[95] Meanwhile, however, I have come to think that this was not a good idea. The reason why I now think that the intentionality criterion is inappropriate is that it defines out of existence the possibility of *intentional influence* which, nevertheless, stops short of being power. The result is a concept of influence which runs very much counter to ordinary usage. One indicator of this is that it is not at all uncommon to speak of *exercises* of influence. But the concept of exercise itself already implies that a purposeful, intentional action is involved. The result of an 'exercise' is not something that merely happens to the exerciser inadvertently or that he even suffers against his will. Wrong's repeated talk of the 'exercise of unintended influence' in the passages cited above therefore has a strange ring.

5. The Normativity-Based Distinction: Ingmar Pörn

If not intentionality, then what? An interesting, rather uncommon alternative criterion for the conceptual distinction between power and influence has been proposed by Ingmar Pörn (1970) and similarly, but less explicitly, by Joseph Raz (1990b).

For the former, power seems to be the more general concept. Power, in his view, can be divided into two subgroups, and one of these is influence. Hence, the proposal apparently belongs into category *(1.a)* and as such is not yet very unusual. But what is unusual is the criterion Pörn chooses for the division of the two types of power he acknowledges: on the one hand, he says, there is *normative power*, defined „in terms of making actions punishable“;[96] and on the other, there is *influence*, which encompasses *all* power phenomena outside of the normative realm (68). Influence can therefore, in turn, come in the forms of „non-coercive (persuasive, suggestive, moral power) and coercive control“.[97]

But, actually, Pörn does not identify influence and control. Rather, influence is for him the broader concept, containing eight basic types, only four of which are types of control (18 f.): 'Control' takes place when some *t* brings it about that some *u* does

[95] Zimmerling 1991, 185 ff.

[96] Pörn dedicates a chapter of his book (ch. 3) to a detailed account of what normative power, punishability, etc. amount to. This is based largely on the work of Felix Oppenheim, whose idea of punishability I will present and criticize in Chapter 3.1.

[97] Ibid., also p. 17; in n. 1 on p. 18, he acknowledges that his 'non-coercive control' is what Oppenheim calls 'influence'.

(does not) bring it about that *p* (not-*p*). These are the four cases of what Pörn calls 'production', 'counter-production', 'prevention' and 'counter-prevention'.

Influence, in turn, also takes place, additionally, when *t* refrains from doing any of this, i. e., it encompasses four more cases: 'toleration' and 'counter-toleration', as well as 'leave' and 'counter-leave'.

It is not entirely clear in Pörn's account whether the fact that influence includes control as well as four other, non-control cases implies that, in fact, influence is not really a subtype of power, after all. In other words, I am not sure whether only the four cases of influence that fall under the heading 'control' are, in his view, at the same time cases of power, and the other four, non-control cases are 'mere' influence, or whether all the eight kinds of influence distinguished by Pörn are thought to belong into the 'power' category. Therefore, my classification of Pörn's proposal into category *(1.a)* may be based on a misunderstanding. If that is the case, then Pörn's view would be exceptional, in that it would assume *neither* complementarity *nor* some relationship of sub- and superordination between power and influence, but rather a partial overlap – a possibility not taken into account in my *Table 2.1*.

In any case, regardless of whether influence is thought to be contained entirely in the broader category of power, or whether the two merely overlap, making *all* cases of control *both* cases of power *and* of influence, Pörn's is certainly a very idiosyncratic view which fares badly if assessed with a view towards established usage, since it is one more of those proposals according to which one could not have or exercise (non-normative) power without at the same time also having or exercising influence.

The very same objection also applies to Joseph Raz's account of the conceptual difference between power and influence. Raz seems to know only two things: normative power, on the one hand, and influence, on the other, where, again, influence is apparently regarded as being a subtype of power in the social sense:

„Influence is exercised by affecting people's reasons for action and their beliefs in them. One typical way in which influence is manifested is by manipulating the circumstances so as to make the realization of certain goals more difficult relative to others [...] Such actions exercise an influence because they change the balance of reasons for or against certain actions, but they are not the exercise of normative powers [...] influence is exercised not only by control over the means by which people must realize their goals. Influence includes the power to affect the goals people have, their desires and aspirations [...] Influence, therefore, need not be power over auxiliary reasons only. It includes power over operative reasons. Normative power, also, includes both power over operative and over auxiliary reasons. Power to enact a mandatory norm is power to create a new operative reason. Power to sell property affects only auxiliary reasons." (Raz 1990b, 99)

Obviously, Raz here mixes up two very different kinds of things which it seems wise to keep conceptually apart, namely, the ability to affect what others believe (about what the world *is* like or *should* be like), on the one hand, and the ability to affect what the world of others is actually like and, thereby, the circumstances under which they will have to perform whatever actions they decide to take.

It is probably the fact that both Pörn and Raz are interested in normative power rather than in the residual category they call 'influence' whicht explains why these authors have not made more of an effort to arrive at a conceptual proposal for the notion of influence that would not be too inconvenient, considering our normal way of talking.

6. Assorted Other Views

We have so far seen several views, held by some prominent advocates, which are, in some sense, special:

(1) The *power-as-ability-to-influence view* (Cartwright, Cassinelli, Katz/Lazarsfeld, French et al., Kliemt) is the *only* variant I am aware of where the 'mode' – ability or exercise – is made the decisive criterion for distinguishing between power and influence. In other words, there are, to my knowledge, no other entries for category *(i)* in *Table 2.1*.[98]

(2) The view that influence is *more general* than power (conforming with category *(1.b)* of the table) is, as far as I know, also held only in the two variants treated above: the *sanction-based* and the *intention-based* view. For each one of them, I have analysed the position of the most prominent advocate I am aware of (Lasswell/Kaplan for the former, and Wrong for the latter).

(3) Another possible conception for which some, but not very many authors have opted, is that of understanding influence as a special case of the more encompassing class of power. In that category, I have been able to find only examples for subtype *(ii)*, i. e., variants of a distinction between power as the more general and influence as the narrower concept based on the type of means on which the respective relationships rely: on *(a)* sanctions, *(b)* persuasion, or *(c)* normative competence. I have presented above only examples of the last of these variants, as they seem to me to be the most peculiar. But the objection I have formulated against them was more general, applying equally to all the other possible subtypes of category *(1.a)*.[99]

What is left now from the categories listed in *Table 2.1* are only conceptions according to which power and influence are *mutually exclusive, complementary* concepts.

(4) Of that larger category, subtype *(i)* has already been taken care of (in Sect. 2 of this chapter, as well as in paragraph *(2)* above).

98 Which does not mean, of course, that there are no other authors who share the power-as-ability-to-influence view; one can find remarks in Harsanyi 1962a/b, Olson 1982, Bernholz/Breyer 1994, or Pettit 1997, to name but a few, which seem to indicate adherence to the same view.

99 An example of a conception of type *(1.a.ii.a)* is perhaps – although that is far from easy to determine – that of the later Luhmann: „By presenting a prospect of sanctions, one can get others to do something they would otherwise not do. This too is still unmediated power [...] But the *restriction* to the production of a behaviour of others means an *increase* in power. We will call this, still very broad, form of power *influence* [...] influence forms of this kind [...] can naturally also occur ad hoc and just once – for instance in the form of a robbery" (Luhmann 2000, 39 f.; my translation). That robbery should be regarded as a matter of 'influencing' seems, to say the least, surprising.
As a defender of a conception of type *(1.a.ii.b)* one can mention Oppenheim (1981).
Kersting's (1991) conception seems to belong somewhere into category *(1.a)*, but it is difficult to say exactly where.

(5) That leaves us, first of all, with subcategory *(2.ii)* of those cases in which power and influence are understood to operate with mutually exclusive classes of means, establishing different kinds of relationships between the agents involved. This category can here be treated very briefly. Two variants of it can be found in the literature, both of them relatively frequent.

– One is the distinction on the line of *sanctions (ii.a)*: if and only if sanctions are involved, it – where this 'it' can be any of a variety of things: changes of behaviour, attitude, opinion, belief, etc., depending on the specific basic definition (which is often not made explicit) – is said to constitute a case of power; otherwise, it is taken to be influence.[100]

– The other variant proposes as a dividing line that of *persuasion (ii.b)*: here, the fixed point is influence, which is said to be involved if and only if 'it' is based on persuasion; otherwise, it is a case of power.[101]

I will not spell out in detail any of the proposals for such conceptions, which can be more or less (mostly less) explicitly found in the literature. The picture presented in the preceding sections, regarding the clarity, precision, and consistency of the analysed conceptions, would only be repeated – I will spare myself and the reader that futile exercise.

In any case, there is a fundamental objection that can be brought forward against all these conceptions: their proposed cut-off points lead to *overly narrow* concepts on the 'fixed' side of the respective pair. When power is conceived exclusively in terms of sanctions, for instance, the important class of *authority* is defined out of the realm of power and into that of influence. That is clearly against much scholarly usage. In any case, if thought to be appropriate, it would have to be argued for. And when influence is conceived exclusively in terms of persuasion, similarly, easily imaginable kinds of relationships that would be regarded by most – laymen and scholars alike – to have something to do with influence, drop out of the picture; this is the case, for instance, with all

100 Representatives of such a conception are (perhaps – remember that in many cases the underlying conceptions are not explicitly presented or discussed, and sometimes they are not consistently held): Bachrach/Baratz 1963, Moscovici 1979, Parsons 1963, Habermas 1988, Hoffmann-Lange 1992. In most cases, by 'sanctions' authors mean negative sanctions, 'deprivations' of some sort; sometimes, however, the possibility of positive sanctions is also taken into account. One such proposal is to distinguish power from influence specifically on that line: „It is appropriate [...] to distinguish between power and influence, the first to mean the ability to move others by the threat or infliction of deprivations, the latter to mean the ability to do so through promises or grants or benefits." (Wolfers 1962, 103; quoted by Rothgeb 1992, 18).

101 With the same proviso as in the previous note, I venture to classify into this category the conceptions of, e. g., Etzioni 1968, 359 f.; 1993, 27; Connolly 1983b; perhaps also Habermas 1988. Connolly contributes an instructive example for the importance of precise distinctions: „What is it we are saying one has, does, or exercises when we attribute to him *power* of a magnitude x, with respect to scope y, over domain z? What changes in meaning occur, if any, when the predicate power is replaced in statements of this sort by predicates such as authority, persuasion, or influence? The statement, 'Colonel House's *power* derived not from any constitutional *authority* but from his *influence* over President Wilson,' changes its meaning when we scramble the underlined terms to read 'Colonel House's *authority* derived not from any constitutional *influence* but from his *power* over President Wilson.' [...] the clause about his constitutional influence hovers on the edge of incoherence" (Connolly 1983b, 86); he then explains that the first form, persuasion, is not a case of an exercise of power *if* persuasion is based on arguments given in good faith and the 'receiving end' freely and on his own conviction chooses his posterior action: under those circumstances, „instances of persuasion are not instances of power" (ibid., 88).

those 'influences' based not on persuasion, but on what one can call *veneration* or *deference* (the already mentioned fashions and fads inadvertently induced by popstars, for example). Sometimes, authors even subscribe to both subcategories at the same time, so that not everything that is defined out of power can find refuge under the concept of influence, and *vice versa*. Therefore, I think that this way of splitting the difference between power and influence simply cannot result in a fully satisfactory solution.

(6) So the very last category that remains unanalysed at this point is that of conceiving of power and influence in a way that gives them mutually exclusive extensions, where the criterion of distinction is found by *focusing on the subject's side* of the relationship, more specifically, on *what kind of impact* is made on that side. Considering that we are interested in *social* phenomena which do 'make a difference', and in relationships on both sides of which – we should assume – we are dealing with *agents*, who ground their choices on *reasons*, this approach seems to me to be, in principle, the most promising.

For a complementarity view, however, the first option given in the table (category *iii.a*: a distinction according to whether the change induced in the subject is or is not the one *intended* by the other side) does not seem to make much sense, for the same reason that this version was already rejected for the subordination view – that it would imply that there can be no intended influence; whenever an intentional influence attempt would be effective, it would by definition have to be understood as a case of power.[102]

As for the second version listed in the table (category *iii.b*: a distinction between power and influence depending on whether the impact made on the subject is induced by an effect on empirical *facts* or on the subject's *opinions*), its adequacy can be questioned on the grounds that, again, impact by *authority* would by definition fall outside of the boundaries of power.[103]

The third variant *(iii.c)*, in turn, which distinguishes between influence and power by looking at whether or not the subject's interests are negatively affected, seems to be the option adopted by Steven Lukes (1974).[104] As indicated already in the previous chapter, this view has the inconvenience that it excludes by definition the possibility that power might also be used precisely to *further* some interest of the subject.

102 However, a kernel of correct insight seems to be contained in that thought. I will come back to this in the proposal formulated in the next section.

103 Some of the things said by Etzioni (1968, 359 f.; 1993, 27), as well as some of those said by Parsons (1967, esp. 361) can perhaps be interpreted on the lines of this distinction between power and influence.

104 This is evident, for example, in his argument against Parsons's and Arendt's conceptions: „According to the conceptual scheme here [i. e., in Lukes's own analysis] advanced, all such cases of co-operative activity, where individuals or groups significantly affect one another *in the absence of a conflict of interests* between them, will be identificable, as cases of 'influence' but not of 'power'. All that Parsons and Arendt wish to say about consensual behaviour remains sayable, but so also does all that they wish to remove from the language of power" (Lukes 1974, 31; emphasis added). However, again, the record is not clear, because Lukes *also* distinguishes between influence and power on the lines of category *2.ii.a*; in fact, he acknowledges that there are „contradictory conceptual pressures" pushing in both directions: „It will be seen that in this scheme power may or may not be a form of influence – depending on whether sanctions are involved; while influence and authority may or may not be a form of power – depending on whether a conflict of interests is involved" (ibid., 32).

And a similar argument seems to apply also to that other variant which does distinguish between the two according to an effect not on interest, but on *freedom* (category *iii.e*).[105]

The remaining variant of the category under review here *(2.iii.d)*, I will not say anything about at this point, since I hold it to be interesting enough to dedicate the next subsection to it.

(7) But before concluding this very cursory panorama of different, on the whole not very plausible ways of going about the distinction between power and influence, for the sake of completeness it must be mentioned that besides the categories listed in my table, and those perhaps useful other categories that might exist and have slipped me by, there is also another basket, of considerable size, containing contributions to the power-influence discussion which I have found myself unable to classify, either because the proposals have a chameleon-like nature, changing freely from one type of distinction to another; or because, at least for my intellectual capacity, they are too confusing.[106]

7. A Subject-Centered View: Mokken and Stokman

The last proposal for a distinction between the concepts of influence and power I will present has been offered, almost three decades ago, by R. J. Mokken and F. N. Stokman, in an article first published in Dutch and shortly thereafter in English (1975). This is a proposal of a conception which can be classified into that last category of *Table 2.1* the consideration of which was still outstanding, that is, category *2.iii.d.* The title of their article promises an analysis of 'Power and Influence', and the authors fully comply with that promise. It is, in my view, until today one of the very best contributions ever published on the topic.

In the present context, it is of some interest that before presenting their own account of how the two concepts should best be understood, the authors explicitly reject *(a)* the power-as-ability-to-influence view, but also *(b)* the sub-/superordination view, in all its possible configurations (36 f.).[107] Instead, they opt for their own particular version of a complementarity view, by defining *both* power and influence, primarily, as *abilities*, but as abilities to do different things, namely, to determine the *elements* of the

105 Although he has not spelled it out, because it was not his particular subject, such might perhaps be the view of someone like Kristján Kristjánsson (1996), for whom – as will be shown in Chapter 3.3 – power and unfreedom are intimately related. Another author who takes freedom into account as a criterion for the distinction between power and influence is Peter Koller (1991). But Koller's is also one of those cases which do not fit easily into the, perhaps overly rigid, frame of *Table 2.1*. He in some way combines a conception along the lines of *iii.e* and *ii.a* with the view that there is a partial overlap of power and influence, both of which are special cases of the more general notion of 'control'.

106 The former is the case, e. g., of Laumann/Knoke 1987, ch. 5, where I have identified at least five of the alternatives given in *Table 2.1*, as well as of Luhmann (2000, esp. ch. 2 and the beginning of ch. 3), especially if one tries to collate this with his earlier work (Luhmann 1975). And as to the latter, I have attempted to take into account, but failed to understand, the proposals of Meier 1979 and Sullivan 1990.

107 Leaving, in terms of *Table 2.1*, only categories *2.ii* and *2.iii* as feasible options.

choice menu of another, in the former, and to determine *which* option from the menu, once it is fixed, is chosen, in the latter case. Hence, in their view, power is

„the possibilitiy to restrict or expand freedom of action, or the capacity to preserve that freedom to a given degree [...] the capacity of actors (persons, groups or institutions) to fix or to change (completely or partly) a set of action alternatives or choice alternatives for other actors“ (37; also 46),

whereas influence is

„the possibility to determine the outcomes of the behaviour of others, without the restriction or expansion of their freedom of action [...] the capacity of actors to determine (partly) the actions or choices of other actors within the set of action or choice alternatives available to those actors.“ (37; 46).

One consequence of these definitions is that power and influence can exist in complete independence of each other. And from the definition, it also follows right away that influence, just like power, can be exercised, and that the *exercise of influence* is linked to a special type of means:

„The exercise of influence takes place mainly by means of persuasion, information and advice. The most important, if not the only, source of influence is in particular associated with strategic locations in the communication and information networks that other actors use for the determination of their behaviour.“ (37)

Power and influence thus defined can also mutually be sources of each other (38):

„*Power itself can be a source of influence [...] Influence can also be a source of power*. This is the case where an actor has a particular influence relation with an actor who holds a position of power with respect to other actors.“ (38)

Note that this is not the same as the *transformation* of influence (or power) into power (or influence) (38 f.):

(1) Power is a *source* of influence when the position of power (i. e., the ability to determine some agents' sets of alternatives) someone has over others is the *motive* for *someone else* to let himself be influenced.[108] (There is then influence in addition to power.)

(2) Influence is a *source* of power in the following constellation: When *A* has *influence* over *B*, and *B* has *power* over *C*, then this gives *A* power over *C* (because *A* can then determine which set of alternatives *B* will determine for *C*, i. e., *A* can indirectly determine *C*'s set of alternatives, by way of determining what *B* does).[109] (A then has power in addition to influence.)

(3) In contrast, influence is *transformed* into power when, for example,[110] an *expert* who is supposed to recommend which decision from a *given* set of alternatives should be taken (in other words: who is conceded *influence*) ends up being able to deter-

108 Mokken/Stokman specifically mention Friedrich's 'law of anticipated reactions' in this context (38, 47).

109 Mokken/Stokman here mention the role of an *éminence grise* (38, 47).

110 The authors' examples are more specific, but seen more generally, they amount to what I am saying.

mine even the set of alternatives from which the final decision is chosen, because only the alternatives he presents to them are taken into account by official decision-makers (that is, he acquires *power*).[111]

(4) Finally, power is *transformed* into influence analogously.[112]

Next, Mokken/Stokman approach the issue of defining specifically *political* power and influence. They note that while sociological approaches have preferred a definition of political power and influence as a special case of the general concepts, influential political scientists have defined power as the matter that distinguishes 'politics' proper from all other subjects (47). The authors think it more plausible to follow the sociological lead. Thus, for them, political power and influence are simply power and influence when they occur in the political sphere, which, in turn, is delineated following Easton's definition (48). Hence, they define *political power* as

„the capacity to fix or to change (partly) a set of alternative value allocations for the members of [a social] system or for parts of it" (49.)

And *political influence*, accordingly, is

„the capacity to determine (partly) within a given set of available alternative value allocations the outcomes of the allocation process" (ibid.).

Concerning political power, they note that besides the „availability of sanctions (positive or negative value allocations) that determine the alternatives open to actors", the instrument of *non-decisions* – which comes in two versions: *non-initiation* (on the „input side", i. e., the agenda-setting process) and *non-implementation* (on the „output side") – is of special importance.

On the other hand, with respect to political influence, Mokken/Stokman observe that it „is strongly associated with the effective aggregation and organization of information, intelligence and expertise and the availability of good opportunities for access to levels of decision-making" (ibid.).

Finally, they also consider the relation between power and influence particularly for the political realm:

„When the political influence of an actor or group achieves a one-sided character in comparison with that of other actors, that influence can be a source of power or it can be converted into power." (ibid.)

Finally, if political influence depends on access and expertise, as has just been said, it can arise on two grounds: either *privileged access* or *privileged information.*[113]

[111] In fact, if there is really a transformation from one into the other, in the end influence should have become power, i. e., there should then no longer be influence. In the case of the expert, it seems that the power acquired then exists *in addition* to the influence, which remains the same as before. The main difference between influence as a source of and influence 'transformed into' power seems to be that in the former case, someone has influence over *one* and power over *another* agent, whereas in the latter case, influence and power are held over the *same* agent.

[112] On this case, the authors' example unfortunately is not very clear.

[113] For both aspects, communication is of fundamental relevance. The authors therefore emphasize a point which at their time of writing (except for some work done by K. W. Deutsch) they found lacking in the literature, to wit: „that positions of power and especially of influence can be traced in the form of critical positions in interaction and communication networks" (50).

So much for Mokken/Stokman's interesting proposal for the distinction between power and influence, in their general social and in their specific political varieties. On the whole, this is arguably the most plausible and consistent approach I have so far come across.[114] It does, however, have one major inconvenience: it defines influence in an overly narrow way, capturing only a small part of what we would usually be willing to call by that name. To use an example already mentioned earlier: it is perfectly common to ascribe influence – sometimes great amounts of it – to the dead. But to say that the dead have the ability 'to determine the outcomes of the behaviour of others' would surely be claiming too much. Therefore, in the last instance, though it contains a number of helpful distinctions and ideas, Mokken/Stokman's conception too cannot be taken as the last word on the subject.

8. A Proposal

In the light of all we have seen so far – particularly, the problems encountered with the different approaches treated above –, it seems to me best compatible with ordinary usage and most useful for theoretical purposes to distinguish between power and influence in such a way as to conceive of them as two *disjoint* categories (i. e., not as two concepts linked by way of super- and subordination), in the following way:

(1) social *power* defined as the ability to *get desired outcomes* by making others *do* what one wants, i. e., by somehow (no matter how) imposing one's own *preferences* on them;

(2) social *influence*, in contrast, defined as the 'ability' to affect others' *beliefs*, that is, their knowledgte or opinions either about what *is* or about what *ought* to be the case, about what is (empirically) true or false or what is (normatively) right or wrong, good or bad, desirable or undesirable.[115]

114 Another proposal that seems to go somewhat into the same direction, although it is not formulated in terms of influence as opposed to power, has more recently been presented by Peter Baumann (1993). Baumann develops a conception of a type of power which, he argues, has been unduly neglected in the past. In contrast to what is usually taken to constitute the „standard case" of social power, namely: the power to sanction *(Sanktionsmacht)*, he makes a case for another, if not *the* standard case of social power, which he calls the 'power of motivation' *(Motivationsmacht)* (160). In an attempt to overcome particularly the defects (above all, the vagueness and indeterminacy) of Lukes's third face of power, and taking into account some useful aspects of what in sociology has become known as the 'power' to define the situation *(Definitionsmacht)*, he develops his concept of the power of motivation. Roughly, the power of motivation is the ability to modify the „desires and preferences" of an agent, whereas the power to sanction can only operate on an agent's „action goals" by shaping his assessment of his external situation, *given* his desires and preferences (27 f.).

115 Concerning the normative side, we also often speak of 'attitudes' or 'judgements'. For simplicity's sake, here I will stick with the term 'normative beliefs'.

Perhaps the most important difference between power and influence thus understood is that in the case of power, there is a direct *conceptual* link (though, of course, *not* a direct *causal* link) between a power-holders *will* and a power subject's *actions*, whereas in influence, there is no such direct conceptual link with either one of the two components.

8.1. RELATIONSHIPS BETWEEN ACTIONS, PREFERENCES, AND BELIEFS

Choices of (purposeful) *action*, very generally, involve an assessment of one's *preferences* (concerning outcomes) *given* one's *beliefs* about which options are available and what their respective properties (among them, their expected consequences) are.

If power is linked to (choice of) action, and influence is linked to belief, then we can see how power and influence are interrelated in social life only if we first sort out the relationships between actions, preferences, and beliefs. In a very rough outline, I think at least the following can be said:

– *Preferences* (concerning outcomes) alone are not sufficient to determine the choice of a purposeful action: if I want to act on my preferences, I must at least have some idea about what that requires, about what I can and/or must do in order to satisfy my preferences, and this means that I must have some beliefs (about how the world *is*, i. e., about what 'is the case' at a given moment, and about how a preferred outcome can be brought about, or preserved, or how an unwanted outcome can be avoided, from the given starting point).

– With *beliefs*, the matter is not quite so simple, since here we must distinguish what kind of belief is at issue:

- Beliefs about how the world *is*, likewise, cannot by themselves determine a purposeful choice of action; empirical beliefs alone do not provide one with a purpose; in addition to the belief, one must also have some kind of preference concerning different possible states of affairs.
- Beliefs about how the world *ought to be*, in contrast, come with an 'in-built' preference, so to speak: if I firmly believe that the state of the world should be x, instead of y or z, then obviously this means that I have a preference for x over y and z. But again, as observed above, even if a preference for an outcome is motivated by such a normative belief, this can only lead to purposeful action if it is combined with some empirical belief about how the world actually is.

It is psychologically possible (and perhaps not even uncommon) that *preferences affect beliefs*; an example would be what is called 'wishful thinking'. This may concern both empirical and normative beliefs; but, again, there seems to be a difference between the two cases:

- To change an empirical belief (about how the world is) merely on the basis of a (change of) preference can never be rational. Rather, such changes, if they occur, are clearly due to a defect in reasoning. Hence, they cannot be brought about by another's reasoning, except perhaps in some rare case where a person is known to suffer systematically from such a defect. For most persons, however, 'wishful thinking' is due only to a slippage in their usual reasoning capacity rather than to a systematic defect. It is not a mechanism on which anyone could generally count for intentionally inducing changes of beliefs in others.

- By contrast, a radically egoistical theory which holds that the world ought to be as one wants it to be (and that, therefore, one may do whatever one wishes to do) is 'rationally' conceivable (whether it is reasonable, or ethically attractive, is another matter). For someone who holds such an 'ultimate' normative belief, it is quite possible that his preferences consistently affect his normative beliefs. In such a case, therefore, it is also systematically possible intentionally to induce a change of belief simply by bringing about an external change which affects the agent's preferences.

Much more common and plausible, however, is the inverse relationship, of *beliefs affecting preferences*:

- *Empirical* beliefs inform us, among other things, about what is possible, and thus a change of belief may, for instance, induce us to abandon preferences for something we have come to believe impossible to attain. More precisely, it may not be able to eliminate our craving for something we believe to be impossible, but the belief may in any case stop us from turning this craving into an 'effective preference' which actually affects our choice of action.
- *Normative* beliefs, likewise, may keep us from pursuing certain outcomes, and induce us to pursue others.

These points are important for the interplay of power and influence:

(I) If power is to be exercised in order to get another to act in a certain way, this can be achieved by affecting either one, or both, of the two elements necessary to determine a choice of action, i. e., *power* can be *exercised* in the following ways:

1. by *affecting* an existing *state of affairs* (constraints, incentives) in such a way that, given another's normative and empirical beliefs, there is a *change in* his *effective preferences* which induces him to act in the desired way (e. g., by a threat of sanction, an offer of reward, by a manipulation of existing resources or some other way of changing the external environment);

2. by *affecting* someone's *empirical beliefs* in such a way that, given his normative beliefs and his preferences, he will come to believe the action desired by the other to be best suited to satisfy his own preferences (e. g., by giving – true or false – information about *technical* matters);

3. by *affecting* someone's *normative beliefs* in such a way that, given his empirical beliefs and his preferences, he will come to believe that the desired action is one he *may* – or is *the* one he *must* – perform.

Taking this into consideration, the proposed distinction can account for the common (though usually unreflected, rather intuitive) view that *one can exercise power through exercising influence*: Since, according to the proposed concept of influence, options 2. and 3. are instances of an exercise of influence, it follows that the exercise of (a very *specific*, *intentional*) influence can be a potentially effective way of exercising power.[116] Note, however, that this does *not* mean that in those instances power and influence are the *same*: they involve different things (*action* in the case of power, *belief* in the case of influence), i. e., they always move in different spheres. It is just that one (the exercise of influence) can be *used* as a means for the other (the exercise of power).

(II) To *have power* (over someone with respect to something), on the other hand, means: to have the *ability* to 'get what one wants' (from that other, within a certain range) by doing, intentionally, any of the things that constitute an exercise of power.

(III) With *influence*, matters are more complicated. Let us first look at the *exercise* of *influence*: Much depends on how broad or narrow an understanding of 'exercise' one has.

- The narrow view would be to understand speaking of an 'exercise' of something as referring exclusively to conscious, intentional action leading to an intended outcome (besides, possibly, any number of unintended consequences). An 'exercise of influence' on this view would mean an *intentional* and *successful* attempt to affect another's beliefs – successful in the sense of leading not to just *any* change of belief, but precisely to the *intended* one (*example*: *A* wants to convince *B* that his belief in *x* is wrong and that instead *y* is true, and therefore brings forward an argument in favour of the truth of *y* which succeeds in changing *B*'s empirical belief from *x* to *y*).
- The broad view, in turn, would be to understand an 'exercise of influence' to mean any occasion at all in which influence actually takes place, i. e., in which something one agent does *somehow* affects another's beliefs. Besides the cases covered by the narrow view, this would additionally include:

(i) all cases in which, although there is an intention of the influencer involved, the intention is *not successful*, but there is instead another, unintended

[116] One can, in other words, (attempt to) use influence strategically, to elicit particular, desired (re-)actions from others. The *Office of Strategic Influence* (O. S. I.) created by the Pentagon shortly after 9/11 to „bring much-needed coordination to the military's efforts to influence views of the United States overseas" was, it can be assumed, intended to do precisely this. Its task was certainly to influence, in the sense defined above; but the ultimate goal was to make certain foreign actors perform, or forbear, certain kinds of actions through this influence. About the tasks and purposes of the O. S. I., cf., e. g., Dao/Schmitt 2002.

effect on the influenced's beliefs (*example*: *A* wants to convince *B* that his belief in *x* is wrong and that *y* is true instead, and therefore brings forward an argument in favour of the truth of *y*, but rather than succeeding to change *B*'s belief from *x* to *y*, what *A*'s argument actually does is convince *B* that both *x* and *y* are wrong); and

(ii) all cases in which, although the influencer does not in any way intend to induce any change in another's beliefs, such a change in fact occurs (*example*: *B* sees how *A*, in whose mental capacities he has great confidence, fervently practices her belief in *y*; *B*, who until now believed in *x*, therefore changes his belief and begins to believe in *y* too).[117]

Perhaps it is merely a matter of taste and intuition rather than one of substance which of the two options one adopts. I myself am more inclined to the former, that is, to restricting the meaning of *'exercise of influence'* to cases where a change in someone's belief is brought about by another's intentional attempt, and to distinguish the other cases from this by using different expressions, such as saying that someone has been (or is) actually *influential*. This has the advantage of *(a)* indicating through language whether the influencer plays a more active or a more passive role in a process of influence, and *(b)* of matching language for the cases of influence and of power: only in the narrow sense of 'exercise' can one say that if someone has the *ability to exercise influence* he can use this ability for the exercise of power; by contrast, if someone is *influential*, but does not know how to *exercise* influence, then his influence is not available to him as an actual means for the exercise of power. It seems helpful in order to avoid conceptual confusion to provide for linguistic means to express these differences from the start, instead of initially calling everything an 'exercise of influence' and then having to sort out the different cases and implications of such exercises.

(IV) Because *effective influence* comes in the two distinguished forms, as the result of *intentional and successful exercises* of influence, and as *unintended influence*, there must also be two different categories of the *'possession'* of influence:

- the first is *having influence* in the sense of the *ability to exercise influence*;

[117] For an illustration of the different examples, assume that *x*, *y* and *z* are religions. The first case, of an intended and successful exercise of influence, could be that of someone who converts from one religion to another as a consequence of a friend's convincing attempts to bring about this change. The second example, of influence taking place, but not as it is intended by the influencer, could be that of a person who, always having believed in one particular religion, suddenly realizes, by being exposed to a friend's attempts to convince him of the truth of another religion, that his friend's arguments in favour of the latter are just as circular as those he himself could bring forward in favour of the former, and that moreover this is necessarily so for *all* possible religons, and therefore not only abandons the religious belief he held before, but also henceforth believes that *all* religions are mere superstitions; in such a case, recalling the proposal made by Steven Lukes concerning power, one could say that the friend did have an *effective* influence although he has not been successful in his influence attempt. The third case, finally, could be that of a non-believer who through observing the conduct of a firm believer in a particular religion (say, by watching a documentary feature about that person on television), comes to believe that this religion must really be true. The new believer could then plausibly say that the protagonist of the movie has exerted great influence on him, although this is not known to, nor was it intended by, that person.

- the second is *having influence* in the sense of *being influential*, as a truly *dispositional* property (where the actualization of the disposition does not depend on the agent's purposeful action, but rather on circumstances external to him – above all: on circumstances concerning the receptiveness of the potential subject of influence).

The former, obviously, is parallel to the case of power ('having power' meaning 'having the ability to exercise power'). The latter pairs the *disposition* of being influential with *actual instances* of being influential.

8.2. On the relationship between influence and action

Someone could argue that this is implausible since it is perfectly common to speak of influences on *actions*, and that what is usually meant by an observation such as '*A* is very much influenced by *B*' refers to the behaviour of *A* rather than merely to *A*'s beliefs. Why not say that 'influence' means affecting action through beliefs? That would, of course, make influence a sub-category of power. What seems to speak in favour of such a conception is above all the fact that, particularly for social-scientific purposes, beliefs are of interest only if, and to the extent that, they are reflected in action. I think, however, that this is not a sufficient reason for linking influence *conceptually* to certain effects on action – namely, those induced by affecting beliefs.

A further argument against linking influence with action is that the *behavioural consequences* of any one single change in belief can be of a very broad range, and, above all, *very dispersed in time*; it would be strange to say in every single instance of such an action that it is the (direct) result of influence. Our beliefs are part of the background conditions which inform our choices; a change of belief can constitute a considerable and *durable* modification of our mental map of the empirical and normative territory in which we move, which subsequently serves to support a myriad of choices. In other words, although in some cases of influence (particularly when influence is intentionally *exercised*) a specific change in behaviour is so closely linked to (and so quickly follows) a specific change of belief that it is tempting to say that what was 'influenced' is the behaviour in question, in many other cases of what we would commonly be willing to call 'influence' just as naturally, such a link between the affected belief and a specific action does not exist. Quite another matter is that we gain *evidence* of occurrences of influence mainly through the observation of changes in behaviour. But in order to identify such a case, we do infer 'backwards' from the change of behaviour to a change in belief.

At this point, it is also convenient to remember a distinction made earlier, in the context of the discussion of Brian Barry's conception of power (cf. above, Chapter 1.2.3., p. 69). When *power* is exercised *through* what I have defined as *influence*,[118] this is even more difficult to trace than in the case of power based on other means, since it does not involve pushing an agent upward on his 'compliance line'. Rather, it is equivalent to a move of the 'zero compliance' point itself. Obviously, this raises enormous

[118] For Barry, it is all power; nevertheless, he recognizes the fundamental difference between changing another's beliefs or preferences and changing another's circumstances of action in other ways.

theoretical problems regarding the question of *freedom* and the ascription of *responsibility* for the actions of an influenced agent.

Finally, the proposed distinction is helpful in accounting for a number of questions we have encountered so far in trying to grasp the differences between power and influence:

(1) It is perfectly consistent with the fact that in ordinary usage it is very common to attribute influence, whereas it makes no sense to attribute power, to the dead. Cervantes is still an 'influential' figure among novelists, because his *Quijote* affects their *beliefs* about how a novel should or should not be written. But it would not occur to anyone to say that Cervantes therefore has power over these writers.

(2) If power can be exercised in some cases through the exercise of influence, this means that someone who *has influence* in the strong sense of a genuine *ability* to change another's beliefs therefore also *may have* power. But whether or not that is the case in a particular situation depends very much on the kind of influence one has, and on the state of awareness of this fact on the part of the holder of influence. An emerging star on the sky of pop music may have gained considerable *influence* on a great number of people without being aware of it: her way of dressing, walking, talking, etc. may change the tastes of her fans (their *aesthetic* beliefs) or their ideas about how one should behave (their *normative* beliefs), or even their outlook on the world (their *empirical* beliefs – e. g., if they start to take the lyrics of her songs as truthful assertions about how the world really is). But as long as she doesn't know this, she has *no power* over them.

PART II
CONCEPTS PUT TOGETHER

[W]here the concepts are firm, clear and generally accepted ..., there and only there is it possible to construct a science, formal or empirical. Wherever this is not the case – where the concepts are vague or too much in dispute, ... – we are at best in the realm of quasi-science.

Isaiah Berlin 1980, 145

Nothing new can ever be learned by analyzing definitions. Nevertheless, our existing beliefs can be set in order by this process, and order is an essential element of intellectual economy, as of every other. It may be acknowledged, therefore, that the books are right in making familiarity with a notion the first step toward clearness of apprehension, and the defining of it the second.

Charles S. Peirce (quoted from Copi 1982, 138)

3. POWER AND FREEDOM

> *LIBERTY, or FREEDOME, signifieth (properly) the absence of Opposition; (by Opposition, I mean externall Impediments of motion;) ... For whatsoever is so tyed, or environed, as it cannot move, but within a certain space, which space is determined by the opposition of some externall body, we say it hath not Liberty to go further ... But when the impediment of motion, is in the constitution of the thing it selfe, we use not to say, it want the Liberty; but the Power to move ... And according to this proper, and generally received meaning of the word,* A *FREE-MAN*, is he, that in those things, which by his strength and wit he is able to do, is not hindred to doe what he has a will to ... *Feare and Liberty are consistent; as when a man throweth his goods into the Sea for* feare *the ship should sink, he doth it neverthelesse very willingly, and may refuse to doe it if he will: It is therefore the action, of one that was* free*: so a man sometimes pays his debt, only for* feare *of Imprisonment, which because no body hindred him from detaining, was the action of a man at* liberty. *And generally all actions which men doe in Commonwealths, for* feare *of the law, or actions, which the doers had* liberty *to omit.*
>
> Hobbes[1]

One of the peculiarities of Thomas Hobbes's account of power and freedom is that the two can hardly clash: an actor remains free as long as no-one puts external (material) obstacles in his way; and doing so is but one, and in political contexts certainly the least relevant and effective, form of exercising power.[2] The fact that on this mechanistic, unpsychological conception, most forms of power simply *cannot* have an effect on freedom goes a long way towards explaining why power (not to be confused with force) is such a relatively innocuous, morally unproblematic feature of social life for Hobbes.

[1] *Leviathan*, Part II, ch. 21, Penguin ed. pp. 261–263. Hobbes's argument is directed above all against Aristotle's much more differentiated view of the voluntary and the unvoluntary, of force and coercion; cf. Nikomachean Ethics, Book III, 1110, where Aristotle expresses doubts about whether one can speak of voluntariness in cases where the only 'options' are to do or omit an action that is accompanied by a severe threat. Besides compliance with an order to commit a crime if otherwise one's parents or children will be killed, Aristotle himself uses the example of throwing valuable merchandise over board if otherwise one's ship will sink.

[2] For Hobbes's definition of power, cf. above the introduction to Chapter 1. Concerning the exercise of power by erecting external obstacles, cf. the remarks on 'physical constraints' in the context of the discussion of Brian Barry's conception of power in Chapter 1.2.

This is certainly not true for most contemporary attitudes to social power. On the contrary, as indicated earlier,[3] today a tendency to general disapproval and even condemnation of power seems to predominate, not only among those who think they have none, or very little, of it and therefore feel subjected to, or vulnerable by, the power held by others, but also among quite a few social theorists.

In the case of the latter, the intuition that to exercise, or even merely to have, power is something 'bad', something to be evaluated negatively, probably contributed in a decisive way to the claim that agreement about the 'universe of application' of that concept is basically impossible.[4] Because, obviously, if power is such a value-laden concept then its applicability to specific cases must necessarily depend, among other things, upon the evaluation one makes of each case. On that conception, then, since power is something morally bad, in order to determine whether or not in a certain social situation we are dealing with a phenomenon involving the existence, or an exercise, of power we must first determine the moral status of that situation: We can then speak of a case of power only when the respective situation is assessed as being morally defective. As a consequence – always according to that same conception –, to the extent that different persons reach divergent moral judgments about some action or state of affairs, their 'descriptive judgments' about whether or not power is involved will have to differ.

However, as I have argued, there are good reasons to reject that view. Let me briefly rehearse only two of them:

(1) On the one hand, we can appeal to the common usage of the term 'power'. It is simply not true that in ordinary language this term always has a negative connotation. On the contrary, statements like 'I wish environmental protection groups had the power to prevent the adoption of policies that have harmful consequences for the environment' or 'Fortunately, Gorbachov had enough power to put an end to the cold war' or 'Unfortunately, democratic countries do not have the power to prevent the violation of human rights in Tyrannia' make perfect sense and are not unusual. Thus, obviously there are situations in which we *desire* or *endorse* the existence, and even the exercise, of power, or lament its absence. And this is true not only for the power to *avoid* or *prevent* certain events, as someone could perhaps infer from the examples given. It also applies to the power to *do* or *promote* things ('Would that he had the power to get me that job!', or 'Fortunately, the UN today has the power to maintain a non-anarchical international system').[5] We thus have a strong empirical argument against the thesis that the concept of power inherently carries an invariably negative evaluation.

[3] Cf. above, Chapter 1, p. 30.

[4] Cf. the discussion of the alleged 'essential contestedness' of the concept of power in Chapter 1.1.

[5] Although it may seem that the power alluded to in the examples is 'power' only in the sense of someone's ability to produce certain states of affairs, in all of them a *social* power relation is involved, in the sense that the states of affairs in question can be brought about precisely because of an ability to provoke certain conducts in other agents. – Lest there be any doubt about it: I do not, of course, mean to claim the correctness of the statements used as examples above; in fact, the empirical truth as well as the evaluative connotation of each one of them could probably be contested on good grounds. But here I am only interested in showing that this *kind* of statements, which imply a *positive* evaluation of some social power-situation, makes sense and can be understood without a problem.

(2) And there is also the theoretical argument. In the realm of scientific work, it is generally advisable to avoid as much as possible the use of *value-laden* concepts, i. e., concepts containing evaluative aspects among their defining characteristics. The only exception to this rule seems to be the field of normative discourse itself.[6] But when the purpose is the description and/or explanation of empirical phenomena, the inclusion of normative elements in the definition of concepts at best does not help, and in the worst case, distorts the perception of empirical reality. This applies to social phenomena and states of affairs just as to natural ones; in both spheres, nothing prevents, in principle, the distinction between their *description* and their *evaluation*. Even in the (not very frequent) case that the evaluation of each and every one of the elements of some category of social phenomena happens to be negative, it is still possible to define the corresponding concept simply by its descriptive characteristics. Think, for instance, of acts regarded as 'crimes' by the criminal law: the acts themselves are defined by certain *descriptive* characteristics which distinguish these acts from others, whereas the corresponding negative connotation results from the fact that the act thus described is *evaluated* as a crime that deserves to be sanctioned by the state.[7] Thus, it is because of certain *descriptive* characteristics that a manslaughter is a 'murder', even though the identification of an act as a case of 'murder' always implies its being evaluated negatively. In other words, the negative evaluation is not a defining, but an accompanying characteristic of the phenomena falling under the concept of murder.[8]

Still, even if one accepts these two arguments, some grain of plausibility seems to be contained in the – in its general version, mistaken – idea that power is *per se* bad, or at least warrants suspicion. I think it is the following:

As is well-known, there are some acts and states of affairs which seem to be *prima facie* morally indifferent (or even praiseworthy) and which therefore call for justification only under exceptional circumstances. And there are others which are assumed to be *prima facie* morally problematic and therefore always need to be explicitly justified. With respect to the latter, perhaps one can say that in each particular case the *suspicion*

[6] For logical reasons, one can derive prescriptive conclusions only from starting points which themselves contain some prescriptive element. Hence, in such a context it may, for some purposes, be of interest to restrict the discourse from the start to classes of objects sharing the same normative status; and in that case it may then also be useful to possess concepts which take that normative aspect into account.

[7] This evaluation, in turn, may, but need not, be based on a negative moral evaluation.

[8] However, cf. Kristjánsson 1996, 190 ff., who – affirmatively citing Kovesi – uses the concept of 'murder' precisely to argue for the opposing view. Kristjánsson's argument is that „the only rationale for distinguishing between murder-motives and other mere-killing-motives is that the former are negatively valued. It is not a contingent fact about murder-motives that they somehow happen to be evaluated negatively" (personal correspondence, Sept. 9, 1998). That may be so; but if the concept of 'murder' is to be of any use for denoting a certain class of social phenomena, then the abstract idea of 'negatively evaluated motives' must be given descriptive content which will, in turn, lead to the *possibility* of a definition of 'murder' by purely descriptive characteristics. Thus, although the negative evaluation of all members of the extension of this concept is not a *contingent* matter, we can get a purely descriptive definition, i. e., a definition in which the valuational aspect need not be mentioned. To the extent that this possibility exists, then, for most social-scientific purposes such a definition is to be preferred over the evaluative alternative. Note that this conceptual reduction of social phenomena to their descriptive characteristics is not to be confused with an operational definition used to 'translate' a descriptive concept into a list of observable indicators: for instance, the definition of 'murder' as 'killing with premeditation and with sexual or sadistic or ... motives' does not contain such operational indicators.

that the evaluation will turn out to be negative holds *until the contrary has been shown*, i. e., until a justification or at least an excuse has been given. And social power seems to be regarded precisely as a phenomenon of that last kind: *prima facie*, its exercise, and perhaps even its mere existence, is generally taken to raise a moral problem. Power phenomena are therefore thought to require justification in each particular case. But, why is that so? Where does the intuition that power is something one must *prima facie* be suspicious of, something basically negative, acceptable or desirable only in special circumstances, come from?

The underlying idea must, of course, be that power invariably and negatively affects some important moral value. And the value social power is most often associated with in this way is *freedom*.[9] The relationship between power and freedom is generally regarded as one of inverse proportion: The *more* power an agent *A* has (or exercises) over another agent *B*, the *less* freedom *B* is thought to possess; and inversely, the *less* power some *A* has (or exercises) over some *B*, the *greater* the latter's freedom. In liberal conceptions, to which the present considerations are restricted, freedom is generally conceived as something positive and desirable, something that counts among a person's basic rights or even as the very foundation on which all those rights are based.[10] The suspicion against power, then, seems to derive mainly from its conception as something necessarily opposed to, or detrimental to, people's freedom.

Given this strong inverse relationship assumed to hold between one side's power and the other side's freedom in a social relationship, it is not surprising that the concept of liberty too is taken by some authors[11] to be one of the 'essentially contested' concepts discussed in Chapter 1 (although in this case, of course, with a value-charge of the oppo-

[9] To give just two examples from contemporary political-philosophy scholarship at this point: Bernard Williams (1993, 154) has maintained that „being free stands opposed, above all, to being in someone's power; and the mark of that [...] is that my choices or opportunities are not merely limited [...] but that they are designedly and systematically limited, by another person who is shaping my actions to his intentions. To lack freedom is paradigmatically not simply to be short of choices, but to be subject to the will of another". Similarly, in Norman Barry's (1989, 87) words, „It is of the essence of power relationships that they involve the diminution of liberty". An interesting variant of this view, based on a definition of power as the ability to determine *another's* set of choices, can be found in Mokken/Stokman (1975, 37): „The freedom of an actor can be defined as his capacity to determine his own sets of action or choice alternatives. In a social organization, the freedom of an actor can then imply power over others in so far as their alternatives are restricted by his freedom. Freedom for Ego implies lack of freedom for Alter. The struggle for freedom and the struggle for power are for that reason two sides of the same coin." These last considerations go a long way toward the insight that, far from a straightforward and invariable inverse relationship between freedom and power, the power of an agent or agency – say, the 'state' – over a collectivity of individuals may for each one of these individuals be at the same time freedom-restricting *and* freedom-enhancing, and that therefore „liberty should be equally exposed to danger whether the Government have too much or too little power", as James Madison formulated it more than two centuries ago; for a stimulating analysis of Madison's ideas about the relation between freedom and power, cf. Read 1995 from whom I have also taken the citation (ibid., 452).

[10] Cf. Miller 1983, 69, for the even more general claim that „our language embodies a presumption that humans should not obstruct one another's activity". An explicit rejection of that 'presumption' in favour of freedom can be found in Oppenheim's critique of Miller's paper; cf. Oppenheim 1985, 308.

[11] Cf., e. g., Miller 1983. Oppenheim 1995, 403, quotes several authors who have adopted that position. For a very useful overview over the debate about the concept of freedom, including the issue of its alleged 'essential contestedness', cf. Carter 1996 and 1997.

site sign of the one attributed to the concept of power). But this is a discussion I do not wish to enter into here.[12]

In this chapter, my purpose is rather to analyse more closely that alleged link between power and freedom that seems to be responsible for making social power in general needy of justification, and for making political power in particular such a fundamental issue of normative political theory.[13] Three authors – Felix Oppenheim, Philip Pettit, and Kristján Kristjánsson – have offered interesting contributions to this topic in recent years. The presentation and discussion of their views will allow me to bring to light and discuss some important points of contention in this context.[14]

1. Felix Oppenheim

Among the contributions of past decades to the elucidation of the fundamental concepts of political science, the work of Felix Oppenheim stands out. In my view, particularly his reflections on the concepts of social power and social freedom deserve more attention and closer examination than they have so far received in political-science scholarship. They constitute a substantial step forward in the clarification and refining process of those concepts; and the great clarity and precision of his presentation also facilitates the identification of some debatable points, the analysis of which may perhaps help us to overcome one or the other of the many conceptual obstacles which still hinder progress in political science.

In 1995, Felix Oppenheim published an article about the concept of 'social freedom'. This essay is partly based on earlier analyses of the same notion presented by the author, among others, in his 1981 book-length study of *Political Concepts*.[15] In view of what has been said earlier about 'essentially contested concepts', it is interesting to note that the explicit purpose of Oppenheim's 1995 paper is to show that, despite the „posi-

[12] In any case, we do not need the notion of an essentially contested concept in order to formulate a logical alternative concerning the link between the *evaluations* of phenomena of power and freedom, depending on how they are thought to be conceptually or empiricall related: Either the alleged inversely proportional relationship between power and freedom holds; in that case, if it is correct, as I have argued, that power is sometimes bad and sometimes good, freedom too cannot always be good. Or else one insists that the value of freedom is necessarily positive, i. e., that all restrictions of freedom are negative; in that case, if power is not always bad, one must give up the idea of the inversely proportional relationship between freedom and power. In other words, what one cannot consistently say is that *(i)* power is sometimes bad and sometimes good, that *(ii)* freedom is always good, and that *(iii)* there is an inversely proportional relationship between power and freedom.

[13] There is another aspect of the relationship between power and freedom that must not be overlooked, although I will not say anything more about it here: In a certain sense, power *requires* freedom, i. e., even if power affects freedom, it can never entirely eliminate it without eliminating itself in the process. Insofar, one does not need to adopt Foucault's concept of power as such in order to agree with his observation (1994, 229) that „Power is exercised only over free subjects, and only insofar as they are free [...] Where the determining factors saturate the whole there is no relationship of power [...] In this game freedom may well appear as the condition for the exercise of power [...] without the possibility of recalcitrance, power would be equivalent to a physical determination".

[14] For helpful critical comments on previous versions of the following two section, I am particularly indebted to Ernesto Garzón Valdés and Kristján Kristjánsson.

[15] In the following, unless indicated otherwise, page numbers given in parenthesis refer to the 1995 essay.

tive valuational connotation of 'freedom'" (419), the concept of social freedom – as well as other concepts of freedom which Oppenheim distinguishes from that of social freedom (among them, above all, that of freedom of choice; cf. 404 f.) – can be reconstructed in purely descriptive terms and that, therefore, it is *not* an 'essentially contested' concept (403).

1.1. THE RELATIONSHIP BETWEEN FREEDOM AND POWER

Let us first see exactly in what terms Oppenheim reconstructs the concept of social freedom, before moving on to his conception of the relationship between this and the concept of social power. The main features of Oppenheim's concept of social freedom are the following:

(i) The aspect which distinguishes the concept of social freedom from any other concept of freedom is that, by definition, it refers to a social relation, i. e., a relation between at least two interacting agents.[16] At a given time, such a relationship can exist with respect to one single action or some set of several actions. In the most simple case, we have two agents and one action. Therefore, the paradigmatic situation of social freedom consists of a triadic relationship between an agent *P*, another agent *R*, and an action *x*.[17] The generic structure of a situation of social freedom thus is as follows: „Wrt [with respect to] P, R is free to do X or to do Not-X" (404).

(ii) In order to explicate what 'being free' means in this formula, Oppenheim takes recourse to a definition *ex negativo*:

a) First, he defines that someone is free to the extent that some other person does *not* make him or her unfree: „Wrt P, R is free to do X or to do Not-X" is equivalent to „P makes R neither unfree to do X nor unfree to do Not-X" (404).

b) He then stipulates what it means to say that someone makes someone else unfree to perform an action: „Wrt P ..., R ... is unfree to do X if and only if P makes it either impossible or punishable for R to do X" (404; cf. also 1985, 307).

Taken together, this yields the following definition of social freedom:

With respect to P, R is free to do x or to do not-x if and only if P makes it neither impossible nor punishable for R to do x and P makes it neither impossible nor punishable for R to do not-x.

It thus becomes clear that the key for determining whether in a given situation we are dealing with a case of social freedom or unfreedom rests with the concepts of the *impossible* and the *punishable*.

[16] They may, of course, be individual or collective agents.

[17] More complex situations involving more than two agents and/or more than one action can always be analysed (in the strict sense of the word) as a set of relations of social freedom of this most simple case. Therefore, here we only need to consider the concept of social freedom for those simple cases. – It should be noted that in the cited works, Oppenheim always uses the letter 'x' to denote the action with respect to which an agent is free or unfree, but he oscilates between the capital and the small letter. In order to avoid confusion, I will always represent it with the small letter, except in some literally quoted passages from Oppenheim.

(iii) According to Oppenheim, there are two quite different senses in which *P* can make it *impossible* for *R* to perform some action *x*:

a) On the one hand, he can make it „strictly" (406 ff.) or „literally" (1985, 307) impossible. Although the author does not explain this further, I think we may safely assume that it means that *P* succeeds in eliminating action *x* from *R*'s menu of choice, that is, *P* in some way brings it about that *R* loses the ability to do *x*.[18]

b) On the other, he can make it merely „practically impossible". In that case, *P* makes it so burdensome or costly for *R* to perform *x* that „any reasonable person finding himself in *R*'s situation" would consider it „too risky or costly or difficult" to carry out *x* (407). Oppenheim illustrates „practical impossibility" with the following example:

> „If P holds a pistol against R's chest and says: 'Your money or your life!' P does not make it strictly speaking impossible for R to risk his life; but if it is fairly certain that P 'means business', R has practically no choice but to hand over his money [...] It seems, therefore, plausible to extend the concept of unfreedom to include relationships making it practically impossible or ineligible for someone to act in a certain way." (406)[19]

Thus, while in the case of „strict impossibility" *x* is no longer among *R*'s options for action, in the case of „practical impossibility" *x* still is an option for *R* – but an option which, through *P*'s intervention, has become so unattractive that any „reasonable" person in *R*'s shoes would consider its choice *unsuitable* or *inappropriate*. In the first case, *x* is „ineligible" in the strict sense: *R cannot* choose to perform *x* anymore, as much as he might want to; in the second case, by contrast, *x* is „ineligible" only in the weaker sense that *R* no longer *wants* to choose it – or at least it is no longer *reasonable* for him to want to choose it –, although he could. In other words: in the former case, *R* no longer has the *factual ability* for performing *x*, whereas in the latter, perhaps one can say that (provided *R* is reasonable) he no longer has the *motivational ability* for doing it.[20]

[18] Thus, this would be the category of power Brian Barry (1991a, esp. 226) called 'incapacitation' through the imposition of 'physical constraints'. Cf. above Chapter 1.2.

[19] Note that 'practical impossibility' in this sense is precisely what Hobbes denied to be a variant of unfreedom.

[20] Of course, the interesting question then is that of identifying the criteria for determining whether or not in a particular situation we are facing a case of strict or of practical impossibility. Although this is a complicated matter which I cannot treat here in detail, at least that much can be said: While the first obviously is a purely descriptive concept (that is, for each given case it can, at least in principle, be empirically established whether or not it falls under that concept), this is not so in the case of the practically impossible, since judgments of practical impossibility presuppose, by definition, not only counterfactual, but hypothetical reflections, based on some particular interpretation of a notoriously normative concept, namely, that of reasonableness. In the first case, for a description of a situation as a relationship of unfreedom of R wrt P to do x to be true it must, basically, be shown that *(i)* at a given time t, R had been able to perform x (that is, all the necessary conditions and some set of jointly sufficient conditions were satisfied) and *(ii)* at a later time t_2, P either eliminated at least one necessary condition or changed the world in such a way as to create some new necessary condition which was not satisfied. In the case of „practical impossibility", in turn, one would need to show the following: *(i')* the same as *(i)*; *(ii')* at time t, under the given circumstances, it would have been reasonable for anyone in R's situation to perform x; *(iii')* at a later time t_2, P brought about some change in R's circumstances of action (but without affecting the satisfaction of all necessary conditions for x); *(iv)* that change affected the set of given circumstances in such a way as to make it unreasonable for anyone in R's position to perform x. In this last case, then, everything depends on what is understood by 'reasonable'. These remarks show that, although the difference between strict and practical impossibility may at first sight only look gradual, the two conditions are, in fact, fundamentally different.

The two kinds of impossibility, taken together, constitute what Oppenheim calls the category of „impediments“ leading to „prevention“ (411).[21]

(iv) Finally, Oppenheim also classifies as situations of social unfreedom those circumstances in which, without making the performance of x impossible in either one of the two senses just presented, P makes it „punishable“ for R to perform x. While in the case of impossibility the relationship with unfreedom was rather obvious, the alleged necessary relationship between the punishability of an action and an agent's unfreedom does not seem very clear and deserves a closer look.

First of all, it is important to note that, contrary to what one may expect, when Oppenheim speaks of the punishability of an action he is *not* referring to the kind of situation where P *threatens* R with a sanction should he perform x, and by doing so perhaps succeeds in deterring R from doing x. According to Oppenheim, cases of threatening must be distinguished from cases of punishability. If P threatens R with a sanction for the performance of x, there are two possibilities:[22]

For a very similar distinction between what Oppenheim calls 'strict' or 'literal' and 'practical' impossibility, cf. Alf Ross's considerations about the statement 'He could not have acted otherwise', as it is sometimes „used as an excuse for an offence committed under coercion“: „[T]he phrase 'he could not have acted otherwise' is used to justify exemption from responsibility in two groups of cases. First, in those cases in which it is actually true that it was not within the person's power to act otherwise (because he lacked the ability or the opportunity or both). Secondly, it is used in cases of external or internal compulsion, in which the statement is merely a figure of speech, the real meaning of which is that under the circumstances the agent could not be expected to have acted other than he did“ (Ross 1971, 255), i. e., „the pressure on him was so great that, according to ordinary standards, he could not have been expected to have resisted it. Although it must be recognized that the person under compulsion could have acted other than he did, it is equally well founded to exempt him from responsibility if the compulsion has been of such strength that, according to ordinary experience and standards, [...] a person with a normally developed intelligence and sense of duty would have acted in the same way in his place“ (Ross 1971, 254). Stanley Benn, though apparently unaware of Alf Ross's essay, has presented the issue in remarkably similar terms, in the context of an attempt to counter the Hobbesian argument that the law, even when accompanied by the threat of sanctions, does not make one unfree: „[S]ystems of norms that are supported by threats would not be regarded as restrictive of freedom unless their penalties in general made the proscribed course so unattractive that by accepted standards of interest and prudence it could be considered ineligible – unavailable.“ And: „It would be quite unreasonable to expect someone to act in the proscribed way if the consequence was imprisonment. Only someone [...] with a disordered set of values or someone of superhuman steadfastness, a saint or a fanatic, would choose such an option. The penalty has made it literally ineligible – one that it would be *inappropriate* for a reasonable, prudent man to choose [...] If he obeys or intends to obey, his own account of his position as unfree invokes an evaluation, that it would be unreasonable to expect anyone in such circumstances not to conform to the law, though admittedly some rash or quite exceptionally resolute individuals might still break it despite the threatened consequences [...] The excuse can be rejected by rejecting the agent's own evaluation and insisting that the threatened penalty did not sufficiently foreclose other alternatives [...] The agent's counterplea might be to deny that the standard being adopted by his accusers should properly be applied to him. Only a saint, a hero, or a fanatic would have disobeyed; one cannot look for martyrs among ordinary men and women.“ (Benn 1988, pp. 144 and 147 f.) Cf. also Williams 1993, 152 f.

[21] Thus, when Oppenheim speaks of 'prevention' or 'impossibility', he actually means literal *or* practical impossibility, that is, impossibility in the strict sense *or* ineligibility; it is therefore not correct when Kristjánsson (1996, 46) counts him among the advocates of what he calls the 'impossibility view'; rather, Oppenheim is clearly a representative of the 'ineligibility view'.

[22] For a detailed analysis of the possible costs and gains for both sides in a threat situation, cf. B. Barry 1991a, esp. sects. VIII and IX.

a) Either the threatened sanction is not sufficiently severe and/or credible to make it *practically impossible* for *R* to perform *x*. In that case, the threat has exactly the same effect as any other „obstacle" *R* may have to face in the course of choosing and performing *x* and which can be „surmounted" (407), and therefore it does not at all affect *R*'s freedom.[23]

b) Or the announced 'punishment' is so severe and/or has such a high subjective probability of application that it does indeed make it *practically impossible* for *R* to perform *x*. In that case, however, we would simply be dealing with one of the situations of prevention presented above:

„By merely threatening R with punishment if he did X, P leaves R free either to comply or to disregard the threat. P's threat is a means to *influence* R to comply; its success depends on its credibility [...] Threats are instances of unfreedom only if they are 'coercive', i. e. if it is practically certain that a threatened severe punishment would be carried out." (410)

Hence, a threat either has *no effect* whatsoever on the social freedom of the threatened person, or it is a 'common' case of prevention, by making some action *practically impossible.*[24] With respect to threats, then, there is no need for a new category. Therefore, the fact that Oppenheim does give the punishability of an action a special treatment implies that his conception of it must be another one. This is also expressed in his explanation that

„Punishability, unlike obstacles, no matter how light the penalty, always indicates unfreedom. The degree of R's unfreedom to do X wrt P depends on the severity of the penalty as experienced [...] by the average person." (412).[25]

Here, Oppenheim invokes the experience of the „average person" in order to protect his conception against a possible objection of subjectivity. Because if one could speak of a „penalty" only when *R* himself „attaches negative utility to the sanction or to the opportunity costs to him of performing the punishable action" (409), then Oppenheim could not uphold the thesis that punishability always implies unfreedom without at the same time converting unfreedom into a subjective concept the applicability of which would always depend on the evaluations made by the agents involved in a particular case. Therefore, he insists that

„whether P's action Y constitutes a reward or a punishment does not depend on R's valuations. R might value a prison sentence positively, and experience being 'rewarded' by being taken to see and hear *Die Götterdämmerung* as a 'punishment' [... W]e must refer to the valuations of average rational agents" (410).

So far, we know that for Oppenheim the punishability of an action always implies unfreedom, even if the affected person regards the penalty as insignificant or if, instead of experiencing it as a deprivation, she enjoys the 'punishment' inflicted on her. But what

[23] The criterion for the distinction between an „impediment" and a „mere obstacle" is, in Oppenheim's words, „whether a normal, rational agent could overcome the impediment, if he desired to do so" (408).

[24] Obviously, a threat alone cannot give rise to a strict impossibility.

[25] Cf. also 1985, 308: „Imposing even a small penalty restricts freedom, but only an obstacle amounting to practical impossibility does so."

we still do not know is *in what sense* punishability necessarily gives rise to some degree of unfreedom. What *is* that alleged difference between a *threat of punishment* in case someone performs a certain action, and the *punishability* of that same action? And how must we understand Oppenheim's thesis that in the latter case, regardless of the quality or quantity of the sanction associated with the action, we have a situation of unfreedom, whereas in the case of a threat, this depends on the severity of the penalty as well as on the threat's credibility?

An indication of how Oppenheim conceives of that difference can be found in his earlier work. There (1981, 57), he briefly explains that 'punishability' of an action means that *if* the action is performed, a penalty is imposed. Thus, punishability is a matter of fact about a certain sequence of events and as such obviously is of another nature as a threat. But Oppenheim's information about this is scarce and vague, and in order to understand what the definition implies, we will need to take a closer look at the relationship between 'punishability' and 'threat of punishment' deriving from it.

I will come back to this matter presently. But first, the presentation of Oppenheim's conception must be completed, because the question that is still open is how his concept of *freedom* is related to that of *power*.

In his more recent paper on social freedom, he is not concerned with power, and therefore does not explicitly discuss that relationship. Nevertheless, it is presupposed from the very beginning, by way of a formulation in which Oppenheim mentions it in passing, as if its involvement were a totally uncontroversial fact. The formulation occurs in the definition of a situation of social unfreedom quoted above. However, in the quotation cited earlier, I deliberately omitted a few words. Here is the complete quotation:

„Wrt P *(a holder of power)*, R (a respondent) is unfree to do X if and only if P makes it either impossible or punishable for R to do X. Wrt P, R is free to do X or to do Not-X if and only if P makes R neither unfree to do X nor unfree to do Not-X." (404; emphasis added)

Thus, Oppenheim implies that situations in which one agent's *social freedom is restricted* by another agent are always at the same time situations of a manifestation of *social power*. Even the letter denoting the agent who makes another one unfree seems not to have been chosen arbitrarily by Oppenheim: it is the 'P' of 'powerful'.[26] Another indicator of this perceived relationship is that the example Oppenheim uses as an illustration for situations of a *restriction of freedom* in the sense of making some action practically impossible – that of the thug with the pistol who says 'Your money or your life!' –[27] is in fact the well-known paradigmatic example for the illustration of certain kinds of *social power* situations.

[26] Note that this is not always the case: Norman (1991) and Kristjánsson (1998a), e. g., use the same letters, but the other way round. Of course, at least since Fritz Heider (1958) the use of 'O' and 'P' has been common for the designation of the participants in a dyadic relationship; but cf., e. g., Cartwright (1969; see also Chapter 2.2) who uses 'O' for the powerful and 'P' for the power*less* actor.

[27] Ibid., 406. Elsewhere, Oppenheim himself invokes „the typical situation of 'Your money or your life'" (1981, 15) as an example for the particular kind of an exercise of power performed by way of a „coercive threat".

In order to realize just how closely related power and (the lack of) freedom are in Oppenheim's view, we must again take recourse to his earlier work and look at his explicit definition of 'social power' which stipulates that

„P has power over R wrt his not doing x iff P has influence over R's not doing x or prevents R from doing x or makes it punishable for R to do x" (1981, 21).

Since, as we have seen, prevention and punishability are the two forms how, according to Oppenheim, one agent can make another one unfree to perform some action, this definition of power, rephrased in terms of freedom, translates into the following:

P has power over R with respect to his not doing x if and only if P has influence over R's not doing x or *P makes R unfree to do x*.

Thus understood, situations of social power and situations of social unfreedom between two agents obviously are not completely interdefinable: some possible situations of power are not situations of unfreedom. Still, all relations of unfreedom (conceptually) imply a relation of power. That means that all the situations presented by Oppenheim of an agent *R* having his freedom constrained by another agent *P* are equivalent to situations in which *P* has power over *R*.

This completes the presentation of the notions of social freedom and social power and the relationship between them, according to Oppenheim. We must now examine some implications of this conception.

1.2. DISCUSSION

(1) Let me begin the discussion with an observation about the relationship between power and freedom. As we have just seen, from Oppenheim's point of view, there are two fundamentally different categories of situations in which one can speak of *social power*: the category of *influence* situations, on the one hand, and that of *restrictions of freedom*, or *unfreedom*, on the other. The problem of the definition of 'influence' is a topic I do no wish to treat at this point. But elsewhere[28] I have tried to show that it is not advisable to conceive of social influence situations as a subcategory of social power situations – among other reasons, because this would mean an unwarranted departure from the common usage of these terms, since in ordinary usage we would not generally be willing to attribute 'power' to anyone who is considered 'influential'. In the present context, this is relevant for the following reason.

If from Oppenheim's conception we eliminate – as I think we should – influence situations as a subcategory of power situations, we are left, *ceteris paribus*, with a concept of social power the *extension* of which is equivalent to that of the concept of social unfreedom. The only remaining difference between the two concepts then regards their *intensions*.[29] They direct our attention to different sides of the relationship in question:

[28] Cf. Chapter 2; for an earlier approach, cf. also Zimmerling 1991, ch. 4.

[29] The thesis that „the locutions 'R exercises power over P' and 'R constrains P's freedom'" should be seen as „extensionally equivalent" is explicitly defended by Kristjánsson (1998a, 264; cf. also 1992e and 1996, esp. 158). I will have more to say about it in Section 3 of this chapter.

'unfreedom' is an attribute of some agent *R* if and only if (and to the extent that) 'power' is an attribute of some other agent *P*. In other words, from the descriptive point of view, the two attributes seem to inform us about different aspects of one and the same relationship: the former about something *R* *cannot* do, and the latter about something *P* *can* do. So, whether we speak of unfreedom or of power seems to depend on which of the parties to the corresponding relationship we are (more) interested in.[30]

(2) Of course, if power situations are identified with situations where freedom is restricted, this has consequences for the question about the evaluation of such situations. On this interpretation, a positive judgment about some relationship of social freedom necessarily implies a negative judgment about its negation, and this means: about the corresponding power relation, and *vice versa*. But from here, we must proceed carefully, and not draw premature conclusions. Because it must not be forgotten that the interdependence of the evaluations of social freedom and social power only applies to *each particular* triadic relationship between some *P*, some *R*, and some *x*. Thus, from this point of view, certainly a negative judgment about a particular power relation between *P* and *R* with respect to *x* is equivalent to a negative judgment about the infringement on the freedom of *R* implied by *that* power relation. But this in no way predetermines the answer to the question of whether or not *R* ought to be free from *any* constraint to do or omit *x*. And, *vice versa*, an argument *against* the freedom of some *R* with respect to some action *x* is no argument in favour of the power of *any* *P* over *R* with respect to *x*. Value-judgments about power or unfreedom relations, thus, can change with each one of the three elements of these relations, as distinguished by Oppenheim. This means that, despite their co-extensionality and interdefinability, the distinction between the concepts of power and (un)freedom continues to be important for our ability to focus on different aspects of such relations.

(3) In addition, there is still a fourth element that may become relevant in the context of the evaluation of a relation of power or unfreedom. I am referring to the different *bases* of unfreedom distinguished by Oppenheim in his definition. Just as it may be of interest for descriptive purposes to distinguish between a relationship of unfreedom based on an *impediment* and another one based on the *punishability* of an action, this distinction may also be relevant for normative purposes.

But before we can assess what kind of (normative) theories may be applicable to what Oppenheim calls situations of unfreedom based on punishability, we must go back to the concept of punishability and try to get a better grasp of what Oppenheim's conception of it and, above all, of its connection with unfreedom, really amounts to. The question we had stumbled over in point *(iv)* of the presentation was that of the difference, alleged by Oppenheim, between the 'punishability' of an action and a corresponding 'threat of punishment', especially as concerns their implications for social freedom.

At this point, it might already be objected that the attempt to establish a distinction between the punishability of an action, as defined by Oppenheim, and a threat of punishment makes no sense, because the two are synonymous: In a certain sense, to say

[30] For more on this, also cf. Section 3.

that the imposition of a sanction is a consequence of the performance of an action, that is, that the action is 'punishable', is exactly the same as to say that the action in question is 'under a threat of punishment'.[31] This is a perfectly common interpretation; and indeed, if this were the only possible conception of the notion of 'threat', Oppenheim's distinction would be incomprehensible.

But there is another possibility, which does permit to draw a distinction between the two concepts. The difference, on that view, seems to be that between a *fact* (here, the fact that an action and a punishment are connected) and a *statement* or report about that fact. A *threat* of punishment, in that sense, is not *punishability* itself, but a statement to the effect that a certain action is punishable.[32] An important aspect of this distinction between the punishability of an action and a threat of punishment is that it underscores the fact that the *credibility*, and with it the *efficacy*, of a threat is *independent* of whether or not the respective action actually *is* punishable. An agent may *wrongly* believe a threat – in the sense of a 'report on punishability' – to be true or false. A threat of punishment, thus, can succeed in deterring an agent from an action that is not punishable, that is, it may be effective even if punishability does not exist; and, *vice versa*, a threat may be ineffective even though punishability actually holds, i. e., it is possible that a threat does not succeed in deterring from the action and that, as a consequence, the agent suffers the penalty. Hence, there are four possible cases whenever an agent *P* threatens another agent *R* with punishment should he perform some action *x*:

		punishability	
		no	*yes*
threat of punishment	*effective*	1) impediment	2) impediment plus (counterfactual) punishment
	ineffective	3) full freedom	4) punishment

Case 1): In the first case, although the action is not punishable – that is, *R* actually would not be punished by *P* for performing it – the threat nevertheless succeeds in *preventing R* from performing the action. In this sense, according to Oppenheim, *R* is made unfree.[33]

[31] This is how Hart (1994, 34), for example, seems to understand it when, without further explanation, he identifies a 'sanction' with a 'threatened evil'.

[32] In that same sense, cf. now also Carter (1999, 229), interpreting Oppenheim: „threats are sincere or insincere statements about the punishability of specific actions or kinds of action, and punishability is an empirical generalization about the tendency of certain kinds of action to provoke sanctions."

[33] To keep things simple, I assume that the agent in question is a 'reasonable' person in Oppenheim's sense and is, therefore, 'impressed' by a threat only when it poses such an enormous obstacle that it makes the action practically impossible.

Case 2): The second case is, so to speak, a case of 'double unfreedom': by *impediment* and, according to Oppenheim, also by *punishability*. Although the agent does not come to 'suffer' because of the second type of unfreedom, since he does not perform the action and, hence, does not provoke the punishment, his unfreedom by punishability nevertheless holds.

Case 3): In the third case, the threat is not effective, hence *R* performs the action; here, the threat is at most a „surmountable“ obstacle that does not affect *R*'s freedom; and since the action also is not punishable, *R* remains *free* with respect to *P* and the action.

Case 4): As in the previous case, in the fourth case *P*'s threat does not affect *R*'s freedom since it is ineffective; therefore, *R* performs the action. But since in this case the action actually is punishable, *R* is not only made *unfree*, despite the fact that the threat is ineffective, but is also *punished* by *P*.[34]

An analysis of these four cases can, I think, take us closer to the desired answer to the question about the nature of the difference between a threat of punishment and the punishability of an action.

(i) One of the differences between the two kinds of unfreedom – that arising from prevention and that arising from punishability – can be perceived if one compares the unfreedom in the case of an effective threat without punishability (case 1) with the unfreedom in the case of punishability without an effective threat (case 4): The unfreedom resulting from an effective threat, according to Oppenheim, consists in the fact that *R no longer can perform* the respective action, where that impossibility is a 'practical' impossibility, that is, *R* cannot work up the necessary *motivation* for performing the action. In contrast, in the case of the mere punishability of an action *x*, the only thing *R* cannot do – and, therefore, the only thing in which, strictly speaking, *P* 'makes' *R* 'unfree' – is to *avoid* that one of the consequences of that action *x* is the imposition of the respective sanction by *P*. In Oppenheim's own words: „P, by making it punishable for R to do x, makes it impossible for R to do x *without being punished* [...]“ (1981, 57). This means that, to begin with, it is *not* act *x* which *R* is no longer 'free' to do when *x* is punishable, but something else (let's call it act *y*) – namely, '*x cum* avoidance of punishment'. In addition, it may also be that a *consequence* of being punished for performing *x* – a second-order consequence of *x*, so to speak – is that subsequently *R* is unable to perform some other act *z*, e. g., because *z* would require financial resources *R* no longer has after having had to pay a fine as a penalty for having done *x*, or because a necessary condition for doing *z* is that *R* can freely decide about his whereabouts, which he cannot do if he is serving time in prison for having done *x*. In that case, again, it is not the punished act *x* itself that *R* is made 'unfree' to do. But remember that Oppenheim's definition of social unfreedom stipulates that the punishability of some act makes an agent unfree to perform *that same act*.

[34] In addition, one could think of the case in which an action is punishable although there is no threat to that effect – the case of 'secret punishability'; this case could be accomodated in the table by regarding it as a borderline case of *3)* (punishability plus ineffective threat).

(ii) A second noteworthy difference can be perceived by comparing the case of an effective threat, when there actually is punishability (case 2) with the cases where the threat is ineffective (cases 3 and 4): An ineffective threat, according to Oppenheim, *does not affect* an agent's freedom at all. In contrast, although in case 2 the punishability is 'ineffective' in the sense that no punishment is inflicted because the sanctioned action is not performed (since it is prevented by the threat), it *does affect* *R*'s freedom, in the sense of having *counterfactual consequences*. In other words, punishability (as the word itself indicates[35]) must apparently be understood as a kind of *dispositional* property of the action in question – a property, that is, which continually exists, with all its characteristics, even when it is not manifest, and which becomes manifest only under special circumstances. According to Oppenheim's conception, then, unfreedom seems to be linked to punishability *as a dispositional property* of an action, and not only to the manifestation of that property in punishment.

(iii) And there is, I think, still a third relevant difference between the punishability of an action as understood by Oppenheim and a corresponding threat of punishment, which is not mentioned by him. It is the fact, already alluded to earlier, that the existence of a threat presupposes some sort of *communicative act*, whereas the punishability of an action only presupposes a *decision* to react in a certain way to certain events – a decision that may well be taken unilaterally by the agent who imposes the penality, without any need of communicating it to the agent who will suffer the punishment.[36]

In view of these three differences, Oppenheim's idea that punishability as he conceives it always implies unfreedom and hence also (the existence of) power has several noteworthy consequences which can perhaps be seen most clearly with the help of some exemplary cases:

(a) Suppose, first, that *P* makes it punishable for *R* to do *x*. The punishability of *x* is a fact which does not depend on *R* knowing about it; hence, suppose, secondly, that *R* does *not* know that he will be punished by *P* if he performs *x*. On the other hand, punishability as a dispositional property of *x* is a fact that is permanently, if only latently 'there', i. e., it 'exists' even when *R* does not perform *x* (and, therefore, does not suffer the corresponding penalty). Hence, let us also suppose that *R*'s own preferences make

[35] As is well-known, words constructed with the morphema '-bility/-ble' usually express dispositional properties.

[36] More generally, perhaps we can say that the prevention of an action – that is, the act of making it strictly or practically impossible – always requires a 'natural act' (which may be a communicative act, as in the case of a threat, or some other act which, besides, must not necessarily be intentional as an act of prevention). In contrast, punishability requires a 'normative act' since the connection of an action with a punitive consequence is nothing but the creation of a punitive norm (an action which is inconceivable without the corresponding intention). For the distinction between natural acts and normative acts, cf., e. g., Redondo 1999, ch. I. – Note, however, that, e. g., for von Wright (1963, 116 ff.) a normative act must necessarily encompass a communicative component, or even directly consist of a „verbal act". On this conception, the creation of a punitive norm is not complete with a unilateral decision of a norm-giver to make some action punishable; it also requires the communication (verbal or other) of the corresponding 'threat' to the norm's addressee(s). This is plausible if one takes into account that there are good reasons to adopt the conceptual position that regulatory norms (norms of conduct) exist only to the extent that they effectively guide the conduct of people and that they can only do so if they are known. In this sense, punishability alone cannot have any practical relevance as long as it remains 'secret'. But that is another topic, which I need not pursue here.

him decide not to do *x* every time he has the opportunity and could do *x*. We thus have a case in which *R*

- always does what he wants (he never wants to do *x*),
- never suffers a punishment by *P* (since he never does *x*), and
- does not even know that he would be punished if he did *x*.

In that respect, *R*'s situation is ideal: He feels perfectly free to do or not to do *x*; the fact that *x* actually is punishable does not change his life in any noticeable way (i. e., it affects neither his actions nor his mental state). And yet, according to Oppenheim, in such a case *R*'s freedom to do *x* or not-*x* is constrained because of the punishability of *x* by *P*.[37]

(b) Second, suppose that the case is as before, only that now *R*, unaware of the risk of punishment, decides to do *x*. He does *x*, *without any impediment* or *obstacle*, and consequently suffers the penalty foreseen by *P* for that case. According to Oppenheim, as for *R*'s freedom to do *x*, this case is no different from the former. He would say that with respect to *P*, *R* is *unfree* to do *x* – although, in fact, *R* performs *x* without any problem (his 'problems', so to speak, begin only *after* he has performed *x*).

(c) Third, assume that *P* now informs *R* of the fact that *x* is punishable, saying something like 'I just want you to know that if you do *x* I will punish you with *y*'. Only then, the fact that *x* is punishable can begin to play a role in *R*'s deliberations about how to act, and can perhaps 'persuade' him to give up the performance of *x*.

From a practical point of view, so far, this shows that the *only* way how punishability might affect the behaviour of a person is through the *communication* of its existence, i. e., through a *threat* (since, as has been observed above, a threat of punishment is basically nothing but an *anticipated information* about the fact that a certain action is punishable).[38] In other words, any effect the punishability of an action may have on the deliberations and decisions of an agent is always only an *indirect* effect, in the sense that it derives only from the threat necessarily implied by the information about the fact of punishability.

(d) Finally, assume that *R*, despite his awareness that *x* actually is punishable by *P*, is not impressed by that threat and performs *x* anyway whenever he feels like it. Assume also that *R* cannot – and knows that he cannot – avoid the punishment and that, still, he consciously decides to 'accept' it, perhaps because he regards it as negligible compared with the pleasure the performance of *x* gives him. Again, Oppenheim would have to say that with respect to *R*'s freedom nothing has changed in comparison with the previous cases: *R* is still unfree to do *x*, simply because of its punishability, despite the fact that there is no impediment.

[37] Oppenheim explicitly insists that „[a] person who feels free may not be a free person" (415, n. 7) and rejects conceptions of freedom (e. g., those of Arneson or Gray) according to which in cases where someone „is made unfree to do only what he does not want to do anyhow" that person's freedom is not restricted (415).

[38] *Pace* von Wright, I think one can safely say that the corresponding 'communicative' act need not be a verbal act: it is, of course, perfectly possible to communicate informations non-verbally, for instance by some kind of regular and observable behaviour. The punishability of an action may thus be communicated – and, indeed, inevitably *is* communicated to anyone with an average capacity of inference – simply through its consistent and observable punishment.

The implications deriving from these four exemplary cases seem to be the following:

As for *R*'s alleged *unfreedom* because of the mere punishability of *x*, this is a kind of 'unfreedom' which actually does not have any notable effect on the *relationship between R and his actions*, since it exists in total independence of *R*'s conduct and, above all, of whether his suffering or not suffering the corresponding punishment is triggered by his own conscious decision or not. In this sense, the 'unfreedom' linked with Oppenheim's conception of punishability seems to have much in common with the 'unfreedom' implied by certain natural causal relationships. In the worst case, the punishability of *x* makes one 'unfree' to avoid the penalty connected with one's performance of *x*, more or less in the same way as the fact that it is raining makes one 'unfree' to avoid getting wet if one goes outside without an umbrella. But in both cases, the action in question (to walk in the rain, to perform a punishable action) is 'eligible', i. e., punishability – just like rain – does not affect the person *as an agent*, but only as a *passive* 'victim' of a consequence. Therefore, if one connects the punishability of an action with the unfreedom of a person, as Oppenheim does, it means, in the last instance, that one gives up the idea that a person's freedom basically concerns that person's *(factual or motivational) ability to act*. It may well be that for certain purposes such a conception has its advantages. But in that case, it would seem advisable also to give up the notion, upheld by Oppenheim, of relationships of social freedom or unfreedom as triadic relations between two agents and an *action*.[39]

And as for the other side of the alleged relation of social unfreedom, that is, *P*'s *power* over *R*, the effective punishability of an action *x* by *P* does, of course, imply a kind of 'power' of *P*, in the sense that it means that *P* really 'can' inflict (or make someone else inflict) a punishment on *R* should he perform *x* (since if he couldn't, he also could not make *x* punishable for *R*). This 'power', however, can hardly be interpreted as an instance of 'social power': In none of the cases presented above we can say that the punishability of *x* gives *P* 'power over *R*' in the sense that *P* succeeds in controlling or guiding *R*'s acts of *x*. With punishability, instead of an ability to *intervene* in *R*'s actions or decisions, *P* only has an 'ability' to *react* to them. In the last case (where *R* consciously defies the threat of punishment although he knows that his doing *x* will trigger a punitive reaction) we could even say with some reason that it is *R* who, because of the punishability of *x*, has a certain power over *P*, because with his decisions to do or not to do *x* he can 'control' *P*'s behaviour with respect to the punitive action. Hence, it seems that from the standpoint of the alleged „holder of power" too, the relationship proposed by Oppenheim between punishability and unfreedom, and therefore also between punishability and social power, does not contribute to the clarity and consistency of the concepts under scrutiny.

[39] Cf. Kristjánsson 1998a for a similar critique of Philip Pettit's idea of freedom as „anti-power" or „non-domination" (Pettit 1996; 1997, ch. 2): His main objection is that Pettit fails to see that the notion of freedom as noninterference, which Pettit rejects, is a conception of the freedom of *actions*, whereas Pettit's notion of freedom as non-domination is a conception of the freedom of *persons*. In these terms, one could also say that Oppenheim, on the whole, defends a conception of freedom of actions, and apparently does not notice that his inclusion of punishability as a defining characteristic of social unfreedom brings with it a shift to a conception of the freedom of persons, thus turning his over-all conception into an indigestible concoction.

(4) There is, however, an alternative to the conclusion that the relation between punishability and unfreedom (and, consequently, also power) is not as Oppenheim argues. It is at least possible that what Oppenheim stipulates does hold if one redefines (at least one of) the concepts. And since it was Oppenheim's conception of punishability that proved to be problematic, it may well be worth the trouble to take a closer look at it. As presented above, Oppenheim's definition makes punishability a kind of dispositional property of an act: *x* is punishable according to Oppenheim ('O-punishable', for short) if, and only if, punishment *in fact* follows the performance of *x*, i. e., if *R* cannot do *x* without being punished. But, what exactly does 'doing *x*' mean here? Although Oppenheim himself does not mention the distinction, it must surely mean that what is O-punishable is an *act-type* or *generic* act *x*, e. g., 'murder' (whereas what is punished can always be only *act-tokens* or *individual* instances of '*x*-ing' – e. g., 'the murder of *Q*'). As we have seen, a (generic) act *x* is O-punishable only if it is „impossible for R to do x without being punished", and that means that *P* makes it O-punishable for *R* to commit 'murder' only if *R* is *de facto* punished *every time* he commits 'a murder'. If one takes this definition of punishability seriously, the implication is that there probably are no O-punishable acts at all; and if there are, in any case we cannot know it. The reason is simple: First, there probably are no O-punishable acts, because the relationship between the performance of a human act and a punishment of that act certainly is never a necessary causal relationship. Performance of some act by an agent is not an empirically *sufficient* condition for the *de facto* infliction of a punishment on him by another; there simply is no 'natural law'-like mechanism that would guarantee that the performance of an instance of a certain generic act invariably and unavoidably is followed by punishment. On the contrary, it is perfectly conceivable that – no matter what some *P*'s intentions may be – a murder is performed by some *R* without subsequent punishment. This is so because whether an act of murder is punished or not depends on a number of contingent circumstances, among them above all on whether the very agent who would be willing and able to inflict punishment is in a position to have reliable and complete information about such acts. Because of this informational requirement, it is extremely doubtful whether there could be any O-punishable acts in the real world. And, second, even if there were such acts, we would not be able to know it, because the most we could know is that all *observed* instances of the generic act in question were indeed followed by punishment; but again, we could never be sure to have complete information about all individual performances of the act in question; moreover, since O-punishability is defined as a property of generic acts, in order to know whether it is the case we would need to have knowledge not only about all past instances, but about all future instances as well, which is clearly impossible. Therefore, while it is very likely impossible to *make* a generic act O-punishable (i. e., to see to it that each and every individual performance of it is in fact punished), it is definitely impossible to *detect* O-punishability, thus defined. This diagnosis holds with one notable exception: the one person who can, of course, make an act O-punishable for *R*, because she always has immediate knowledge of *R*'s acts, and who can also be said to 'know' about the O-punishability of *x* for *R*, is *R* herself.[40] But

[40] But note that even in this case, *R* could know about this case of O-punishability only by introspection, i. e., by knowing that she follows a 'rule' of punishing herself for the performance of the generic act in question,

punishability by *self-punishment* involves no social situation and, therefore, certainly falls outside of Oppenheim's object of consideration.

A possible objection against this interpretation of Oppenheim's few statements about the concept of punishability could turn on the fact that Oppenheim himself has not explicitly said that punishability is conceived by him as a dispositional property of *generic* acts. The interpretation could, therefore, be rejected as too demanding or strict. If one drops the idea that punishability in Oppenheim's sense is a property of generic rather than of individual acts, then the indicated problems disappear: It is, of course, perfectly possible to make one single individual act ('the murder of *Q* here and now') O-punishable, just as it is possible to find out about that fact.

But the problem with this objection is that it makes the concept of punishability completely useless. If punishability is predicated of individual acts only, then that an act *x* is punishable means nothing but that this particular single act *is* punished when it is performed; and whether or not that is the case, i. e., whether or not some *individual* act is O-punishable, can only be verified *post actum*. Hence, a well-founded statement about the punishability of an act could never be a statement in the present tense; it would always have to be in the past tense; therefore, it would be entirely equivalent to a statement to the effect that a particular act *has in fact been punished*: '*x* was punishable' would mean exactly the same as '*x* has been punished'.[41] The notion of punishability in that sense would, therefore, have no function at all and be completely redundant.

Another possible objection could be to accept that O-punishability is a dispositional property of generic acts, but to say that my interpretation of O-punishability makes 'much ado about nothing', since dispositional properties are well-known kinds of properties,[42] and punishability is a dispositional property like any other. Why, then, should it be a more problematic concept than, say, that of solubility? Solubility is the property of a solid to dissolve in a liquid ('Sugar is soluble in water' means 'Sugar, *when* mixed with water, dissolves'); and statements about the solubility of some substance are nothing but empirical hypotheses arrived at by induction from observed cases – hypotheses which can be confirmed or falsified by each new observed case, but never verified. Analogously, punishability would be the property of some action to be followed by a punishment *whenever* it is performed; and statements about the punishability of an (generic) action would, consequently, be empirical hypotheses arrived at through the observation of individual instances of the action in question which were followed by punishment. That the punishability of an action in this sense is dependent on the contingent conditions (above all, the informational requirement) mentioned above could easily be taken care of by including them among the necessary circumstances of punishability,

and not by way of empirical evidence: although *R* has complete evidence of all past individual instances of the act in question followed by self-punishment, not even *R* can have evidence about the generic act to which O-punishability would have to be attributed. Generic acts as such simply are not a kind of entities one can have evidence about.

[41] The assertion that '*x* is punishable' in the sense of '*x* will be punished when performed' would be entirely speculative since there are no conceivable empirical indicators for this being the case: any sequence of events observed on other occasions would concern other (individual) acts that have no bearing on the case under consideration.

[42] On dispositional properties, cf., e. g., Garzón Valdés 1988, ch. I.1; Heil 1992, Mumford 1998. For a classical example, cf. Hobbes who explicitly defines the justice or injustice of a man – as distinguished from that of an action – as a „disposition" which exists „before it proceed to Act" (Leviathan, ch. 15).

i. e., by refining the definition. 'Punishability' would then be something like 'the property of an action to be followed by a punishment *when* the action is performed, *provided* its performance is known by an agent who is able and willing to inflict a punishment on some other agent every time he knows about his having performed the action in question'. Thus, if one finds that in the past an action *x* performed by some agent *R* has been punished by another agent *P* every time *P knew* about *R*'s action and was able (i. e., had all the necessary resources) to inflict the punishment, then one has good reason to induce that *x* has the dispositional property of being 'punishable' (for *R*, by *P*).

However, there are two inconveniences with this objection. First, it does not remedy the indicated problem with Oppenheim's conception, i. e., that a concept of punishability linking an action only to *future* events (namely, to the punishments *following* each performance of the action) cannot – for logical reasons – refer to something that infringes on the agent's freedom with respect to the performance of that same action. And, secondly, this conception has an interesting precondition, with considerable consequences for the concept of punishability. Because, as we have just seen, for an action *x* of *R* to have the dispositional property of being punishable in Oppenheim's sense, it must be the case that there is some agent *P* who not only has the ability, but also, so to speak, the 'disposition' to punish *R* every time *P* knows that *R* did *x*. This necessary link of the dispositional property of an action to be punishable to the 'disposition' of an agent to punish it is what makes punishability differ fundamentally from solubility: *P*'s disposition to punish *R* for *x* (and, therefore, the disposition of *x* to be 'punishable') is not based on a *causal* stimulus-response kind of relation between *R*'s action *x* and *P*'s punitive action, but on *P*'s *willful choice* of and *commitment* to a certain line of action. Thus, that *P* makes it O-punishable for *R* to do *x means* that *P* follows a kind of *rule* stipulating something like 'Every time *R* does *x*, *R shall* be punished'.

There is a notable advantage in taking this into account for Oppenheim's own purposes, because seen from this perspective, we can understand punishability as a property linking an action to something *prior* to each individual performance (i. e., to *P*'s disposition or *commitment* that performance of the action by *R should* have a certain consequence), rather than merely with (contingent) subsequent events. And this means that it is now at least *logically possible* that the punishability of *x* infringes on the freedom of *R* with respect to that *same* action *x*.

Now, what happens if we find an instance of a performance of *x* by *R* which, though known to *P* under circumstances in which *P* has the ability to punish *R*, *P* does *not* punish? If we stick strictly to Oppenheim's definition of punishability, this would have to count as evidence against the hypothesis that *x* is punishable (for *R* by *P*). But if, instead, we focus on the disposition of *P*, two different interpretations are possible:

On the one hand, *P*'s failure to punish a performance of *x* under those conditions could mean that *x*, indeed, is *not* O-punishable because *P* in fact does *not* have the corresponding disposition. In that case, the assertion that there exists an effective rule for *P* stipulating that 'Every time *R* does *x*, *R* shall be punished' is false.

But on the other hand, there is also the possibility that *P* nevertheless has adopted the rule and there has been only a slippage on his part, perhaps out of negligence, in the particular case. It is then not the assertion that 'Every time *R* does *x*, *R shall* be punished' that is wrong, but *P*'s action. Here, the rule still stands, but *P* has 'violated' it.

The difference between the two interpretations turns on the word 'shall': In the first case, the 'shall' clause is understood as a *predictive* statement about what *in fact will* happen under certain circumstances (i. e., as asserting an *empirical regularity*), whereas in the second case it is interpreted as a statement about what *ought* to happen, i. e., as a *prescriptive norm* – the norm that *R should* not be able to do *x* without being punished for it (by *P* or some agent of *P*).

This latter perspective, finally, gives us what we have been searching for: an alternative possibility for the conception of punishability. Instead of defining punishability as a dispositional property of an action – a conception which does not allow of 'exceptions' in the punishment-follows-action sequence whenever the corresponding circumstances obtain –, we can define punishability as a *normative* condition attached to an action, i. e., as the fact that there exists a norm to the effect that performances of that action *ought* to be punished.[43] This definition of punishability has at least two considerable advantages:

First, in contrast to O-punishability, if punishability is defined in terms of the existence of a punitive norm, an action can be punishable even if it is not in fact *always* punished when performed. Thus, we do not need to stipulate any ackward circumstantial conditions (especially concerning *P*'s information about *R*'s individual acts of *x*-ing) to take care of (at least some) instances of punishable, but unpunished actions. Moreover, it becomes perfectly possible to find out empirically whether or not a (generic) act *x* is punishable. In order to do this, what must be determined is the existence of a punitive rule or norm. And regardless of whether one understands it in the systemic or in the social sense,[44] this is something that can, at least in principle, be found out through empirical evidence.

Secondly, this definition is also – again, in contrast with O-punishability – in accordance with the ordinary, and particularly the legal, usage of the term. To this Oppenheim might object that, while conformity with ordinary usage can generally be considered an advantage, in this case the advantage is outweighed by the disadvantage that in ordinary and legal usage 'punishability' refers to (social or legal) rules and norms, which is precisely what social scientists should do without and what he himself therefore has been so careful to avoid in his analysis. But this possible objection has no bite. Perhaps it is Oppenheim's (in my view, very reasonable) suspicion against prescriptive statements in empirical science that has made him overlook that while norms

[43] The definition of punishability in terms of the existence of a norm, of course, leads to a number of questions concerning the necessary relativity of norms to some normative system, the identity of the norm-giver and the norm-enforcer, etc. These are common questions of normative theory which it is neither necessary nor possible to treat here. Good places to start looking for answers to those questions are, e. g., Hart 1994, von Wright 1963, Alchourrón/Bulygin 1971. Cf. also Chapter 4.

[44] In the systemic sense, a norm 'exists' if it is a valid member of a given normative system, i. e., if it „satisfies all the criteria provided by [that system's] rule of recognition" (Hart 1994, 103) – for instance, if it has been enacted by a competent authority, following prescribed procedures, or if it derives logically from the set of norms thus enacted (cf. Alchourrón/Bulygin 1971, 54 ff.). In the social sense, in turn, a norm can be said to 'exist' if there is a corresponding „general though not necessarily invariable" behavioural regularity, deviations from which are „generally regarded as lapses or faults" (Hart 1994, 55), or, in other words, a „social practice comprising both patterns of conduct regularly followed [...] and a distinctive normative attitude to such patterns of conduct" (Hart 1994, 255).

themselves may have a prescriptive content, their *existence* is a matter of *fact* in social life that can be treated in a perfectly 'empirical' way. Hence, what empirical scientists need to avoid are *norms*, not *normative propositions* (i. e., descriptive propositions *about* norms).[45]

Summing up, then, in view of the insurmountable problems Oppenheim's conception of punishability as a dispositional property of an action poses, and of the considerable advantages the ordinary conception of punishability offers, I think there is good reason for discarding the former in favour of the latter.

Now, where does this leave us with respect to Oppenheim's contention that the punishability of an action always infringes on a person's freedom with respect to that same action? In fact, it seems that the conception of punishability I have argued for also conforms much better than Oppenheim's own explanation to his idea that, besides strict and practical impossibility, there is still another way of making an agent unfree to perform an action. As we have seen, Oppenheim's text does not succeed in elucidating what this third mode could be. But once we understand punishability as a normative qualification of an action – linked to a normative attitude of an agent willing and able to impose, or make someone else impose, a penalty –, then this points immediately to another kind of *impossibility* not mentioned by Oppenheim,[46] namely, so-called *deontic* impossibility: To say that an action is punishable, in the normative sense that it *ought* to be punished every time it is performed, amounts to saying that within the normative system in question it is *prohibited*: on *threat* of punishment, it *must not* be performed. As Oppenheim himself explains at an earlier point of his study,[47] the very idea of punishment is that of a harm inflicted on an agent *because* he has performed a certain action. The specific purpose of a penalty may be that the mere threat of it operates as a deterrent, or that its infliction satisfies a desire for retribution, or that it serves as a penance; yet, these different conceptions of the function of punishment have one thing in common: they all rest upon the presupposition that the punishable action is an action that *should not* be, or have been, performed, which means that it is prohibited.[48]

Here, then, we finally have what Oppenheim is arguing for. By implying a prohibition, *punishability* makes an action 'deontically impossible', and that is independent of whether or not the *threat* of punishment accompanying the prohibition is effective as a deterrent, i. e., whether it actually imposes a *practical* impossibility. Hence, when an

45 On the distinction between norms and normative propositions, cf., e. g., von Wright 1963; Alchourrón 1969; Alchourrón/Bulygin 1971; Bulygin 1982.

46 Oppenheim at one point mentions „legal impossibility", but he presents it as just another variant of 'practical impossibility', i. e., in the sense of ineligibility on the grounds of excessive costs (1981, 25).

47 1981, ch. 2.1.3, where he presents a detailed explication of the concept of punishment.

48 This does not necessarily mean that, *vice versa*, all prohibited actions must be punishable. Although a prohibition not connected with a penalty may not be very effective, it is perfectly conceivable. – One of the pathological features of systems of state terrorism or tyranny is precisely that the conceptual link between punishment and prohibition is severed: it is an integral aspect of terror that aggressions not connected to any prohibited act are presented as 'punishments'. Mario Vargas Llosa, in his recent novel about the Dominican Republic under the dictatorship of Rafael Leónidas Trujillo (*La Fiesta del Chivo*, Madrid: Alfaguara 2000) has masterfully captured this pathology in one single sentence: „How could he punish him for obeying?" – that is the question torturing one of the characters, a loyal follower who has suddenly and for unknown reasons fallen into disgrace with the *Generalísimo* (p. 279).

action x is made punishable by P for R, what, in a very general sense, infringes on R's freedom – besides whatever possible surmountable or insurmountable obstacles creating inconveniences, if not strict or practical impossibilities – is the fact that P contests R's right to determine what actions he may or may not do, i. e., P claims *normative authority* over R.

In this context, it is interesting to note that Kant already saw, and Murphy – siding with Kant against Locke's idea that a right to punish already exists in the state of nature – more recently elucidated, that the very concept of punishment is necessarily linked to such a claim.[49] But that, in turn, can only be made within the context of a given normative system:

„[...] surely mere conscientiousness does not give a man the authority to punish. And this is so, in part, for purely logical reasons: If we say that each man in a state of nature is an authority with respect to punishment, then when Jones says 'Martin deserves punishment' and Smith says 'Martin does not deserve punishment', they are *both* – if equally conscientious – issuing binding judgments. But this is incoherent. Where everyone is said to be an authority, the concept of authority operates without sense."[50]

Hence, that an agent P makes an action x punishable for another agent R, *conceptually* implies that there exists a normative system from which P derives his normative authority (which, to say it once again, is not to be confused with his effective social authority) to issue punitive norms (for R, concerning x) and, in this manner, restrict R's freedom. In this sense, there is, thus, a conceptual link between a relationship of *unfreedom* and a relationship of *power* implied in the punishability of an action: When P makes x punishable for R, P exercises a *normative power*[51] in order to restrict R's freedom in the sense

49 Murphy 1994, 95 and 98 f.: „For [...] punishing in a state of nature is [...] conceptually impossible [...] Punishment must be authoritative, because only in this way can punishment proper be distinguished from the kind of infliction of social harm that is found, for example, in the activities of certain vigilante groups [...] Punishment demands, at a minimum, three conditions: a system of rules, authorities to apply these rules, and authorities to enforce sanctions for breaches of these rules"; ibid., 107: „As Kant views the state of nature, it is characterized by certain pathologies. In the first place, there is no fair way to guarantee that one natural right we have – freedom. In the second place, there is no way to legitimately acquire other rights and powers. And so government, with its Rule of Law, is to be viewed as a cure for these social pathologies. Government allows the acquisition of a right to punish and thus secures freedom fairly. And it provides a fair way for exercise of powers that are lacking in a natural state." In other words, if a harm inflicted on R by P following R's performance of x is to be regarded as a 'punishment' for x, what P cannot answer to the question 'Why did you do this?' is 'Because I just happened to feel an urge to hurt him' or 'For no particular reason' (in these cases, the action of P would not even be connected with the prior action of R), nor 'What he just did suddenly made me furious, so I wanted to hurt him' (here, although the two actions are linked, P's act is a spontanous reaction rather than a systematic punishment). Instead, P would have to say something like 'Because I can't stand it when he does x, and I hope that will teach him not to do it again'. – Note that in our example, for reasons of simplicity, P is at the same time both the norm-giving and the norm-enforcing authority. Obviously, that must not necessarily be the case: the agent or agency making an action punishable need not be the same as the one in charge of doing the punishing. In any case, since what is at issue here is punishability, we only need to focus on P's condition as a norm-giving authority.

50 Murphy 1994, 100. Oppenheim recognizes this in part when he explains (1981, 19) that the concept of punishment is linked to the idea of an „offense", and that offenses „are defined by man-made rules"; but he does not seem to have seen the full implications this has for the power relations implied.

51 Cf. Chapter 4 for a discussion of normative power. If we say, very tentatively, that normative 'authority' is 'power' based on norms, then in the realm of *factual* social power authority is *one of several* conceivable kinds of power, whereas in the normative realm itself, authority and power coincide.

of making it *deontically impossible* for R to do x. This means that the adoption of the 'normative' concept of punishability proposed here is perfectly compatible with the two conditions stipulated by Oppenheim: that punishability always means an infringement on freedom, and that as such, it is conceptually linked to an exercise of power.

(5) On this interpretation of punishability and its effects, we can now see that the distinction between Oppenheim's 'practical impossibility' and 'punishability' is almost identical to the one made by H. L. A. Hart, between 'being obliged' and 'having an obligation'. Whether or not someone is *obliged* to do a certain thing is a matter of judgment, of motivation and beliefs (Hart 1994, 83), particularly beliefs about the credibility of threats connected with the action in question: an effective threat 'obliges' one to refrain from certain actions in the sense that consideration of the expected consequences makes the actions „less eligible" (ibid., 82). Just as for Oppenheim, for Hart too this is a matter of reasonableness:

> „[W]e should not think of B as obliged to hand over the money if the threatened harm was, according to *common judgments*, trivial in comparison with the disadvantage or serious consequences, either for B or for others, of complying with the orders [...], for example, if A merely threatened to pinch B. Nor perhaps should we say that B was obliged, if there were no *reasonable grounds* for thinking that A could or would probably implement his threat of relatively serious harm." (Hart 1994, 82 f.; emphasis added)

This passage clearly suggests that a judgment saying that someone is obliged to *perform* an action in Hart's sense is exactly the same as a judgment saying that the actor is subjected to a practical impossibility, in Oppenheim's sense, to *omit* the action.[52] What the quotation also implies is that since such judgments may differ from one person to another, depending on their beliefs and motivations, it is perfectly possible that an actor may *feel* obliged to something although an external observer would not think that he actually *is* obliged.[53]

By contrast, in Hart's terminology, that someone has an *obligation* to do a certain thing refers not to a mental, but to a *normative* state of affairs. Regulatory norms make behaviour „non-optional or obligatory" (Hart 1994, 82) in the sense that they assign deontic predicates to actions. Depending on how the concept of a regulatory norm is understood, Oppenheim's punishability condition seems to coincide with this idea, if not fully, at least partly.[54] It is therefore not surprising to find that Hart underlines as one important difference between 'being obliged' and 'having an obligation' exactly what

52 Analogously, one could say that someone is *forced* to perform a certain action if it is *strictly impossible* for him to omit that action.

53 As already briefly mentioned earlier, in presenting Oppenheim's idea of 'practical impossibility', this difference raises important questions about the objectivity or subjectivity of freedom and, consequently, also about the attribution of responsibility for the corresponding actions – questions I cannot pursue here. Oppenheim evades these questions by stipulating that practical impossibility is in the eye of the reasonable observer, not of the – potentially unreasonable – actor himself. Particularly, he does not consider in what sense an actor who has power over another insofar as she can make him believe, *wrongly*, that she has made a certain action practically impossible for him and, therefore, can make him discard that action from his choice menu, could be said to infringe on his freedom too.

54 In fact, if the condition of punishability is thought to apply only to a subset of the cases where there is an obligation, this would only mean that Oppenheim's condition is cut too tightly.

has been explained above for the case of practical impossibility and punishability, concerning their different implications for an actor's behaviour:

„[W]hereas the statement that he had this obligation is quite independent of the question whether or not he in fact [complied with it], the statement that someone was obliged to do something, normally carries the implication that he actually did it." (Hart 1994, 83)

Thus, Hart brings out more clearly than Oppenheim himself that if both *practical* impossibility and punishability in the sense of *deontic* impossibility, are to be seen as conditions of unfreedom, they must refer to two very different kinds of unfreedom and, by implication, also two very different kinds of power: one that does, and another one that does not, necessarily affect an actor's conduct.

1.3. CONCLUSION

The analysis of Oppenheim's conception of social freedom and its relationship to social power has led to an interesting result. For the most part, Oppenheim's account has withstood the examination of its internal consistency, with the exception of one specific part: the part where, in the widest sense, normative questions are inevitably involved. The reinterpretation of this rather obscure part of Oppenheim's work with the help of one or two very basic ideas taken from the theory of normative systems has, I think, clarified and simplified Oppenheim's classification of the different kinds of social unfreedom. Three such kinds can be distinguished. In all three kinds, in the most simple, paradigmatic case, an agent infringes on the freedom of another by making it in some sense *impossible* for him to perform certain actions; what is different in each case is the *kind* of impossibility involved. An agent can restrict another agent's freedom by making an action *strictly* impossible, or *practically* impossible, or *deontically* impossible:[55]

- In the case of *strict* impossibility, the action is made *factually* ineligible.
- In the case of *practical* impossibility, though remaining a factual option, it is made *motivationally* ineligible.
- In the case of *deontic* impossibility, without affecting its factual or motivational eligibility, it is made *normatively* ineligible, i. e., *prohibited.*

To these three different types of impossibilities and ineligibilites correspond three different types of power:

- In the case of unfreedom as *strict* impossibility, the power required is a *factual* control over some of the affected agent's empirical circumstances, i. e., a *control over facts*.

[55] In other words, Oppenheim's way of presentation, suggesting that the relevant line of delimitation separates matters of modality (possibility – impossibility) from something entirely different (punishability), obscures the fact that in all cases, the question of freedom is a question of possibility or impossibility.

– In the case of unfreedom as *practical* impossibility, it is power as a *factual* control, so to speak, over a part of the agent's mental situation, i. e., *control over preferences* (which may, but must not, be based on power over facts).
– In the case of unfreedom as *deontic* impossibility, the required power is *normative power.*[56]

This distinction of three different kinds of social unfreedom and power seems to me the most interesting aspect to be derived from Oppenheim's account of unfreedom and its relationship with power.

But different as they may be, as we have seen, in Oppenheim's conception the three types of unfreedom do share one important feature: in all three cases alike, the existence of a situation of unfreedom implies that the agent who *makes* another unfree not only *has* the corresponding kind of power, but also *exercises* it. On this view, unfreedom in the social sense conceptually implies an active *interference* of one agent in another's options for action; and inversely, freedom requires no more than the absence of such interference through the exercise of power.

Oppenheim is certainly not alone in defending such a negative concept of freedom as *non-interference*, but he is arguably the political scientist who has offered the most explicit and articulate formulation of this conception and its consequences for the related fundamental political concepts, such as that of power. But it is precisely this view of social freedom that has also been extensively discussed and sharply criticised. If at all acknowledged, Oppenheim's conception is therefore usually treated critically, as a clear example of that allegedly inadequate view. The two alternative accounts presented next can be seen as two particularly sophisticated examples of such criticism, from two very different points of view.

2. Philip Pettit

A conception of the relationship between power and freedom which – for reasons related to the last point, but otherwise quite different from those exposed in the previous analysis – is critical of the position held by Oppenheim has been developed by Philip Pettit. In fact, the two approaches could hardly be more different: Pettit proposes a concept of freedom that is constructed in explicit opposition to the kind of concept Oppenheim advocates;[57] and his purpose in doing so is, also explicitly, that of reconstructing what he considers to be a *normative ideal*,[58] as opposed to Oppenheim's intention of defining a purely descriptive, non-normative concept. What is similar in both approaches, however,

[56] For details on the distinction between power over facts and power over preferences, cf. above, Chapters 1 and 2, as well as Zimmerling 1991. For more about normative power, cf. below, Chapter 4.
[57] Surprisingly, however, although Oppenheim's recent conceptual proposal is a prominent example of precisely the kind of conception he argues against, Pettit makes no specific reference to it.
[58] On the assumption „that freedom is an ideal that state and society ought to foster", the question is not, Pettit says, what ordinary usage of the term is, but rather „how we should best think of freedom" if it is claimed to be such a public ideal (1998, 277). [Unless otherwise indicated, all references in this section will be to works by Pettit.]

is that the authors seem to hold it to be almost self-evident that power and freedom are closely related.

Pettit's conception is interesting not only in contrast to Oppenheim's, but in its own right, and deserves a closer look.

2.1. THE RELATIONSHIP BETWEEN FREEDOM AND POWER

Pettit's concern about freedom is embedded in his more general interest in a „republican" – or, as he has also called it, a „social democratic" (1987) – theory of the state. In that context, of course, the freedom Pettit is interested in is not just any kind of freedom, it is „a social as distinct from an asocial conception of freedom" (1989, 161).[59] And it is not even just any kind of social freedom; rather, it is social freedom as restricted to the political realm, that is, what Pettit (1989) calls „the freedom of the city". The ideal to which, in Pettit's view, a state should aspire is that all its subjects – more precisely, „all current adult residents" (1989, 143) – enjoy „full" freedom in this sense. That is the „personal good" an ideal state should promote above all; and it is this perspective Pettit holds to be the characteristic feature of his own political philosophy (1989, 141).[60]

Drawing on ideas formulated by C. S. Lewis and Charles Taylor, Pettit explains that the freedom he is thinking of is practically synonymous with „franchise" or „citizenship": A person fully has that „freedom of the city" to the extent that she enjoys full franchise and therefore is a full citizen (1989, 142 and 165, n. 3).

In order to explicate what freedom in the indicated social sense means, Pettit reconstructs „an intuitive notion of what full citizenship involves" (1989, 142). The basis of freedom as franchise is thought to be negative liberty, defined in the following terms.

Negative liberty

An agent *A* has the negative liberty to perform some action *x* if and only if (1989, 144):

[59] In this respect at least, Pettit's and Oppenheim's concepts coincide.

[60] For a very critical assessment of Pettit's idea of republicanism, cf. the review article by Roger Boesche (1998, esp. 861–866). Boesche detects „many mistakes" in Pettit's presentation of the „republican ancestry of his ideal" and of traditional liberal thinking: „Whereas his ideal denounces any potential interference, he sees liberalism objecting only to *actual* interference [...] This in fact is a sweeping – and highly dubious – indictment of liberal thought and action [...] I doubt that a single liberal would agree with Pettit that liberals are only trying to protect individuals from actual arbitrary interference and not potential arbitrary interference" (ibid., 863). Boesche also contests the 'social democratic' conclusions Pettit draws: „he seems to think he can deduce from the principle of nondomination other ideals and institutions [...] Pettit thinks that a 'welfare state' follows somewhat logically from his principle of freedom. One problem with Pettit's discussion is that a central component of his argument, namely, an active state, does not follow logically at all from his principle of nondomination" (ibid., 865). For support of Pettit's conclusions against Boesche, cf., e. g., Robert Goodin 1988 who has argued that the most plausible and cogent justification of the welfare state is the idea that vulnerability and dependency – i. e., the main causes of unfreedom, according to Pettit – ought to be eradicated.

A more balanced and, on the whole, positive review of Pettit 1997 is Christman 1998. His main critical point is that in Pettit's critique of liberalism „Kantian Liberalism" is left out of the picture; and in Christman's view, Kantian liberalism is precisely what Pettitian republicanism is advocating.

(1) A normally (i. e., when unimpeded, but also unaided by anyone or any special circumstance) has the ability to do *x*, and

(2) there is no other agent *B* such that

(2a) B would knowingly (contribute to) „prevent or frustrate“ an attempt by *A* to do *x*, *were A* to undertake such an attempt, or that

(2b) B „credibly threaten[s]“ *A* with „such prevention or frustration“.

By 'preventing' someone from doing something Pettit understands making it „physically impossible“ for that person to do that thing, i. e., „removing that option from his feasible choice set“ (ibid.); to 'frustrate' another's action, in contrast, is thought to mean to affect negatively the other's chances of reaching the end(s) for which he has chosen (or would choose) to perform that action. In other words, while 'preventing' operates on the *possibility* of performing the action itself, 'frustrating' operates on the *utility* one can expect to derive from an action, either by increasing expected costs („imposing an appropriately heavy punishment on the agent“) or by reducing expected benefits („ensuring that the prospects which made the choice attractive are appropriately unlikely to be realized“) (ibid.).

***

Since this definition, as will be seen, is only of minor importance for the final development of Pettit's conception, I will not come back to it later. However, it deserves a few comments which I interpolate here by way of a brief *excursus*.

Obviously, Pettit's definition of negative liberty in some respects ressembles Oppenheim's definition of social freedom. Like Oppenheim's, it is basically a definition *ex negativo*, i. e., a person's negative liberty consists in not being made unfree in a certain sense. Also, Pettit's second and third condition, stipulating what it means to be unfree in that sense, remind one of Oppenheim's conception of unfreedom as strict or practical impossibility. At this point, the main difference between Oppenheim's non-intervention account and Pettit's non-domination account of freedom are not yet fully visible.

Still, the differences between the two notions are considerable. One of these is that Oppenheim's concept is a concept of freedom of one agent *relative to another agent*, and Pettit's notion of someone's negative liberty is formulated in *absolute* terms, with respect to *all* other agents. At first sight, this may not seem a very relevant difference. After all, Pettit's definition can, in a way, be extended to bilateral agent-agent relationships: if an agent enjoys full negative liberty in the sense defined, then he is free with respect to each and every other agent *B*; hence, if an agent does *not* enjoy negative liberty there must be at least one agent *B* (and possibly more agents *C*, *D*, ...) from whom that lack of liberty emanates, and therefore one can say that in this case the fact that the agent does not have negative liberty *in general* is due to the fact that he is unfree *in particular* with respect to *B* (and, perhaps, also *C*, *D*, ...). Of course, if negative liberty is defined in Pettit's way, i. e., as a *general* condition of an agent, then strictly speaking one cannot, at the same time, call that agent's situation with respect to some *individual* agent 'negative liberty' too. But negative liberty in the general sense implies a specific kind of relationship between the agent in question and all other individuals; in fact, it is actually defined as the *conjunction* of relationships of this kind with every other individual. Hence, each conjunct, referring to one other individual agent, 'contributes' to negative liberty, that is, represents a 'part', relative to one other agent, of the agent's overall negative liberty, and in this sense it would be a straightforward extension of Pettit's definition to say that an agent who has negative liberty in the general sense has 'negative liberty with respect to' all other agents. From here, it is then only a small logical step to break the concept down into bilateral relations, defining something like 'agent-relative negative liberty'. The advantage of such a conception of negative liberty – of which Oppenheim's 'social freedom' is an example – over that of Pettit is that it enables one to distinguish different *degrees* of negative liberty (or the lack thereof), depending on the quantity and quality of the agents relative to whom one does or does not have the negative liberty to perform some action *x*. Of course, since impossibility is an all-or-nothing affair, it does not make any difference for the specific choice-situation of an agent who wishes to do *x* whether he is prevented from the performance of *x* by just *one*, by *many*, or even by *all* other agents. It does, however, make a considerable difference for an agent's chances to reach overall negative liberty to do *x* whether he starts from a situation of 'partial negative liberty' with respect to *all but one* other agent, with respect to *most*, or with respect to only a *few* agents around him. Therefore, at least for some purposes it will be desirable to be able to express not only that an agent does or does not have the negative liberty to perform some action *x*, but also with respect to which other persons (or groups of persons) he does or does not have the corresponding relationship. Concerning this aspect, thus, Oppenheim's definition of freedom or unfreedom relative to some other agent seems preferable over Pettit's, since it incorporates this possibility of differentiation and at the same time offers a direct possibility for describing situations of overall negative liberty, whereas the conceptual extension from the overall to the relative case, although rather obvious, is more complicated to explicate.

A second difference which, at first sight, seems to give an advantage of precision to Pettit's concept concerns Pettit's first condition, which delimits the domain in which 'negative liberty' operates, to contain only those actions an agent is 'normally' able to perform. The question is, however, whether that requirement really does any work. For example, let *x* be the action of reading a certain book written in a certain language. According to Pettit's definition, one can predicate someone's negative liberty to read that book only if that person knows the language the book is written in, knows how to read, is not incapacitated (for instance, by some eye ailment), and would 'normally' have access to the book. Such a person would have the negative liberty to read that book if her attempting to do so would not be prevented or frustrated by anyone else and if she would not be deterred from undertaking such an attempt by a credible threat of such prevention or frustration. Now, suppose the condition is not satisfied – for instance, think of a case where a person has access to the book, knows the language, has no eye impairment, but is unable to read the book because she doesn't know how to read. Could such a person be prevented (or coerced into refraining) from reading that book? Certainly not: the concept of preventing presupposes an event which, if unprevented, would take place; to say that something was prevented implies the counterfactual assertion that, had it not been prevented, the event in question would have occurred. And that is not the case with an action someone is unable to perform. Similar arguments apply to the other cases mentioned in Pettit's conditions two and three, i. e., to attempts at performing some action (if I do not know how to read, I also cannot *attempt* to read) and to being coerced from performing an action (I cannot be coerced from performing an action I do not know how to perform and, therefore, cannot even attempt to perform). Pettit's first defining condition of negative liberty, therefore, seems to be *redundant*, since it is already entailed in his other defining clauses. To this, Pettit could possibly object that a person who does not know how to read *now* cannot *now* be prevented from reading; but such a person may some day learn how to read; and therefore one can very well assert *now* that *were* she ever to attempt reading that book (after having learned to read) she *would* be prevented from doing so or that *should* she ever acquire the necessary reading skill she *would* still not read that book because of a *standing* (now, and then) credible threat of prevention. After all, the definition does not say that someone has negative liberty to do *x* if he *is* not prevented from doing *x*, but if he *would* not be prevented from doing it should he ever attempt to do it and if he *would* not be deterred from trying to do it because of a credible threat of prevention. Thus, there is a sense in which defining conditions two and three do make perfect sense even if defining condition one is not actually satisfied (and the notion of negative liberty in Pettit's sense therefore is not applicable. But this argument raises another question, namely that of whether it makes sense to speak of someone's negative liberty to do some action *x* only in case he actually possesses the *ability* to do *x*, or whether this notion should not be extended to the case where an agent does not yet have the ability, but does have the *capacity* to (acquire the ability to) perform *x*.[61] For someone who does not know how to read, it does, of course, make no actual practical difference whether or not reading a certain book is under a threat (either in the psychological or in the factual sense) of being prevented or frustrated. But does that already mean that it makes no sense to say that she does or does not have the liberty to read that book? Suppose there is a persistent credible threat of prevention for reading that book, and some day our person acquires the ability to read. Of course, her *choice* situation has now changed: whereas before she *could not* have chosen to read that book, she now *can* choose this; and therefore it does make a difference for her now that she is prevented from reading, or even attempting to read, that book (although that difference has a *practical* effect only when reading the book is what the person actually wants to do, or when the option of reading the book at least occupies a

[61] Cf. von Wright 1963, p. 50 (emphasis added): „It is within a man's *capacity* to do a certain thing, we may say, when he can acquire the *ability* or skill needed for doing this thing, although he does not yet possess it."

place in that part of her preference order that is relevant for some of her actual choices). But would it be a plausible description of the change that has taken place to say that she is now unfree to read that book, whereas this was not the case before – although the only thing that has actually changed is her reading ability?

***

The definition of negative liberty is only the beginning of Pettit's account of freedom as franchise. In fact, what matters for Pettit is not people's negative liberty as such, in its absolute or full form, but what he calls their „prospect" of negative liberty, where a prospect of something seems to be nothing but what elsewhere would probably be called the 'expected quantity' of that something,[62] a person's prospect of negative liberty being the *amount* of negative liberty at issue, multiplied by the *probability* that one will actually get that amount.[63]

Only with the notion of a 'prospect of negative liberty' thus in place can we try to understand Pettit's concept of freedom as franchise, or citizenship.

Freedom as franchise

According to this concept, an agent has „full" freedom if, and only if,

„1 he enjoys no less a prospect of negative liberty than is available to other citizens;
2 he enjoys no less a prospect than the best that is compatible with the same prospect for all;
3 it is common knowledge among citizens that the first two clauses obtain" (1989, 142 f.).[64]

62 The idea of 'expected utility' is, of course, prominent in economics and in rational-choice approaches, but this does not mean that it necessarily has an 'economistic' flavour; for a perfectly general account of 'expected value', cf., e. g., the 10th edition of Copi's *Introduction to Logic* (Copi/Cohen 1998, ch. 16.5).
63 1989, 143: „if a person has a one-in-ten chance of getting ten units of liberty, then he enjoys the same prospect as someone who has a one-in-five chance of getting five units."
64 Obviously, the first clause is in charge of ensuring a certain degree of *equality*; the second, of guaranteeing a certain *minimum level* of freedom, and the third of guaranteeing *transparency* and the possibility of *consent*. Note, however, that this definition means different things, depending on whose freedom we look at: If we look at only *one person*, then she enjoys full freedom in Pettit's sense if *(1)* she enjoys an equal *or greater* prospect of negative liberty than all others, and *(2)* this prospect is also equal to *or higher* than the maximum an equal distribution of prospects would yield, and *(3)* that fact is common knowledge. But as soon as we look at the joint prospects of *two persons*, the picture changes: in order to satisfy clause *(1)*, the prospects of both persons *must* now be equal (otherwise, the clause is violated for one of the two) (or should „no less than that available to others" rather mean: no less than *some* other, i. e. would it already be satisfied if there is *one* other person with the same low prospect or an even lower one?); however, their prospects may still be higher than those of all others, and they may still be higher than the 'maximin' required by clause *(2)*. Third, if we look at the joint prospects of *all citizens* in a society, if *all* of them are to enjoy full freedom, then in order to satisfy clause *(1)* they must all enjoy the same prospect of negative liberty; that prospect can, in principle, be lower than or equal to the minimum required in clause *(2)*, but it can, by definition, no longer be higher (since it is an equal distribution, it cannot be on a higher level than the highest possible equal distribution). If it is lower, then clause *(2)* is not satisfied and *no-one* has full freedom. Therefore, all citizens have full freedom only if we have an equal distribution of the prospects of negative liberty *and* those prospects cannot be raised for all at the same time anymore. On this view, full freedom for everyone in a society may thus require that the distribution of prospects of negative liberty is Pareto-suboptimal: it may well be the case that from the highest possible level of an *equal* distribution of prospects, it could still be possible to raise *some*, though not all, people's prospects without lowering those of others.)

We thus have a *relative* concept of freedom with a *counterfactual* component.[65] Whether a person has full freedom on that account cannot be determined by merely analysing her own situation and the impediments or frustrations she may in fact be subjected to. Rather, by definition, the assessment involves the determination and comparison of the prospects of negative liberty *actually* enjoyed by (all?) other citizens, on the one hand, plus the *hypothetical* assessment of the highest prospect that *could* be reached if prospects *were* equally distributed, on the other.

Accordingly, full freedom for *all* citizens at the same time would be attained only if, indeed, everyone's prospects of negative liberty were *equal at the highest possible level*, and this were common knowledge among all.

This is where the relationship between freedom and *power* comes into play, because in Pettit's view, full freedom for everyone, in the sense just reconstructed, is compatible only with particular distributions of power:

„The requirement that people know that they enjoy a prospect of liberty no less than that available to others places severe restrictions on how power can be distributed. It puts constraints on the procedure for the distribution of power and constraints on the pattern of power's distribution." (1989, 154)

Note that Pettit seems to think that it is the *common-knowledge* requirement of his concept of freedom as citizenship, rather than the requirement of an *equal distribution* of prospects of negative liberty itself which imposes such constraints on the distribution of power. This, precisely, is the point where, in Pettit's own view, his „republican theory" departs from other current liberal theories. For someone to be free, on his conception, it is a *necessary*, but *not a sufficient* condition that this someone has a certain prospect of negative liberty, that is, a certain chance of being able to perform certain actions undisturbed by interventions of others. Freedom is not only „having negative liberties", but also „being assured [...] of having them" (1989, 158). One is free only if one can confidently go about performing certain actions because one *knows in advance* – and others know it too, and everyone knows that the others know, etc. – that the action will neither be prevented nor frustrated. The situation of a person who is free in this sense is certainly different from that of someone who is free to perform a certain type of action (act-category) in the sense that, on a case-by-case basis, she discovers *ex post factum*, each time anew, that an action (act-individual) of that kind was *de facto* neither prevented nor frustrated by anyone.

This conception of freedom, presented by Pettit in 1989, already shows two characteristic features which acquire even more relevance in his more recent writings: It is *not* a conception of freedom as *merely actual non-interference*, but a much more

[65] Note also that Pettit defines 'freedom' with the help of 'liberty', as if these were two naturally different things; but he can do this only because of a peculiarity of the English language. In other languages – for instance, in German or in the Romance languages – 'freedom' and 'liberty' translate into the same word (or, more precisely: the vocabulary is limited to words from *either* the 'free-' *or* the 'liber-' family). This already indicates that not all is well with Pettit's definition. At the very least, since he seems to be making a systematic difference between the two terms – rather than using them interchangeably, as most authors do –, one should have expected an explanation. For an illuminating explanation of the etymological genealogies and subtle differences in meaning of 'freedom' and 'liberty', cf. Pitkin 1988.

demanding one.[66] And freedom, thus understood, to some extent is compatible with, and even requires, the imposition of behavioural constraints through public institutions – a „suitable legal order“ (1989, 158) – since, to the extent that they serve the „mutual assurance of non-interference“, such institutions cannot be regarded as infringing on people's freedom (1989, 160 f.).

How exactly freedom, in Pettit's sense, and power are related is spelled out most clearly in his later essay „Freedom as Antipower“, the title of which already indicates the main thrust of the argument (1996).[67] Here, Pettit is concerned with the variety of power he calls „dominating“ or „subjugating“. Just as, earlier, he had defined a *social* concept of freedom, this is, of course, a *social* concept of power: dominating power is something an agent – who may be a „personal, corporate, or collective agent“ (1996, 578) – has *over* another agent (who must be „a person or group of persons, not just a corporate body“).[68] And, as already underlined in 1989, it is the absence of such *power*, rather than the absence of *interference* by other agents, that is essential for a person's freedom: „freedom is defined as the antonym of domination“.[69]

Hence, only by knowing more about the power the absence of which constitutes such freedom can we know more about the conditions under which a person can be free in that sense, and Pettit consequently dedicates a substantial part of his essay to a careful, step-by-step explication of the concept of dominating power (1996, 578–588).

Dominating power

Basically, Pettit says, an agent has dominating power over another if she has

- „the capacity to interfere“
- „with impunity and at will“
- „in certain choices that the other is in a position to make“ (1996, 578).

This definition, once again, contains a number of terms in need of more precise specification.

66 In Pettit's later view, in fact, there is no less than a „gulf“ between freedom as „the simple absence of interference by others“ and freedom as „invulnerability to an arbitrary power of interference on the part of others“ (1998, 275).

67 Much of the material of this paper reappears in ch. 2 of Pettit 1997. However, there are also some changes between the 1996 and the 1997 versions, not the least of which is that Pettit has chosen to give yet another name to the freedom he is interested in. Thus, he has evolved from „freedom as franchise“ in 1989 through „freedom as antipower“ in 1996 to „liberty as non-domination“ in 1997.

68 Note that the fact that Pettit characterizes the relationship he is interested in here as a power 'with an adjective' implies that he must think that, at least in principle, there is also a variant of social power which lacks the feature indicated by this adjective, i. e., a non-dominating variant of power; this implication is confirmed by several remarks he makes in passing. What it is that makes power 'dominating' will be explained below. For a systematic classification of types of power according to Pettit, cf. the appendices in 1996, 603 f.; 1997, 78 f.

69 1997, 273; see also 1996, 578: „Under the conception of freedom as antipower, I am free to the degree that no human being has the power to interfere with me [...]“

(1) In order for something to count as an 'interference', Pettit stipulates that it must be a „more or less intentional" action,[70] where the intention must be to „worsen" the other's choice situation.[71] This means that interference, and with it dominating power, is not a value-free concept: the identification of an instance of interference presupposes an evaluation, a comparison of an agent's situation *ex ante* with his situation *ex post*, in order to determine whether or not the latter is 'worse' than the former; and it also requires the imputation of a certain intention to the interfering agent. As Pettit explains, there are three ways how one can go about worsening another person's choice situation: A choice situation is defined by the *range of options* one has (or believes to have), by the *payoffs* one *expects* each option to yield, and by the payoffs each option *actually* offers. Therefore, a *reduction* in either one of these three elements is said to worsen an agent's choice situation.[72] What Pettit wants to see excluded from the concept of interference with the help of the 'worsening' idea are instances where an agent changes another's choice situation by offering rewards of any kind. Therefore, the only possible methods of interference, according to Pettit (1996, 578 f.; 1997, 53), are physical or psychological „coercion" or „manipulation".

(2) Pettit is also careful to note (1996, 580; 1997, 54) that when he invokes the „capacity to interfere", he is speaking of an effectively existing skill, not of a virtual capacity in the sense of some as yet unawakened, untrained talent or potential. Strictly speaking, that is, Pettit's 'capacity' is not a capacity, but an ability.[73]

(3) Next, in Pettit's 1996 view, there is dominating power only where an ability to interfere can be exercised „with impunity", that is, where there is „no penalty, and indeed no loss" resulting for the interferer from his interfering action (1996, 580). As Pettit observes, this actually implies two quite different things: on the one hand, neither the affected nor other agents must be in a position (i. e., able *and* willing) to impose a sanction on the interferer (in other words, to interfere with the interferer in a certain way), with the consequence that the interferer does not have to 'answer', cannot be made 'respons-ible' for his doing; on the other hand, there must also be no non-penalty kind of „loss" to the interferer from his action. Pettit does not specify whether he is thinking only of *net* losses or of *any* kind of losses, although his remark that the impunity condition means that „the interferer does not have to [...] renounce any benefit in order to practice the interference" (ibid.) seems to imply the latter. That is, however, not very plausible in the light of the fact that *all* action is bought at least at the 'price' of oppor-

70 The awkwardness of this clause is so obvious that it does not deserve further comment. I will take it to mean simply „intentional".

71 Ibid.; also 1998, 276: „Interference, as I understand it, involves intentionally or quasi-intentionally worsening someone's choice scenario by reducing the options available – say, by obstruction or manipulation – or by raising the actual or expected costs attached to one of those options, as in coercion."

72 „All interfering behaviors [...] are intended by the interferer to worsen the agent's choice situation by changing the range of options available, by altering the expected payoffs assigned to those options, or by assuming control over which outcomes will result from which options and what actual payoffs, therefore, will materialize. Context [...] fixes the baseline by reference to which we decide if the effect is indeed a worsening." (1996, 579; 1997, 53 f.)

73 Cf. above, n. 61, for von Wright's distinction between capacity and ability.

tunity costs: interference always 'costs' energy, time, and possibly other tangible assets and, in that sense, always implies renouncing at least to the benefits that could be expected from some alternative use of those resources. On the other hand, if Pettit were thinking of net losses only, then the first part of the impunity condition – i. e., that only interferences not accompanied by a penalty qualify as an expression of dominating power – would not be plausible: as long as an agent could disregard an existing threat of punishment when deciding about an interference because, all things considered, the interference, even when punished, would still result in a net benefit, it would be difficult to see why this case should be treated analytically in a substantially different way from a case where, while there is no penalty, the resulting net gain, perhaps because of higher opportunity costs, is no greater.[74]

However this may be, soon after the 1996 publication of his essay in *Ethics*, Pettit must have become aware of the problems the impunity condition, quite unnecessarily, creates for his concept. By 1997 (52 and 55 ff.), he had already quietly dropped it, and in 1998 he explicitly acknowledged that it had been „a mistake to introduce the reference to impunity at the definitional level" (282).[75]

(4) From the second clause of his definition of dominating power, therefore, only the 'at will' condition has survived, reformulated into an *arbitrariness* condition. In 1996 (580 f.), and still more clearly and extensively in 1997 (55–58), Pettit explains his main concern: What makes power 'dominating', in his view, is not the ability to interfere as such, but the basis on which it can be exercised. Where this ability is unchecked, unlimited, not controlled in a *specific* way, it is „arbitrary" and, therefore, dominating. Dominating power, in other words, is the ability to interfere at one's „pleasure", one's „own whim", or „arbitrium".[76] From this it follows that a non-dominating form of power would be an ability to interfere in the lives of others, not arbitrarily, but checked by another than one's own „capricious" will.

[74] Note that Pettit does not say what kinds of 'penalties' he is thinking of. Imagine a case where certain interferences by an agent are punished with the penalty of, say, social ostracism. As long as the interfering agent does not care whether he is well liked or not, this penalty will have no effect on him. It is a penalty alright, in the sense that it is intended and *usually* also functions as such, that is, it usually does impose a 'cost' on people, since most persons do care about their social standing; and the agent in question may even recognize that the others' behaviour is intended to punish him, and in that detached sense may 'feel' that he is being punished. From this perspective, then, the agent could not act with impunity and therefore would not have dominating power in Pettit's sense. And yet, since the penalty in the assumed case has no effect on the interferer, his situation would be exactly the same as if there were no penalty at all for his interference; hence, the interference takes place anyway, and the only thing the penalty it triggers does is to impose an extra cost *on the punishing agent* (since, as all action, the imposition of a penalty too is never entirely free of 'costs').

[75] However, that the elimination of the impunity condition is not an unmixed blessing has been pointed out by Kristjánsson: „If it is sufficient for domination that R can interfere arbitrarily in certain choices that P is in a position to make, then it seems that almost any R can hold dominating power over any P, as long as that particular R happens to be indifferent to the harmful consequences to himself that would ensue if he interfered with P. Ascriptions of domination and unfreedom (in Pettit's sense) would thus become a purely subjective and psychological affair [...] I prefer Pettit's earlier formulation, including the impunity condition, as a specification of *domination* – even though it cannot be fully equated with personal unfreedom." (Kristjánsson 1998b, 295).

[76] „And in particular, – Pettit adds (1997, 55) – since interference with others is involved, we imply that it is chosen or rejected without reference to the interests, or the opinions, of those affected."

While the impunity condition, now dropped, had been unable to capture this idea comprehensively, it had already indicated the thrust of the argument: For prudential reasons, an agent who is liable to be effectively punished by others for what they perceive to be a misconduct cannot entirely disregard those others' opinions or interests in her decision-making. Depending on the severity and probability (on the 'prospect', as Pettit might say) of the penalty, she will – provided she is rational – have to take those opinions or interests into consideration. The prototypical example of an agent with dominating power over another person is, of course, the slave-holder (within a slave-holder society): slaves are *unable*, and the rest of a slave-holder society is *unwilling*, to check in any way a master's arbitrary interferences with his slaves. Hence, in the treatment of his slaves, the master does not need to take into account anyone else's opinions, wishes or interests, least of all those of the slaves themselves.[77] He may, of course, sometimes happen to decide something that coincides with the slaves' own wishes or interests; but he certainly does not *need* to do so.[78]

On the basis of this conception of arbitrary, 'at will' action, Pettit (1997, 55) then stipulates that „an act of interference will be non-arbitrary to the extent that it is forced to track the interests and ideas of the person suffering the interference [...] – at least forced to track the relevant ones".

Two important practical questions with respect to dominating power are treated only briefly by Pettit. The first concerns the identification of the phenomenon, the second the possibility of eliminating or preventing it.

(i) Since the difference between arbitrary and non-arbitrary interference lies exclusively in the factors taken into account in the decision-making process of the interferer, it is, as Pettit acknowledges, rather tricky to tell them apart empirically, especially when it comes to interferences by the public powers into the lives of citizens – interferences which in order to be non-arbitrary „must be triggered by the shared interests of those affected" (1997, 56). Although it may be difficult to determine whether or not dominating power exists in a particular instance, involving complex evaluations and interpretations, Pettit says, it is in any case a matter of *fact*.[79] An adequate „test" for arbitrariness, he suggests, must be a procedural, „political" one: the openness of public discussion (ibid.).

(ii) As for the problem of keeping dominating power at bay, Pettit sees two general possibilities for constraining power in such a way as to make it non-arbitrary: procedural „filters" which effectively „screen out" acts of arbitrary interference (i. e., which

[77] However, cf. Joshua Cohen (1997, 98 and 99): „But slaves were not entirely powerless – mere extensions and instruments of another's will [...] Running away was particularly important as a display of power, [...] because it showed the costs that slaves could impose on masters (masters lost a considerable capital investment and needed to increase their investment in enforcement)".

[78] „Even with a benevolent master, and a wide space of actual options, the slave is no less unfree, because any choices remain at the master's discretion." (Ripstein 2004, 8)

[79] Christman (1998) observes that since it is Pettit's explicit purpose to present a *normative* conception of freedom (and, consequently, also of unfreedom), and dominating power is said to be what makes people unfree, it is inconsistent to say that dominating power is a purely factual matter. This is, of course, basically correct. But what Pettit seems to mean with his assertion that the presence or absence of domination is a 'factual matter' is that the negative evaluation of dominating power – wherever it exists – notwithstanding, it is a matter of fact whether or not a phenomenon of the kind defined as dominating power exists.

see to it that such acts *cannot* occur), on the one hand, and the imposition of sanctions on behaviour constituting arbitrary interference – a provision which does not necessarily eliminate such behaviour, but makes it liable to „exposition“ whenever it occurs –, on the other (1997, 58).

(5) Finally, the last clause in Pettit's definition of dominating power merely calls attention to the fact that such power may have a restricted domain. Dominating power, thus, is not an all-or-nothing affair; rather, it comes in degrees, depending on the extension and the quality of its domain (1996, 583; 1997, 58). Besides being „more or less extensive, depending on the range of choices affected“ (1997, 272), the dominating power of one agent over another may also be „more or less intense, depending on the severity and ease and arbitrariness of the interference available“ (ibid.).

So far the *definition* of dominating power. A remarkable feature of this kind of power, in Pettit's eyes, is the fact that its existence is likely to be a matter of *common knowledge*. This is so, Pettit argues (1996, 582–584; 1997, 58–61), because dominating power is basically a matter of unequal access to certain resources, where – with one notable exception – those resources are easily detectable, and because, regardless of which end of a dominating-power relationship one may be at, it is highly important to be informed about existing power structures. The combination of these two conditions – *interest* in knowing and *ability* to know – makes it likely that in fact everyone knows (and everyone knows that everyone else knows too, and so on) who has dominating power over whom and to what extent. Pettit seems to think that the exception he mentions is not of great importance for his case, since he hardly says anything about it. In fact, however, it covers a substantial part of what he had earlier identified as the methods for interfering with a 'worsening' intention, namely that of „manipulation“, as distinct from the methods of physical and mental coercion. Strictly speaking, Pettit asserts that the exception concerns only what he calls „backroom manipulation“ (1996, 583; 1997, 60); but since manipulation in general is something that works only as long as it is not discovered for what it is, the word 'backroom' does not seem to stand for any effective restriction of the method. Thus, what Pettit actually says is that when dominating power is based on means of coercion, its existence can be expected to be common knowledge, whereas when it is based on means of manipulation, no such assumption can be made.[80]

[80] Note that this makes for an unexplained difference between the common-knowledge condition in Pettit's early (1989) definition of 'freedom as franchise' and his later conception of dominating power and 'freedom as antipower': In the early paper, common-knowledge about the appropriate distribution of the prospects of negative liberty was, as we have seen, an integral *part of the concept* of 'full freedom', and from this Pettit inferred that only certain distributions of power are compatible with citizens' full freedom. But when he comes to dominating power (and antipower, as will be seen below), he no longer seems to understand common knowledge about the distribution of power (and, therefore, about people's degree of freedom) as a conceptual necessity; rather, he now seems to regard it only as a probable, but nevertheless *contingent empirical fact*. With respect to this aspect, Pettit's two conceptions thus do not fit very well together. In my view, it is an improvement over the earlier definition of freedom that Pettit has now dropped the common-knowledge condition as a defining characteristic, and defines freedom directly as the absence of dominating power. But this change does have consequences for Pettit's arguments, which he does not seem to have noticed. As I will explain presently, Pettit strongly emphasizes the psychological consequences of common knowledge about relationships of domination; in fact, these consequences seem to be his main argument for insisting that even

If there is common knowledge about existing power relations of the dominating kind, Pettit observes (1996, 584), this has psychological consequences which can hardly be overestimated. Such knowledge leaves the power-holders with an „awareness of control" and those who are dominated by them with an „awareness of vulnerability"; moreover, it means that there is also mutual awareness of that awareness, i. e., those who are powerless know that the power-holders can interfere with them arbitrarily *and* that they are aware of that ability. To both sides of the relationship, it is thus perfectly clear who „live[s] at the mercy" of whom and, therefore, those who are dominated „cannot enjoy the psychological status of an equal" (1996, 586; 1997, 63 f.), their „subjective self-image and intersubjective status" is impaired; as Pettit somewhat dramatically puts it,[81] they feel like, and are perceived by others to be, „a nobody" and therefore cannot „look the other in the eye" (1997, 71).

Were it not for the assumption that domination is usually a matter of common knowledge and therefore has detrimental effects of the kind just indicated, it would be difficult to understand why in Pettit's view domination, i. e., „exposure to an arbitrary power [...] of interference on the part of another", is something that is always „suffered" (Pettit 1998, 276). After all, as long as dominating power is not *exercised*, the subject's situation is not *actually* worsened. And one could at least imagine a case where not only the dominating power one agent has over another *is not* exercised, but where the subject also can be confident – perhaps because he knows that the powerful agent is a practising Kantian – that it *will never* be exercised. In such a case, then, the subject does not even 'suffer' in the sense that he would be *afraid* of possible arbitrary interferences. But even then, dominating power in Pettit's sense exists insofar as the power-holder *could* interfere arbitrarily if she wanted to. And the only way in which this can possibly be understood to make the subject of that dominating power 'suffer' is by way of the purely psychological effects of people's common knowledge about it.

Non-dominating power: Antipower

A person subjected to the dominating power of another is unfree. And such unfreedom persists, Pettit argues, as long as one agent has the ability to interfere arbitrarily with the decisions or actions of another, even if the power-holder never actually exercises that ability, or at least never does so in an 'arbitrary' way, i. e., without taking into account the affected person's interests. Power relationships of the dominating kind exist whenever certain means which *could* be used for coercive or manipulative purposes are at the disposition of some, but not of others.[82] Since, in Pettit's view, an ideal state should as much as possible promote the freedom of its members, this means that it should strive to eliminate, or at least reduce, the existence of such situations.

dominating power that is never exercised has detrimental effects on a person and that, therefore, the freedom-as-noninterference account is inadequate. This argument obviously loses much of its strength when it is realized that common knowledge about dominating power is only a contingent fact.

81 This description of the situation of the powerless *vis-à-vis* those holding dominating power under conditions of common knowledge is reminiscent of the description given by Avishai Margalit (1996) of what it means to be 'humiliated'.

82 Note that this means that such a relationship may exist even against a power-holder's own will.

But how can this be done? If dominating power results from an unequal distribution of certain means, such that some do and some do not have those means, it would seem that there are, in principle, two possible ways of approaching that goal, namely: either by controlling the distribution of means, seeing to it that the means necessary for effective antipower are in fact available to everyone equally; or by somehow 'neutralizing' the power-enhancing effect of the means held 'in excess' by some agents.

As far as the task of the state to enhance the social, and especially political, freedom of its citizens is concerned, this can only be done by way of an appropriate framework of *institutions*. Of the two available strategies, that of transferring a sufficient amount of „empowering" means to individuals, in order to „give [all citizens] equality in basic capabilities", and hence „reciprocal power", is, Pettit says, a rather recent idea, its form of implementation having become known by the name of 'welfare state'.[83] Traditionally, if at all, states have used the other option: that of neutralizing the resources and means of the 'powerful' by regulating and/or granting protection against their use for domination, i. e., through the *regulatory* or *protective rule of law* (1996, 589 ff.).

In any case, whatever the option chosen, the promotion of social freedom places special requirements on the institutional framework of a state as well as on the institutions operating within that framework:

„Freedom as antipower [...] requires a specific sort of law and polity in which the powers that be are denied possibilities of arbitrary interference, and if it is to be a universally enjoyed ideal, it requires attention to the patterns of domination associated with such contexts as marriage and the workplace." (1996, 602)

Finally, much for the same reasons as in the case of dominating power, Pettit holds that the existence of antipower too is usually a matter of common knowledge, and that it therefore has positive effects on the self-esteem as well as the social status of those who enjoy it (1996, 594).

Freedom as antipower

Since on Pettit's conception freedom thus implies non-domination, and non-domination in turn implies antipower, Pettit finally proposes to call a person 'free' only insofar as she has such countervailing power; that is, he proposes to take a conceptual shortcut and directly understand 'freedom as antipower' (1996, 597).

In his view, the advantage of such a conception of freedom is that it accounts for two important insights: on the one hand, as already mentioned, it directs attention to the fact that there may be reason for concern about someone's freedom even if no actual interference with the affected agent's choices or actions can be observed;[84] on the other, it also underscores that not every kind of (ability for) interference poses a threat to the

[83] Of course, „reciprocal power" could also be promoted by individuals in a decentralized way, and until 1996, Pettit advocated such a strategy. But since then he has come to argue that non-domination should be promoted and ensured not individually, but by constitutional means (cf. 1997, 95).

[84] „[W]hereas freedom as noninterference is consistent with the benign dictator [...] freedom as antipower is not" (1996, 600).

freedom of the agent who is (or could be) interfered with.[85] This has an interesting consequence for the ethical evaluation of political systems and institutions. Instead of saying that all political power necessarily restricts the freedom of those subject to it, and that therefore all political regimes face basically the same problem of justification, on Pettit's view of the relationship between power and freedom it becomes possible to argue that there are certain kinds of constitutional authorities who do not infringe on, or – to use Pettit's terminology – „compromise", the freedom of their subjects. After all, as long as legislators and administrators cannot rule 'arbitrarily', but must take into consideration the interests of those they interfere with, they possess only non-dominating power.

Theoretically, Pettit's account thus offers a clear criterion for a sharp distinction between systems based exclusively on power that cannot dominate and systems which work (at least to some extent) by domination. The common denominator of all political systems is, of course, that they necessarily imply power structures;[86] but this common characteristic should not, as Pettit sees it, make one overlook the fact that the decisive question is not that of the existence of power as such, but whether or not that power is dominating. Only dominating power, because of its detrimental effect on freedom, raises the question of justification. This precisely is one of the reasons why Pettit insists on his 'republican' nondomination account of freedom, against what he holds to be a specifically 'liberal' noninterference account. He fears that equiped with the noninterference account „enthusiasts about liberty" – he particularly mentions libertarians – will criticize *any* kind of apparent constraints on freedom, even if they are not arbitrary (as, for instance, those imposed by a just legal order). Therefore, in order to fend off the criticism such unconditional supporters of freedom may bring forward against just legal constraints, he prefers to conceive of freedom in such a way that, by definition, it is simply *not* impaired by nonarbitrary interferences (1998, 281).[87]

85 Cf. 1996, 595 ff.; also 1998, 276 f.: „On this view, free action is nondominated action, not noninterfered-with action [... An] action may be unfree, even if it is not interfered with [...] And [...] an action may be free, even if it is subject to interference." Most recently, in a paper published when this book was just about to go to the press, he has elegantly referred to this as „the orthogonal relation between agency-freedom and option-freedom" (2003, 396; to be sure, in this currently latest turn of his thinking about freedom he distinguishes not two, but three different conceptions: freedom as non-interference, freedom as non-domination and, newly, freedom as non-limitation, and the citation refers to the relation between the latter two of them; but it seems to me that when the consideration is restricted to freedom as a *social* concept, as it has been throughout the present investigation, the first two conceptions conflate).

86 See already Pettit 1989: „Differences of power arise with the political organization of a society. Once there is an allocation of the rights of coercion implicit in such organization – the rights of legislation, adjudication and administration – then there is already a hierarchy of power. That hierarchy creates a problem, for it introduces new possibilities of corruption, usurpation and all the melancholy ills of the political world" (1989, 154), and „if a state is oriented by the philosophy of promoting franchise, then it will be suitably sensitized about the problem created by difference of power [...] There is a need to reflect on what constraints are currently required for the maximization of franchise" (1989, 155).

87 Margalit (1996, 13 f.) has recently summarized the anarchist position in the following terms: „For the anarchist [...] the very possibility of coercion – that is, the very fact that people are subject to the good graces of an authority – constitutes humiliation. In order for people under authority to be humiliated it is not necessary for the authority to actually be coercive – it is enough that it constitutes a permanent threat hanging over the people under the institution's authority". Pettit offers an account which perfectly agrees with the position sketched by Margalit as far as its anti-noninterference aspect is concerned, but which counters the claim that it must therefore follow that *no* state authority can be justified because it is always „humiliating" (i. e., dominating).

And, of course, if the ideal is that the state should promote citizens' social freedom, it should not do so by means which themselves restrict freedom; the state, that is, should not seek to eliminate or curb the dominating power *between* citizens by wielding that same kind of power *over* them:

„[T]hose in power should not be able to interfere at will and with impunity in the affairs of citizens; their power over others should not be a power of arbitrary interference." (1996, 600)

Compromising freedom vs. conditioning freedom

The mistake of those who regard *all* public power as constraining freedom and, therefore, like the libertarians, constantly and indiscriminately clamour for less rather than more state is not to see the different effects of dominating and non-dominating power on the citizens' freedom. Pettit attempts to elucidate this difference by introducing yet another interesting conceptual distinction.

He begins by pointing out that there are, of course, several different meanings in which the term 'free' is used in ordinary language „to mark salient differences among choices and actions" (1998, 278). Definitions of freedom differ, depending on what one takes to be the *most important* difference in some context. For Pettit himself, as we have seen, for the purposes of normative political theory what matters most is whether or not an agent's choice is *dominated.* The existence of dominating power is, therefore, the criterion he advocates for distinguishing between free and unfree choices. For the reasons explained, he thinks that domination is more important than interference, whereas others insist that what matters most is actual interference and thus favour a freedom-as-noninterference account. These were the two rival conceptions discussed so far.

But, Pettit now acknowledges, there are still other differences between choice situations which are sometimes expressed by people in terms of 'freedom', and it is important not to confuse the different concepts implied in such usage. Pettit singles out one of them as especially salient: There are, of course, many factors in the world, „in particular, [...] natural limitations and obstacles" (ibid.), which, although they do not make one unfree either in the sense of freedom-as-noninterference or in that of freedom-as-nondomination, still *constrain* one's choices, in that they determine the availability, or the terms of availability (i. e., the costs), of certain choice options. Often, such constraints are seen and referred to as limitations of a person's 'free choice'.

Rather than ruling out such a usage of language as confusing, Pettit opts for distinguishing between two quite different ways how 'free choice' can be affected:

On the one hand, whatever one adopts as the *main* criterion for distinguishing freedom from unfreedom[88] is, he says, what determines whether or not in a particular situation a person's freedom is „compromised". Note that such a 'compromising' of someone's freedom must not necessarily result in any change in choice behaviour: a dominated person may make exactly the same choices as she would if she were not sub-

[88] He mentions as options only the two criteria dealt with before: interference or domination; but there is no reason why the same should not apply to any other possible criterion someone might accept as *the* criterion for freedom. What seems to be important – though Pettit does not especially mention the point – is only that the criterion may *not* merely be whether or not there exists *any* sort of constraint on an agent's choice.

jected to domination, as long as the dominator makes no use of his power; and a person may even defy an actual attempt to make her change her ways by interfering with her choice situation. Thus, freedom may be 'compromised' – at least on the freedom-as-nondomination or freedom-as-noninterference accounts – even if choices are left unchanged.

On the other hand, there may be constraining factors which do, indeed, induce a change in choices, by eliminating some option or by making its choice excessively costly (and thus 'practically' eliminating it from the choice menu, as Oppenheim would say). Hence, their effect is that one is no longer 'free to choose' that option. But as long as such constraints have nothing to do with the adopted main criterion of freedom (i. e., as long as they are not produced by someone's interference, or someone's ability to interfere arbitrarily, respectively), they obviously do not 'compromise' freedom in the sense just defined. Rather, what they do is set the *conditions* under which the agent can then make his choice; for short, they „condition" his freedom of choice.

Pettit must be thinking of something like the following: if you are stuck in a traffic jam then all the other cars standing around you and blocking your way certainly prevent you from stepping on the accelerator and moving ahead; but the cause of your being deprived of that option is not that anyone has interfered, or could arbitrarily interfere, with your choice (in Pettit's sense of *intentionally worsening* your choice situation). In this sense, while standing in a traffic jam 'conditions' your freedom of choice by making certain actions impossible, it does not 'compromise' your freedom – neither on a freedom-as-noninterference nor on a freedom-as-nondomination account. And in the case of the latter, mere 'conditioning' can even go much further and include actual intentional interferences, provided they are not, and could not be, 'arbitrary'. Thus, on this view even Ulysses, tied to the mast and deprived of the option of changing his instructions to his crew, can only be said to have his freedom 'conditioned', but not 'compromised': he is effectively and intentionally prevented by his men from doing things he would perhaps now want to do, and his choice options are reduced practically to zero (his freedom of choice thus being 'conditioned' in an extreme way), but the interference he is subjected to is carried out on his own orders and for his own good, and assuming that sailors depend on the well-being of their captain if they want to have a chance of reaching their home port safely, the crew cannot interfere with him in an arbitrary way – a fact which, besides, is common knowledge on that ship. Thus, on Pettit's nondomination account, here we have a man whose freedom of choice is almost entirely 'conditioned' away, but who nevertheless has his freedom 'uncompromised'. And, what's more, for Ulysses, *having his freedom conditioned in this way is a necessary precondition for not having his freedom compromised*: the constraints are imposed on him precisely in order to protect him from falling under a dominating power. In an analogous way, Pettit argues that those who in the name of freedom call for an indiscriminate elimination of state power actually do freedom a disservice: some framework of non-dominating power structures is necessary in order to *condition everyone's freedom* in such a way as to ensure that *no-one's freedom is compromised.*

With this final element, the outline of Pettit's conception of freedom as nondomination and, therefore, as antipower, is complete.

2.2. DISCUSSION

As it has evolved over the past decade, Pettit's has certainly become a very complex conception of freedom and its relationship to (dominating) power. In the following discussion, I will consider only a few of the aspects mentioned in the above presentation, to assess the usefulness and plausibility of his account, especially with a view towards its possible contribution to a better understanding of the concept of power.

Prospects of negative liberty

The first important element of Pettit's early conception of 'freedom as franchise' was the *prospect of negative liberty*, the idea being that for someone to have 'full' freedom the distribution of such prospects among citizens must fulfil certain criteria of equality.

Even if one accepts the underlying idea that freedom, especially political freedom, is something relative rather than absolute, which in itself certainly is not entirely self-evident, problems arise as soon as one tries to pin down exactly what it means for a person actually to have a certain 'prospect' of liberty. A prospect of that kind, Pettit tells us, is an *amount* of negative liberty, discounted by the *probability* that the person in question will really be able to enjoy that amount. But what does that mean? To find out, we must start, I think, by looking at Pettit's definition of negative liberty, to identify those elements of it to which the concept of *probability* can possibly apply, i. e., elements which may arise with more or less certainty. The only element in Pettit's definition which has this property is the *actual interference* (by way of prevention, frustration, or the threat thereof) by another agent that *might* take place should the action in question be performed. That such interference will, or will not, occur can, indeed, be more or less probable.

Secondly, since negative liberty, as defined by Pettit, consists in being able to perform actions without being prevented from, or frustrated in, doing so, the 'amount' of liberty one enjoys can, it seems, only refer to the *actions* one can freely perform. The most straightforward possibility apparently is that the *amount* of negative liberty someone has varies with the *number* of different actions he is free to carry out, i. e., that the „units" of liberty Pettit mentions in this context are simply (generic) actions. On this interpretation, then, an agent's prospect of negative liberty would merely be a function of the size of the set of actions he can perform freely, and of the probability that he can really perform all actions from that set freely. On a more complex conception, one could also take into consideration that not all actions are equally important for a person's liberty. In this case, actions would have to be attributed different weights, and the corresponding 'units' of liberty would have to be based somehow on the 'liberty-enhancing capacity' of actions.

One problem with this account is that, of course, the probability of interference may (and usually does) differ from one action (or group of actions) to another. What happens, for instance, if one and the same person has, to use Pettit's own terms, a nine-in-ten chance of getting ten 'units' and a five-in-ten chance of getting another five 'units' of negative liberty; that is, if a person can count rather confidently on being able to perform a certain set of actions without impediments, and, in addition, can hope with somewhat less confidence also to be able to perform some other set of actions freely? What is the overall 'prospect' of negative liberty for such a person? Is it whichever of the two 'prospects' is the higher one? Or the lower? Or their average? Also, what happens if someone is completely sure of being at liberty to do one single action and has a zero chance of performing any other imaginable action without being interfered with, while someone else has a very small chance of doing whatever may occur to him without being prevented from or frustrated in it? In this case, for the former, $p = 1$ for *one* action, and $p = 0$ for *all others*; for the latter, $0 < p << 1$ for *all* actions. How do the prospects of negative liberty of such two persons compare? And what does it mean for their respective situations? Surely, it will not do simply to translate the question of 'comparative liberty' into an 'amount-times-probability' formula. Negative liberty does not come in nicely packaged, homogeneous 'units' and with a single, across-the-board probability of non-interference. Pettit does not provide any clue for answering those questions.[89]

However, the basic idea apparently on Pettit's mind, that social freedom is not an all-or-nothing affair, but comes in degrees, and that the extent of a person's liberty is determined not only by *what* actions she is free to do, but also by *how probable* it is that she will really be able to do them without being interfered with, is certainly not entirely implausible.

But in 1989, though already working on the intuition that an account of freedom purely as non-interference has serious shortcomings, Pettit seems to have been still in the process of spelling out an appropriate conception; and therefore, he rather clumsily formulated a definition where in a first step (negative) 'liberty' is defined by the *actual* absence of interference, and in a second step, this clear *freedom-as-noninterference* conception is then weakened by linking it to probability, in order somehow to get rid of the actuality of interference. In any case, this was still a far cry from the *freedom-as-nondomination* conception which, despite the questions it gives rise to, certainly is a great improvement over the earlier account.

Interference

The next aspect worth analysing more closely is Pettit's conception of *interference*. In his view, there is interference only when there is an intentional attempt to „worsen" another agent's choice situation, where this means either eliminating some option(s) from the agent's choice menu or reducing the expected *or* the actual payoffs of some option(s) (that is, by raising their costs). Several objections to this view easily arise.

First, Pettit apparently thinks that reducing *expected payoffs* and reducing *actual outcomes* of choices are two notably different ways of interfering with an agent. In fact, however, it is hard to see how a reduction of the *actual* payoff from a particular available option (Pettit's own example is a punishment inflicted for a certain behaviour) worsens the *choice* situation of an agent, unless that agent is *aware* of the reduction, that is, unless the (subjectively) *expected* payoff is reduced too. The reduction of actual net payoffs as such certainly changes a person's *situation ex post*, but not her *choice* situation *ex ante*. Choice, and subsequent action, to the extent that it is based on some sort of cal-

[89] For a study of the possibilities of measuring freedom, cf. Carter 1999. However, Carter explicitly rejects Pettit's – and, generally, any republican or value-based – conception of freedom (ibid., ch. 8.6).

culus or deliberation about consequences at all, can always be affected only by *expected* consequences. Therefore, as far as the choice situation of an agent is concerned, reducing the actual payoff for certain actions cannot be seen as an independent means of interference – at least not if interference is thought to have anything to do with freedom of choice or action.

Second, since for Pettit a reduction in the number or range of options, without any further condition, counts as a 'worsening' of an agent's choice situation, he seems to think that it is *always* better to have more rather than less options (regardless of what the options are). This amounts to saying that with respect to choice options, 'more' and 'better' as well as 'less' and 'worse' always coincide. But what can such a necessary coincidence be grounded in? A simple conceptual stipulation will not do, since this would merely amount to a confusion of the categories of *quantity* and *quality*. Therefore, what is needed is a plausible substantive foundation of the idea that changes in the *quantity* of choice options are invariably connected with changes in some *qualitative* respect. This leads us necessarily to a consideration of the *content* (or still more directly: the outcome) of the options in question. In other words, although an agent's *choice situation ex ante* is, of course, to be distinguished from his *situation ex post*, the former cannot be evaluated in complete independence of its connection with the latter. Pettit would have to argue somehow along the line that, whatever the content of an option, it is always worse for an agent not to be able to realize it than to be able to do so. At best, this would result in a notion of 'worsening', where even the elimination of an option so unattractive that the affected agent would not dream of ever seriously considering it in his decision-process would be regarded as a 'worsening' of his choice-situation. But such a weak notion does not seem to be very interesting. A mere reduction in the range of available options can count as a 'worsening' of an agent's choice situation in an interesting sense only if the eliminated options would have offered better (expected) outcomes than the remaining ones, or if they would at least have been positioned sufficiently high on the agent's preference order to be serious contenders for choice. *Vice versa*, if I have, say, ten options to choose from, all of which I consider fairly attractive, and someone offers me an eleventh, rather unattractive option in addition, my choice situation can hardly be said to have 'improved' by that mere numerical extension of options. And, what's more, even if someone adds to an agent's menu of choice an option which the latter then actually chooses over the options he had before, this must not necessarily constitute an 'improvement' of his choice situation. Imagine that someone points out to you a new option you had not been aware of before and at the same time succeeds in 'manipulating' your perception in such a way as to make the subjectively expected payoff from this new option seem very high, while it will actually be low. In such a case, you would seem to have been better off before that 'broadening' of your range of options, as it may lure you into a decision which will result in a (relative) *worsening* of your *post-choice* situation. Such examples show that, when it comes to choice options, it is simply not very plausible to say that 'more' or 'less' always readily translates into 'better' or 'worse'. Whether the existence or non-existence of a specific option in an agent's choice set makes any appreciable difference for that agent's choice situation depends, among other things, on the quantity and quality of the remaining available options and, above all, on the potential position of the option in question, relative to the other existing options, on some value-based scale.[90]

Third, Pettit's conception of interference as the intentional worsening of another's choice situation is rather vague. Pettit's own example for a particular case of interference is the pharmacist who decides to „exploit" another's urgent need for a scarce drug by asking an unusually high price for it. But this is only an – extreme – case from a very large class of basically similar situations. Taking Pettit's definition literally, one could argue that not only the greedy pharmacist, but any grocer who raises the price of, say, cabbage 'interferes' with his potential clients because he, indeed, 'intentionally worsens' their choice situation in that very same sense, by making a certain option more costly: obviously, he raises the price with the clear intention of increasing his turnover, and he is certainly aware of the fact that customers are, however insignificantly, negatively affected by such action.[91] What becomes apparent here is that everything depends on what is taken as the „baseline" against which payoffs and costs are compared in order to determine whether or not there is interference. To be sure, Pettit acknowledges this; but he does not provide any substantial information or argument about what that baseline could possibly be. Lacking such information, the pharmacist might argue that, far from exploiting anyone, what he actually does is make a generous *offer* of a benefit to the needy patient (after all, he is not responsible for the patient's urgent need, and instead of offering to sell him the drug, he could just as well have closed his shop and gone home). In any case, whether generous or not, what Pettit explicitly regards as an exploitative interference is, at the same time, certainly an offer of some sorts, and that brings with it yet another problem.

Because, fourth, there is Pettit's restriction of the concept of interference to the methods of coercion („of the body" or „of the mind"; 1996, 578) and manipulation. Pettit's intuition seems to be that these are the only ways by which a person's choice situation can be 'worsened'; specifically, he maintains that the offer of a reward (or a bribe) can never constitute such a 'worsening'. It is not entirely clear from his texts what exactly Pettit understands by 'coercion' (especially 'of the mind') and 'manipulation'. But we know that the 'worsening' of someone's choice situation for him consists in reducing either the range of available options or (some of) the payoffs connected with them. Therefore, we can take a look at what such reductions involve and see whether all the possible ways of bringing them about can be understood, on an ordinary-language account, to fall naturally under those two headings, i. e., whether the employment of one of these methods is a *necessary condition* for bringing about a 'worsening', and especially whether offering a reward is, indeed, *not sufficient* to do so:

The *elimination* of an option from an agent's choice menu can be obtained by physically blocking her from performing the necessary action, which is, clearly, coercion

90 For a brief, but clear statement and discussion of the two main philosophical positions on this question, cf. Mills 1998. A *locus classicus* for a carefully argued – and, in my view, convincing – negative answer to the question „Is more choice better than less?" is G. Dworkin 1988a.

91 After all, that is why the grocer must (and knows that he must) keep an eye on his competitors and be careful not to raise the price of his cabbage – normally, not an especially scarce good – too much; in a sense, then, he must actually 'track' the interests of potential buyers, and therefore this is not an 'arbitrary' interference in Pettit's sense; but it still has all the defining characteristics of an interference spelled out by Pettit.

of the body; or by depriving her of some of the necessary means, which may perhaps be called 'manipulation'; or by changing the world in such a way that the means at her disposition are no longer sufficient for the option in question to be available, which, again, could perhaps be called 'manipulation'. Thus, the reduction of the range of available options seems to be the territory of physical coercion and of manipulation – manipulation, that is, 'of the world', not of the 'backroom' variety mentioned earlier.

The reduction of *payoffs*, on the other hand, is a much more complex matter. To begin with the most simple case, suppose only one single action is available, i. e., the agent can only choose whether to perform or to omit that one action. Suppose also that if there were no intervention from anyone, he would choose to perform this action, i. e., he would have an effective preference – for whatever underlying reasons – for performing it over omitting it. Now, as long as it stops short of eliminating an option completely from the agent's choice menu, any intervention of the kinds listed above (by physical coercion or manipulation of factual circumstances) may result in an increase of the costs of performing that action or in a reduction of the benefits to be expected from it, since what these methods boil down to is that, if not outright impossible, at least they make it in some way *more difficult* for an agent to perform the action in question or to bring about certain desired consequences by performing it. Obviously, the effect this can have on an agent's choice is that at some point the balance between performance and omission may tip and he may change his preference in favour of omission, because he no longer expects to be able to gain anything from performing the action; in other words, the (subjectively) expected *net* payoff from the performance of the action (considering the increase in costs and/or the reduction in gains caused by the intervention) may no longer be perceived to be higher than that of the other option. Thus, even when we consider only one action and the corresponding options of performing or omitting it, the choice between these options – if it is a 'choice' in the strong sense: a deliberate, consciously taken decision – must somehow be based on an assessment of *relative* expected payoffs. And this result extents quite naturally to the case where more actions form part of the choice menu: the effect of direct interventions in the sense of physical coercion or manipulation of the world, as long as they do not completely eliminate options, is an effect on the *relative* positions of the available options in a person's preference order.[92]

But besides such physical coercion or manipulation, there are also other ways how the benefits to be derived from an action can be reduced and/or its costs increased, i. e., how expected net payoffs can be lowered and an agent's choice situation can possibly be 'worsened': of course, this can be achieved by deliberately and systematically attaching certain side effects – what is usually called a 'sanction' or a 'disincentive' – to the performance of a particular action. As already indicated, in this context Pettit himself specifically mentions the infliction of a punishment. But here, the observation made in the first objection applies: a punishment can have an effect on a person's *choice* of action only insofar as the *threat* of its infliction reduces *expected* net payoffs.[93] To the

92 And again, as in the case of the elimination of options, interventions of this kind make a noticeable difference for an agent's actual choice only if they affect the options that occupy the top positions in that order.

93 Cf. above the discussion of Oppenheim's conception of 'punishability', and my objection that a punishment as such does not have any effect on a person's freedom of action; however, a *threat* of punishment, as Oppenheim correctly observes, can either constitute a „surmountable obstacle" to an action or make it „prac-

extent that it is effective, this may perhaps be what Pettit would call 'coercion of the mind'. In such a case, again, what happens is that the intervention brings it about that an option which otherwise – i. e., except for the threat – would have been chosen ceases to be the most preferred option and another is chosen. It is the change of *relative* positions in a person's preference order which leads to the change in action.

But if the effect of disincentives is seen in this light, one could object against Pettit that what happens when a reward or a bribe is offered for the performance or omission of some action(s)[94] is not substantially different: to the extent that such an offer is effective, the agent's mind is 'coerced' just the same, by an intentional change in the relative expected payoffs of some available options, into choosing an option he would not otherwise have chosen.[95] If, as Pettit asserts, an agent's freedom is not only 'conditioned', but 'compromised' when another can 'arbitrarily' wield the stick of negative sanctions, why should one not also regard this to be the case when an agent's choice is determined, in the last instance, by another's 'arbitrarily' wagging carrots in front of him? In other words: if one's freedom is thought to be infringed upon by the threat of a sanction which places such great expected costs on the *performance* of an action that it is thereby, on all reasonable accounts, made 'practically impossible', why should it not be plausible to say likewise that a person's freedom is affected by the offer of a reward which attaches such great expected benefits to the performance of an action that its *omission* is, on all reasonable accounts, made 'practically impossible' – i. e., by the proverbial offer one cannot refuse? When the *pressure of intentionally created external factors* is sufficiently great to make the choice of a certain option 'practically' inevitable, an agent's freedom seems to be affected, regardless of whether those external factors are incentives or disincentives and whether what is made practically inevitable is the performance or the omission of an action. In this sense, an effective offer seems to 'worsen' an agent's choice situation just as much as an effective threat.[96]

tically impossible". Note that because of this, Pettit's definition of 'negative liberty' (1989, 144) is, strictly speaking, redundant insofar as a credible threat with the prevention or frustration of another's attempt to perform some action *is* a contribution to the frustration of that action, rather than *another*, alternative way of making someone unfree to perform that action. – To prevent misunderstandings, let me make it clear that my use of a 'utilitarian' terminology in this context is not intended to suggest that such disincentives must necessarily consist of a material or physical harm to the agent himself; they may just as well involve, e. g., a threat of harm to a third party and the *moral* discomfort this produces in the agent.

94 Or when the performance of an action is somehow made easier by another agent; for simplicity's sake, I will not treat this variant separately.

95 In this sense, in legal theory – a field with special competence for the concept of sanctions – it is generally taken as self-evident that a sanction may be negative (a punishment operating as a disincentive) *or* positive (a reward or *premium* operating as an incentive). Cf., e. g., Kelsen 1960, pp. 26 ff.

96 Cf. Benn 1988, pp. 136 ff., for an attempt to argue against such a uniform answer: in his view, offers don't usually, but do *sometimes* worsen another's choice situation, thus constituting a freedom-affecting interference. Specifically, he argues, exploitation (taking advantage of another's lack of choice options) does *not* infringe on freedom (although, he says, it is unjust for other reasons), whereas extortion does. The decisive difference, according to Benn, is that in the case of extortion, the extortionist himself is responsible for the absence of alternative options that makes the other party exploitable. But note that in the case of offers, the two notions necessarily collapse, since, in the absence of other options, it is *the offer itself* which fixes the choice situation; therefore, on Benn's own terms, to the extent that an offer leads to exploitation, it is an extortion, and thus infringes on the exploited person's freedom.

Pettit could counter this objection by pointing out that, however similar the two methods may appear from the perspective just explained, there still remains a decisive difference between them: in the case of a threat, the change of positions in the agent's preference order is brought about by *reducing* the expected payoff of the previously highest-ranking option. This means, *ceteris paribus*, that after an interference with a credible threat of punishment the expected net payoff of the then most-preferred alternative is necessarily *less* than what it had been before. In contrast, in the case of an effective reward, the consequence is that, while there is no change in the expected net payoff from the previously best option, some previously less-than-best option now promises an *even higher* net payoff. In this sense, then, an agent's choice situation is clearly *improved* by the offer of a reward. If we take the *situation before the intervention* as the 'baseline', then in the case of an effective threat of punishment an agent *can* still perform the action he previously preferred most, but *only at a cost*;[97] and if he discards that option and chooses what under the obtaining circumstances has become the best alternative, the expected payoff will in any case be *lower* than the best feasible outcome without the threat. If we then look at the case where a reward is offered, we see that, again, the agent *can* still choose what he previously preferred most, and he can even do so *at no cost*, compared with the baseline of his *ex ante* situation;[98] only that, *in addition*, there is now an *even better* option available to him. Hence, in this sense, indeed, only a threat of punishment, but not an offer of a reward entails a 'worsening' of an agent's choice situation.[99]

If we take the objection and the counter-objection together, this means that the offer of a reward, although, just as a threat of punishment, it works – if it works – by 'coercion of the mind', nevertheless does not count as an infringement of an agent's freedom, because freedom is compromised only by (certain kinds of) interferences, and the offer of a reward is not an interference in Pettit's terms since it does not constitute a 'worsening' of the agent's choice situation. This result is remarkable because it reveals that on Pettit's account it is *not* the *coercion* element that is antagonistic to freedom, but only the 'worsening' of the choice options, regardless of how this is brought about.

The problem with this view is not so much that it may seem unusual.[100] Above all, there is a problem with the baseline it presupposes; because there is at least one kind of action which, though it does *not* fall under Pettit's acknowledged methods of interference, can nevertheless result in a situation that would have to count as a 'worsening',

Steiner (1974/75) agrees with the argument that there is no decisive qualitative difference between the effects of offers and threats on preferences and, thus, on freedom; but instead of concluding from there that *offers as well as threats* can infringe on a person's freedom, he draws the opposite conclusion: that *neither offers nor threats* compromise freedom (cf. Kristjánsson 1996, 40).

97 In Pettit's terms, he is not 'prevented' from performing the action, but 'frustrated' in attempting to reach a certain outcome.

98 In other words, there is neither 'frustration' nor 'prevention'.

99 However, Pettit cannot argue in this way if he wants to uphold his 'greedy pharmacist' example. For the example to stand, he must accept at least something like Benn's view that offers can impair freedom at least in some cases. – I will have more to say about the status of offers as compared to threats in the discussion of Kristjánsson's account, in the next section.

100 Against the common view that unfreedom is primarily related to coercion („impediments and constraints") and in favour of the view that it is basically a matter of available options, cf. also Benn 1988, 132.

namely, *sincere and truthful information* or *reasoning*, which can hardly be regarded as an instance of either coercion, in its physical or mental variety, or manipulation, whether of the world or of the mind. Suppose, for instance, that *A* realizes that *B* has an illusory view of his own available options and/or of the outcomes to be expected from them, and *A* succeeds in (truthfully) *convincing B* to adopt a more realistic outlook. For *B*, this may indeed lead to a reduction of his *perceived* range of options and/or *expected* payoffs – a reduction clearly intended by the intervening agent. There is thus a 'worsening' in Pettit's sense (which was defined as just that: a reduction in the perceived number of options or in the payoffs to be expected from certain options, as compared with the situation before the intervention). But would it not be extremely odd to say that to have a realistic view of one's choice situation is 'worse', in terms of one's freedom, than to have an embellished, unrealistic one?[101] Here, it seems, we have one of the cases which remind us that concerning (perceived) choice options 'less' is not always 'worse'.[102]

In summary, we have seen that there are cases where there is coercion, but no interference because there is no 'worsening' (the case of offers of reward); and there are cases where there is neither manipulation nor coercion, but 'worsening' in Pettit's sense, though to call it that seems strange (the case of disillusioning conviction). Therefore, neither are the methods singled out by Pettit as the only methods of interference the only ones capable of bringing about a 'worsening' in his sense, nor is his conception of 'worsening' a choice situation evaluatively convincing.

[101] By this, I do not mean to say that it is always and under any circumstances best to have complete and truthful information about one's condition. Certainly, there are situations where it may arguably be better – subjectively preferable, or objectively more advisable – for a person to hold on to a mistaken belief, to an illusion, and not be 'enlightened'. In matters of love and death, for instance, we sometimes have good reasons to demand to be allowed to keep our „cherished ignorance" (Garzón Valdés 1999). But those are precisely situations of *impotence* where there is no hope for a change to the better, i. e., where we either have no choice at all or where all available options are so unattractive that the cost of deliberating on them is perceived to be higher than any possible gain from a deliberate choice. But when it comes to situations where deliberate choice can make a difference, it always seems best to be able to choose on the basis of the most complete and correct information about available options and their probable consequences to be had (at reasonable cost).

[102] This is precisely why paternalism can be morally justified: paternalistic interventions 'worsen' an agent's choice situation in Pettit's sense by reducing the number of options or the payoffs to be expected from certain actions, and they do so intentionally, sometimes even using coercive means. Hence, according to Pettit, they constitute interferences. But in the case of justified paternalistic acts, the purpose of restricting the agent's choice options is to protect him from 'himself', preventing him from making 'self-harming' choices. Cases of justified paternalism, thus, show that sometimes one can regard a person to have been made *better* off by having her choice options *restricted* (cf. VanDeVeer 1986, Garzón Valdés 1990). To call this a 'worsening' intervention hardly seems warranted. On the other hand, the fact that there is such a concept as 'temptation' indicates that on some occasions we would regard it, at least in some sense, as a *worsening* of our choice situation if someone were to *add* certain kinds of options to our choice menu. The fact that one succumbs to the temptation constituted by an 'unrejectable' offer does not necessarily mean that one is happy to have been made the offer in the first place (why else would anyone think of pleading not to be led into temptation?). Hence, the argument that the decisive distinction between threats and offers lies in the agent's second-order preferences – i. e., in the fact that agents mind acting under a threat, but do not mind acting on an offer and that, therefore, an effective threat makes choice unvoluntary and unfree whereas an effective offer does not (G. Dworkin 1988b, 155) – is not true for *all* offers of incentives; Dworkin himself is careful enough to claim only that this is „normally" the case; but „normally" is not enough for an argument intended to establish a *systematic* difference between threats and offers.

Because of these problems with Pettit's conception, I think that if we want to get a plausible, useful concept of interference (and, subsequently, of freedom and power), we must drop the 'worsening' requirement and replace it with some other condition.

If we keep in mind that the purpose of the whole exercise is the reconstruction of a plausible concept of freedom of choice and/or action, then perhaps Pettit's worsening clause should be changed to something like the following: We can speak of an 'interference' of one agent with another when the former intentionally acts in such a way as to either eliminate certain actions from the latter's choice menu (prevention) or make them *relatively less attractive* (frustration). The latter can, obviously, be brought about either by disincentives (making the undesired action itself less attractive, by making it more costly or less profitable) or by incentives (making some *other* option more attractive, e. g., by offering a reward for its performance), by persuasion (which may be regarded as a kind of 'manipulation of the mind') or by truthful information (conviction).[103]

The concept of interference which results from this modification of Pettit's proposal is, I think, still compatible with his general purpose, and may even serve it better. It can account, as I think Pettit's own conception cannot, for the intuition that interferences may be for better *or* for worse. And it does not affect in any way his distinction between interferences which do and those which do not compromise a person's freedom.

Arbitrariness

This distinction, in turn, is based, as we have seen, on the notions of *arbitrary* versus *non-arbitrary* interferences. In my view, this is the weakest point in Pettit's reconstruction of freedom and its relationship to power. His distinction between arbitrariness and non-arbitrariness contains, I think, a fundamental flaw, which I will try to explain presently. In order to prepare the argument, however, I will first raise another point which, though perhaps of lesser importance, has some bearing on the following.

(1) As I have pointed out, Pettit is aware of the fact that it may not always be easy to know whether someone's ability to interfere with others, or some actually occuring interference, is of the arbitrary or the non-arbitrary kind. When political issues are openly debated in public, he says, that may be as good an indicator as we can get for the (actual) non-arbitrariness of political decision-making. And he recommends two ways how a possibly existing dominating power (i. e., an ability to interfere arbitrarily with others) can be reduced: on the one hand, certain kinds of arbitrary interferences can be made *impossible*, he suggests, by procedural „filters"; on the other, they can be made liable to „exposition" through the imposition of sanctions.[104]

[103] On the threat-offer issue, then, I think Swanton (1992) has a point when she argues that much of the discussion has been misguided because of a „failure to appreciate that offers and threats should be understood as illocutionary acts" (108) (i. e., that the conceptual difference between them basically relates to their different kinds of illocutionary force), whereas „Whether or not threats and offers limit freedom depends on their perlocutionary effects" (109). If one accepts this interpretation, it follows *logically* that threats *and* offers, regardless of the intentions pursued with them by their issuer in each case, sometimes *do* and sometimes *don't* infringe upon the other side's freedom. I will come back to this issue in the next section.

[104] Cf. Pettit 2001, ch. 7, for an extended presentation of his ideas about such mechanisms and resources.

First, concerning Pettit's procedural filters, it should be noted that there is only one sense in which purely procedural means can make certain actions 'impossible', and that is, once again, the *deontic* or *normative* sense. This becomes immediately evident when one considers what exactly it is that procedural provisions *do* – at what point and how they manage to function as 'filters'. When a certain procedure is required for the performance of a certain act (say, an act of 'legislation'), this means no more and no less than that, as long as that procedure is not observed, whatever motions one may go through simply will not *constitute*, will not *count as*, such an act.[105]

For the present purpose, the relevant point is that what procedural constraints obviously cannot accomplish is to eliminate the factual ability of performing the 'motions'; all they can do is 'disempower' someone from performing certain *acts* by going through certain motions. Therefore, Pettit's procedural filters can only operate on the ability of arbitrary interference through *institutional* (as distinct from *natural*) acts.[106] Hence, where an interference consists, so to speak, of the naked motion itself, purely procedural filters cannot reduce dominating power.[107] The possible role of procedural barriers in reining in arbitrary interference is, thus, doubly limited: it applies only to institutional acts, and it eliminates only a normative possibility, not a factual ability. The great challenge for the ideal freedom-enhancing state envisioned by Pettit is, so to speak, to *make the institutional prevail over the natural*, and *the normative over the factual* in matters of (horizontal or vertical) interference. And that is something procedural requirements as such have no grip on.

Where procedural constraints are inapplicable, we are left with the second strategy acknowledged by Pettit: the imposition of sanctions. But sanctions, to say the obvious once again, function only *post hoc*, and if they are to have any *ex ante* deterring effect on the actual performance of arbitrary interferences (making them, if not impossible, at least less likely to occur in the future) it can only be through the constitution of a *credible threat*: The expectation of a harm or inconvenience produced by the infliction of the sanction must provide a sufficient disincentive to those who would be in a position to perform arbitrary interferences. Here, the problem is, however, that such an effect can only arise if the actions of powerful agents are *reliably monitored*, that is, if violations of the non-arbitrariness clause *can*, and generally *will*, be detected. But that is very unlikely, considering that not only is there no sure test for arbitrariness: even open public debate – the criterion recommended by Pettit – cannot accomplish very much. After all, arbitrariness cannot be inferred in any way from the external manifestation of an inter-

105 That is, of course, from the point of view of the normative system which stipulates that the procedure is required, i. e. the system to which the procedural rule belongs. I will not say anything more at this point about the conceptual questions this raises, since it would lead us too far away from the subject at issue here. For some more details, cf. below, Chapter 4, on the concept of normative power.

106 For a discussion of this distinction cf., e. g., Redondo 1999, ch. I; Ruiter 1993.

107 A procedural filter may, for instance, make it (normatively) impossible for someone to 'punish' another, by reserving the imposition of 'punishments' to certain especially empowered agents; whatever anyone else does will then not count as a 'punishment'; but that does not, of course, make it impossible for the agent in question to 'go through the motions of punishment', e. g., by inflicting the same physical pain which, if preceded by the right procedures, would constitute a punishment. Or, to say it differently, that the state has the monopoly on the *legitimate exercise* of violence does, obviously, not mean that it has a monopoly on the *exercise* of violence.

ference, since it is *conceptually* linked not to an action's result or consequences, but to the agent's subjective *reasons* or *motives* for performing it. And Pettit's non-arbitrariness clause, rather than stipulating that an interference is arbitrary whenever it does not *effectively serve* the interests or opinions of those affected by it, only prescribes that those interests or opinions must be *taken into account* when deciding about what action to take (interferences „must be triggered" by the consideration of those interests or opinions, must be „forced to track" them). And whether or not that has been the case is not only not manifested in the action itself; it cannot even be inferred from the action's *consequences*, because an agent may *err* and in effect harm someone's interests even when he has not violated the non-arbitrariness clause; and, *vice versa*, an agent may bring about effects which (happen to) serve the interests of those affected even when he interferes arbitrarily and simply does what, for some reason, he considers to be appropriate, without considering the wishes, interests or opinions of those affected. Neither actions nor their consequences can thus be regarded as reliable indicators for arbitrariness.

For the *justification* of an interference, one could perhaps argue that it is necessary that it be 'triggered' by the *intention* to avoid harm (to the person subjected to the interference herself *or* to others), i. e., by a consideration of the interests of those affected, but that *an additional* necessary condition is that there must also be a high probability of *success*, and that, therefore, if negative consequences for those affected result, arbitrariness may be *presumed* unless the interferer can present convincing evidence to the contrary.[108] Hence, the accountability of decision-makers in open public debate may be an important device for testing the *justifiability* of political decisions. But for arbitrariness in Pettit's sense, only the first condition applies, and its satisfaction can hardly be ascertained through public debate. Therefore, the threat of exposition Pettit holds to be linked to the imposition of sanctions on arbitrary interferences does not seem to have much bite.

Taking into account that the effective imposition of a negative sanction (i. e., the regular infliction of a harm) for a particular kind of behaviour is indicative of the existence of a norm prohibiting that behaviour, the problem with the prohibition of arbitrary interference backed by an effective threat of sanction boils down to the problem of knowing for particular states of affairs whether they are cases to which such a norm is applicable.

And there is still another general point. Even if a threat of punishment were an effective deterrent from arbitrary interference, it could as such never – not even when accompanied by actual sanctioning in case an arbitrary interference is believed to *have* taken place – affect the *existence of dominating power* in Pettit's sense. Because, as Pettit himself has underlined, for his conception it is not sufficient that no arbitrary interference *does* in fact occur; it must also be the case that no-one has the *ability* of performing such interferences. And factual *ability* is, of course, not affected by a threat of punishment. What is affected, at best, is the *disposition* to act on that ability. The idea that a threat of sanction can be an effective way for countering dominating power, i. e.,

[108] Such a 'reasonable chance of success' condition only reflects the ancient wisdom that the road to hell is paved with good intentions. For a more recent elaborate arguments why good intentions are not enough for a justification of interferences in the affairs of others, neither on the harm-to-others nor on the harm-to-self basis, cf. Garzón Valdés 1990, 1991.

for destroying the ability of arbitrary interference, perhaps indicates that, despite having been eliminated from the definition, the *impunity* clause still lingers in the back of Pettit's thoughts about dominating power. That is, of course, not a totally implausible idea: Surely, the 'master' who is liable to a sanction should it occur to him to whip his 'slave' is not really a master over a slave anymore, in the strict sense of the terms. But the reason for this is not that he *could* no longer treat the other person in an arbitrary way; rather, it is that it may be reasonably expected that he *will* in fact not do so, because of the external constraints (the incentive structure) he is facing. In other words, a threat of sanction, when effective, does not take away the factual *ability*, but only the *motive* to act toward others in an arbitrary way.[109] And regardless of whether or not it succeeds in erecting an effective threat, the imposition of a sanction, just as in the case of procedural constraints, makes arbitrary interference *impossible* only in the *deontic* sense.

Since Pettit gives such a prominent role to constitutive and regulatory norms in his account of the workings of dominating power, arbitrary interference and antipower, it seems important to keep in mind these characteristics of the operation of such constraints. They can, at best, reduce the *actual exercise* of dominating power, but they cannot reduce the *existence* of such power.[110]

(2) The preceding observations point out some problems Pettit's account of how arbitrary interferences can be curbed would have to confront even in the *best possible case*, i. e., if his conception of arbitrariness and non-arbitrariness were as such acceptable. I will now attempt to show, however, that its acceptance is not warranted.[111]

As we have seen, for Pettit, 'arbitrary' interference is interference at the interferring agent's own will (however capricious it may be), at his own *'arbitrium'*.[112] Besides this positive definition of arbitrariness, which is vague enough not to be implausible at first sight, Pettit also tells us what condition an interference must satisfy in order to be 'non-arbitrary', that is, if it is to *lack* the property of arbitrariness: interference is non-arbitrary, he says, to the extent that it 'tracks' the interests of those suffering the interference.

With the positive and the negative definition thus placed side-by-side, the problem with this conception leaps to the eye: What is wrong here is that, contrary to linguistic convention (and without any apparent reason), arbitrariness in Pettit's sense (here-

109 Think of the case of Augusto Pinochet who, to his own surprise, was subjected, if somewhat belatedly, to international and domestic criminal investigations. High hopes were raised by the possibility that he may have to stand trial – hopes, that is, regarding the future effects this may have on dictators all over the world. But, of course, these hopes cannot reasonably include that the end of impunity for state terrorists such a trial might signal will take away anyone's *ability* to torture and kill, where that ability already exists; in *this sense*, the demonstration of punishability can do nothing to reduce dominating power in the world. One can only hope that the loss of impunity will make those who *have* dominating power think twice before they decide to *exercise* it, and that in *this sense* it would 'force' them to take into account the interests and opinions of others (i. e., to act non-arbitrarily toward them) *in their own interest*, for purely *prudential* reasons.

110 The unsatisfactory account given of the workings of sanctions and the threat therewith could be regarded as another similarity between Oppenheim and Pettit.

111 In trying to sort out the problems of Pettit's account of arbitrariness and non-arbitrariness, I profited very much from discussion with Ernesto Garzón Valdés whose objections forced me to refine my points.

112 I have used the word 'arbitrary' in the discussion so far precisely in that vague sense.

after: *P-arbitrariness*) and non-arbitrariness in Pettit's sense (hereafter: *P-non-arbitrariness*) do not negate each other; instead, P-non-arbitrariness requires more than the mere absence of P-arbitrariness, i. e., P-non-arbitrariness is only a *special case* of non-P-arbitrariness. The consequence is that, if one adopts Pettit's definitions, one can easily think of a case where an interference is *neither arbitrary nor non-arbitrary*.[113] This can best be illustrated with an example: Suppose there are three agents: an interfering agent *A*, an interfered-with agent *B*, and a third party *C*. When *A* interferes with *B on behalf of C* (say, because *A* is eager to please *C* and, therefore, carefully 'tracks' *C*'s interests in deciding her own actions), *A*'s interference with *B* is *not P-arbitrary* since, *ex hypothesi*, *A* does not act on her own whim; but it is also *not P-non-arbitrary* since the interests *A* tracks in interfering with *B* are not those of *B*.

This observation might be regarded as an attempt to split hairs, were it not for the consequences this peculiarity of Pettit's conception of arbitrariness and non-arbitrariness has for his account of the relationship between *dominating power* and *freedom*. After all, dominating power is defined in terms of P-arbitrary interference. Therefore, the absence of dominating power implies the absence of P-arbitrary interferences; but as we have just seen, that is still a long way from a situation where the only possible interferences are P-non-arbitrary. But P-non-arbitrariness of interferences is what Pettit himself expressly mentions as a necessary criterion for freedom. Hence, contrary to what Pettit claims, on his own definitions the absence of dominating power does *not* imply freedom, although the presence of dominating power does imply unfreedom. Hence, if he takes his own definitions seriously, Pettit cannot uphold his idea that freedom is *equivalent* to non-domination. And if he does not want to give up that idea, he must change his concept of arbitrariness and/or his concept of non-arbitrariness.

Since the function of 'non-' in ordinary language is to indicate negation, I think it is advisable in any case to opt for the second alternative, restoring the relationship of contradictoriness between 'non-arbitrariness' and 'arbitrariness'. In order to see how this can be done, we must identify more precisely the source of the problem in Pettit's definitions. As we have seen, the problem is basically that there is some sort of gap between them. If arbitrariness is taken to mean 'acting on one's own whim, pleasure, or *arbitrium*', then the negation of this is certainly not 'acting in consideration of the interests, opinions, or wishes of those affected by the action'; rather, it is simply '*not* acting on one's own whim, pleasure, or *arbitrium*', but on some other kind of criterion. Pettit must be aware of this, and his account of non-arbitrariness must surely be intended to spell out what exactly it means not to act on one's own whim.[114] But I think in his interpretation Pettit has made one unfortunate choice and one mistake. The unfortunate choice is that he has focused attention exclusively on *whose will* or *interest* decides about action: if what is decisive in arbitrary interference is *the will of the interferer*, then logically what must be decisive for interference to be non-arbitrary must, naturally, be *something other than the will of the interferer*; and Pettit has chosen to interpret this as 'someone

113 This is similar to defining 'green' in a way as to designate the colour green, and 'non-green' in a way that boils down to designating the colour red, with the consequence that there are then plenty of objects (blue, yellow, purple, ...) which are neither 'green' nor 'non-green'.

114 Nothing Pettit says indicates that it was his *intention* to make 'non-arbitrariness' mean something different from 'absence of arbitrariness' (i. e., to use 'non-' in an unusual and counterintuitive way).

else's interest'. And from there, he makes the mistake of a logical jump, stipulating that this must be not just *anyone* else's will or interest, but specifically that of the interfered-with person or group of persons. This mistake, obviously, is what is responsible for the gap between P-arbitrariness and P-non-arbitrariness; and, therefore, the problem encountered with Pettit's definitions will disappear if one 'jumps back', so to speak, and eliminates the reference to specific persons in the definition of non-arbitrariness. This is not to say, of course, that the interests of those who are interfered with are irrelevant when we think about freedom and power (especially in the political context); it is only to say that by incorporating it into non-arbitrariness, Pettit has clearly overburdened that concept.

However, the stipulation that 'non-arbitrariness' is simply 'not acting on one's one whim' is still extremely vague and does not quite capture the specific meaning transported in ordinary usage by words from the *arbitrium* family. When someone is said to have chosen something 'arbitrarily', it is usually implied that the choice was *unpredictable* for an observer (and perhaps even for the chooser himself) because there seem to be *no systematic, consistent reasons* for having made *that* choice and not another. And as soon as we realize that someone's choices of action in recurring situations follow some regular pattern, we would not normally continue to call them 'arbitrary'. The prototypical example of arbitrariness is that of 'treating like cases *not* alike': The slave-holder who, for no apparent reason, sometimes does and sometimes does not whip a slave who refuses to call him 'Sir' acts (or at least seems to act) arbitrarily. By contrast, the slave-holder who always (and therefore, after a while, predictably) whips such a slave clearly does not; instead, he seems to be following a kind of *rule* – a rule he may, in fact, have established 'at his own whim' and which others may find abominable, but a rule nevertheless. Rule-following eliminates (or at least reduces) choice and discretion, since rules predetermine what option is to be 'chosen' (or at least restrict the range of admissible options) in certain choice situations; by following a given rule decisions are 'ruled' by certain given criteria rather than by spontaneous, *ad hoc* preferences.[115] That,

[115] Under the 'rule of law', e. g., one of the foremost duties of judges is to produce legal certainty, which requires that like cases are treated alike and not decided „on impulse, at random or so that the pattern of decisions falters in unexpected ways", and judges are therefore restricted in their decisions, among other things, by the demand that „arbitrariness be avoided" (Aarnio 1987, 3). In this context, as Aulis Aarnio (ibid., 4) observes, „arbitrariness is the same as randomness and the resulting unpredictability". Note that this is a characteristic of law, independently of the law's substantive content. Even law which, for some reason or other, might be considered „bad law" has this „redeeming feature that at least it *replaces arbitrariness* [...] *by a rule*", thus providing the subjects with a „shield from the despot's caprice" (de Jasay 1998, 207; emphasis added). For the direct identification of 'arbitrary power' with 'lawless power', cf. already 'Cato' in Letter No. 25 (1721) (Trenchard/Gordon 1995, 179–188).
The idea that rule-following is what 'negates' arbitrariness is, of course, not restricted to the consideration of law. For instance, as all consumers of detective stories know, the serial killer who has a problem with blondes and therefore selects his victims according to the rule 'Blondes only!' can, because of this element of non-arbitrariness which makes his actions more predictable, be caught more easily than the serial killer whose only purpose is to spread terror and who therefore selects his victims arbitrarily, without following any perceptible rule of choice. The distinction between the psychotic and the terrorist also serves to show another meaning sometimes given to the terms 'arbitrary' and 'non-arbitrary': insofar as the psychotic acts under a compulsion which makes it impossible for him to control his own conduct, he can be said to act non-arbitrarily (not on the basis of a willful decision), whereas the cold-blooded, calculating terrorist would be acting arbitrarily, i. e., based on a willful choice. *Arbitrariness-as-capriciousness* and *arbitrariness-as-willfulness* are two very

then, seems to be, at the most general level, the meaning of non-arbitrariness as the negation of arbitrariness: a decision is non-arbitrary if, in view of a plurality of effectively (factually) existing choice options, it is not entirely open and unpredictable which option will be chosen by the agent in question, *because* his 'choice' is, at least to a certain extent, predetermined by some kind of decision rule to which the agent is committed.[116]

But, of course, the fact that someone acts according to a rule does not imply anything at all yet about the particular *content* of that rule. This is precisely where Pettit's mistake lies: In his definitions, he 'jumps' from action which is arbitrary, i. e., *not regular* at all, to action according to a *very specific rule*, namely that of taking into account the interests of a specific person or group of persons.

As far as I can see, there is only one possible way of arguing that this does not constitute an unwarranted logical 'jump', and that is to restrict the consideration from the very beginning to a certain *class* of reasons or criteria and, consequently, decision rules. This is not an uncommon strategy for assessments of arbitrariness. When one says that someone has acted 'arbitrarily' on a certain occasion, what one means to deny is often not that the agent in question did not act according to any decision rule at all, which, should a sufficiently similar situation arise again, would lead him to repeat that same choice.[117] Rather, what one means to say is that whatever decision rule he may have acted on 'does not count' because it is not of the right kind.[118] If in some context only a certain class of reasons is admitted as *appropriate*, a choice based on some other kind of reason may be regarded as arbitrary, but the arbitrariness is then *relative* to the class of exclusively admitted reasons (e. g., when the verdicts of a judge who, in a secu-

different notions which must not be confused. The concept Pettit had in mind clearly is the former rather than the latter.

116 Three remarks are in order at this point: *(1)* The term 'rule' must not be taken in a strict technical sense here (as defined, e. g., in von Wright 1963, ch. I., where it is distinguished from other types of norms), but in a loose and general sense, referring merely to the provision of some kind of *reason* or *criterion* for consistently choosing a certain kind of action in a certain kind of recurring situation, as opposed to pure *ad hoc* decisions. *(2)* Of course, not all regular (and, therefore, predictable) behaviour is rule-following behaviour in that sense. Habits, for instance, are manifested in regular behaviour too; but habitual behaviour is more similar to reflex-like reactions to certain characteristics of a situation functioning as stimuli than to a conscious, deliberate choice of action. The qualification of something as 'arbitrary' or 'non-arbitrary', however, applies only to genuine choices, or actions based on such choices. For non-arbitrariness in the strict sense, thus, the mere regularity of conduct does not seem to be sufficient; behaviour must not only 'look' *as if* the agent may be following a rule, it must actually be triggered by the agent's *commitment* to a rule. In a weaker sense, however, one could perhaps say that it is sufficient for a behaviour to be non-arbitrary that it *conforms* to a rule, regardless of whether or not *compliance* with the rule is intended by the agent (for the distinction between conformity and compliance, and for the view that „what matters is conformity", cf. Raz 1990b, Postscript; the quoted phrase is on p. 190). *(3)* It is often difficult to know whether someone acts arbitrarily or not; it is not even always readily perceptible whether a behaviour is regular or not. Decision rules can be quite complex, and they may refer to non-obvious characteristics of a choice situation, thus leading to behaviour the regularity of which can be recognized as such only *after* the underlying rule is known.

117 Understood in this very general sense, arbitrariness is probably an almost inexistent phenomenon. Most people most of the time do seem to act on some kind of reasons which have at least some degree of consistency and stability.

118 Thus, for instance, for Wilhelm von Humboldt „arbitrary" state action was simply state action „not grounded on proper motives" (von Humboldt 1993, 116).

lar legal order, bases her judicial decisions on religious rather than on legal grounds, are said to be arbitrary, this must be understood to mean 'arbitrary as far as legal reasons are concerned' or, for short, 'legally arbitrary').

In this sense, one could perhaps think that what Pettit was trying to get at all along was not arbitrariness in general, but a specific version of it, namely *moral* arbitrariness.[119] When it comes to the moral justification of actions, it may be possible to argue that choice based on an agent's own interests is *morally arbitrary* (i. e., that the mere consideration of one's own interest does not provide a defensible moral rule for the justification of one's actions), whereas basing it on the interests of all those affected by an action makes it *morally non-arbitrary* (that is, that they may, or even must, form part of such a rule). If one were to understand Pettit's conception in this limited way, it would mean the following: I am unfree to the extent that others can interfere with me according to their own interests, and this means: in a *morally unacceptable* way; and I am free to the extent that no-one can interfere with me except in a *morally acceptable* way, *and* that is always the case whenever my own interests are given their due weight in the other's deliberation prior to a choice of action.

This interpretation would eliminate the logical jump from arbitrariness to non-arbitrariness; but the advantage would be bought at a high price. It would mean that an entire moral theory were hidden behind Pettit's talk of arbitrariness; and in that case, for the sake of transparency, it would be advisable to replace the terms 'arbitrary' and 'non-arbitrary' directly by 'morally justified' and 'morally unjustified', respectively. I think, however, that this is really not what Pettit intended, because on this reading his account of freedom (understood as the absence of the ability for 'arbitrary', i. e., morally unjustifiable interference) would come very close to a 'moral responsibility' view of freedom. And *that* is a view Pettit himself, in his controversy with Kristjánsson,[120] has vehemently criticized.

Thus, we seem stuck with the general concept of arbitrariness and the problems encountered with Pettit's conception of it. One important consequence of this conception for Pettit's overall view has not been mentioned yet. The observations made above about the severe limitations of the applicability of procedural provisions for the reduction of dominating power were *general* remarks about such provisions; they did not *specifically* take into account the application to 'arbitrary' interferences. But as soon as one accepts that 'arbitrary' behaviour primarily means 'non-regular' behaviour, it follows immediately that if 'dominating power' is defined as nothing but the 'ability to interfere arbitrarily', there can never exist dominating power concerning *institutional* actions, simply because such actions cannot exist without rules: they are constituted on the basis of rules.[121] Therefore, to speak of 'arbitrary institutional actions' is a *contradictio in terminis*, and, hence, with respect to the exercise of dominating power (i. e., *arbitrary* interferences) procedural constraints cannot even play the limited normative role ascribed to them above: institutional actions, on which alone procedural provisions can operate, are themselves always already somehow procedurally constrained and are there-

119 After all, his expressed interest is to elaborate an *ideal* rather than a neutral concept of freedom.

120 Cf. the next section of this chapter.

121 Cf. the references to Kant and Murphy in the previous section.

fore non-arbitrary in the strict sense; they may be constrained *in a different way*, by a different set of rules, of course; but that has nothing to do with a reduction of arbitrariness.

In view of these problems with Pettit's conception of arbitrariness and of the central position this conception occupies in his construction of freedom as the absence of dominating power, if his entire argument is not to unravel, the idea of arbitrariness must be replaced by another one, better suited to support the construction. What we need, then, is a criterion for the distinction between two kinds of power relations: those that leave the freedom of a subject intact, and those that do not. Pettit's basic insight was that agents are free to the extent that they are assured that no-one else can interfere with them without taking their interests into consideration. The question is what this view implies for the needed distinction between types of power. So let us see whether what Pettit himself says about what such assurance involves contains any helpful clue.

Antipower

In Pettit's view, the absence of dominating power – i. e., of one's ability to interfere with another without 'tracking' the latter's interests – can be guaranteed only by antipower, that is, by a non-dominating kind of power capable of „blocking" another's dominating power:

„The fact that antipower is not itself a form of domination [...] does not mean, of course, that antipower is in no sense a sort of power. On the contrary, antipower will represent a form of control that a person enjoys in relation to her own destiny [...] and such control represents one familiar type of power: the power of the agent who can make things happen [...] Their antipower gives [those who have it] the capacity to command non-interference [...]"[122]

According to this formulation, the 'things' antipower is thought to allow an agent to 'make happen' are only *omissions* – the omission of certain kinds of interferences by others: when *B* has antipower, then for any *A* who might have the factual ability to interfere with *B*, *B* has the means to control *A*'s *exercise* of that ability and thus prevent undesired interferences from happening.[123] But what precisely does this mean? How is the interplay between (a potential of) dominating power and antipower thought to work?

As explained earlier, one possibility for an agent to have such antipower is that he has the means negatively to affect another agents' choice situations. The idea behind this option seems to be the following: *A* can interfere arbitrarily with *B*'s actions only as long as *A* is *invulnerable* to whatever *B* may do to him in reaction. As soon as each side has the means to interfere with the other (in Pettit's strict sense of 'interference' as 'worsening' the other's choice situation), neither can do so 'arbitrarily' (1996, 588); instead, in their own interest both sides must *strategically* take the other side's interests into account. In such a case, therefore, each side has a certain power over the other, but

122 1996, 589; also 1997, 272: „Non-domination involves the absence of domination in the presence of other people: it is a social ideal which requires that, though there are other people who might have been able to interfere with the person on an arbitrary basis, they are blocked from doing so."

123 According to the passage quoted, it would not make sense to speak of antipower if the other side did not have the ability to interfere: to „command non-interference" would then be superfluous.

that power is *not dominating*; rather, it is a power which merely prevents the other's power from being dominating – an 'anti-power power', so to speak. At first sight, this may sound plausible. But a closer look reveals that the idea is not unproblematic. After all, such antipower must simultaneously satisfy *two* conditions: it may not itself be dominating power; and it must, at the same time, have the effect of preventing the power of another from being dominating. How can that be?

Suppose some agent *B* has this kind of antipower against another agent *A*. If the antipower is not to be of a dominating kind, then while *B must* be able to interfere with *A*'s choices, he *must not* be able to do so in an 'arbitrary' way. But if the only way to prevent that someone's power is dominating, in this sense, is the possession of antipower against it, then, if it is to be excluded that *B*'s antipower against *A* is, in turn, dominating, either *A* himself or some other agent ready to act on his behalf must also have antipower against *B* – 'anti-anti-power power', so to speak. Thus, first of all, for conceptual reasons, *antipower* (being, by definition, a nondominating kind of power) *is not something that can exist only on one side of a social relationship*. That *A* has such antipower against *B implies* that *B* (or someone else on *B*'s behalf) also has antipower against *A*. But what does *this* mean? According to Pettit's conception of non-arbitrariness, it means that *B* must not be able to interfere with *A* without taking into account – without 'tracking' – *A*'s interests. But, in the case of antipower, this does not seem to make sense: if the power *B* has over *A* is to serve to prevent *A* from interfering arbitrarily with *B*'s choice situations, how can this power of *B* in any way be subjected to the interests of that same *A*? The very idea of antipower seems to be that the agent who has it can use it to prevent another agent from taking certain actions she might otherwise take – that is, to prevent her from doing certain things she might perceive to be 'in her interest'. In other words, antipower is needed precisely to protect *one's own interests* against those of someone else. Therefore, it would seem absurd to require that *B*'s antipower *against A* should in any way be constrained by *A*'s interests.

Thus, it seems that either antipower, if it is to be effective, must be an ability to interfere 'arbitrarily' in Pettit's sense, i. e., that it must be a dominating power, or else non-arbitrariness must be defined differently, that is, not necessarily referring to the interests of the person 'suffering' an interference.

2.3. CONCLUSION

The preceding discussion of Pettit's conception has shown, perhaps even more than that of Oppenheim's, how very difficult it is to come up with a coherent set of conceptual proposals that does not only appear superficially plausible, but can withstand closer scrutiny.

But, objections and questions aside, Pettit's approach has been shown to have several features which, at least for some purposes, specifically those of normative political theory of liberal leanings, make it look more attractive than Oppenheim's.

From the outset, considerations are restricted to questions of *political* freedom. Besides, Pettit adopts a *liberal* point of view from which such freedom is seen as an *ideal*. He thus fully subscribes to the idea that freedom is valuable, and that constraints on freedom therefore require justification. So here we have a view of the kind I mentioned in the introductory remarks to this chapter: a presumption in favour of freedom which (depending on the stipulated conceptual relationships) possibly affects the assessment of power phenomena.

A further choice Pettit makes from his specifically *political* vantage point, with considerable consequences for his entire construction, is that of attaching the concepts of freedom and power, so to speak, to *structures* (relationships) rather than to *events* (actions and their consequences). That is, of course, a decisive step away from Oppenheim's proposal. It is based on the insight that what matters, primarily, for the moral evaluation of political *systems* is the *distribution of power*, in the sense of the *ability* to affect others' choices in certain ways; actual *exercises* of power, in contrast, matter on another level, of secondary importance for the purposes of political theory, concerning the *performance* of agents *within* a given system.[124]

With respect to the concept of power as such, Pettit has not contributed any new proposal; but his decisions have one very clear and straightforward consequence: At least to the extent that the moral evaluation of power phenomena is linked to the question of freedom, it is not warranted to uphold a presumption against power in general. Only *certain kinds* of power phenomena have a negative effect on freedom. Hence, distinctions must be made.

The problems and questions Pettit's account has given rise to in the previous discussion concerned precisely the criteria for those distinctions. In this respect, there seems to be a need for clarification and modification. Above all Pettit's idea that not only unfreedom, but also freedom is constituted by a particular type of power ('dominating power' in the former, 'antipower' in the latter case) turned out to pose a major logical problem.[125]

In summary, just like Oppenheim, Pettit has offered in his work a wealth of interesting and important considerations about power and its relation to freedom, emphasizing certain aspects which are of special relevance for the purposes of political theorists. In many respects, his empirical assertions and theoretical decisions seem plausible. But, also just as in the case of Oppenheim, a discussion of details revealed that the superficial

[124] Obviously, if only the *exercise* of power mattered, then a dictatorial system could get the same marks, regarding its record on freedom, as a liberal democracy, provided the successive dictators are benevolent enough to restrict their *exercise* of power correspondingly (cf. above, the quotations in nn. 78 and 84).

[125] Again, as in the case of the problem with Oppenheim's punishability condition, this problem can, I think, be avoided – *ceteris paribus* – only by moving from the factual to the deontic level. The distinction between dominating power and anti-power falls into place when it is not based on the factual ability, but on the deontic 'ability' – the permission or prohibition – of interference. If freedom is the assurance that there are limits to others' interferences in one's actions, this can, if taken seriously, be only a normative, not an empirical assurance; and if the assurance is to be grounded in anti-power against such illegitimate interferences, then this anti-power, if it is not to be dominating power itself, can only be a (restricted) normative power, i. e., the *permission* to employ coercive means against certain kinds of interference. – Ripstein (2004) recently argued for such a rights-based, Kantian conception of the interplay between freedom and coercion. When he observes that „Kant explains the idea of coercive enforcement in terms of the hindrance of a hindrance", where „those who hinder the freedom of others [...] may be prevented from doing so", that „In an ideal world, no person hinders the external freedom of another [...] because, if it does, it is hindered directly" and that „the claim about hindering a hindrance is [...] an explication of the idea of a limit" (ibid., 22 f. and n. 28), the analogies to Pettit's idea of assuring freedom – absence of dominating power – through anti-power are obvious. Ripstein himself refers to Pettit's notion as „a related idea of freedom as independence" (ibid., n. 14).

appearance is misleading. Pettit has, no doubt, made a valuable contribution to an important line of discussion in political theory. But, again, the merits of the work seem to lay more in the questions it raises than in the answers it provides.

3. Kristján Kristjánsson

The third author whose conception I will present and discuss argues in favour of a position that is located somewhere between those of Oppenheim and Pettit. His views are of special interest to the present discussion, on the one hand, because he explicitly criticizes the conceptions of these two authors. On the other hand, the particular interest of his analysis of the concepts of freedom and power for the present purpose is that he derives the latter directly from the former. In that sense, as we will see, Kristjánsson's proposal implies the strongest of the three different kinds of relationships between power and freedom to be found in the three views discussed in this chapter.

Like Pettit, Kristjánsson is primarily interested in the concept of social *freedom*; hence, as in Pettit's case, his analysis of power is an offshoot of his discussion of freedom. Throughout the first half of the 1990s, he developed his views in a series of articles which evolved out of a doctoral thesis (1990) and can in turn be seen as preparatory work leading to a book-length publication of a conceptual study on *Social Freedom* (1996). The following presentation will therefore mainly refer to that monograph, as the endpoint of a longer intellectual trajectory.[126]

More recently still, an exchange between Kristjánsson and Pettit precisely on these conceptual issues was published in the *Journal of Theoretical Politics* (Kristjánsson 1998a and 1998b; Pettit 1998) which also bears on the relationship between power and freedom and will be given due consideration in what follows.

3.1. THE RELATIONSHIP BETWEEN FREEDOM AND POWER

Kristjánsson raises objections against the conceptions of Oppenheim and Pettit on two different levels: on a more general level concerning their basic approach or method, and on a more specific level concerning the particular content they give to their respective concepts. His own concepts of freedom and power, and his conception of the relationship between the two, derive to a large extent from these objections.

The methodological foundation

Kristjánsson rejects both Oppenheim's and Pettit's approach to the conceptualization of social freedom, although he is perhaps somewhat closer to the latter than to the former.

It is certainly one of Kristjánsson's great merits that he takes methodological matters seriously. Consequently, he has devoted an entire chapter of his 1996 book to

126 Cf. Kristjánsson 1992a (now partly incorporated into chs. 1, 2, and 5 of 1996), 1992b (reworked as ch. 3 of 1996), 1992c (now basically ch. 4.1–4.3 of 1996), 1992d (now incorporated into ch. 5.3–5.7 of 1996), 1992e (an early version of ch. 6 of 1996), 1993 and 1995 (both early versions of ch. 7 of 1996). In this section, page numbers without further specification will refer to Kristjánsson 1996.

such questions. Particularly in this context, he deals extensively with Oppenheim who is presented as one of the most prominent contemporary representatives[127] of an approach to the formation of concepts which Kristjánsson himself considers fundamentally misguided (at least for certain basic concepts of the social sciences), namely, *operationalism* (168–172).[128] The charges brought forward against the operationalist method of conceptual analysis in general, and against Oppenheim's approach to the analysis of social freedom and power in particular, are primarily two:

(1) its futile insistence on a construction of purely descriptive, entirely value-neutral concepts; and
(2) its, in Kristjánsson's view, unnecessary departure from ordinary usage (i. e., stipulation instead of reconstruction).

At least with respect to the concepts in question, the second of these defects is regarded as a consequence of the first since, as Kristjánsson argues, in ordinary language 'freedom' is *not* used as a value-neutral term.

It must be noted, however, that this second objection does not make Kristjánsson a representative of ordinary-language analysis. Rather, the method he endorses is a combination of Aristotelian naturalism, Rawlsian 'reflective equilibrium' and Kovesian functionalism – what he calls 'naturalistic critical revision' (cf. esp. ch. 7.3).

***

This is not the place to enter into a lengthy general methodological discussion, or particularly a discussion of Kristjánsson's argument for his own approach. However, the latter is interesting enough to deserve at least a brief, summarized description: Adequate conceptual work must, according to Kristjánsson (3, 167), satisfy at least four criteria:

(1) it must start from ordinary common usage;
(2) it must, if – but only if – necessary, modify that usage with a view to coherence;
(3) it must result in „serviceable and non-relative" definitions, and
(4) it must show why the concept in question may be, or may have been, contested.

Ordinary-language analysis satisfies condition *(1)*, but generally not the other conditions (it particularly violates the non-relativity condition). *Rawlsian reflective equilibrium* satisfies both conditions *(1)* and *(2)*,[129] but fails on the remaining two (mainly because the underdetermination of reflective equilibria gives rise to very broad, overly „permissive" concepts – a defect for which particularly Swanton 1992 is criticized; cf. 179 f.). Therefore, the method of reflective equilibrium must be complemented, Kristjánsson thinks, by a kind of *functionalism-cum-naturalism* adapted from Kovesi and, ultimately, from Aristotle, particularly by the insight that „definitions are *created* to serve a purpose" (194), that the grouping together of one set of properties rather than another – which is what the definition of a term in the last instance boils down to – makes sense only if it enables us to refer to something that is of interest from some particular point of view, and that such purposes or points of views are ultimately related to facts, i. e., to the *nature* of the world (including, e. g., the nature of social relations); hence, condition *(3)* („serviceable and non-relative") is satisfied if a concept can be shown to be useful from a point of view that „*is* or *should be* of interest to people, given their

[127] Perhaps even the only one remaining? In any case, he is the only one mentioned.
[128] However, cf. Oppenheim 1981, ch. 9.2.1 for an explicit rejection of operationalism.
[129] It is „first and foremost a *coherence method*" (178).

human nature" (193) because it is then „objectively useful" (194) and in that sense non-relative.[130] Finally, for the satisfaction of condition *(4)* it is argued that no more than the insight in the *open texture* of language is needed.[131]

***

Although this may sound like a rather idiosyncratic approach, at least one of its main tenets is, I think, perfectly reasonable and as such hardly controversial: it „requires that ordinary usage be respected unless one has good reason for abandoning it" (1998b, 290). The controversial question is, of course, what is to count as a 'good reason'. Whatever a defensible general answer to this question might be, Kristjánsson makes it very clear that in any case, in his view, the particular reason for departing from ordinary usage which he attributes to Oppenheim does *not* qualify as such a good reason: he dismisses it as „an outdated positivist search for value-free definitions" (1998a, 264).

On the other hand, Kristjánsson also rejects – again, mainly with a view to what he holds to be respectable common usage – what he calls a directly 'moralized' concept of social freedom, that is, a concept on account of which freedom is *by definition* necessarily and invariably good and any infringement on someone's freedom, therefore, necessarily bad (19 f.; 32 ff.). But this is precisely how our second author, Philip Pettit, has proposed to understand social freedom: As we have seen in the previous section, Pettit conceives of freedom as an *ideal* and sees an infringement on someone's freedom only where there is power that *should not* exist – specifically, the kind of power he calls 'dominating'; constraints brought about by nondominating power, in contrast, do not count as restrictions of freedom for him. Pettit's reason for stipulating this link between freedom and the absence of dominating power was, as we have also seen, his rejection of *another* equally 'moralized' concept of freedom, namely, the libertarian ideal of freedom as the absence of *any* socially imposed constraint. In other words, Pettit disagrees with the libertarians concerning *which* constraints on an agent's action are to be evaluated as morally unjustified, and therefore he also disagrees with them about the concept of freedom. Kristjánsson, in turn, thinks that *both* Pettit's and the libertarians' conceptions are mistaken because they are merely different proposals for a moralized concept of freedom (1998a, 1998b).[132]

130 Cf. 198 ff. for an extensive argument attempting to establish that this constitutes not just an explication of, but a substantial addition to the Rawlsian method of reflective equilibrium.

131 194 ff.; particularly, what is *not* needed is the thesis of essential contestedness, which is sharply criticized on pp. 180 ff. (with good reason, I think; cf. above Chapter 1.1).

132 Kristjánsson agrees with Pettit that there are some conceptions of freedom which do not see a significant difference between arbitrary and nonarbitrary interferences (he too names especially „libertarian" versions: „Perhaps there is after all something to Pettit's worries [...] about the many recent writings about freedom which imply that any infringement of freedom is a moral wrong – such writings being tacitly driven by a libertarian conception of free action" [1998b, 296]). But, Kristjánsson argues, this is not an unavoidable implication of a non-interference account of freedom; rather, it is a problem of „a moralized definition of a constraint on freedom" according to which „all constraints on freedom become unjustified by definition" (1998b, 294). Therefore, he contends, Pettit's objection against the non-interference view is fired againstt the wrong target. – Besides, at this point, Pettit is also confronted, just like Oppenheim, with the verdict that „if for no good reason an advocate of a particular conception of freedom knocks his head against the wall of ordinary usage, this should weigh distinctly against that conception", concerning his conception's implication that under certain circumstances a perfectly unconstrained particular action must be regarded as unfree if there is

Now, one might think that the alternative between either a purely descriptive or a moralized concept exhausts our menu of choice concerning types of concepts. But Kristjánsson argues that there is, indeed, a third option, a middle road between the two, and that is the alternative of what he calls not a 'moralized', but a *moral* concept of freedom. The difference Kristjánsson draws between a moralized and a moral concept refers precisely to the aspects I have drawn attention to in the introductory remarks to this chapter: On his account, a concept is *moralized* if the moral evaluation of the members of its extension is, so to speak, hard-wired into the definition and therefore *fixed once and for all*. In contrast, the actions or states of affairs a *moral* concept refers to merely *raise a moral question*, while the answer to this question is not conceptually predetermined. However, the fact that such a moral question arises at all does imply that, unless satisfactory arguments to the contrary can be given, a presumption that the moral evaluation must be negative will hold.

And this is precisely what Kristjánsson takes to be the case with the concept of social freedom, or rather, for a start, with its contrary, i. e., the concept of (socially imposed) unfreedom. He reflects on the „point" of talking about freedom, on what our interest in that concept is all about, and his main thesis in this context is that there is, indeed, as some authors (Benn/Weinstein, D. Miller, Connolly) have argued, a „'presumption of freedom' embodied in our language" (26). Consequently, he asserts, the idea of a constraint on freedom is a moral concept in the sense just explained: „It refers to something that is considered wrong prima facie and challenges us to bring forth some relevant justificatory considerations" (25). But this should not make one „overlook one of the more central aspects of most nondomination conceptions of freedom, which is that infringements of freedom are not necessarily moral wrongs" (1998b, 294). Constraints on another's freedom do require justification – that is what it means, in Kristjánsson's terminology, to say that freedom is a *moral* concept –, but in some cases they can in fact be justified – that is what it means to say that freedom is *not* a *moralized* concept.

The concept of freedom

This methodological starting point obviously has direct consequences for the possible *substance* of a concept of freedom: moral questions arise only where moral agents are at work and must respond for their acts (actions as well as omissions) and/or the states of affairs they bring about through them. *Responsibility* is therefore the key ingredient of such a concept of freedom. Interestingly, in reversal of what we have seen to be the case on the methodological level, on the substantial level this brings Kristjánsson's conception in some sense closer to that of Oppenheim than to that of Pettit, because Oppenheim's concept of freedom is, likewise, a concept based on the idea of responsibility. The shared idea that social freedom, or rather its absence, is best understood as conceptually linked to actions that can be imputed to particular agents is what leads both Oppenheim[133] and Kristjánsson to propose a negative, *non-interference* account of free-

no assurance that actions of the same kind by the same agent will remain unconstrained in the future (1998b, 291).

133 Cf. esp. Oppenheim 1985, 305, who expresses his agreement with Miller that „Only obstacles 'attributable to human agency' constitute limitations of freedom".

dom. Nevertheless, the resulting conceptual proposals are very different. That is so because responsibility can be understood in a *moral* or in a *non-moral* sense. And after what has been explained above, it is not surprising that Oppenheim and Kristjánsson part company precisely on the question whether one or the other is the better candidate for an adequate foundation of a responsibility view of freedom. Oppenheim, strictly opposed as he is to definitions with „valuational overtones“ (1985, 305), emphatically opts for the idea of *causal* responsibility.[134] For Kristjánsson, in contrast, after what has been said, only *moral* responsibility can be a plausible choice. Consequently, in his view, an agent *makes* another *unfree* to act in a certain way if, and only if, he is morally responsible for some constraint on that action; and therefore, formulated positively, an agent *is free* relative to another agent (and a certain action) if the latter is *not* morally responsible for any obstacle to the respective action.

At this point, without knowing more about exactly how Kristjánsson defines such responsibility, we can already see where he must disagree substantially with Pettit (besides the fact that he rejects his moralized concept of freedom): On Kristjánsson's account, since an *ability* is not, as such, something the possession of which an agent can be held morally responsible for, an ability alone cannot give rise to another's unfreedom – regardless of what other kinds of effects (provoking fear, caution, restraint, envy, etc., in others) it may have. Agents have moral responsibility only for what they do or don't do, or for the (foreseeable) consequences thereof. But this already goes some way towards weakening Pettit's objection that advocates of a non-interference view of freedom have nothing to say about dependency relationships(at least not in terms of freedom), as long as these do not manifest themselves in active interference. Because *if* the mere existence of such a dependency relationship does impose *constraints* on the dependent side's choices of action *and* the other, privileged side *could* do something to eliminate those constraints, it is very well possible that the latter could be held morally responsible for *not* eliminating them – i. e., that he constrains the other's freedom even on Kristjánsson's non-interference account (for this and related objections to Pettit's conception, cf. 1998a, 266 ff.).

Now, let us go back and take a look at the details of Kristjánsson's approach. He is not the first to have proposed a moral-responsibility conception of freedom. In fact, he mentions several others who have done so before him (29). But his view is different from those others, and he singles out the conception proposed by David Miller, as the strongest of these alternative accounts, to show why and how he disagrees. In contrast to the rest of the book under discussion, his thoughts on this matter are not always entirely transparent (at least to this reader), but the central points are clear enough: If „an obstacle counts as a constraint on an agent's freedom if and only if there is another agent who can be held *morally* responsible for the existence of the obstacle“ (63; 1992c, 104),[135]

134 „I accept [...] 'that any obstacle for which human agents are in some way or other causally responsible should be regarded as a constraint on freedom' (p. 74) – causally, not morally, responsible.“ (Oppenheim 1985, 306; the reference is to Miller 1983); cf. also above, Sect. 1. – Recently, Pettit (2001) has also come to embrace responsibility in connection with freedom, but from the perspective of free – i. e., causally undetermined – agency as a conceptual prerequisite of social freedom.

135 Kristjánsson notes that one can be responsible for the existence of something in different ways: either by *bringing* it into existence oneself, or by *refraining from preventing* someone else from bringing it into exist-

as both Kristjánsson and Miller propose, then obviously the decisive question that must be answered in order to determine whether an agent is free or unfree in a particular situation is what it means to say that someone is morally responsible for something, and that is where Kristjánsson disagrees with Miller.

On Miller's account, an agent is morally responsible for an action if there is at least a *prima facie* obligation involved; specifically, an agent is morally responsible for the existence of an obstacle to another's action (and therefore constrains that other's freedom) if he has a *prima facie* obligation to suppress the obstacle. A *prima facie* obligation may, of course, be overridden, and thus the failure to suppress an obstacle one is morally responsible for in that sense may in some cases be perfectly justified; in others, there may at least be an excuse for it. Hence, according to Miller's conception, moral responsibility does not necessarily imply culpability or blameworthiness – a point that, as we have seen, is of great importance to Kristjánsson (32 f.; 65 ff.). Miller thereby avoids the objection that his is a moralized concept.

Nevertheless, Kristjánsson thinks that the resulting concept of unfreedom still leaves something to be desired. He sees primarily two disadvantages which, in his view, make the concept, on the one hand, overly broad and, on the other, at the same time overly narrow.

Let us first see why Kristjánsson finds Miller's account too broad. He agrees with Miller that responsibility, and therefore also freedom, is an all-or-nothing affair: either one does or one does not constrain another's freedom concerning some way of action (45 ff.). As a consequence, it does not matter for the distinction between freedom and unfreedom whether an obstacle is small or large; what matters is only whether there is any obstacle at all and whether or not someone is responsible for it. The problem Kristjánsson sees with Miller's account, however, is insufficient clarity about the meaning of 'obstacle', which may lead one to think that freedom can be constrained by an *offer*, as long as someone is responsible for it and it makes the subject's choice of certain options sufficiently difficult. Kristjánsson wants to avoid this conclusion, with the following line of argument: The key of the matter is the notion of 'obstacle'. For Kristjánsson, nothing can be a constraint unless it is an obstacle, and the main characteristic of obstacles is that they „narrow down possibilities or close options" (52). Since that is what threats do, threats constitute obstacles. Offers, in contrast, „open new possibilities and extend the range of options" (ibid.). Hence, they cannot be obstacles and, consequently, they cannot be constraints on freedom. However, he acknowledges that there is a particular type of offers – 'final proposals', in his terminology (57) – which, although they have all the manifest properties of a 'genuine' offer, contain an element that performs like a threat. Such offers therefore do, indeed, impose obstacles. But, then, Kristjánsson argues, they do not do so in their capacity as offers proper, but only because of their threat component. And since it is possible, at least analytically, to separate this component from the genuine offer component, it is preferable to say that threats, but not offers impose obstacles. The inclusion of offers among the factors which can constitute constraints on freedom makes the concept of freedom too broad.

ence, or by *refraining from repressing* its existence. For the sake of linguistic simplicity, he uses the single term 'suppression' to refer to an omission in either one of these three different senses; thus, an agent 'suppresses' an obstacle if she either refrains from erecting it, or prevents another from doing so, or eliminates an obstacle that already exists (63). I will adopt this usage where convenient in what follows.

Now, this objection of excessive breadth is not so much directed against Miller's conception of freedom and unfreedom as such, as against a certain interpretation of the notion of obstacle. More directly aimed at the core of the concept is the contrary objection, i. e., that Miller's account is too narrow. More precisely, this second objection is that the criterion of the existence of a *prima facie* obligation to suppress an obstacle is too demanding. In Kristjánsson's view, an agent can constrain another's freedom by failing to suppress an obstacle even if he does *not* have a *prima facie* obligation to that effect. His task, then, is to propose a criterion which includes *prima facie* obligations as a subcategory (because he does not deny that such obligations are a *sufficient* condition for moral responsibility; 74), but is defined in a more encompassing way, and still deserves to be classified as a *moral* kind of responsibility. Now, on a common understanding of the meaning of 'moral', the latter condition implies that, somewhere and somehow, obligation must continue to play an essential role in the criterion, and Kristjánsson seems to be aware of this since he observes at least twice that his own conception too „presupposes a theory of moral obligation" (73, 78). So he must find a way, so to speak, to throw obligation out and at the same time keep it in. Obviously, the only way to do so is by throwing it out *in one place*, only to reintroduce it *in another*, and this is exactly what Kristjánsson does. On his account, an agent is morally responsible for an obstacle not (only) if he has an *obligation* (at least *prima facie*) *to suppress* it, but whenever he has an *obligation to justify* its non-suppression (78). The main element of Kristjánsson's definition of freedom thus is the burden of justification concerning the existence of an obstacle:

„When it can be placed on a specific person, *A*, that person is responsible for the given obstacle to *B*'s choice and, hence, *A* has constrained *B*'s freedom." (79)

But this has only apparently solved the problem, because now we need to know what it is that allows one to place the burden of justification for an obstacle on an agent in some situations, but not in others. What Kristjánsson has provided with his reference to the obligation of justification seems to be merely a *reformulation* of the notion of 'moral responsibility' (that is, the moral obligation to respond for one's acts) itself, instead of an answer to the question under what conditions such responsibility arises. Miller's criterion – the existence of an obligation to suppress an obstacle – was an answer precisely to *that* question, and having rejected Miller's criterion, Kristjánsson still needs to provide an alternative to it. Of course, the kind of thing he must say about such an alternative in order to be consistent with the rest of his argument, as just presented, is that, while the existence of the *obligation to suppress* an obstacle may be *one* reason for an *obligation to justify* its non-suppression, there may also be *other* reasons for such an obligation. And Kristjánsson is perfectly consistent – this is exactly what he says:

„An agent *A* is morally responsible for the non-suppression of an obstacle *O* to *B*'s choices/action [...] when there is an objective *reason*, satisfying a minimal criterion of plausibility, why *A*, given that he is a normal, reasonable person, could have been expected (morally or factually) to suppress *O* – however easily overridable this reason is." (74; 1992c, 113)

This – obviously, itself rather broad – criterion of moral responsibility leads to a concept of unfreedom, and therefore also of freedom, that has, according to Kristjánsson, several advantages:

(1) Whether someone is or is not *made unfree* does not depend in any way, as it does on some other accounts, on the affected agent's *preferences* or „desires“; here, it makes no difference to a restriction of freedom whether or not the affected cares very much about it, or whether he would ever wish to exercise the corresponding freedom. In this sense, it is clearly not a subjective, but an *objective* concept.

(2) Whether an agent does or does not *make another* unfree also does not depend on the former's *intentions*. Thus, this conception allows us to speak in terms of unfreedom of obstacles brought about merely „through inattention and mindlessness“ (117); this is an important advantage over the 'intentionality view' of freedom which, Kristjánsson claims, often points towards the wrong agents when it comes to knowing why someone is unfree, and thus does not get at the „prime malefactors – the real powerholders“ (118). An agent may be responsible for someone else's unfreedom without having intended to make that person unfree, simply by thoughtlessness, producing unfreedom as an unforeseen (though foreseeable) side-effect. On the responsibility view, agents who are responsible in that sense can be identified and the corresponding cases diagnosed as situations of unfreedom (117 f.; 1992a, esp. 229).

(3) Moreover, this conception also extends the universe of unfreedom to the full range of the non-suppression of obstacles. Since responsibility for an obstacle may arise not only from erecting it oneself, but also from *not* eliminating it or from *not* preventing its erection by others when one could be expected to do so, an agent can constrain another's freedom even by mere passive negligence, e. g. by *omitting* to prevent the erection of, or to remove, an existing obstacle.[136]

The contours of Kristjánsson's ideas about concepts in general, and the concept of freedom in particular should now be sufficiently clear to enable us fully to understand his account of the relation between freedom and power.

[136] In fact, that „omissions can never give rise to unfreedom“ is for Kristjánsson one of the greatest disadvantages of a conception of freedom based on the *causal* responsibility view (21). Oppenheim (1985, 306 f.), for example, advocates „subsuming under constraints of freedom only cases of preventing, not those of failure to enable“: if someone is locked into a room because the door, which can be unlocked only from the outside, was blown shut by the wind, then relative to all those who do not enable her to leave by unlocking the door from the outside that person is merely 'unable', but not 'unfree' to leave the room. Someone who knew about the situation, had the key to the room, was even officially in charge of making sure that no-one gets locked up accidentally overnight, and yet did not let the person out, could thus be blamed for a number of things, such as neglect of professional duties, malevolence, even murder (if the lock-up lasted long enough), but *not* for having deprived the person of her freedom to leave the room. On a *moral* responsibility view such as Kristjánsson's or Miller's, in contrast, mere inability in that case would apply only relative to those who have no moral responsibility to unlock the door, whereas any agent who can be argued to have such a responsibility and who fails to unlock the door could be said to constrain the person's freedom. Kristjánsson puts this line of reasoning to interesting use in his ch. 4.3 in order to argue that unfreedom can arise from *poverty* even in cases in which responsibility for the *causation* of poverty cannot be attributed to any particular agent.

Freedom and power

Kristjánsson devotes a whole chapter of his book (ch. 6) to this topic which he has elsewhere qualified as a „neglected area of research within the contemporary freedom debate“ (1998a, 264). His own conception of power and its relationship to freedom is given shape mainly in the second of the chapter's three sections.[137]

The fact alone that Kristjánsson gives so much room to a discussion of power in the context of an analysis of the concept of freedom already indicates that he must hold the relationship between social freedom and social power to be very close. In fact, he professes to see „a much closer relationship between power and freedom than has been suggested by previous writers“. In his view, they are even „too intimately related for each of them to be worked out in isolation from the other“ (151). It is therefore no surprise that, in analogy to his concept of freedom, Kristjánsson also advocates a concept of power based on the idea of moral responsibility. Moreover, as in the case of freedom, in the case of power too the object of the responsibility involved are obstacles to the actions of others:

> „*A* exercises power over *B* if and only if *A* is morally responsible for the non-suppression of an obstacle *O* that restrict[s] *B*'s options“ (151).[138]

Since according to this definition, the conceptual condition for an *exercise of power* is exactly the same as the conceptual condition for *making another unfree*, it implies that for Kristjánsson power and freedom are conceptually as close as two different concepts can possibly be. As he himself remarks, „the locutions 'R exercises power over P' and 'R constrains P's freedom' are best seen as extensionally equivalent“ (1998a, 264; similarly 1996, 151, 158, 160).

From this it would seem to follow that everything we could wish to say about power can equivalently be expressed in terms of freedom, and that therefore no more needs to be said specifically about power. But Kristjánsson duly reminds the reader that this is true only to a point, and that there is one aspect of power for which it is not the case. This is the aspect of *having*, as opposed to *exercising*, power over another.

137 In the first section, Kristjánsson discusses different conceptions of power, all of which are found wanting, for a variety of reasons: He dismisses Arendt's definition as too far removed from common usage. He then objects against Russell's insistence that exercises of power necessarily involve the production of intended effects; Connolly is mentioned as having presented a convincing example where power is exercised without intention, merely by negligence. His objection against Weber's definition rests on the common mistaken reading in which resistance is seen as a crucial element. Dahl's concept is regarded as too broad because it includes persuasion and advice among the forms of exercising power. Therefore, Benn's definition, which combines elements of the definitions of Russell, Weber, and Dahl, is also rejected. Oppenheim's proposal for a coherent web of definitions for several 'power concepts' is, of course, criticized on the ground that he offers „arbitrary, stipulative definitions“. In the account of Steven Lukes, Kristjánsson also finds more defects than virtues, the most important of them being that Lukes adheres to the 'essential contestability view' while arguing for the superiority of his own account. Cf. above Chapter 1 for my own discussion of most of these points. In the third, final, section of the chapter, Kristjánsson discusses the problem of measuring different degrees of freedom and power and the question of a non-relational account of aggregate or 'total' freedom.

138 Kristjánsson acknowledges that Lukes correctly saw that „to locate power is to fix responsibility for consequences“, but criticizes him for not having seen the difference between (moral) responsibility and culpability (150 f.).

First, he draws attention to a linguistic peculiarity: If on the level of events or processes power and freedom are so closely related that statements about the *exercise* of power can be equivalently translated into statements about *constraints* on freedom and *vice versa*, one should expect that a similar relationship also holds, and is manifested in linguistic usage, on the level of states of affairs, i. e., that there is also some equivalent in terms of freedom for the common notion of *having* power. But this, Kristjánsson thinks, is not the case:

„It is noteworthy that we have no term corresponding to 'having power over' in the case of unfreedom, meaning that *A* has in general the opportunity to constrain *B*'s freedom (in a particular field) or that he frequently does so. To describe such a state, we would simply say that *A* has power over *B*. This is, I believe, one more indication of the logical affinity between 'exercising power over' and 'constraining freedom' [...]"[139]

The conclusion Kristjánsson seems to draw from this observation is that the notion of 'having power over' can be dismissed as being, at most, of minor importance. But that needs some explaining, because (as we have seen in Chapter 1) it seems almost natural to think that one can *exercise* only an ability one *has*, and that therefore *having* power is, in a way, more fundamental than *exercising* power. Kristjánsson, in contrast, argues that in order to exercise power over someone, one does *not* necessarily need to 'have power' over him. In fact, he says, everyone can, if he really wants to, erect an obstacle to anyone else's actions:

„If an individual *A*, however 'insignificant' a person he may be, sets all his energy at hampering or annoying person *B*, he will most likely succeed, however powerful *B* is."[140]

In other words, everyone can exercise power over anyone else. But it would surely be absurd to claim that everyone also 'has power over' everybody else. Now, if 'having power over' does *not* refer to the ability that is actualized in exercises of power, what *does* it refer to? Kristjánsson seems to be unsure about how to answer this question, and the reason is probably that his starting point – common usage[141] – is ambiguous. As he observes,

139 154 f.; similarly, 1998a, n. 3. Kristjánsson does not stop to say anything about the range of languages for which he would want to claim the truth of his assertions on this point. If he meant to claim that it is true only for English, it would be a very weak argument indeed for making a conceptual point. Besides, it is not even obvious that it is true for English: remember Pettit's – at least linguistically, not implausible – idea that 'to have (dominating) power over' is equivalent to 'compromising' freedom (cf. above Section 2.1).

140 155. Kristjánsson does not bother to mention that, at the very least, some kind of 'access' – physical or motivational – is a necessary condition for such an event. Besides, whether – consistently with Kristjánsson's own definitions – mere „hampering or annoying" already amounts to an exercise of power is questionable.

141 He does not comment on Oppenheim's alternative proposal for a distintion between the ability to 'exercise power over', on the one hand, and to 'have power over', on the other. (On Oppenheim's account, one 'has' power over someone to the extent that something one has done in the past – which must not necessarily have been an exercise of power itself – continues over time to have an impact on another's choices; although he mentions the phenomenon of 'anticipated reactions' as a case in point, Oppenheim apparently does not think that such effects are simply consequences of an awareness, on the part of the subject of power, of the power-holder's ability to exercise power; cf. Oppenheim 1981, 21 ff.). But had he done so, he could have been expected to reject it, once again, on the ground that it is contrary to common usage.

„the locution 'having power over' [...] is commonly used to denote the general tendency or ability of an agent *A* to constrain *B*'s freedom in a certain respect" (161).[142]

A 'tendency' is, of course, something very different from an 'ability'.[143] But the two share an important characteristic: they are both latent properties. Hence, in Kristjánsson's words, „the locution 'having power over' [...] tends to denote relations of a *dispositional*, rather than *episodic*, nature" (153; 1998a, 264). But the definition of a particular dispositional property depends on the prior definition of the kinds of 'episodes' it is counterfactually linked to. Hence,

„the locution 'having power over' [...] designates a dispositional relation, parasitic on the point of the episodic 'exercising power over'" (155),

and, therefore,

„while the dispositional concept 'having power over' can mean a number of different things, it always depends logically on the more basic and easily definable 'exercising power over'" (154; 1998a, 265).

Kristjánsson has thus established the kind of relationship between having and exercising power that he needs: he has found a way how 'having power over' can be interpreted as derivative, secondary to 'exercising power over'. The fundamental, relevant concept is the latter; *that* is the concept intimately related to that of freedom. It is enough to link freedom and power on the *episodic* level, he seems to imply; our linguistic usage provides evidence that we have no need to refer to a *dispositional* dimension of freedom, and hence the *dispositional* view of power does not need to be reined in accordingly. It doesn't really matter whether it is used to refer sometimes to one and sometimes to another type of latent feature; in any case, such features matter only insofar as they direct our attention *somehow* to potential exercises of power, because only such 'episodes' can give rise to moral responsibility, and attention to moral responsibility is the whole 'point' of power-talk as well as freedom-talk.

3.2. DISCUSSION

Kristjánsson's attempt to steer a middle course between the conceptions of Oppenheim – with whom he agrees on the usefulness of a *non-interference* account of freedom – and Pettit – with whom he shares the basic idea that the concepts of freedom and power should best be seen from a *moral point of view* – is, on the whole, carefully considered;

142 Note that in the citation, quoted earlier, about the lack of a corresponding expression in terms of freedom, the enclosed definition of 'having power over' was somewhat different, „meaning that *A* has in general the opportunity to constrain *B*'s freedom (in a particular field) or that he frequently does so". Having a tendency to do something and doing it frequently can, *cum grano salis*, be regarded as equivalent; but an opportunity and an ability to do something are clearly different things.

143 Kristjánsson even makes out yet a third meaning in which the expression 'having power over' is supposedly used, which is reference to the fact that someone has *authority* over another. Kristjánsson did not realize that the most plausible and coherent way of accounting for this usage is to conceive of authority as a specific subcategory of power and that it therefore does not indicate a third, independent meaning of 'having power over'. On the conceptual relationship between power and authority, cf. below, Chapter 4.

his conceptual decisions are backed by arguments, which often refer to the disadvantages and inconveniences of particular alternatives. Still, there are several points on which Kristjánsson's account provokes comments or even raises serious questions and doubts. It is not always obvious that his proposals satisfy even his own criteria of conceptual adequacy – above all the first two of them, requiring respect for common usage and coherence. In the following discussion, I will, with one exception, content myself with the consideration of aspects that are specifically related to his conception of power.

Extensional equivalence of power and unfreedom

The first issue that deserves a comment concerns an aspect that may be of minor importance for Kristjánsson's construction as a whole, but should still not be overlooked.

Statements about exercises of power can be formulated also as statements about constraints on freedom, Kristjánsson remarks. There is always an *extensionally* equivalent pair of such statements. The possible objection that his definitions of freedom and power therefore go „against conceptual economy" he counters by pointing out that, even if the extension of 'exercise of power' and 'constraint on freedom' is the same, they are still two different concepts, „bringing our attention to different aspects of the relation between *A* and *B*; 'exercise of power' shifting the focus to the powerholder, *A*; with 'constraint on freedom' relating more to *B* and the obstacles that restrict his options" (158).

It must be noted, however, that in this specific case, we are not dealing *merely* with extensional equivalence. In fact, the difference between the two concepts in question, as defined by Kristjánsson, is at most the difference between a formulation of one and the same thing in an *active* or in a *passive* mode. Except for this difference of emphasis, the two concepts seem to be not only extensionally, but also *intensionally* equivalent.[144] And it is not even entirely correct to claim the general existence of *that* difference. After all, on Kristjánsson's conception, one can use *both* terms in sentences in the active mode with *no* difference of emphasis, that is, with exactly the same intension: '*A* exercises power over *B*' *means* exactly the same, by Kristjánsson's definition, as '*A* constrains *B*'s freedom'.[145] In a way, then, one could say that they are not really two different concepts at all.

144 Not all extensionally equivalent concepts display also such a very close intensional similarity: A standard textbook example of a pair of concepts which are extensionally, but not intensionally equivalent is that of evening star and morning star: the reference is the same – namely, the planet Venus; but they differ regarding the features by which they identify it: visibility on the Western sky in the evening, on the one hand, and visibility on the Eastern sky in the morning, on the other.

145 In Kristjánsson's words, „an obstacle counts as a constraint on an agent's freedom if and only if there is another agent who can be held *morally* responsible for the existence of the obstacle" (63). This can be rearranged into: 'If and only if there is an *A* who can be held morally responsible for the non-suppression of an obstacle *O* that restricts *B*'s options, the obstacle is a constraint on *B*'s freedom.' Together with Kristjánsson's definition of an exercise of power, this yields: '*A* exercises power over *B* if and only if *A* constrains *B*'s freedom' – the meanings of the two phrases are the same; unlike in the case of morning star and evening star, nowhere in Kristjánsson does one find two independent, intensionally different definitions of 'exercise of power' and 'constraint on freedom'.

The only genuine difference in the common usage of 'exercise of power' and 'constraint on freedom' seems to turn up in *incomplete* references to a relationship of power or unfreedom, respectively, i. e., in statements in which one of the two sides of the relationship is left unmentioned. Following ordinary usage (but with Kristjánsson's definitions in mind), one would say '*A* exercised power', rather than '*A* constrained someone's freedom', in order to make a statement not about the relationship involved, but only about what happens on the side of *A*; and, analogously, in the opposite case one would say '*B* was unfree', not '*B* was subject to an exercise of power'. However, nothing is wrong *linguistically* with the unusual expressions; their only 'defect' seems to be that they make it quite obvious that some information is missing and almost automatically provoke questions ('Whose freedom?' in the former, 'By whom?' in the latter case) asking for the completion of the account by filling in the missing information about the counterpart of the respective relationship. This is not the case if we use the corresponding equivalent, but more common formulations. In that sense, what common usage permits us to do is neglect or occult the fact that there *is* another side. And that seems not irrelevant, e. g. in view of the further fact that only if we possess information about all the elements and circumstances of such a relationship, a well-grounded moral assessment of it becomes possible.

I think this is the only possible way to explain the fact that statements about exercises of power and about constraints on freedom are used in such different ways – unless, of course, one loosens the intensional connection between the two concepts.

Omissions as 'exercises of power'

While the previous, first point was only a comment, to draw attention to an interesting feature of Kristjánsson's conception of the intimate relationship between power and freedom, the second concerns a real problem regarding his view of the relation between omissions and exercises of power.

Kristjánsson insists that one substantial advantage of his account, e. g., over that of Oppenheim, is that another's freedom can be constrained not only by actions, but also by omissions (namely, by omitting to suppress an existing obstacle). While *causal* responsibility can refer only to actions, *moral* responsibility can arise both from actions and from omissions. It is, thus, an advantage of a moral-responsibility view that it can invalidate an important argument against non-interference views of freedom.

Usually, it is held that the *exercise* of power requires, or consists in, *action*. On such an account, if constraints on freedom are conceptually linked to exercises of power, it follows that freedom can be constrained only by actions. Oppenheim is a representative of such a view. For anyone who, by contrast, agrees that the concepts of freedom and power are intimately related, but thinks that freedom can be constrained even in the absence of action, there are then two alternatives:

(1) One is to uphold the idea that exercises of power necessarily imply action and therefore to give up the view that it is the *exercise* of power that is linked to constraints on freedom. In other words, this is the alternative of abandoning the idea that unfreedom can be brought about only by active interference in another's options and that, consequently, freedom must be conceived in terms of non-interference. But if power is not

linked to unfreedom through its *exercise*, then it can only be linked to it through its *possession*. As we have seen earlier, that is the alternative adopted by Pettit.

(2) The other option is to take exactly the opposite road, that is, to maintain the link between exercises of power and constraints on freedom – to stick to a non-interference view of freedom – and to drop, instead, the link between exercises of power and *actions*. This is the option Kristjánsson advocates: on his conception, exercising power and constraining freedom are equivalent; and since freedom can be constrained by omission, it *must* follow that power can also be exercised by omission.

The problem with this view is its implication that in order to *refrain* from constraining someone else's freedom, i. e., in order *not* to exercise power over another, one may not only have to omit, but actively to *do* certain things.[146] First of all, this would lead to the bizarre situation that in some cases one might, e. g., have to reject praise for helping another by pointing out that 'All I'm doing is omitting to exercise power over him'. Secondly, it would then not seem very plausible to uphold the general presumption against unfreedom which serves as a basic support for Kristjánsson's conception, since while it is possible to *omit* any number of actions at the same time, one can always only *perform* very few actions at any one time. Hence, at least concerning the vast area of unfreedom-by-omission which would then exist, we should expect that it is more often than not morally inobjectionable; and this, in turn, should have some effect on the presumption itself. Finally, it seems that the very notion of 'exercise' refers, at least in common usage, to a process of actualizing some latent property or feature in a way that leads to some *change in the course of events*; omissions, in turn, are characterized precisely by *not* changing the *status quo*, or *not* modifying the course of an on-going process. What one is responsible for in case of an exercise of power is a *change* in another's situation; what one is responsible for in omitting to suppress an existing obstacle is, by contrast, the *absence of a change*, i. e., the continuation of a *state of affairs*.

With a view towards coherence, it therefore does not seem to have been a very good idea of Kristjánsson's to design his conceptual construction in a way that allows an omission to be regarded as an exercise of power. Perhaps the price he has paid for linking power so strongly to his peculiar concept of unfreedom will yet turn out to have been too high.

Exercising power vs. having power over another

This impression is reinforced when we turn to a third aspect, directly related to the former, which, I think, needs to be given some thought.

As we have seen in the previous section, the relationship between power and freedom, as Kristjánsson sees it, concerns only the episodic level, i. e., the level of *exercise*. For him, there is no conceptual relationship between an exercise of power and an *underlying* latent condition of 'having power'. On the contrary, he sees the exercise of power as the more basic notion, from which the concept of 'having power over' someone is derived. On the other hand, he also does not want to deny that an 'exercise' must,

146 Remember that on Pettit's account, in contrast, there may not even by anything at all an agent *could* do to refrain from constraining another's freedom since such constraints are independent of his actions and omissions.

in turn, be based on something, on some latent ability. But he claims that the latter has nothing to do with 'having power over':

„the capacity exercised in exercises of power is not the capacity designated by the locution 'having power over' [...] The capacity required for exercises of power to take place is simply *power to* [...]" (154)

His argument for this peculiar, counter-intuitive conception is surprising: it is that 'having power over' *cannot* be the ability on which 'exercising power over' is based, „for having power over is here not a 'capacity' at all, in Morriss' sense, but rather a disposition" (ibid.). So, now we must look at his arguments in support of *that* claim, and here the trouble starts.

As I pointed out earlier, when presenting his view, Kristjánsson acknowledges that 'having power over' is used in ordinary language in different senses, sometimes indicating an *ability*, sometimes a *tendency*, and sometimes an *opportunity*. The *only* 'argument' he offers, as far as I can see, against the first of these three different senses – which is, after all, the most common – is the reference just quoted to Morriss's conception. Indeed, as Kristjánsson explains a few pages before the quoted passage (152), Morriss argues that the ability at the root of exercises of power is 'having power *to*' do certain things; 'having power *over*' is not even mentioned in that context. Hence, it is true that 'having power over' is not *the* ability Morriss sees as fundamental to exercises of power. But, of course, that *statement* of Morriss's view in itself is not an *argument for* adopting it, and much less is it an argument for the further claim that 'having power over' is *no* ability at all. Kristjánsson, however, apparently thinks that with his reference to Morriss, he has definitely dismissed the *ability view* of 'having power over'.[147]

This leaves him with *two* other senses: the *tendency view*, and the *opportunity view*. About these, their respective merits, and their adequacy as 'dispositional' concepts, Kristjánsson remains silent. He seems to think that he does not need to say anything more about the notion of 'having power over' because for the purposes of his study, he is interested only in that mode of power which can give rise to moral responsibility, and that is the mode of 'exercising', not the mode of 'having' it – regardless of whether the latter refers to an ability, a tendency, or an opportunity (cf. 156 f.).

But even though I think he is right in holding that 'having power over' someone is not something anyone can plausibly be held morally accountable for, he is wrong in thinking that, therefore, he needs to pay no attention to this concept. Since his most fundamental criterion for conceptual adequacy is maximal respect for common usage, he should not neglect the fact that 'having power over' another is most commonly thought to mean precisely the *ability* to 'exercise power over' that other.[148] Except for the pseu-

147 Only to reintroduce it, seemingly without being aware of it, a page later when he explains that „*A has* power over [...] basically means that he has the power *to* exercise power *over*" *B* (155). What does 'having the power to' do something mean other than being *able*, having the *ability* to do it? Cf. also 1998a, 267 f., where he adopts, apparently without any problem or second thoughts, Pettit's ability view of 'having power over' someone, and combines it with his own responsibility view of 'exercising power over', when he says that „we identify R as having power over P because we know that *if* R chooses to exercise power over P, which R can do arbitrarily and at will, R's action will stand in need of a justification."

148 Thus, the assertion that someone *has* power over another is usually not taken to *answer*, but rather to *provoke* questions about the inclinations of the powerholder to *exercise* that power. It is, for instance, common

do-argument mentioned above, he has not offered any argument against that conception. Hence, we seem to have no reason for giving it up. But, unfortunately, it is a conception that is hardly compatible with his own account of 'exercising power over' as something for which one does *not* need to 'have power over' in any non-trivial sense.

I think this problem is due to the fact that Kristjánsson has focused somewhat too firmly on what he calls the *episodic* character of exercises of power. This has led him to overlook an important distinction. Of course it is trivial to say that for any particular exercise of power over someone, one needs to be able to – or, in other words, one needs to 'have the power to' – perform that very action: *performing* an action implies *being able to perform* it (in the particular circumstances, at that particular location and time). And Kristjánsson is perfectly right in noting that *that* ability is not meant when it is commonly said that someone 'has power over' another. The ability one necessarily (and, therefore, trivially) manifests in performing a particular action refers only to the action as an *act-individual* or *act-token*. In contrast, the ability that is commonly meant when someone is said to 'have power over' another does not refer to an act-token, but to an *act-type* or *act-category*: I 'have power over' you, with respect to a certain matter, to the extent that *whenever* an opportunity arises and I decide to do so, I am able to exercise power over you, i. e., to perform (a token of) the (generic) act 'exercising power over' you.

Now, Kristjánsson *must* say that if 'having power over' is understood in *this* sense, then one does not need to *have* power over another in order to *exercise* power over him in *his* sense. It is, of course, possible (at least sometimes, under some circumstances) to constrain another's freedom on a particular occasion, even if one does not have a 'generic' ability to do so, over a certain stretch of time.[149]

In other words, one *cannot* consistently hold, at the same time, both that an exercise of power over another is always an actualized instance of the underlying ability denoted by saying that one 'has' power over that other, *and* that exercizing power over another is (at least extensionally) equivalent to constraining the other's freedom. Concerning the concept of power, the question then is, again, whether there is a good reason to insist, as Kristjánsson does, that the choice between these alternatives should be decided in favour of the latter, even though common usage supports the former and has not been invalidated as incoherent by any argument.

As we have seen, Kristjánsson elaborates on the point that there is no linguistic equivalent on the side of freedom talk for the 'having – exercising' pair on the side of

knowledge among political scientists that within the French political system, the president *has* a great amount of power; but precisely because of this, one interesting question about French politics has always been *to what extent* a particular president has been inclined to *exercise* that power. On the other hand, a credible assertion to the effect that someone does *not have* power over another is usually taken to preclude all questions about possible exercises of power. The question 'Oh, but don't you think he still might exercise power over me sometimes?' seems a strange reaction – to put it mildly – to the assertion 'Don't worry – he has no power over you'. If 'having power over' would refer merely to an *inclination* to exercise power frequently, however, the question should be perfectly natural.

149 Imagine a case in which an otherwise very weak agent uses up all the resources available to her in order to erect one big obstacle to another. After having completed that feat, she will never again be able to muster the strength to do so. In that case, she would have exercised power on that one occasion in Kristjánsson's sense; but she would certainly not 'have power over' the other in the sense indicated above.

power talk. He interprets this as a confirmation of his view that it is the *exercise* of power that is conceptually linked to constraints on freedom, and that, since 'having power over' has no equivalent in terms of freedom, it can be dismissed as a secondary, derivative notion devoid of independent importance. This is, however, only one possible conclusion to be drawn from that linguistic fact. It seems at least equally plausible to draw exactly the opposite conclusion: that since ordinary usage reflects the idea that power talk refers to a very special kind of relationship between agents which comes, so to speak, both in a latent ('having') and a manifest ('exercising') version, and since nothing equivalent exists on the side of freedom, a forced equivalence, by definitional decision, between exercises of power and constraints on freedom fails to capture an important dimension of the 'point' of speaking of *power relations* (instead of merely isolated instances of someone somehow prevailing over another).

At this point, the comment I made earlier about the fact that on Kristjánsson's account, exercising power and constraining freedom seem to be not only extensionally, but also intensionally equivalent, may yet acquire some weight. Perhaps Kristjánsson has been looking at the wrong place for the conceptual difference between the two. The weak account of the difference between power talk and freedom talk as being merely a matter of emphasis, as well as the question of how to accomodate the notion of 'having power over' both disappear as soon as one takes ordinary usage seriously, as recommended by Kristjánsson himself. If 'exercising power over' is admitted to have the feature of being necessarily (conceptually) linked to 'having power over', and if nothing similar can be said for (un)freedom, then it seems that 'exercising power over' should, at most, be conceived only as a *special case* of infringing upon another's freedom. On such a conception, a close link between exercises of power and constraints on freedom can be upheld, but it does not amount to extensional equivalence. Power can then still be defined in terms of constraints on freedom, but constraints on freedom do not necessarily involve exercises of power – someone's freedom may be constrained, for instance, either by a use of *force* or by an exercise of *power*. The switch to such a conception would not even oblige Kristjánsson to give up a *responsibility* view of power. Hence, there seems to be no reason why he should be reluctant to take this conceptual step.

Power and intention

But that impression is mistaken. Because the conception according to which an *exercise* of power over someone is always a manifestation of an underlying latent *relationship* of power between the agents involved – of one side 'having power over' the other – has further implications.

Kristjánsson not only conceives of power in a way that makes it possible for it to be exercised by omission. He also argues against the requirement that an exercise of power, in order to be such, must be „successful" (147). In other words, he thinks that even if an interference *fails* to bring about a desired result, as long as the other defining characteristics obtain, it is still to be regarded as an exercise of power. And this is a view that would be incompatible with a conception according to which 'exercising power' refers to an actualization of an underlying condition of 'having power' in the ability sense. After all, what could 'having power' in that sense mean other than precisely the ability to 'exercise' it *successfully*? Or, the other way round: What could the observation of a *failed* attempt to exercise power over another be taken to indicate if not a *lack* of power on the part of the respective agent? Moreover, on a more general level, that an *attempt* to perform some action *x fails* means that action *x* was *not performed*; in that sense, for logical reasons, only a 'successful' attempt to exercise power can be regarded as constituting an actual exercise of power.

Kristjánsson could surely not deny this; therefore, he must be talking about the success or failure of exercises of power in some other sense. In fact, on his definition of 'exercise of power', there is a way how the possibility of unsuccessful exercises of power can be made comprehensible. If, for example, one sets out to erect a certain obstacle to another and fails to bring it about, but in the course of it one manages – perhaps inadvertently – to erect *another* (different, smaller ...) obstacle instead, then one has 'exercised power over' the other in Kristjánsson's terms although one has failed in one's attempt to bring about the desired result. In other words: in such a case, one intended to perform *one* exercise of power, but has actually performed *another*. In a sense, then, one has, at the same time, been successful *and* unsuccessful in attempting to exercise power over the other.

But this ambiguous state of success and failure already indicates that it is doubtful whether on Kristjánsson's account it even makes sense at all to speak in terms of success when referring to exercises of power. In fact, Kristjánsson himself should reject the language of success concerning the exercise of power, because the very concept of success has a component that is highly inconvenient for his view. After all, he denies that the exercise of power necessarily requires the agent's *intention* – a view for which he offers at least three different arguments:

(1) Power can be exercised by *negligence* and thoughtlessness, because that is how, among other things, constraints on freedom can come about (158).

(2) Besides, this is also what the responsibility view of power suggests: one is morally accountable not only for the intended effects, but also for the (foreseeable) *unintended side effects* of one's actions; hence, a distinction along the lines of intention would be arbitrary (158 f.).

(3) Finally, the 'exercise' involved in exercises of power is not of the kind for which an agent must be „actively engaged" in an action (159); instead, he argues, 'exercising power over' is a *relational* concept, and for such concepts, 'exercise' means nothing but the fact that the respective relationship is „'actual' as opposed to 'potential'", which is the case whenever there is an obstacle for whose non-suppression someone can be held accountable (160).

The notion of success, however, is parasitic on that of intention: success and failure are *comparative* concepts, and what is compared in declaring one or the other is what an action *did* bring about, on the one hand, and what it was *intended to* bring about, on the other. Therefore, Kristjánsson's rejection of an intentionality view of power *logically implies* that success or failure cannot (at least not generally) be predicated of exercises of power. Hence, there is no need for him even to raise the question of success as an independent issue, requiring independent arguments.[150]

The more important question, however, is whether his three arguments really succeed in making a convincing case against the intentionality view itself. In my view, they do not withstand closer scrutiny:

* The *first* argument depends entirely on the presupposed conceptual intimacy of 'exercise of power' and 'constraint on freedom', the adequacy of which was already put into question in the previous considerations.

* The same applies to the *second* argument. As soon as one admits that not *all* constraints on freedom are necessarily constituted by exercises of power, one can also admit an intentionality view of power without having to give up the idea that obstacles existing by way of unintended side effects of someone's action may, nevertheless, give rise to accountability.

* And the *third* argument is, in my view, another surprising case of disrespect for well-established usage. Indeed, Kristjánsson's conception of 'exercise of power' is so far removed from anything one would usually call an 'exercise' that it is hard to imagine how he could hope to convince even fellow-philosophers of its adequacy and usefulness as a viable proposal for a future conceptual convention. Remember that in his view accountability is not culpability; one may, for instance, be accountable for states of affairs one is not even aware of. Hence, on Kristjánsson's interpretation of 'exercise' in the relational version,[151] if a third person erected an obstacle to your freedom which I could, for some reason, be expected to suppress, and I don't, because I am *unaware of its existence*, I would be 'exercising power over' you.

A conception so radically detached from common usage would need very strong arguments in its favour to gain some plausibility; but such arguments are nowhere to be seen. Indeed, besides the fact that Kristjánsson *needs* such an account of 'exercise' in order to be able to uphold his definition of 'exercising power over', there seems to be no explanation for its existence at all. But far from being an argument *in favour* of that strange conception of 'exercise', this fact rather seems to be another argument *against* his definition of power.

Power as a disposition

In view of the specific problems we have so far encountered in Kristjánsson's account of power as related to freedom, much seems to speak in favour of the well-established conception of power as referring to an ability that is manifested through its successful exercise, and the exercise of which, in turn, implies a corresponding intention on the part of the exercising agent.

150 The arguments Kristjánsson does offer (147 f.) can therefore perhaps be seen as evidence that he is not fully aware of the implications of his own approach.

151 It is not even clear in what sense Kristjánsson can regard 'exercising power over' as a *relational* concept at all, considering that he denies that it is based on an underlying relation (i. e., on 'having power over').

Now it is time to return to another interesting aspect, which has earlier been mentioned merely in passing. It is an aspect that is relevant, regardless of the position one adopts concerning the previous questions. In his discussion of the relation between 'exercising' and 'having' power over others, Kristjánsson repeatedly asserts that the latter denotes a *disposition.* He cannot bring himself to decide what *kind* of a disposition it is,[152] but nevertheless uses the alleged fact *that* it is one as an argument in favour of his conception of power. Apart from this peculiarity, his view that 'having power over' is of a dispositional nature is shared by many other authors.[153]

Of course, the term 'disposition' is another ambiguous word. One of its common lexical meanings is merely that of a synonym for 'tendency' or 'inclination' to behave in certain ways. Clearly, this is one of the meanings Kristjánsson has in mind when he says that 'having power over' may denote the 'tendency' to exercise power; but just as clearly, this is *not* the sense in which the phrase 'having power over' is usually understood. The same is true for Kristjánsson's suggestion that 'having power over' is a dispositional concept in the sense that it refers to an opportunity: this too is not the sense in which 'having power over' is usually employed; but in addition, it is also, as far as I am aware, not the kind of thing that would fit under any common conception of a disposition.

This leaves us with the third possible understanding of the (allegedly) dispositional concept 'having power over' – the ability view. This is the view Kristjánsson *explicitly discards.* But note that it is also the view the author on whom he relies for the distinction between episodic and dispositional concepts, Dennis Wrong, *explicitly endorses.*[154] Here is what Wrong has to say about it:

„Power [...] is unmistakably a 'dispositional' term in Gilbert Ryle's sense, referring not to an actual performance but to a capacity, latent in the actor even when not being exercised, to produce a particular kind of performance.“ (Wrong 1988, 1)[155]

And again:

„[P]ower when thought of as a capacity is a dispositional concept. What Gilbert Ryle says about 'knowing' and 'aspiring' also applies to power conceived of as a capacity to control others: [...] Ryle calls verbs such as 'to know', 'to aspire', and 'to possess' *dispositional* words that refer to recurrent tendencies of human beings to behave in certain ways, in contrast to the *episodic* words we employ to refer to specific behavioural events. The distinction between 'having power' and 'exercising power' reflects the difference between viewing power as a dispositional and as an episodic concept.“ (Wrong 1988, 6)

Unfortunately, this formulation is not very clear. It sounds as if Wrong wanted to hold that power is an ability, and at the same time *also* a tendency, where the tendency account is claimed to follow Ryle. In fact, Wrong's „recurrent tendencies of human beings to behave in certain ways“[156] may have misled Kristjánsson into thinking that Wrong

152 Cf. above: after discarding the ability view, the tendency and the opportunity view were left.

153 Among the authors who regard power explicitly as a dispositional property are, e. g., Nagel (1975, 31), Koller (1991, 114), Morriss (1987, 14). Cf. also Chapter 1.

154 So do most other writers who conceive of 'having power over' as a dispositional concept.

155 The reference is to: Gilbert Ryle, The Concept of Mind, New York: Barnes & Noble 1949, 116–125.

156 To offer yet another hair-splitting comment: since 'tendency' already refers to something recurrent, it is difficult to know what a 'recurrent tendency' could be other than simply a tendency.

and Ryle support his idea that 'having power' refers to a tendency to exercise power frequently. He apparently did not realize that this interpretation cannot be reconciled with the fact that 'to know' or 'to possess' are given as examples of the dispositional concepts Ryle has in mind.[157] It is true that Ryle's idea of such concepts has something to do with 'tendencies', but not with tendencies in the sense Kristjánsson seems to have read out of Wrong's description; what Ryle says instead is that such words as 'believing' or 'aspiring' are dispositional in that they refer not directly to actions, nor to abilities for certain actions, but rather to a kind of (latent) states of mind, or conditions, which become manifest only when under certain circumstances they make people behave in specific, typical ways.[158] He thus suggested that certain concepts which are otherwise difficult to grasp can perhaps best be understood *in analogy* to such ordinary dispositional properties as being soluble, brittle, magnetic, or irascible.

But Ryle's idea of dispositional concepts obviously refers neither to opportunities, nor to tendencies in the sense of inclinations to certain actions, nor to abilities. Hence, under none of the three possible conceptions of 'having power over' mentioned by Kristjánsson, it could be a dispositional concept in Ryle's sense. Consequently, if it is to be a dispositional concept at all, we must look for another account of dispositionality. And the natural place to look seems to be that basic notion of 'dispositional property' Ryle refers to as the inspiration for his analogous account.

Taken seriously, such 'dispositional properties' are tricky things. A number of eminent epistemologists have tried to solve the puzzles they give rise to. Their special characteristic is, in Wilhelm Essler's words, that they have no „explicit definition"; instead, a „dispositional predicate" can be captured only by a kind of „conditional definition" – „a partial, or conditional, determination of its meaning" (Hempel 1974, 33) – which is „usually" an „operational" definition „consisting in the specification of a *test condition* and of a corresponding *test result* in the positive case" (Essler 1970, 127 ff.).

***

EXCURSUS: DISPOSITIONAL PROPERTIES

From an epistemological point of view, such properties are far from trivial. For instance, a logical problem arises if what has just been said about them is translated into a schema for operational definitions, shown here with the example of intelligence, of the following form:
„For all persons x: x is intelligent if and only if whenever x is subjected to test condition Tb then x brings about result Rs." (Essler 1970, 128)

The problem with this schema is that it leads to a paradox, since in case an *x* is *never* subjected to the test condition, according to the logic of implication the disposition would have to be ascribed to it; but the same would also be true for the contrary. Thus, an *x* that has never been, and will never be, subjected to the test would have to count as *both* intelligent and unintelligent at the same time.

Carnap, „in order to avoid such inadequate results" (ibid., 128 f.), proposed that dispositional predicates should not be reconstructed by a definition as in the above schema; instead, he suggested to reconstruct them with the help of two 'reduction sentences' of the following kind:[159]

[157] The same objection applies to Wrong's account.
[158] In other words: a person's actions to some extent reflect her beliefs and/or her aspirations; and under certain circumstances, how someone behaves also reflects that he is in possession of certain things.
[159] Ibid., 129; for similar accounts, cf. Hempel 1974, 31 ff.; Nagel 1975, 24 f.; Stegmüller 1983, 161.

(1) „If at some time t a person x is subjected to test condition Tb and if x is intelligent, then at that time x brings about result Rs", and
(2) „If at some time t a person x is subjected to test condition Tb and if x is not intelligent, then at that time x does not bring about result Rs".

The conjunction of these two sentences is logically equivalent to another schema:

„If at some time t a person x is subjected to test condition Tb, then x is intelligent if and only if at time t x brings about result Rs."

The decisive difference between the two schemata thus characterized is that, while the former gives rise to the above-mentioned paradox, according to the latter the dispositional predicate is merely *undefined* for persons never subjected to the test condition.[160]

***

So the question is: Can one plausibly say that the power of an agent – his 'having power over' another – consists in his *disposition* „to react to a condition *C* by the characteristic response *R*" (Carnap 1960, 243)? If this were indeed the case, then one would have to specify such a condition and a corresponding 'characteristic response' that would constitute a manifestation of power. But, in fact, a characteristic response does not seem to be what an agent's having power over another is about.

Moreover, generally speaking, it seems that an *ability* cannot be a *disposition* in the above sense – an ability is just not the kind of thing that is invariably (or even only frequently) triggered as a response to certain circumstances. But, someone might object, isn't my ability to close doors manifested in my successfully closing a door whenever I seriously set about it? Generally, isn't an ability to do *x* manifested in *successfully doing x* whenever one *attemps* to do *x*? And, therefore, isn't the fact that *A has* power over *B* manifested precisely in bringing about whatever it is that an *exercise* of power by *A* over *B* is supposed to bring about, *whenever A attempts* to exercise power over *B*? In that sense, could one not say that an ability is a disposition after all, namely, the disposition to react with the 'characteristic response' of successfully doing the thing in question to the 'condition' of attempting to do it?

To say the least, this would seem to be a rather strange way of putting it, especially if one translates it into Carnap's formulation: the ability to do *x* would then be the disposition 'to react to the attempt of doing *x* by the characteristic response of actually doing *x*'. The strangeness of this resides in conceiving of the successful doing of *x* as caused or 'triggered' by the attempt to do *x*. A disposition in Carnap's sense refers to a

[160] The deeper problems of the task of finding criteria for the ascription of dispositional properties which are themselves based exclusively on manifest properties of the respective subjects, and the relations between dispositional predicates and counterfactual conditionals, have been treated by Nelson Goodman in the first of his famous 'Special Lectures in Philosophy' at the University of London (1953), which was later published as the second chapter of *Facts, Fiction and Forecast* (Goodman 1955). – An entirely different, but no less intriguing question is that of explaining where a disposition comes from, what it is based on. On this, cf. Ruben's (1990, ch. VII) considerations about „disposition explanations", i. e., about „the explanation of why an object has a dispositional property in terms of its structural features"; he explains dispositions by pointing to the microstructure of things, reminding the reader that „two objects can have the same dispositional feature, like water-solubility, in virtue of two different microstructural bases" (ibid., 226), and then goes on to discuss whether the disposition-structure relationship is a causal one.

causal relation between some condition, as the *cause*, and some characteristic reaction, as the *effect* or *consequence* of that cause. But in the case of a human ability to perform certain kinds of actions, the attempt to perform such an action is *not* the cause which brings about, as its effect, the successful performance of that action; rather, the successful performance of an action is the *result* of an attempt of such a performance.[161] Or perhaps it would be still more accurate to say that whenever an attempt to do *x* is successful, then *doing x* and *attempting to do x* is simply the same thing.

Thus, instead of talking about an ability as a disposition, it seems more to the point and less awkward to say that the ability to perform some (generic) act *x* is shown by the successful completion of (individual) attempts of doing *x*. This is all there is to it.

Interestingly, however, Carnap himself uses the example of an 'ability' precisely to demonstrate what he calls the „method of dispositional concepts":

„For example, let *X* be an automobile and *D* be the ability for a specified acceleration on a horizontal road at a speed of 10 miles per hour. The hypothesis that the automobile has this ability *D* may be tested by either of the following two procedures. The behavioristic method consists in driving the car and observing its performance under the specified conditions. The second method consists in studying the internal structure of the car, especially the motor, and calculating with the help of physical laws the acceleration which would result under the specified conditions."[162]

As the example suggests, the difference between a disposition and an ability, as the terms are commonly used, perhaps resides in that a disposition is thought to lead, under certain circumstances, *necessarily* to a certain reaction, whereas an ability opens a *possibility*, but does *not* entail the *necessity* to react in a certain way to certain circumstances. A person who 'can' (knows how to) play the piano may nevertheless not have the disposition (be under no compulsion) to do so; under certain circumstances she *could*, but *need not* do it. Likewise, someone who has the *ability* of controlling the actions of another may nevertheless decide never to do so. In other words, when it comes to human actions, the *ability* to do something is certainly a *necessary*, but *not a sufficient* condition for doing it; a *disposition* to do a certain thing *presupposes* the ability to do it, but not *vice versa*; the ability may well exist without the disposition.

In the above quote, Carnap does not mention this distinction – probably because he is thinking exclusively of purely causal relations in which, so to speak, the 'ability' to react in a certain way to a certain condition is not only a necessary, but also a sufficient condition for a particular effect (as in the case of accelerating a car: if the car *can* accelerate at a certain rate under specified conditions, then it also *will* invariably thus accelerate under these conditions – if it doesn't, then the conditions under which it can do so simply do not obtain). But this does not apply to human actions, where doing what one *can* do is subject to one's *choice*.

In the case of 'having power over', there seems to be only one sense in which the idea that it is a *dispositional concept* acquires some plausibility, namely, when it is understood as being, in a certain sense, an *ability* of one agent, but at the same time also

161 On the decisive conceptual distinction between effects, on the one hand, and consequences and results of actions, on the other, cf. von Wright 1984, ch. III.2.

162 Carnap 1960, 243; for pioneering discussions of dispositional properties in the same sense cf. also Carnap 1936/37 and 1956.

as referring to a particular kind of *relationship* between that agent and another, to wit, a relationship involving precisely the ability of the former to determine (or control) certain actions of the latter.[163] Thus, if *A*'s 'having power over' *B* is defined as *A*'s ability to make *B* behave in certain ways, then the fact that *A has* power over *B* manifests itself in that whenever *A* does certain things (namely, *exercise* his power) this 'triggers' a particular kind of reaction by *B*.

In *that* sense, 'having power over' can perhaps be seen as a dispositional concept in Carnap's understanding: the 'test condition' for showing that an agent *A* 'has power over' another agent *B* is that *A* attempts to 'exercise power' over *B*; and the 'test result' which indicates that *A* does indeed 'have power over' *B* is that *B* reacts in a certain way to such an attempt.[164] But this would mean that although it is *A* who has the *ability* in question, the *disposition* would be on the side of *B*.[165] So even on this account, we have a situation that is substantially different from the kind of situations the concept of 'dispositional properties' refers to.

It seems, therefore, that not much is to be gained (besides perplexity and confusion) from insisting on the dispositional nature of 'having power over', and that for this reason too, it is advisable simply to stick with the ability view.

The status of offers

The last aspect of Kristjánsson's conception of power that deserves discussion is the status of offers, i. e., the question whether offers as well as threats can constrain freedom and therefore, in his view, constitute exercises of power. In my view, Kristjánsson's answer to this question is not convincing.

When offers adversely affect a subject's freedom, that is so, he argues, only because they obliquely contain an element of threat, and it is only *this* component which erects an obstacle and can therefore be responsible for the infringement of freedom. His account of the specific characteristics of such 'offers' as compared to genuine, 'pure' offers can be reconstructed as follows: The types of offers we are concerned with here are

163 Cf. Dowding 1991, 15 f.: „This fact that some properties of individuals also denote relations between people seems to confuse some analysts [...] It is a fairly common denotational error to think that some property, such as power, is *either* a property of an actor *or* a relation between actors [...] When we come to describe (or 'model') the power structure we describe actors by their relationship to other objects, including other actors [...] the structural description is what explains individual and group power; but that power is still individual and group power and not structural power."

164 Note that there is one remarkable difference between dispositional properties as envisaged by the epistemologists mentioned above, and power as a dispositional property in the sense just explained: in the case of power, the reactions of *B* which count as positive test results for the disposition '*A* has power over *B*' may be substantively variable. It is not that there is one single reaction by *B* as an indicator of *A*'s power over *B*; rather, what is 'characteristic' about those reactions by *B* is the *relation* in which they stand to *A*'s prior action, i. e., to the 'test condition'.

165 In addition, *awareness* on the part of *B* of the fact that *A has* power over him may itself, independently of any possible *exercises* of that power, produce certain behavioural dispositions in *B*, in the sense of anticipated reactions and the like. Such reactions, however, are not really linked to *A*'s power, but rather to *B*'s *beliefs* about that power and about *A*'s desires concerning *B*'s conduct (beliefs which may be true or false), and they must therefore not be confused with the reactions involved in the question whether or not having power is a dispositional property.

conditional offers,[166] i. e., proposals which can be translated into some variant of a sentence of the form 'If you do *x*, I'll do *y*', where *y* refers to some action that is assumed to be beneficial to the addressee. Now, Kristjánsson thinks that offers should be distinguished according to what they imply about possible alternative ways of securing the benefit of *y*: what he calls 'tentative proposals' link *y* to the performance of *x* in a non-exclusive way, leaving it open whether *y* might also be provided if the stipulated condition is not satisfied; such tentative proposals, he says, hence constitute „pure" offers. In contrast, when an offer implies that the benefit can *only* be secured if the condition is satisfied ('If *and only if* you do *x*, ...'), this is a 'final proposal'. Such final proposals, in Kristjánsson's view, although they look just like genuine offers, actually contain both an offer *and* a threat. The reason why he thinks so can be assumed to be that if the 'if and only if' clause is spelled out in extensive form, the corresponding proposal reads 'If you do *x*, I'll do *y*, *and* if you don't do *x*, I won't do *y*', where 'not *y*', being the withdrawal or cancellation of a benefit, amounts to a harm or deprivation, and therefore the second part of the proposal constitutes a threat.

But this account is unsatisfactory. Kristjánsson is certainly right in claiming that most authors overlook the fact that a distinction between strongly and weakly conditional offers can be made, that weakly conditional offers ('tentative proposals') are not entirely irrelevant,[167] and that they do not foreclose any options, i. e., do not impose obstacles. But that is only an argument against the thesis that *all* offers are necessarily freedom-constraining. For the weaker claim that *some* offers constitute a constraint on freedom, one can, I think, concede that only offers in the sense of final proposals, with firmly fixed conditions, must be taken into account. The real issue is Kristjánsson's reason for thinking that *all* 'final' offers potentially constrain freedom.[168] And the problem with his reason is that it is a *structural* reason, to wit, that such offers invariably have the complex structure of a genuine *offer* combined with a *threat*. In my view, this interpretation of final proposals is untenable. In order to see why this is so, we need to take a closer look at the general structure of threats and offers.

Note, first, that it is impossible to tell a threat from an offer simply by looking at the external *structure* of a proposal, without considering also its *content*. Take the following four basic forms of conditional proposals (let us assume they are all final proposals in Kristjánsson's terms) that can be made to an addressee *A* by an issuer *I*:

(1) 'Iff you do *x*, I'll do *y*.
(2) 'Iff you don't do *x*, I'll do *y*.'
(3) 'Iff you do *x*, I won't do *y*.
(4) 'Iff you don't do *x*, I won't do *y*.'

166 Unconditional offers are not of interest here because they make no specific demand whatsoever on the addressee's conduct; they can be accepted or rejected, or even simply ignored.

167 Kristjánsson is apparently thinking mainly of bargaining situations in a market, where suppliers of goods make successive 'tentative' offers, testing the addressee's willingness to satisfy the condition for obtaining the good, until they reach their 'final' offer which stipulates the minimum condition the addressee must satisfy if he is to obtain the good in question.

168 They do so only *potentially*, because here too, of course, the decisive criterion for considering an obstacle a constraint of freedom is that of moral responsibility.

Without making any assumptions about the substance of *x* and *y*, and particularly about *A*'s attitudes towards them, we have no way of deciding in each of the four cases whether they constitute a threat or an offer; each of these conditionals could be either one. Or, more precisely, without attributing to an *I* any *assumptions* about the attitudes of an *A*, we cannot decide whether *I*, in issuing any such proposal, means to threaten *A* or to make an offer to *A*.

So let us consider what the structure of these assumptions must be, for each of the four cases, if it is to be interpreted as a threat or as an offer, respectively. One can certainly think of all kinds of sophisticated variants of offers or threats based on complex assumptions about the addressee's attitudes and preferences. But in order to see the structural point I'm driving at, we can restrict the analysis to the most primitive, straightforward interpretation for each case.[169]

(1) 'Iff you do x, I'll do y'

(1t) If this is meant to serve as an effective *threat* from *I* to *A*, *I* must assume that without the threat, *ceteris paribus*, *A* would do *x*, but that if the choice is between the conjunctions of doing *x* and having done *y*, on the one hand, and *not* doing *x* and *not* having done *y*, on the other, *A* prefers the *latter*.

Example: 'If you reject my bill today, I'll reject your's tomorrow.'

(1o) If this same type of sentence is meant to serve as an effective *offer* from *I* to *A*, *I* must assume that without the offer, *ceteris paribus*, *A* would *not* do *x*, but that if the choice is between the conjunctions of doing *x* and having done *y*, on the one hand, and *not* doing *x* and *not* having done *y*, on the other, *A* prefers the *former*.

Example: 'If you endorse my bill today, I'll endorse your's tomorrow.'

(2) 'Iff you don't do x, I'll do y'

(2t) If this is meant to serve as an effective *threat* from *I* to *A*, *I* must assume that without the threat, *ceteris paribus*, *A* would *not* do *x*, but that if the choice is between the conjunctions of doing *x* and *not* having done *y*, on the one hand, and *not* doing *x* and having done *y*, on the other, *A* prefers the *former*.

Example: 'If you don't endorse my bill today, I'll reject your's tomorrow.'

(2o) If it is meant to serve as an effective *offer* from *I* to *A*, *I* must assume that without the offer, *ceteris paribus*, *A* would do *x*, but that if the choice is between the conjunctions of doing *x* and *not* having done *y*, on the one hand, and *not* doing *x* and having done *y*, on the other, *A* prefers the *latter*.

Example: 'If you don't reject my bill today, I'll endorse your's tomorrow.'

(3) 'Iff you do x, I won't do y'

[169] It should be clear that in these cases nothing is implied here about the *correctness* of *I*'s assumptions about *A*'s attitudes, nor about the actual *effectiveness* of the respective offers and threats.

(3t) If this is meant to serve as an effective *threat* from *I* to *A*, *I* must assume that without the threat, *ceteris paribus*, *A* would do *x*, but that if the choice is between the conjunctions of doing *x* and *not* having done *y*, on the one hand, and *not* doing *x* and having done *y*, on the other, *A* prefers the *latter*.

Example: 'If you reject my bill today, I'll not endorse your's tomorrow.'

(3o) If this is meant to serve as an effective *offer* from *I* to *A*, *I* must assume that without the offer, *ceteris paribus*, *A* would *not* do *x*, but that if the choice is between the conjunctions of doing *x* and *not* having done *y*, on the one hand, and *not* doing *x* and having done *y*, on the other, *A* prefers the *former*.

Example: 'If you endorse my bill today, I'll not reject your's tomorrow.'

(4) 'Iff you don't do x, I won't do y'

(4t) If this is meant to serve as an effective *threat* from *I* to *A*, *I* must assume that without the threat, *ceteris paribus*, *A* would *not* do *x*, but that if the choice is between the conjunctions of doing *x* and having done *y*, on the one hand, and *not* doing *x* and *not* having done *y*, on the other, *A* prefers the *former*.

Example: 'If you don't endorse my bill today, I won't endorse your's tomorrow.'

(4o) If this is meant to serve as an effective *offer* from *I* to *A*, *I* must assume that without the offer, *ceteris paribus*, *A* would do *x*, but that if the choice is between the conjunctions of doing *x* and having done *y*, on the one hand, and *not* doing *x* and *not* having done *y*, on the other, *A* prefers the *latter*.

Example: 'If you don't reject my bill today, I'll not reject your's tomorrow.'

The resulting pattern of the assumptions connected with the different forms of threats and offers can be seen more clearly when the characteristics of the different cases are collected in a table.

Table 3.1 Threats and offers, ordered by type of case

Case	A would	Assumed preference relation
1 t	x	x & y < not x & not y
o	not x	x & y > not x & not y
2 t	not x	x & not y > not x & y
o	x	x & not y < not x & y
3 t	x	x & not y < not x & y
o	not x	x & not y > not x & y
4 t	not x	x & y > not x & not y
o	x	x & y < not x & not y

Table 3.1 gives a shorthand presentation of the cases and their characteristics as just spelled out, maintaining the above order. The ordering in *Table 3.1* reveals something about the pattern *within* each pair of threats and offers. We see that in each of the four cases, the *difference* between the threat and the offer concerns *both* the assumption about what the addressee would do without *I*'s intervention (he *would not* do in case of the offer what he *would* do in case of the threat) *and* the assumption about *A*'s preference concerning *one and the same* pair of options (he prefers one side in case of the threat and the other in case of the offer).

But perhaps a still more interesting pattern is one that cuts *across* different cases, as shown next in *Table 3.2*, where the entries are regrouped accordingly.

Table 3.2 Threats and offers, combinations of characteristics

Assumed preference relation	A would	Case
not x & not y > x & y	x	**1t** and **4o**
x & y > not x & not y	not x	**1o** and **4t**
x & not y > not x & y	not x	**2t** and **3o**
not x & y > x & not y	x	**2o** and **3t**

How is this pattern to be interpreted? What the table shows at a glance is that there are only four different combinations of characteristics, each of which appears exactly twice, once in a threat and once in an offer. Consider the first of these types. It reveals that the characteristics of a type *(1)* threat and of a type *(4)* offer are exactly the same: in both cases, *A* would – absent the threat or offer, respectively – presumedly do *x*; but if the only available options are the conjunctions of doing *x* and having *y* done, or of *not* doing *x* and *not* having *y* done, then *A* is assumed to prefer the latter package to the former.

Now, let us look once again at the corresponding basic formulae, beginning with that of the *offer*:

An offer of type *(4)* was of the kind 'Iff you don't do *x*, then I won't do *y*'. But that is, as has already been explained, equivalent to the extensive form 'If you don't do *x*, then I won't do *y*, and if you do *x*, then I'll do *y*': *If you don't reject my bill today, I'll not reject your's tomorrow;and if you reject my bill today, I'll reject your's tomorrow.*

Secondly, take now a threat of type *(1)*: 'Iff you do *x*, I'll do *y*'; if we spell this out in the extensive form, we get as its equivalent 'If you do *x*, then I'll do *y*, and if you don't do *x*, then I won't do *y*: *If you reject my bill today, I'll reject your's tomorrow; and if you don't reject my bill today, I'll not reject your's tomorrow.*

What this means, obviously, is that as long as we restrict our consideration to final proposals, a threat of type *(1)* can be transfered, merely by changing the order of the components of the proposition, into an equivalent offer of type *(4)* and *vice versa*; as long as they concern the same alternatives, in their extensive forms the two are indistinguishable. And the same applies also to the other three pairs of threats and offers sharing the same characteristics.

Hence, it is not that a final offer is an 'impure' offer in the sense that, besides an offer, *additionally* it also contains a threat component that can be separated analytically from the 'genuine' offer component; seen in that light, one would also have to say, analogously, that a final threat is always 'impure' in that it additionally contains an offer component. Rather, what we have seen is that the *content* of a final offer can always be *equivalently* expressed in terms of a final threat, and *vice versa*. But, then, it does not seem logically plausible to hold that there is a fundamental difference between (final) threats and offers concerning their possible effect on an addressee's freedom. If a particular threat (perhaps) constrains freedom, then it would be strange to say that in any case the offer that is *equivalent* to that threat does not; and if an offer does not constrain freedom, it would be equally strange to say that the *equivalent* threat (perhaps) does.

Nevertheless, we do distinguish between threats and offers, and it makes good sense to do so. The key to understanding in what way they are different things, despite the equivalences we have just seen, has been provided most satisfactorily, in my view, by Christine Swanton, with her argument that the *illocutionary* and the *perlocutionary* aspects of threats and offers must not be confused (cf. above, n. 103): The *conceptual* distinction between a threat and an offer is a matter of the former, whereas whether or not one or the other does or does not constrain freedom is a matter of the latter; and it is *that* level where the equivalences revealed in the previous analysis occur. What distinguishes freedom-constraining from freedom-neutral offers and threats is that the former, but not the latter, take advantage of – or exploit, if you wish – a *vulnerability* of the addressee, in the sense that the satisfaction of an urgent desire or need is granted on condition that the addressees do something which they could not be expected to consent to under less pressing circumstances. And whether such an act is to be regarded as a threat or an offer depends on *other* aspects of the relationship between the agents involved, above all on the assessment one makes concerning the situational baseline, i. e., on whether or not granting the satisfaction of that need or desire is (factually or morally) expected of the agent who issues the condition.[170]

This is, of course, a general result, applying not only against Kristjánsson's account of the difference between threats and offers, but against all authors who hold that offers cannot constitute exercises of power because they do not restrict, but expand options.[171] But since Kristjánsson's basic approach to the analysis of freedom and power

170 As Onora O'Neill (1996, 109) observed, „Well-organized exploitation of others' vulnerabilities is often coupled with bare-faced assertion of their invulnerability: the powerful assume, accurately enough, that the weak must go along with their proposals, yet then interpret their compliance, outrageously enough, as evidence of informed, legitimating consent." When such distorted interpretations are couched in the language of 'offers', their persuasive force can be explained as a confusion of the two levels distinguished by Swanton. On the intertranslatability of threats and coercive 'offers' that exploit particular vulnerabilities, cf. also O'Neill 1991, esp. 189 ff. (and notes 1 and 9 for more references).

171 Cf., for instance, Caporaso/Levine 1992, ch. 7; although these authors use different words, I think their account nicely fits the preceding analysis: As they very clearly expose, there is a tendency to ignore questions

gives so much importance to factual or moral expectations, it is perhaps more surprising in his case than in the others' that he has missed that point when treating the question of the status of offers.

Moral responsibility

In fact, although my specific interest in this study is Kristjánsson's view of power, a discussion of his contribution cannot properly end without some comment precisely on his basic approach. The final point I will discuss therefore constitutes the exception I announced at the outset: it is only indirectly related to Kristjánsson's concept of power. It concerns a more general matter which affects the very foundation of his entire construction, namely, his idea of moral responsibility.

In his view, as we have seen, an agent is morally responsible for some act (action or omission) whenever there is so much as a minimally plausible reason for requesting a moral justification for it; the existence of a *prima facie* moral obligation to act to the contrary (i. e., to omit the action that was performed, or to perform the action that was omitted) is a sufficient, but not a necessary reason of that kind. This way of viewing moral responsibility raises several questions to which, as I see it, Kristjánsson offers no conclusive answers.

(1) First, note that Kristjánsson proposes a concept of moral responsibility according to which such responsibility *continues* to exist even after a justification or excuse for an act has been given. This is clearly not in accordance with predominant usage:[172] it is usually thought to be an important function of justifications and excuses precisely that they *exempt* from responsibility. The question, on Kristjánsson's own criteria, then is whether he has a good reason for such a departure from a very widespread usage. Is it really incoherent to say that once a justification or excuse for what someone has done has been given there is no longer any reason to make that agent 'respond' to further questions about it, i. e., that he is then exempted from moral responsibility for it? Or is it, at least, more plausible to say that a justification or excuse is nothing but the answer to a question, and that the fact that such an answer exists does not make the corresponding question inappropriate?

Kristjánsson clearly thinks that at least the second and probably also the first question should be answered affirmatively. After all, he considers it a sign of conceptual

of baseline and vulnerabilities in accounts of market relations based on the idea of voluntary exchanges between 'consenting adults'. This explains, they argue, why for many economists 'power' is not a relevant concept – as reflected, e. g., in *The New Palgrave: A Dictionary of Economics*, about which Robert Heilbroner, in a review essay with the telling title „Economics without power" (in: *The New York Review of Books* 35:3 [March 1988] 23–25), „notes a striking fact: In a collection that runs over 4,000 pages and has 2,000 entries, there is no entry for 'power'" (Caporaso/Levine 1992, 178). That markets are 'power-free zones' (and, hence, also 'moral-free zones': cf. Gauthier 1986) only under the ideal conditions of perfect competitiveness typically presupposed in economic scholarship, but never attainable in real life, Caporaso/Levine point out, is often obscured by the language of the 'voluntary' acceptance of market 'offers' and the implied assumption of Pareto-efficiency.

[172] For some recent work on normative responsibility with numerous passages supporting this assertion, cf. Fischer/Ravizza 1993; Garzón Valdés 1997; Hart 1998, esp. 225 ff.; Larrañaga 2000; Lucas 1993; cf. also the quotations from Alf Ross above, in n. 20.

confusion to link moral responsibility to blameworthiness and culpability. But it is precisely blameworthiness and culpability that are defused by justifications and excuses. Hence, the idea that justifications and excuses affect responsibility must seem to him like part of that same conceptual confusion.

In fact, however, he appears to be the victim of a conceptual confusion himself, as he fails to realize that the term 'responsibility' is commonly used quite naturally in a number of different senses and that, therefore, ambiguity can be avoided only by way of its further qualification. The two meanings at issue here, for example, have been clearly distinguished already in 1975 by Alf Ross[173] as *liability-responsibility*, on the one hand, and *accountability-responsibility*, on the other. While 'being responsible', or 'bearing responsibility', in the latter sense only means that one can legitimately be requested to account for one's conduct – and thus amounts to responsibility in Kristjánsson's sense – , 'being responsible' in the former sense means to be culpable of, and liable to recrimination for, some violation of duty – i. e., responsibility precisely in the sense Kristjánsson lightly dismisses as 'confused'. This ambiguous usage is a lexical fact, and it therefore does not seem to reflect a particular respect for common usage to claim exclusive plausibility for one of the two without further argument.[174] Besides, it seems unnecessary to make such a claim, since at least in English it is not at all uncommon to use the term 'accountability', instead of 'responsibility', to denote precisely what Kristjánsson seeks to express.

(2) An additional problem is that that, at least at times, when using the term 'responsibility' Kristjánsson himself unwittingly seems to slip into the view he characterizes as confused. Here, I am referring particularly to those passages where he carries over to the notion of responsibility a distinction which in ethical theory is commonly defined precisely for duties or obligations.

Note, first of all, that on his account, one can distinguish three different possible states regarding an agent's moral responsibility for some act:

(a) there is *no responsibility* at all, i. e., there is not even a minimally plausible moral reason to request an account; or

(b_1) there is such *responsibility*, but the requested account can be given in a morally satisfactory way, i. e., there is *no reason for blame*; or else

[173] My account relies on the presentation of Ross's views in Larrañaga 2000, 59 ff.

[174] An argument that has been given, according to J. M. Fischer (1999, 95), by Marina Oshana ('Ascriptions of Responsibility', in: *American Philosophical Quarterly* 34 (1997) 71–83) for an accountability view of responsibility very much like Kristjánsson's is that it is etymologically „more basic" than the liability view. But this argument seems questionable. As H. L. A. Hart explains in an essay first published as early as 1967, „though some sense of 'answer' is connected with all the main meanings of responsibility it is not that of answering questions, and the connexion though systematic is indirect [...] The original meaning of the word 'answer', just like that of the Greek 'ἀποκρινεσθαι' and the Latin *respondere*, was not that of answering questions, but that of answering or rebutting accusations or charges [...] There is, therefore, a very direct connexion between the notion of answering in this sense and liability-responsibility [...] The other senses of responsibility are variously derived from this primary sense of liability-responsibility [...]" (Hart 1998, 265). Hart therefore does not even bother to include accountability-responsibility in his classification of different types of responsibility (which, besides causal responsibility and liability-responsibility, in its legal and its moral version, also contains role-responsibility and capacity-responsibility; cf. ibid., 211–230).

(b_2) there is *responsibility and* no satisfactory account can be given, i. e., there is also *blameworthiness*.

In order to distinguish linguistically between the two cases in which responsibility exists, Kristjánsson proposes to speak of 'imperfect' and 'perfect' responsibility (cf. 65, 75, 88 f.). In this context, he explicitly refers to the well-known distinction, of Kantian origin, between perfect and imperfect moral duties and even acknowledges that his proposal amounts to a „quasi-Kantian terminology" (65). Moreover, the example he uses for explaining the difference between his two types of responsibility – the alleged 'imperfect responsibility' of the Icelandic government with respect to poverty relief in Ethiopia because it has decided to spend all the resources it can reasonably be requested to dispense for poverty relief on assistence to Cabo Verde – is actually a perfect example of a case of imperfect duty.[175]

Although Kristjánsson is apparently unaware of it, I think the use of this kind of example is not accidental. With it in mind, it is easy, both for the author and the reader, to accept the proposed distinction as plausible and to overlook a problem it raises for Kristjánsson's own account. Because it is just the right kind of example to occult the fact that, unless the 'minimally plausible reason' necessary for responsibility in his sense to arise at all is the assumption that a corresponding moral duty exists (at least *prima facie*), the proposed distinction between imperfect and perfect responsibility makes no sense. That is, were moral responsibility (in Kristjánsson's sense) in some particular case to arise for *another* reason, not related to a duty or obligation, it would have to be *neither perfect nor imperfect* – a possibility Kristjánsson himself does not seem to envisage. That the distinction is difficult, if not impossible, to conceive outside of a context of duty or obligation also becomes apparent if one simply applies it to what we have seen Kristjánsson's idea of responsibility ultimately to refer to, namely, 'accountability'. What could it mean to have 'imperfect accountability'? It seems that either there is or there is not a minimally plausible reason for requesting an account of someone for something, i. e., someone either is or is not accountable. Why should the *content* of the account that may possibly be given in the former case be able to qualify the *fact of accountability* as such? In other words, what could the content of the answer *(ex post)* have to do with the type of accountability, if accountability was defined as depending only on the existence *(ex ante)* of a minimally plausible reason for asking?

Thus, it does not seem possible to transport the 'perfect-imperfect' distinction from the conceptual realm of obligation to that of responsibility without maintaining precisely those links between the two realms which Kristjánsson wants to deny. Or, using Ross's terminology: it is, indeed, a short step from perfect/imperfect obligation to perfect/imperfect liability-responsibility; but there is no way from there to the distant shore of accountability-responsibility.

175 Cf. Mill (1992, 158): „duties of [...] imperfect obligation [...] being those in which, though the act is obligatory, the particular occasions of performing it are left to our choice; as in the case of charity or beneficence, which we are indeed bound to practise, but not towards any definite person, nor at any prescribed time." For a more detailed discussion of the notion of imperfect and perfect duty, cf., e. g., Garzón Valdés 1987, to which I owe the reference to Mill.

(3) Doesn't all this speak heavily against the broader *accountability* view of responsibility *à la* Kristjánsson, and in favour of a more narrow *liability* view, such as the one advocated by Miller, as an adequate foundation for the concept of freedom? Kristjánsson would probably deny this even if he accepted the points I just made, because besides the charge that it is excessively narrow, he also holds another fundamental objection against Miller's account of freedom, namely, that it is „radically relativised" (85).

In Miller's view, whether someone is free in the face of an obstacle depends directly on whether or not someone else has a *prima facie* moral obligation to suppress that obstacle. But, Kristjánsson argues, what counts as a moral obligation differs, depending on the moral theory one accepts; hence, on Miller's account freedom or unfreedom is necessarily *relative* to a particular moral theory. And an adequate concept of freedom, though a moral concept, should be *objective*, in the sense that everyone – no matter what moral theory he holds – should be able to agree, concerning any particular case, on whether it is a case of freedom or of unfreedom. That is why no more than a condition of 'minimal plausibility', which supposedly can be recognized by everyone, from every imaginable moral point of view, can be stipulated for the reasons on which the attribution of responsibility may be grounded:

„An agent *A* is morally responsible for the non-suppression of an obstacle *O* to *B*'s choices/action when it is appropriate to request from *A* a justification of his non-suppression of *O* [...]" (74);

and whether or not it *is* appropriate is not a relative, subjective matter, depending on a specific point of view, but a matter of *objective reasons*, as the continuation of the citation, already quoted earlier and repeated here for the reader's convenience, asserts:

„[...] and that in turn is when there is an objective *reason*, satisfying a minimal criterion of plausibility, why *A*, given that he is a normal, reasonable person, could have been expected (morally or factually) to suppress *O* – however easily overridable this reason is."

On the other hand, remember my earlier interpretation in the sense that Kristjánsson apparently thinks that he has taken care of the 'moral' quality of his view of responsibility by locating the necessary 'obligation' component in the *justification* of the action (rather than in the *action* itself). This would mean that it must be 'appropriate to request a justification' precisely when the other side has the *obligation* – and what kind of obligation could that be, if not a *moral* obligation? – to comply with such a request. But now we can see that this is something Kristjánsson cannot consistently claim. So perhaps my interpretation was wrong, and the moral quality of his concept of responsibility is actually based on something else, which we still need to look for.

(4) As I said before, what Kristjánsson has given us so far is only a reformulation of the meaning of 'moral responsibility'. The question, therefore, remains unanswered: When exactly does such responsibility arise, when *is* a reason objective in that sense, what *does* a minimal criterion of plausibility require? Somewhere in the answer to this complex question we should also expect to find the morality of his view.

Unfortunately, however, Kristjánsson does not offer more than his intuitions about what reasons would actually satisfy the condition (77; also 1992c, 114). And in the course of it, another inconsistency seems to have crept into his argument. He thinks that „placing the onus of justification on the constraining agent“ means the same as that such an agent „is liable to blame unless he can supply us with a morally acceptable reason why he did not suppress the obstacle“ (83). Hence, we must distinguish *two* kinds of reasons involved in the determination of freedom or unfreedom:

(i) reasons for placing the burden of justification on someone, which – according to the definition quoted above – may be based on *moral or factual* expectations; and

(ii) reasons given for the action in question (the non-suppression of an obstacle), which must, in any case, be *morally* acceptable.

Now, suppose in a particular case, concerning step *(i)*, the *only* reason one has for requesting an account of why someone did not suppress an obstacle is not a moral, but a *factual* expectation[176] (satisfying the minimal-plausibility criterion) that he would suppress it. In such a case, why should, in step *(ii)*, a *morally* acceptable response be required at all? Why should the mere fact that in a certain situation someone has not done what another (or even everyone) might have expected a „normal, reasonable person“ in such a situation to do (i. e., the fact that someone's actual motivation was different from most people's motivations in similar circumstances) create a *moral* obligation for that person to give a *morally* acceptable account of her unusual choice of action? Disappointed *factual* expectations should only trigger surprise and provoke requests of *explanation*. If, in addition, they also provoke *suspicion* and 'appropriate' requests of *justification* (in the strong sense), this already implies an involvement of prescriptive rules and, correspondingly, a *normative* expectation, rather than mere empirical regularities, from which factual expectations derive.

Thus, it seems that in Kristjánsson's account of moral responsibility, the variant based on *factual* expectations should be eliminated for reasons of inconsistency. That leaves only those cases in which it is appropriate to request a justification because a minimally plausible reason for some *moral* expectation was disappointed. But what can 'I morally expected you to do *x*' mean if not 'You had (I believe) a (*prima facie*) moral obligation to do *x*'?

In summary, then, on the side of *factual* expectations, Kristjánsson's account runs into trouble with the requirement of consistency, and on the side of *moral* expectations, it leads us right back to the liability view of responsibility which Kristjánsson rejects because of its alleged relativism.[177] This is not a very satisfactory result, of course. But it

[176] An expectation, that is, of a purely empirical kind, based on certain assumptions about the agent's motivation, regardless of what that motivation may be grounded in.

[177] But consider the two cases of prospective students whose applications are turned down by a university: Kristjánsson seems to agree that a student who cannot study because he is too poor to pay the required tuition may be unfree with respect to some agents who are morally responsible for his poverty not only in the accountability, but also in the liability sense; on the other hand, he thinks that a student who cannot study because he does not satisfy the required intellectual prerequisites cannot be said to be unfree, because „the people in charge [...] cannot, in general, be held morally responsible for setting and enforcing some standards

does not come entirely unexpected, considering Kristjánsson's attempt to define an *objectively* applicable concept of *moral* responsibility while upholding *moral relativism*.

3.3. CONCLUSION

If the objections presented in the preceding pages are not mistaken, Kristjánsson's account, as it stands, is flawed and, just like those of Oppenheim and Pettit, would require substantial revisions in order to become coherent and plausible.[178] This regards his fundamental conception of moral responsibility as much as the concept of social freedom constructed on that foundation and the idea that freedom and power in the social sense are but two sides of one and the same coin.

But, again, this is very far from saying that Kristjánsson's contributions to the conceptual debate is therefore useless – on the contrary. In my view, his is perhaps the most interesting and important of the three accounts reviewed in this chapter. His project is the most ambitious and the most radical, and he pursues it boldly, employing his analytical weapons forcefully against whatever obstacle he encounters. That he can't avoid cutting a few corners in the process is only to be expected.[179] But that is not for the worse, since, in the last instance, it is the questions and doubts provoked by the ensuing idiosyncrasies and inconsistencies which provide reasons to probe deeper into some of the issues involved.

Thus, the fact that some of these problems could be traced back to the close link between his definitions of power and of freedom suggested that relating the two concepts in this way does not capture fully what the language of power is usually meant to refer to. Generally, because his analysis and discussion is, on the whole, very lucid and clear, whenever it became awkward and obscure there seemed to be reason for skepticism about his conclusions. And this, in turn, has helped to clarify, at least to some extent, several aspects of major relevance in the analysis of the concept of power in general, such as the relationship between having and exercising power as well as between exercising power and intention, the often repeated idea that power is a dispositional concept, and the no less frequently formulated thesis that one can exercise power (and constrain freedom) through threats, but not through offers.

Perhaps the most important of all these points Kristjánsson's account forces the reader to think about is that of the complex triangular relationship between having power, exercising power, and constraints on freedom. Though he has, I think, drawn the

of competence for prospective students" (1996, 119). It seems that this is an answer Kristjánsson could not have arrived at without himself tacitly relying on some substantive moral theory providing him with a criterion to distinguish between morally relevant and morally irrelevant features of people. – Also, if arguments from moral obligation are inevitably relativist, as Kristjánsson argues, he cannot hold that the existence of a moral obligation to suppress an obstacle is, if not a necessary, at least a sufficient reason for moral responsibility. In order to do so, he would have to admit that such an obligation is a minimally plausible *objective* reason for requesting an account.

178 His assessment of Pettit's account therefore applies, I think, also to his own proposal: it is „an account which looks promising but eventually turns out [...] to be unsatisfactory" (Kristjánsson 1998b, 297).

179 I hasten to add that on many questions which are outside of the scope of the present considerations, especially with his objections against a number of 'classical' arguments in the discussion of the concept of freedom, Kristjánsson offers very intelligent and plausible analyses. His 1996 study is therefore a sourcebook of arguments for and against many of the standard aspects in the debate about freedom.

wrong conclusions from it, with his observation about the linguistic asymmetries of power talk and freedom talk Kristjánsson has pointed to much more than merely an empirical epiphenomenon devoid of deeper significance. Because insofar as the observation is true, the conclusion from it must be the following: To the extent that a concept of freedom is made to involve power either exclusively in the 'exercising mode' or exclusively in the 'having mode', a discussion of social phenomena – such as, e. g., political systems – in terms of freedom, and not in terms of power, must necessarily fall short of capturing all relevant aspects, especially with regard to normative questions.

4. Conclusions

In this chapter, I have presented, to the best of my understanding, three recent views about the relationship between power and freedom. What the three authors under review have contributed to this topic is, no doubt, among the best to be found about it anywhere in the social sciences as of today – a fact apt to increase rather than reduce the surprise and perplexity about what we are left with after this analysis.

We have seen three authors of great originality and erudition, endowed with considerable reasoning powers, spend great efforts on the subject. And yet all three accounts turned out to be insatisfactory. At least for myself, this was a surprising result.

We have also seen three very different, even mutually incompatible approaches to power and freedom. All three of them have strengths as well as weaknesses. And the differences between them make it impossible simply to pick out the positive aspects of each and combine them to a new, less problematic conception. Hence, once my surprise subsided, perplexity took its place.

But if perplexity is not to end in resignation, we must find a way to turn this result into a starting point for new considerations. And that is possible, because from the accounts reviewed here, at least two lessons can, I think, be learned.

(1) The first lesson is of a very general kind. The fact that three scholars of the intellectual standing of Kristjánsson, Oppenheim and Pettit have presented accounts none of which can be regarded as a sufficiently plausible proposal to be used as a ready-made conceptual basis for further, substantive work attests, above all, to the enormity of the task. In this sense, the result of the preceding analysis supports and complements the rationale of the present study. Not only is conceptual analysis more important than some political scientists like to acknowledge; it is also more difficult than many seem to realize. *Empirical* political science can, to some extent, simply avoid the issue by relying on more or less *ad hoc* operational definitions.[180] For *normative* political science, in contrast, a state of affairs in which fundamental concepts such as freedom and power and the relationships between them are undetermined is untenable if any claim of significance is to be made for the products of that subdiscipline. The first lesson, therefore, is that continued efforts need to be made to get our concepts right and, thereby, stabilize the very foundations on which our theories must be built.

180 However, as I pointed out in Chapter 1, that is not a cost-free strategy.

(2) The second lesson is specific. Regarding the concepts particularly at issue here, the analysis of the three different conceptions has also, taken together, given some hints about promising directions for further reflection. We have seen that the three approaches are very different. It is difficult, if not impossible, to find a common denominator regarding their positive contributions. Their respective shortcomings too are very different; but here, at least one common denominator can be indicated. It seems to me that, in the last instance, their different inconsistencies and implausibilities can be traced back in most cases to a failure to make important *distinctions*:

(i) Oppenheim failed to see that if the possibility or impossibility of performing an action is a decisive criterion in the determination of two varieties of freedom and power phenomena ('strict' or 'practical' impossibility), then the third variety distinguished by him should also best be captured in the same terms. He thus failed to look for a third variety of possibility or impossibility, and missed the important distinction between factual and normative power. Besides, he also failed to see that where *causal* responsibilities are involved (as he claims for phenomena of power and unfreedom) nothing short of *strict* impossibility should be sufficient for a consistent account.[181]

(ii) Pettit did make a number of important distinctions, such as between morally problematic and other phenomena of power, between freedom conditioned and freedom compromised, etc. But he too failed to give an explicit account of the distinction between normative and factual power, without which particularly his ideas of procedural constraints on power and of antipower are incomplete, if not entirely incomprehensible. Also, he makes the distinction between having and exercising power, but only to concentrate almost exclusively on the former. One consequence of this is that responsibility – whether causal or moral – is not an issue he pays any attention to. And this, in turn, as I will try to show presently, also prevents him from seeing a potentially relevant distinction.

(iii) And, finally, for Kristjánsson, in a certain sense, the same applies: Among the many distinctions he made were, e. g., those between different ways of exercising power and imposing constraints on freedom (threats, sanctions, physical coercion, negligence, non-suppression of poverty ...). But although his whole approach proved to rest on a great awareness of the importance in that domain of normative questions, he did not see that one distinction of great theoretical consequence is the more general one between *de facto* and *de jure* ways of exercising power over another. And although in his account, responsibility of a *moral* kind plays a decisive role, he only looked at the responsibility of *one* of the two sides involved in a relationship of power or unfreedom. In other words, concerning a relationship of some *A* exercising power over some *B*, he took it for granted that only *A*'s responsibility matters, and overlooked the fact that questions about the responsibility ascribed to *B* for acts performed *under* such a relationship of power may provide useful clues for a distinction of substantially different kinds of situations.

In the remaining part of this study, I will try to show in what way these two ideas may be relevant and how they could perhaps become a promising starting point for further con-

[181] Cf. the discussion about the adequacy of causal views of power in Chapter 1.3.2 for more information on Oppenheim's peculiar conception of the causality involved.

siderations. In the next chapter, the distinction between factual and normative power will be considered. And in the final chapter, I will formulate some observations about the problem of political power and influence, taking into account, among other things, the question of responsibility.

4. SOCIAL POWER AND LEGAL POWER

1. Introduction[1]

In an instructive article published some years ago, Dutch legal theorist Dick Ruiter pursued the question what legal institutional theory and economic institutional theory can learn from each other.[2] In his view, economic institutional theory can, above all, learn two things from legal institutional theory:

(1) on the one hand, the distinction between two different kinds of institutions, namely – to use Ota Weinberger's terms – between 'real' institutions (i. e., social practices, regularities of behaviour), and 'normative' institutions (i. e., complexes of rules), and

(2) on the other, the notion of 'validity', which is extremely useful, for instance, when it comes to explaining what it means that an institution 'exists'.

That legal institutional theory has something of interest to offer beyond its strict disciplinary boundaries, especially with the two notions just mentioned, applies, I think, not only to economic, but also to political theory. The topic I wish to treat in this chapter, with these ideas in mind, is that of the concept of *power* and its conceptual 'relative', *influence.* As a political scientist, I am, of course, interested above all in that particular type of power called 'political power', and that (as I have argued in Chapter 2, related, but not identical) thing called 'political influence'. Something peculiar seems to be the matter with power and influence in the political sphere – something that makes the phenomena denoted by those terms especially difficult to grasp, since, as we have seen in the previous chapters, to this day scores of scholarly contributions have not been able to settle the debate about these concepts.

The idea I shall focus on in what follows is that part of what makes the concept of political power so special, and so difficult to handle, is perhaps the fact that it is located at the intersection of two rather different kinds of power, namely, *factual social power* and *normative* – or, more specifically: *legal* – *power.*[3] Precisely because of this

[1] For helpful comments on previous versions of this chapter, I am grateful to Ernesto Garzón Valdés, Luitgard-Berenike Holst, Guillermo O'Donnell and Annette Schmitt as well as audiences at the Departments of Legal Philosophy at Pompeu Fabra University in Barcelona and the University of Alicante.

[2] Ruiter 1994. Prominent representatives of *legal* institutionalism mentioned by Ruiter are Hans Kelsen, H. L. A. Hart, Neil MacCormick and Ota Weinberger; of *economic* institutionalism, James Buchanan, Gordon Tullock, Geoffrey Brennan and Viktor Vanberg.

[3] I will here be concerned mostly with normative power in its particular legal version, although most of the following considerations can probably be extended to the more general case. Since that is not relevant for my topic here, however, I will basically disregard possible conceptual differences between generally normative

awkward position at the crossroads of different concepts referring to different phenomena, it is far from clear what is meant by the widespread common-sense understanding that 'What politics is all about is power'.[4]

In a first approach to disentangle the often confused conceptions of the relationship between power and politics, I think we can safely say at least the following:

One sense in which 'politics is about power' refers to the basic purpose of all politics (or political systems and political processes): Expressed in terms of power, the purpose of politics, in the last instance, is invariably the *control*, up to a certain point and in certain respects, of the *power of individuals or groups of persons over each other*; in other words, it is the restriction of the free-floating, private social power *de facto* existing in every society at any moment in time. This, however, is not what people usually seem to have in mind when they say that power is the central element of politics. Rather, they seem to be thinking about a second sense in which 'politics is about power': This sense refers to the fact that politics itself aims fundamentally at the exercise of power – since political decisions are intended to be converted into 'outcomes' that 'make a difference' in the social world – and, consequently, also to the assumption that the aspiration of those actively involved in politics is to reach a position where they can exercise as much power as possible.

But *that* power, the one exercised in politics, is of a special kind. Political processes, in the strict sense of the term 'political', are concerned with the enactment of binding norms for a society – with the „authoritative allocation of values", as David Easton's famous definition of politics had it. Hence, the power exercised in this context is what can be called 'normative' or, more specifically, 'legal power'.

Thus, on this highly abstract account, we have the control of (private) factual social power as the main *purpose* – or, at least, one of the main purposes – and the exercise of (public) normative power as the typical *means* of politics.

The advantage of this very simplified sketch is that it enables us to see immediately that some crucial element must be missing from it, because the means and the end just stated obviously do not 'match': pure normative power simply is not the kind of thing, by itself, to make an effective means for attaining the end of controlling factual social power. The two kinds of power belong to different realms, and without the introduction of some additional factor it is impossible to understand how power on one level (the normative) can come to have any effect on power on the other (the factual) level.[5]

But before we can even begin to grasp what is missing in this overly abstract account, we must, first of all, reach an understanding of *(a)* what 'normative' or 'legal power' and *(b)* what factual 'social power' means, and how these types of power operate. Only then can we say something more about how the two kinds of power interact –

and specifically legal matters and sometimes use the terms somewhat loosely, as if they were synonymous. – On the interplay between *de jure* and *de facto* power as well as between legal, political, and societal powers, cf. also, from a somewhat different perspective, the instructive essay by Tom D. Campbell 1997.

4 This idea has also been reproduced, less common-sensically, in scholarly publications. An example can be found in Michelangelo Bovero who begins his essay on 'Politics and Power' with the following assertion which, he says, is „almost a *consensus humani generis*": „Politics and power constitute an inseparable twofold. Power is the basic material or substance of the universe of entities we call 'politics'" (Bovero 1985, 37; my translation).

5 For interesting insights into this same problem from a sociological point of view, cf. Baurmann 1999.

that is, how 'political power' as a whole functions – and, finally, in view of the negative connotation often attached to that common saying that 'politics is about power', perhaps also about how the functioning of political power may give rise to problems for the justification of a political system.

2. Distinguishing the Two Kinds of Power

So, first of all, we must look into the two concepts of power in question: 'normative' or 'legal' power, on the one hand, and 'factual' social power, on the other. The concept of social power has already been treated extensively in Chapter 1. But I think a small degree of redundancy is convenient – more convenient to the reader, in any case, than constant references to specific passages of that previous chapter. The following will therefore include a short section with a brief review of those aspects of social power that seem relevant to the present context.

Since we are dealing with two varieties of one and the same thing called 'power', it is advisable to begin by examining their common core, i. e., the meaning of 'power' at its most general. For brevity's sake, a handy approach to this task is to look at ordinary usage. And here, it is interesting to note that in a number of languages – though, curiously, neither in English nor in German – the word corresponding to the English noun *power* is the same as the word corresponding to the English verb *can*.[6] Consistent with this linguistic finding, the common core of the meaning of different conceptions of power seems to be that it is some kind of 'can do' – an *ability*.

2.1. NORMATIVE OR LEGAL POWER

On this basis, let us now take up that variety of power qualified with the adjective 'normative' or 'legal'. In order to keep things as simple and brief as possible, I will present my understanding of it on the basis of a few quotations which elucidate the meaning commonly attributed to this term in legal theory and which, at the same time, also provide information about the conceptual controversies that still persist:

„In the act of issuing a competence norm, *i. e.,* a permissive norm of higher order, the superior authority of higher order may be said to *delegate power* to a *sub-authority* of lower order. 'Power' here means 'competence', by virtue of norm, to act as an authority of norms. I shall also speak of it as *normative* competence or power." (von Wright 1963, 192)

„Legislation is an exercise of legal powers 'operative' or effective in creating legal rights and duties. Failure to conform to the conditions of the enabling rule makes what is done ineffective and so a nullity for this purpose." (Hart 1994, 31)

„It is a commonplace feature of legal systems, and other norm-governed organisations, that particular agents are empowered to create certain types of states, by means of the performance of specified types of acts [...] empowering is [...] a standard feature of any norm-governed organisation where selected agents are assigned

[6] E. g., in Spanish, French, and Italian: *poder, pouvoir, potere*. The German noun for 'power' *(Macht)* is, instead, etymologically related to the verb 'to do, to bring about' *(machen)*; but doing, of course, also implies a 'can do'.

specific roles [...] An adequate account of the mechanisms by which an organisation conducts its affairs will have to incorporate, one way or another, the phenomenon of *institutionalised power*, as we shall here choose to call it.“ (Jones/Sergot 1997, 349 f.)[7]

From these quotes, which stand for many other, similar ones one could draw upon, we can derive the following defining properties of ‘normative’, or ‘legal’, or – as Jones/ Sergot prefer to call it – ‘institutionalized’ power:

(i) It is a power produced within a normative (legal or other) system.
(ii) It is, therefore, produced *by way of norms*, more precisely: by way of a special kind of norms, referred to by Hart as „power-conferring rules“ which he understands to be „enabling rules“, and by von Wright as „competence norms“.
(iii) An exercise of this kind of power brings about a change in the corresponding normative system (i. e., the modification, addition or subtraction of some norm[s] of the system).
(iv) Hence, this kind of power consists in the „competence [...] to act as an authority of norms“.[8]

This, then, is what seems to be the shared understanding of the conception of normative or, more specifically, legal power. But, as legal scholars know and the above quotations reflect, there is also much controversy in legal theory about the exact nature of normative or legal power.[9] That controversy concerns above all the question of what precisely is to be understood by ‘competence’. Here, two main contenders are facing each other:

(1) For Hart and those inclining towards his side, since it is produced by an *enabling* rule, this kind of power must necessarily consist in the possession of an *ability*: the ability, that is, to create certain rights and obligations, or to perform certain acts.[10]

(2) For von Wright and others on his side, by contrast, the competence norms which confer normative power on an agent are *permissive* norms, and therefore, in their view normative power consists in having the *permission* to create such rights and obligations or to perform such acts.

7 In one version of his several theories about the „ideal form“ of legal norms, Hans Kelsen has even suggested that the ‘basic’ mode of *all* legal norms is the creation of a legal power, not a legal obligation, i. e., that all legal norms expressed in terms of commands could be reformulated in terms of empowerments. Cf. Paulson 1988.

8 Parsons’s assertion that „power is in certain circumstances convertible into money, for example through taxation“ (Parsons 1967, 380) is, therefore, at best, an inadequately sloppy formulation: the power of taxation is a *legal* power and as such, obviously, cannot be ‘converted’ into money (or any other tangible asset, for that matter): effective legal power can, of course, be *used* to raise money; but ‘conversion’ implies a process whereby the input is *replaced* by the output, and the power of taxation, as a normative competence, certainly does not *disappear* when it is exercised.

9 For further readings about this controversy, cf., e. g., the contributions by N. Bobbio, J. Raz, D. W. P. Ruiter, N. MacCormick, and A. Carrino, to ‘Part V. Power, Legal Powers, and Empowerment’ of Paulson/Litschewski Paulson (eds.) 1998.

10 For Kelsen, likewise, ‘competence’ is synonymous with ‘legal capacity’; cf. Kelsen 1949, Part One, VII (90 f.)

Although being enabled to do something and being permitted to do that same thing is clearly not the same, and although the two competing conceptions have different implications for the logical properties of legal systems, for the present purpose not too much depends on that distinction.[11] One point, however, deserves to be mentioned here:

If it is true that the core meaning of the general term 'power' in ordinary language, as indicated above, is that of an ability to do something, then those who share von Wright's conception of competence norms as permissive norms, and consequently also of normative competence as a permission rather than an ability to do certain things, should perhaps better refrain from speaking of normative 'power'.[12] This would not only be more consistent with the accepted usage of the term 'power' in ordinary language; more importantly, it would also eliminate the danger of – wrongly – linking the phenomena they mean to refer to with that other kind of power, usually known as 'social power' or designated simply by the term 'power' without any further qualification, to which I will now briefly turn.

2.2. SOCIAL POWER

With respect to social relationships, the common core of the meaning of 'power' as an ability seems to be almost universally accepted. For instance, to quote a prominent author not already mentioned in Chapter 1, John Dunn, in the context of his reflections on Western political theory, expresses this very general conception when he says that „the root meaning of power is simply capability, the capacity to act for the better as well as for the worse, for the worse as well as for the better" (Dunn 1993, 113). Whatever Dunn may specifically have meant with this somewhat mysterious remark: for almost any purpose, this „root meaning" is much too broad for being of interest. Just as in the case of normative power, social power too, to be a useful concept, must be conceptualized in more narrow and, thus, more substantive terms.

One representative example of such a specification of social power, which we have seen in Chapter 1, is the definition proposed by Brian Barry, who understands it to be simply „the ability to cause things to happen when the object is actions by other people" (Barry 1991a, 223). This causal definition and its many existing equivalents, which at first sight might seem perfectly adequate, do, however, have at least one important flaw. In a way, instead of being overly broad, they are now overly narrow. As I have argued in Chapter 1.3.2, causal conceptions cannot capture fully what is at issue when human agency and interaction are involved.

Whether for this or for any other reason, the best-known and most widely accepted definitions of 'social power' are not framed directly in terms of causation – in fact,

[11] On the controversy between the advocates of the two conceptions, cf., for example, Bulygin 1992; Atienza/Ruiz Manero 1994 and 1997, ch. 2; Moreso 1998, ch. III; or the contributions of Caracciolo, Mendonca/ Moreso/Navarro, Atienza/Ruiz Manero, and Ferrer in Comanducci/Guastini 1995. A particularly transparent presentation of the two positions can be found in Mendonca 1995, ch. 4.

[12] In the same vein, Caracciolo (1995, 203) observes that if 'deontic power' is understood in the sense of 'normative competence' and this, in turn, as the *permission* to perform certain acts, then to call this a 'power' is only „a way of talking", since „it does not suppose any special ability".

they do not even mention causality:[13] Recall that Max Weber's famous definition characterizes it merely as „any ability to impose one's own will in a social relationship, even against opposition, regardless of what that ability is based on" (1922, 28);[14] and that according to Robert Dahl's no less famous definition, „*A* has power over *B* to the extent that he can get *B* to do something that *B* would not otherwise do" (1957, 202 f.). And the same applies to all the 'faces' of power earlier presented.

Despite the fact that all these proposed conceptions have been much discussed and criticized (often with good reason, as I have shown in Chapter 1), we here need to make a decision about the conception we will rely on in what follows, and I have recommended to take what I think is the greatest common denominator of them all – with the possible exception of Peter Digeser's four-faces conception which, in the last instance, coincides with Foucault's notion: the common core of the different conceptions of social power that have come to be more or less widely accepted in the social sciences, and specifically in political science, seems to be that agents have such power if they can, somehow, effectively control some behaviour(s) of some other agent(s). Hence, for the present purpose – paying the greatest tribute to Weber, who in my view, already had pretty much the right intuitions – I have defined social power as the ability to get desired outcomes by making others behave as one wishes, i. e., by imposing one's own preferences on them, through whatever means (cf. above, p. 141).

3. Political Power at the Crossroads of Legal and Social Power

After this quick glimpse at the meanings of (normative) legal power and (factual) social power, let us now go back to the question of the 'mismatch' between the *exercise of legal power* as the means to the purpose of *controlling social power*.

(1) A first point worth mentioning is the following: If the purpose is to *constrain (private) factual social power* – i. e., to restrict the scope of what the members of a society can do to each other, and especially what they can force, or induce, each other to do –, then this means precisely to *control the behaviour* of people (in the 'private' realm). Therefore, this purpose itself presupposes the ability to make certain other actors do or omit certain actions or activities, and this, in turn, means that what is required for the task is *(public) social power*. Note that this is so not for empirical, but for conceptual, i. e., logical reasons. Thus, if the purpose of constraining (private) social power is reached, then that *means* that (public) social power is exercised or, at least, exists in the latent sense and through its mere existence produces the desired effects.

This may sound trivial. After all, any normative system as such, without the property of efficacy, is totally irrelevant from the practical, empirical point of view; some

13 This does not mean, of course, that the authors may not have a causal conception in mind – but whether or not they do can only be ascertained by looking at their further explications of the concept and the contextual usage they make of it; in any case, their definitions are sufficiently open to allow another interpretation.

14 The very same idea appears in an even more condensed formula in Barry Hughes's definition of social power as „the ability to elicit desired behaviour from others" (1978, 202).

even say that as long as it is not efficacious it is, strictly speaking, 'inexistent'. And this is certainly no less true in the case of politics and legal systems.

Still, it is important to have perfect clarity about the nature of that efficacy, i. e., about the fact that it can be expressed in terms of public social power. This helps alert us to the relationships between different *loci* of social power, which is interesting for conceptual reasons, but also acquires special relevance when we come to the problem of the justification of a politico-legal system.

(2) The fact that *normative power* must be accompanied by, or transformed into, *factual public social power* in order to be able to fulfill its purpose of controlling *private social power*, is not the only point of 'intrusion' of factual social power into the realm of legal power. Another such point results from the fact that, just like factual power, normative power, understood as competence, requires a base or foundation. While in the case of factual social power, the base consists in certain physical or mental resources which are agent (or at least are believed by others to be) at the command of the 'powerful', in the case of normative power the foundation consists of certain norms – the already mentioned 'norms of competence':

„[T]he concept of *competence* inevitably alludes to the existence of provisions that confer certain powers on certain legal authorities. To say it in the words of Carrió, 'the idea of a competence without rules from which it derives is like that of a child without parents'.“[15]

But to say that the basis of normative competence is always a norm is to open a kind of Pandora's box, filled to the brim with new theoretical problems, which it is impossible and unnecessary to address here. I will mention only one implication of this conception, because it does play some role for my present purpose:

The idea that normative power, or competence, is itself based on norms necessarily leads to the decisive question of *all* arguments from hierarchy: What is the foundation of the last, ultimate or supreme, element in the respective chain?[16]

The various proposals advanced within the theory of normative or legal systems as possible answers to that question are well-known, and it is not my purpose to present them here. On the contrary, at this point, I wish to abstract from that specific knowledge for a moment, and look only at the range of logically possible answers that can, in principle, be given to the question.[17] They can, I think, be of three different kinds:

(i) One possibility is to insist that normative power or competence is a property that can without exception be conferred only by norm and, therefore, to hold that the supreme normative power of a legal system must itself be grounded in a power-conferring norm. In that case, if the requirement is not to be hopelessly paradoxical, the competence norm in question obviously cannot belong to the *same* normative system.

15 Mendonca 1995, 46, quoting from Genaro R. Carrió: Sobre los jueces y su status normativo, in: M. Laclau and D. Cracogna (eds.), *Teoría General del Derecho. Sus problemas actuales. Estudios en homenaje a Julio C. Cueto Rúa*, Buenos Aires: Heliastra 1966, 49.

16 The corresponding question to Carrió would, obviously, have to be: Where do the procreators of the first 'child' come from?

17 A good place for a political scientist interested in these questions to start reading is, e. g., Ruiter 1993.

This possibility, thus, implies a *transition* from one normative system to another. And such a transition, again, brings with it a number of problems that make any solution of this kind look rather unconvincing.[18]

So what are the alternatives? Any alternative to *(i)* must, first of all, drop the requirement that normative power is a property that can *only* be acquired through a norm. The question, then, is *how else* normative power in general, and the normative power of a legal system's supreme power-conferring norm in particular, can be conceived to arise.

(ii) It may seem that if the foundation is not to be a norm, then it can be nothing but a *fact*. But a descent to the realm of facts must surely be anathema to anyone interested in keeping the realm of normative systems 'pure' (whether for fear of naturalistic fallacies or simply out of respect for disciplinary boundaries), not to speak of those who even reject alternative *(i)* on the grounds that it 'trespasses' from one system into another (though both of them of a normative kind). Such purists must, therefore, look for another alternative, one that amounts to a foundation *neither* in a norm *nor* in a fact. And, indeed, with a bit of imagination one can think of a possibility that is non-normative and yet stops short of a foundation in any 'hard', real-worldly fact. Thid possibility is a foundation in a kind of *fiction*, a thought or hypothesis – a *mental fact*, so to speak.

That is, of course, the well-known alternative chosen by Hans Kelsen with his „basic norm" which is, itself, not grounded in any norm or fact, but in a *presupposition.*[19]

But even Kelsen, who, for all purposes of legal knowledge and legal theory, insisted on the purely normative nature of legal systems and admonished legal scholars not to „ventur[e] into non-legal fields in search of answers to legal questions" (Paulson 1990, 35), acknowledged that

18 To mention just two of these problems: One can argue that it is *conceptually* questionable in what sense a power-conferring norm can really be said to belong to a normative system *other* than that of the norms to which its conferral of normative competence gives rise; or, in other words, that it is precisely the chain of power-conferrals which determines the boundaries of a normative system. But even if one were to accept that the founding norm of the supreme normative competence of one system can belong to another system, the problem of foundation would not be solved; it would, of course, begin all over in that second, higher-level system.

19 Another interpretation of this case – perhaps more in agreement with Kelsen's own view – would be to say that the need or even the possibility of a foundation is in that case denied altogether: the basic norm is *not founded* on anything at all; rather, it 'arises' merely in the form of a presupposition. Instead of three possibilities of foundation – on norm, on fact, or on fiction – we could then say that there are only two such possibilities – on norm, or on fact –, *plus* the alternative of denying that any further foundation is possible or necessary. (In Kelsen's construction, for instance, what *does* need a foundation is, of course, the supreme norm of the legal system in question; and *that* foundation, in Kelsen's view, must be a *norm*; but then, the question of foundation naturally turns on that ultimate founding norm, and it is *this* question which, according to Kelsen, makes no sense: the ultimate norm cannot and need not be founded. It must simply be presupposed because that is the logico-transcendental condition for us to be able to interpret a set of norms as a valid normative system, and specifically as a legal system). Although I find it more plausible not to argue away the need for a foundation, I think the two interpretations basically amount to the same. Helpful summaries of the main features of Kelsen's conception, can be found, e. g., in Ross 1958, 66 f. or Garzón Valdés 1998.

„while the legal validity of the constitution stems from the presupposed source norm, its content stems from the empirical acts of will of the constituting authorities"[20]

and that, in the last instance,

„the basic norm, in a certain sense, means the transformation of power into law".[21]

So, what we have here are empirical acts of will, laid down in norms with the corresponding content, and a *de facto* ability to impose those norms (i. e., that will) in a society;[22] and what the presupposed basic norm apparently 'adds' to these ingredients is a kind of mental device for providing factual power-holders with the normative power, or competence, necessary for the 'foundation' of what can be interpreted to be a legal system.[23]

(iii) This points directly to the third and, I think, last option for a foundation of the supreme power-conferring norm of a legal system: For those who, for the indicated or other reasons, discard possibility *(i)*, and who also wish to avoid resorting to fiction and having to deal with the severe problems that recourse implies, there is, in any case, the possibility of turning directly to the *facts* mentioned above. The foundation of a supreme power-conferring norm, according to this option, must be understood to refer

20 Kelsen, *Das Problem der Souveränität*, Tübingen: Mohr 1920, reprint Aalen: Scientia 1960, vii; quoted here from Paulson 1990, 35 (Paulson's essay also contains an interesting reconstruction of the evolution of Kelsen's conception of the 'source' or 'basic' norm).

21 Kelsen 1949, 437. On this point, cf., e. g., Bobbio 1985, 34 f. (my translation): „[F]or Kelsen the function of the basic norm is to transform power into law. What does that definition mean? It means that if we do not presuppose a norm that closes the system, that is, if we do not presuppose that the legal system is closed by norm rather than by sovereign power, the relationship between commander and commanded remains one of *de facto* power, a relationship of pure force. In other words, the basic norm [...] functions as a criterion of legitimacy"; and Bobbio 1998, 449: „Kelsen [...] cannot help but specify that, notwithstanding the basic norm, the legal system is valid overall only if it is also efficacious, that is, only if those who have the power to create the norms of the system also have the power to enforce them [...] the Pure Theory of Law makes it known that, at the apex of the system, law can no longer be separated from power, and, indeed, it becomes increasingly difficult to make out where one ends and the other begins". (Obviously, Bobbio is here speaking of social rather than legal power.) In the same context, cf. also Habermas (1997, 289) who refers to „that normative authority [which power] gains through its internal connection with legitimate law" and argues precisely that „political power" can be legitimate only if it is more than merely institutionalized factual „social power".

22 I assume that this is what Kelsen means by 'power' when he speaks of the „transformation of power into law"; I simply see no other possible interpretation – which may, however, be due to a lack of imagination or information on my part.

23 For a critique of Kelsen's 'formal idealism' which argues precisely that, with his recourse to the *Grundnorm*, or „initial hypothesis", he fails to address the question of the relationship between legal power and factual social power, cf. Ross 1958, esp. 70: „As long as we remain on the lower steps of the legal system, it is possible to postpone the problem of the validity of the norm by referring back to a superior norm. But this procedure cannot be employed when we come to the initial hypothesis. At this point the question of the relation of the norm to reality becomes inescapably urgent. If the system is to make sense, it is clear that the initial hypothesis cannot be chosen arbitrarily. Kelsen himself says that it must be chosen in such a way that it covers the system which is actually in effect. But it is then clear that, in reality, effectivity is the criterion for positive law; and that the initial hypothesis, once we know what is positive law, in reality only has the function of investing it with the 'validity' which is demanded by the metaphysical interpretation of legal consciousness, though no one knows what it is [...] By making validity an internormative relation [...] Kelsen has at the outset precluded himself from dealing with the heart of the problem of the validity of the law – the relation between the normative ideal content and the social reality." More generally, Ross (1958, 69) notes that it is an eternal problem of 'idealistic' legal philosophy „to explain how it is possible that the act of legislation as a social phenomenon can produce anything more than social effects".

to an empirical, 'real-wordly' fact, namely, to the fact that some individual or group not only stipulates certain norms, but also succeeds in obtaining (with respect to power-conferring norms) *recognition* for and (with respect to regulatory norms) *compliance* with those norms at least from some relevant group of people – in other words: to the *de facto* acceptance of a claim to normative authority.

A prominent representative of this kind of ultimate foundation of a normative system is Georg Henrik von Wright. In the construction proposed by von Wright (1963, ch. X, esp. 194-202), the chain of delegations of normative power goes all the way back to a supreme norm which does not itself rest on a delegation of power, i. e., is not founded on a power-conferring norm. Instead, the supreme norm rests exclusively on the empirical *datum* of its effective social imposition.[24]

This alternative, which consists in a bold step from the realm of norms to that of facts, is the most straightforward and, in my view, the most adequate one when what is at issue is not merely the *logical* properties of 'pure' *normative* systems (where the fiction, or axiomatic presupposition, of a founding norm is all that is needed in order to close the system and thereby to determine the boundaries of the object of analysis), but

[24] I am referring to von Wright rather than to Hart because von Wright exposes the 'factual end' of the chain of competence norms even more straightforwardly than Hart with his idea of a 'rule of recognition'.
Note that, just as for Kelsen it makes no sense to ask about the validity of the basic norm, in von Wright's view, likewise it makes no sense to speak of the validity of the supreme norm of a normative system. Von Wright, like Kelsen, defines validity in terms of normative delegation; hence, 'validity' is inapplicable to norms which cannot be traced back to a higher-order norm. Therefore, the supreme norm of a legal system is not valid but 'sovereign'. Still, because of their different concepts of the existence of norms (a normative one in the case of Kelsen, a social one in the case of von Wright) this is much less a problem for von Wright than for Kelsen: Kelsen distinguishes the *validity* of a norm from its *efficacy*, and identifies the *existence* of a norm with its validity; thus, for him a norm that is not valid does not exist. In Kelsen's view, that is, there can be no 'invalid norms' – the expression itself is a *contradictio in terminis* (though he acknowledges that there may well be invalid rules, i. e., rules which fail to be norms). Von Wright too distinguishes validity and efficacy, but instead of linking the existence of a norm to its validity, he opts for the other alternative and identifies it with its efficacy. Thus, whereas validity is associated with normative delegation, existence is associated exclusively with social facts. Consequently, according to von Wright there can be norms which are *not valid*, and such norms are either *invalid*, i. e., issued in violation of some higher-order norm, or *sovereign*.
On this account, von Wright can be considered much more of a legal positivist than Kelsen, who is often regarded as *the* legal positivist *par excellence*. For an account of the difference between 'true' legal positivists and Kelsen which focuses precisely on their different conceptions of the relationship between legal power and factual power (or, as the author formulates it, between 'law' and 'power'), cf. La Torre 1998, chs. I and III. For a very clear and concise presentation of von Wright's conception of the existence and validity of norms and his intermediate position between Kelsen and such realists as Axel Hägerström or Alf Ross, cf. Garzón Valdés 1965, 314 ff., esp. 317. For an analysis of the issue of legal validity and the ultimate foundation of competence or power-conferring norms, including a detailed discussion of the similarities and differences between Kelsen's 'basic norm' and Hart's 'rule of recognition', cf. Ruiter 1993. Ruiter clearly comes down on von Wright's side of the argument (apparently without being aware of it; he refers to von Wright's *Norm and Action* only with respect to some logical and conceptual issues); he even uses the same 'test case' as von Wright, namely that of the establishment of a new legal system, i. e., a revolution (Ruiter 1993, 224 f.): „History teaches us that a certain person or assembly typically proclaims the establishment of the new legal system's constitution. What is the linguistic nature of such a proclamation? [...] the self-assignment of the constitutional authorities of a new legal system is not the performance of a validity-conveying act-in-the-law. Rather, it is the performance of an *assertive* speech act about *factual recognition* of legal validity, which is true or false, and which grants no reprieve in the latter case. This is why establishing a new legal system is such a hazardous undertaking, as many a revolutionary can attest."

the actual functioning of *political* systems, where the legal system effectively 'in force' in a society at any given moment depends, in the last instance, on the factual ability of its 'enforcement'.[25] The important consequence here, for the present purpose, is that at least at this point, then, normative power is no longer a matter of permission, but of ability, i. e., of what earlier has been defined as *factual social power*.

Note that this connection between the legal system as the realm of normative power and the 'brute facts' of social power is a *necessary* connection; it represents, so to speak, an 'undestructible bridge' from social power to normative power, and therefore, of course, also a possible way of intrusion by which the 'usurpation' of the latter by holders of the former can take place.

(3) Finally, if we go back to the metaphor, quoted above, which compares normative competence with human offspring, we can say that with the *contents* of legal norms, it is just as with children: It is usually perfectly possible to trace them back to their 'issuing source'. But what can never be known with certainty is exactly when, under what circumstances, and with whose collaboration they were conceived.[26]

What I mean to say with this is that it is possible that those who actually 'make' a norm are not those who have the normative competence to issue it, but some other agents. In that case, we would have to say that the latter too possess a kind of 'normative power'. But this 'normative power', to actually bring about the creation of norms with a particular content, is then, obviously, not a competence conferred on the respective agents by some norm; rather, it consists merely in their *factual* ability to 'dictate' the content of the norms in question to the respective competent authorities. This apparently is what Francisco Laporta (1996, 441) is hinting at when he says that:

„It seems to be undeniable that those who create and enact the norms of the *law* exercise a certain kind of *power*. But it is also considered general wisdom that those who have *power* are the ones who determine what the content of the *law* is to be."[27]

[25] Besides, it should not be forgotten that in all conceptions stipulating *social efficacy* as a necessary condition for the existence of a legal system, the step to the world of empirical facts is already implied.
To avoid misunderstandings, it should be mentioned that all this does not yet imply anything at all for a possible 'foundation' of such a system in the sense of its *justification*: If normative power is ultimately based on social power, i. e., on the factual ability of imposition, then justification must turn on the question of *how* this imposition is accomplished. After all, social power can have very different bases, ranging from *force* to voluntary *consent*. As is well-known, some approaches make the justification of the social power exercised through a politico-legal system depend on the factual consent of the norm-subjects; one consequence of this is that there is then a close relationship between the efficacy (by voluntary compliance) of the corresponding norms and their 'validity' (in the sense of their justification by the very consent which also motivates compliance). It is in this sense that one can say that the foundation of normative power „à la Habermas and many others [as] legitimation through constitutionally-bounded majority decisions" is „both a normative and an empirical grounding" (Guillermo O'Donnell, private correspondence, June 1998). However, for analytical purposes, I think it is advisable to distinguish between questions of motivation and of justification, as well as between the latter and conceptual questions.

[26] With respect to this, we can always rely only on 'presumptions' – which can, of course, play an extraordinarily helpful role, in legal theory as well as in the practical maintenance of social peace and order.

[27] Cf. also Atienza/Ruiz Manero 1997, 7: „On the one hand, legal norms can be seen as the result or effect of certain social relations; on the other, legal norms themselves shape the relations between subjects by con-

The 'power' Laporta is indiscriminately speaking of here seems to be of two very different kinds: one normative, the other factual.

So far, we have seen that on several sides normative power offers points of infiltration – or 'dock-on points', somewhat like cells that offer 'dock-on points' for certain viruses – for factual social power: at the very *beginning* of the chain of the competence norms which confer normative power; at the *end* of that chain, when regulatory norms enacted by normative authorities effectively control social behaviour; and also *in between*, to the extent that the content of norms is determined by the will of agents whose identity remains largely indeterminate and who neither have, nor pretend to have, the *de facto* authority enjoyed by the supreme guarantor of the normative system in question nor *normative* power conferred on them by some intra-systemic norm of competence.

4. On Justifying Political Power

For the sake of completing the panorama, in what follows, I will present a sketch of how the preceding reflections may come to play a role in a justificatory theory of political power.

Normative power as such, in the 'pure' sense of normative authority (competence) *de jure*, within some theoretically constructed and closed normative system, obviously does not raise questions of justification. But as soon as it appears in a practically existing normative system, i. e., whenever it effectively controls (some of) the behaviour of (some) people and is thus duplicated into (public) factual social power – whether by being accepted *de facto* as normative authority or by affecting in some other way the reasons for action of the agents involved – normative power needs to be justified. The following considerations about the justification of normative power will be limited to one single case: that of a liberal representative democracy under the rule of law.[28] Such a system can, I think, be justified basically along the following lines:

(1) The factual social power that consists in the ability of the political system to elicit – mediated through the authority of its legal system and, where necessary, through its law-applying and law-enforcing organs – widespread compliance with the system's regulatory norms is justified to the extent that, in the last instance, the ultimate foundation of that public power has certain well-defined characteristics.

(2) Above all, that ultimate foundation may *not* itself refer to some factual social power (held *de facto* by some 'first' normative authority). But then, since this means that it may be based neither on social power nor on some other normative power, for the required mediation between normative power and factual social power the only possible

ferring powers and protecting the interests of some against others; and, finally, the power given to some individuals (or groups) by legal norms is used to change – or, more generally, to affect – social relations themselves. This third way of approaching norms – more closely linked to the sociology of law or the ideological critique of the law – is usually missing in the main currents of contemporary legal theory. In our view, that is a substantial deficit."

28 In fact, I think this is the only political system that has a chance of being justifiable, and therefore it is also the only case worth analysing. However, that is a thesis which I cannot even begin to argue for here.

realm that is left is that of 'thought', in this case that of the *forum internum* of every individual agent: instead of a control of one's behaviour by someone else, it must consist in mutual *self-restraint*, that is, so to speak, in every person's 'power over herself', by way of an *autonomous commitment.*

(3) But certainly such self-restraint cannot reasonably be expected to be forthcoming unconditionally, without good reason. And in the case under scrutiny, such reasons can only be certain *normative* ideas. On the other hand, although it is a normative system, those ideas cannot be provided by the very politico-legal system the justification of which is at issue. Rather, they must be *moral* ideas.[29]

(4) Finally, the system to be justified – liberal representative democracy under the rule of law – must be able to accomodate a wide variety of people with a plurality of interests and viewpoints, or 'conceptions of the good'. Hence, what is needed for the task is a moral base which is as neutral as possible concerning those interests and conceptions of the good – anything else could be subject to reasonable objection by the representatives of those interests and ideas which are given less consideration than others.

The type of morality with the *least* amount of metaphysical presuppositions, and thus the *most* demanding one for a justificatory grounding of social constraints to individual behaviour, is one that is, if possible, based exclusively on reason.[30] From the point of view of such a morality, the normative ideas we are looking for can perhaps be formulated, very briefly, as follows:

> *(i)* To some extent, the control of 'private' social power is desirable for everyone.
> *(ii)* But, of course, the 'public' social power necessary for implementing that control should itself be controlled as much as possible.
> *(iii)* Such a 'control of the controllers'[31] can, in principle, be obtained through
> – certain procedural constraints[32],

29 There can be no such thing as the 'self-justification' of a normative system; the politico-legal system, for instance, simply does not contain the 'material' or 'tools' needed for its own justification. More directly, one could also argue that what is needed are moral ideas (principles or norms) since what we are interested in here is the *autonomous* imposition of restrictions on behaviour, and that is, *by definition*, precisely the realm of morality.

30 A recent promising attempt to argue for the possibility of a universalist and substantive moral theory founded on nothing but reason is O'Neill 1996.

31 Awareness of the problem of controlling the controllers is so old that, rather than being attributable to the insights of any one person, it can be regarded as a kind of 'folk' wisdom. To mention just one of the classical formulations of the problem, cf. Kant's very lucid, prudently pessimistic remarks in the Sixth Proposition of his *Idea for a Universal History from a Cosmopolitan Perspective* (Kant 1784). More recently, cf. Sorokin/Lunden 1959 who have made the question 'who shall guard the guardians' the main focus of their considerations on power and morality.

32 For instance, a system of procedures amounting to a 'representation' of all citizens. Another prominent idea which immediately comes to mind is that of 'checks and balances', meaning that the 'controllers' themselves will 'control' each other, an idea which has been expressed most clearly by James Madison when he said that „the great difficulty lies in this: you must first enable the government to control the governed; and in the next place oblige it to control itself" (*Federalist* no. 51; I was reminded of this passage by reading a recent draft paper by Guillermo O'Donnell.)

– certain content-related, material constraints on normative competence[33], and

– finally, in the remaining area of normative power that is free from formal or material constraints, through the requirement that there be a certain kind of relationship – which I will presently say more about – between the content of the norms issued and the interests (or, if you prefer, the wishes or preferences)[34] of each and every individual subject to the political power in question (i. e., above all, to the *factual* social power accompanying that normative power).

These are, I think, roughly the basic kinds of constraints on *legal* power that can and must be operative if the *factual* social power exercised through a political system is to be morally justifiable.

However, there is a formidable 'catch' to this idea, because any claim of constraining the normative power of the ultimate or supreme norm-authority in a normative system – and, with it, also the *legitimate* social power of such an authority – in any one of the three spheres mentioned runs into conceptual problems (not to speak of practical difficulties).[35] For the question of the relationship between legal power and social power, the most interesting of these spheres seems to be the last one, which makes the justifiability of a political system, as a system of the institutionalized possession and exercise of factual social power, depend on a particular aspect of the respective norms' content – an aspect which refers not to their 'absolute', but to their 'relative' content, that is, to the relationship between the content of the norms and the content of certain valorations made by the norm-subjects.

In practical politics, I think it is precisely this last condition that is the underlying reason for certain constitutional provisions as, for example, that very peculiar norm contained in Art. 38 I of the German Basic Law (GG), which stipulates that the representatives in the *Bundestag* are „representatives of the people as a whole [...] and subject only to their own conscience“.[36]

I think it is not too farfetched to interpret this provision of the German Basic Law in the sense of the justificatory condition just mentioned: that the normative power conferred on German federal legislators is restricted – among other things – by an obligation to take into consideration, in their legislative decision-making, the interests of each and every member of 'the people'[37] and to decide not according to the dictate of any in-

[33] That is, an „off-limits“ – to use the term coined in this context by Ernesto Garzón Valdés 1989, 157 – for majority decisions, which serves to protect and guarantee basic rights, i. e., especially those rights which are indispensable for the satisfaction of people's basic needs.

[34] In a more detailed analysis of this specific aspect, one would have to examine whether what should be taken into account are interests, wishes, or preferences. But for the present purpose, not much depends on the distinction.

[35] On the *logical* impossibility of legally restricting the sovereign's normative competence, cf. Garzón Valdés 1981. A similar insight seems to underlie de Jasay's (1998, 211) observation that „A state bound by a 'law of laws', being at the same time the monopolist of all law enforcement, can always untie itself. It would not be sovereign if it could not“.

[36] „Sie sind Vertreter des ganzen Volkes [...] und nur ihrem Gewissen unterworfen.“

[37] Note that the idea here is not that the interests of all those subject to the political power of the system, or all those affected by a norm, but only those of 'the people' must be taken into consideration. The political power exercised, for instance, over *foreigners* thus would, in any case, need some other (moral) foundation.

dividual or group, nor according to their own personal interest or arbitrary fancy, but on a careful, conscientious consideration of all the interests involved. But if interpreted in that sense – as I think it must be, according to the justificatory conditions of a representative democratic system – the norm raises enormous problems.

Given that in German politics constitutional provisions are generally taken very seriously, it can be seen as an indicator of these problems that this particular constitutional provision is hardly reflected in established political practice. And it is no secret that Art. 38 I GG is not very efficacious. Legislators do, in fact, normally follow the dictate of their respective party,[38] the decisions of which, in turn, often seem to cater to special interests (especially in matters that fail to gain the attention of so-called 'public opinion', i. e., of the mass media). But the inefficacy of that constitutional norm apparently is not believed to have negative consequences for the legal validity of the norms enacted by the *Bundestag*.[39] Strictly speaking and from a purely *systemic* point of view, norms issued by the German Federal Parliament in violation of Art. 38 I GG are invalid (and therefore, on some accounts, even inexistent *qua* norms), because the

38 It does not help to argue that fact away by saying that this, then, seems to be precisely what the representatives' conscience is dictating them to do. Often enough, representatives let it be known that they feel *obliged* to vote the way their party wants them to, even though their conscience, or their reason, tells them something else. And only on rare occasions parliamentary party leaders explicitly release their members from the generally expected 'discipline' of voting along party lines and 'encourage' them to vote according to the dictates of their conscience. This would not be necessary, it seems, if voting in accordance with Art. 38 I were taken to be self-evident and the rule. There can, of course, be no officially acknowledged and much less a written norm binding representatives to party decisions, since this would be clearly unconstitutional and therefore, from the legal point of view, „without effect" (cf. Katz 1992, RN 357). And, of course, while parties cannot recall a representative during a term, representatives who wish to escape party pressures can – at least in theory – always leave their party while staying on in parliament as independent members. But the costs to a representative of such a step, which would inevitably lead to a loss of all party support, are enormous, and experience shows that 'unorthodox' voting puts a representative's political career at risk. Hence, although parties lack the *normative* power to issue certain norms for their group in parliament, they do have great *de facto* power over 'their' representatives. In fact, it seems that the expectation that representatives, as a rule, vote in accordance with party directives has evolved into a *social norm*, in the technical sense of the term, within the German system of parliamentary democracy. But the road between *Fraktionszwang*, which is regarded as unconstitutional, and *Fraktionsdisziplin*, which is not, is short and slippery, and the dividing line is not very clear. Of course, it is argued that party discipline is necessary in a parliamentary democracy for the sake of government stability as well as for protecting individual representatives from external pressures and temptations; and that, besides, most matters voted on by the legislators are not 'really' questions of 'conscience'. My claim here is not that these are bad arguments. My point is only that there seems to be a permanent tension between that social norm and the constitutional norm of Art. 38 I GG, that is, the constitutionally granted legislative power; that the constraint on legal power involved in this issue is of great importance for the justifiability of a political system as a whole; and that, therefore, the problems we encounter in the implementation of the constraining provision deserve to be taken very seriously and not to be dismissed as a matter of allegedly secondary importance.

39 The same applies, of course, to legislative bodies in other countries, as a recent incident in Spain graphically illustrates: On occasion of the final vote on a bill for a new Telecommunications Law, the deputy majority whip in the *Cortes* „in charge of indicating to his party colleagues whether they should push the 'Yes', the 'No', or the abstention button, first ordered to vote 'Yes', but immediately afterwards made the gesture for a 'No' vote". The consequence of the legislators' mechanical compliance with a mistaken 'order' was that an amendment proposed by the Government was rejected with the help of the 'No' of almost half the Government majority's own votes, including that of the President of the House and at least two cabinet members, thus leaving a law which had already been passed with an important regulatory gap. On this „parliamentary accident", cf. articles by S. Carcar and C. Valdecantos in *El País* (Madrid) of April 11, 1997, 40.

normative power conferred on the German legislators is constitutionally restricted by the provisions of that article, and the violation of the clause is therefore clearly a „Failure to conform to the conditions of the enabling rule" which according to Hart „makes what is done ineffective and so a nullity for this purpose".[40] However, as long as the validity of these norms is not contested by any competent organ, for all *practical* purposes they appear to be perfectly valid, insofar as they succeed in being effective.

Of course, on a less justificatory and more legal reading of the provision of Art. 38 I GG, the phrase „are subject only to their own conscience" may perhaps be interpreted to mean only that a representative's vote may not be subjected to *judicial* scrutiny, i. e., that the law may neither stipulate nor enforce any *external* constraints (e. g., by a party) to a legislator's decisions, and that the votes of representatives are thus not subject to any *legal liability*. On this account, social norms which *de facto* constrain a representative's vote would be legally *permitted* (in the weak sense of not being explicitly prohibited), although they would not be legally *enforced*. A representative complying with the rule of party discipline would then not act in violation of Art. 38 I GG.

But this would eliminate only the legal, not the justificatory problem. And *that* problem is a serious one, because not only is it difficult to understand what compliance with a provision in the line of the 'strict' interpretation of Art. 38 I GG could mean for a human agent (one might even ask whether it is humanly possible). What's more: even if this last difficulty could be overcome, because of the very nature of the provision it will always be impossible to *know* in a particular case whether or not it has been complied with, since it entails neither a perceptible procedural constraint nor a substantive constraint on the content of norms, but a *conditional* constraint on normative content, where the condition refers to the *mental process* preceding a legislator's decision. So, what we have here is a restriction of normative competence that is, in principle, *impossible to control* (and just as impossible to enforce through the means and mechanisms of the usual systems of social control).

On the other hand, we must remember what has been said earlier: that one of the main purposes of a political system is the control, in different ways, of people's behaviour, i. e., the exercise of public social power. Now, if we start from the fact that, rather than perfect celestial harmony in which there would be, at most, a need for coordination, what we usually have in social life are divergence and even conflict of interests, then it follows directly that it is in everyone's interest to do everything possible to assure that the norms issued by the competent authorities coincide with his or her own interests. Thus, we must expect that there are always more or less strong incentives for attempting to gain control over the respective norm-authorities. And the higher the stakes for an agent, the stronger these incentives will be for him.

Now, in a system of representative democracy under the majority principle, where the degree of 'normative control' that can be exercised by any single, individual member of a norm-creating body is usually very low,[41] it is difficult – if not outright impossible – to gain control over the content of the norms to be enacted simply by the

40 See the passage of H. L. A. Hart quoted earlier.

41 Except for agents in very special political roles, such as some Presidents, or the German Chancellors with their 'directive competence' *(Richtlinienkompetenz)*, who do possess a relatively high degree of individual control over the decisions in their competence.

usual legislative ways, that is, by becoming oneself (part of) a norm-authority and using the officially recognized means for changing outcomes, namely one's own vote and one's skills of persuasion.[42]

From this, it follows that in such political systems it is to be expected that there will be particularly strong incentives for seeking to gain the desired control – and this means: *political power* – by other means. And if such an attempt is successful, then we have, so to speak, a 'pure' case of the *usurpation of legal power by factual social power*. The original system will then have been perverted, since from the point of view of that system, the norm-authorities, i. e., the holders of normative competence *de jure* (for instance, the legislators in parliament), should be the *only* sources of political power. Above all, there should be no hidden 'dictators'.[43] And this means that not only

42 Cf. esp. B. Barry 1991b, 270: „power is more important to an actor, in relation to luck, the more uncertain that actor is of the likely alignment of forces within the relevant period of time." But, in voting under the majority rule, each individual voter must, indeed, be very lucky if he is to get what he wants (ibid., 301): „Even the most utopian set-up, if it gives equal power to everyone, is going to mean that [...] the capacity of a single individual to overcome the resistance of others is going to be confined to those cases where the strength of his allies is very closely matched with the strength of his opponents." Also (ibid., 300): „If power is not an end in itself, it would seem that it is better to have powerful friends than to be powerful yourself – provided, of course, that you have some way of being sure that they will remain your friends." If you have 'powerful friends', you don't need to exercise (or even have) power yourself in order to get what you want, i. e., you are „lucky". And apparently, the more powerful your friends are, the fewer of them you will need in order to be successful. Therefore, when votes are taken in large committee settings, but final decisions are also 'filtered' through decisions made by smaller groups or even individuals at some higher level of the power-hierarchy, the small power consisting in participating, with equal power, in the large-setting vote may promise much less success than having the luck of an *amigo* in the higher echelons of power. – Ronald Dworkin (2002, esp. 190 ff.) refers to the distinction between the legitimate and the illegitimate ways of affecting political outcomes in a democracy when he speaks of „political impact" and „political influence" as two dimensions of „political power", where political impact is defined as the difference one can make with one's own vote or choice, political influence the difference one can make on political outcomes (decisions) through intervening – in any imaginable way: persuasion, threats, ... – with others.

43 It has been argued by some observers that never has this condition been violated more blatantly in the United States than by the George W. Bush administration. Cf., e. g., Suskind 2004; Chait 2002/3, 16–19: „the administration is subservient to economic pressure groups to an extent that surpasses any administration in modern history [...] In fact, if you look at the major economic issues of the Bush presidency, in every instance Bush's position has been identical to that of whichever interest group applied the heaviest political pressure [...] His energy bill was written in consultation with energy producers and reflected their desires almost perfectly [...] Since he's taken office, government and business have melded together as one big 'us'. Scores of mid-level appointees [...] oversee industries for which they once worked [...] lobbyists have in some instances literally taken over the responsibilities of governing [...] On virtually every issue that has come before him, Bush has sided with the intense preferences of the well-organized minority." Chait (2002/3, 17) also suggests an explanation for the visible contrast in this respect between this administration and, for instance, the Clinton administration: „It's the deep asymmetry between the two parties' financial support. The Republicans receive support from business or from groups [...] that don't oppose business's agenda [...] Democrats, by contrast, draw financial support from a broader range of interests [...] the president's [Clinton's] dogged pursuit of soft money was seen both by liberals and conservatives as the apex of political sleaze. But, in fact, the breadth of Bill Clinton's fund-raising is precisely what insulated his decision-making from undue influence [...] on most issues, it was at least *possible* for him to make a detached judgment on the merits. That is precisely what Bush cannot do." The slope from there to the extremes of direct political corruption is seen by some as very slippery: Darrell West has argued „that we now have a 'checkbook democracy', a form of government in which money has hijacked the campaign process. It is a system characterized by large contributions, secret influence, citizen cynicism, weak public representation, and increasingly unaccountable elected officials. Big money tied to private interest groups has disrupted democratic elections [...] Checkbook

should there be no *coercion* nor *de facto normative authority* over those who have normative power: they should also not be subject to any *other* kind of factual power, held by virtue of whatever other means – for instance, to a factual power based on *epistemic authority*, gained by way of certain *intellectual skills* or (perceived) *superior knowledge*.

This last aspect is, I think, the one that causes the greatest problems for the desired 'control of the controllers' in a representative democracy. Because what should play no role at all is *factual* social power (over norm-authorities) that would derive from such means. But, at the same time, those very same types of skills and expertise are precisely what democratic authorities must rely on in order to be able to take justifiable political decisions. In other words, the *illegitimate* control of norm-authorities by *de facto* power-holders largely operate with the same means and basically through the same mechanisms as those influences that are desired and even necessary if norm-authorities are to take adequate decisions in a representative democracy.

This inherent 'dual use' quality of political channels of influence is, if only implicitly, a standing topic in the literature on lobbying, as exemplified in an especially clear way in the following observations by Richard Smith about the impacts of interest groups on the U. S. Congress:

„The extent to which the lobbyists of an interest group can influence the public positions of members of Congress during a lobbying campaign depends upon the extent to which they can influence the interpretation and explanation processes of members of Congress. Lobbyists try to influence the interpretation process by formulating and presenting arguments for their group's position. These arguments are designed to advance interpretations of the consequences of the group's position that the lobbyists believe members of Congress will find more appealing than the interpretations for alternative positions [...] The lobbyists of an interest group try to influence the explanatory process by making those members of Congress who view the interest group as an important audience believe that they would have to explain to the officials and members of the interest group any public position contrary to the position advocated by the group. The intent of the lobbyists is to get members of Congress to conclude that they cannot successfully explain an opposing position and must, instead, publicy support the position of the interest group." (Smith 1993, 186)

„Clearly, the standard statistical approaches used to study interest-group influence, such as regression, logit, or probit models, do not capture well the influence relationships described here. They cannot represent the hypothesized relationships in which the presence of defection conditions is necessary for public defection and the absence of defection conditions is sufficient for public agreement. Indeed, they would understate the actual level of influence that an interest group has [...] I have shown how interest-group influence is strongly structured by the interpretation and explanation processes. Therefore, my results indicate *how the public positions of members of Congress and their reactions to the lobbying efforts of an interest group can be responses to both argument and pressure; to both the desire to make good public policy and the need to be politically expedient*." (Smith 1993, 206; emphasis added) [44]

democracy weakens the leadership accountability that is such a crucial part of our [the U. S., RZ] political system [...] It is this legitimization and institutionalization of corruption in our political system that represents such a vital threat" (West 2000, 7); cf. also Etzioni 1987, ch. 2: „The Ways Private Power Penetrates"; ch. 3: „Retail: Buying Vote by Vote".

[44] For an analysis of the particular difficulties of measuring the power of lobbyists, which are found to be much greater than many previous analysts have thought, cf. recently Ward 2004. He argues that, because of possible strategic behaviour, „what lobbies push for cannot be assumed to be a guide to what they prefer; and without independent knowledge of their preferences, it is difficult to make judgements about the degree to which counterfactual outcomes have been changed in desired directions" (45).

Hence, the decisive theoretical task for a refinement of normative democratic theory with a view towards the justificatory problems arising from political influence, would be, first, to distinguish clearly and precisely between the two phenomena and, second, to invent appropriate 'filters' for effectively preventing illegitimate influence without at the same time blocking necessary influence. Whether and to what extent this is possible at all, however, still seems wide open to question.

5. Conclusion

Summing up the argument, we can say that the concept of political power refers to a complex chain of power relations in which two different kinds of power are interlocked.

One part of that chain is the sub-chain of the positions of normative, or purely legal, power, the elements of which are linked to each other through delegations of that same type of power, by way of 'norms of competence' or 'power-conferring norms'. At the end of this chain, as the outcome of its workings, there should be some constraint on (private) factual social power.

This means that the system of normative powers itself somehow 'transforms' into factual social power. But that transformation from one kind of power into another is justifiable only if at least two possible points of intrusion of factual social power are blocked:

(1) The chain of normative powers may not begin with a relation of factual social power; instead, it must begin with a normative relation – although of a different normative dimension: a sort of self-restraint, of 'power over themselves', so to speak, on the parts of the subjects.

(2) And it can only be expected that people may voluntarily enter into such a normative relationship if the holders of normative power are, in turn, constrained in certain ways. In this respect, the most important aspect mentioned was that norm-authorities must not themselves be subject to any factual social power.

If this is correct, then I think we have scant reason for optimism: As we have seen, between desired influence and undesired power, there are no empirically perceptible differences that could guide the construction of the necessary 'filters'; nor can we expect that the subjects of political power, for whom often much is at stake in legislative decisions, will voluntarily give up attempts to 'usurp' normative power by exercising any factual social power they happen to possess.

Some time ago, Adam Przeworski suggested what would be required to change that expectation: „A central distinctive task of democratic institutions, – he said –, is to counteract increasing returns to power" (1995, 40). This assertion shows the predicament we are in, because „to counteract increasing returns to power" is an *impossible quest* – not for factual, but for conceptual reasons: If 'social power' means something like the „ability to elicit desired behaviour from others", as the definition by Hughes quoted earlier stipulates, then „increasing returns“ are implied by the concept.[45] Hence, until that problem can be solved, the question must remain open whether *really existing* political systems – even of the 'best possible' kind, i. e., those aspiring to satisfy the conditions of liberal, representative democracy under the rule of law – come close enough to the *ideal* model of such a system to still fit under that model's 'justificatory umbrella'.

[45] Cf. Pierson 2000 for an illuminating discussion of the importance of increasing returns processes for politics in gernal, and for the development of the social distribution of power in particular.

5. INFLUENCE AND POWER: A MESS TRANSFORMED?

> *[L]et us not forget Lilliput [...] In the third phase of Modernity, the name of the game will be* influence, *not* force; *and, in playing on that field, the Lilliputians hold certain advantages.*
>
> Stephen Toulmin 1992, 208

If what I have said in the preceding chapters, especially my proposal for a distinction between power and influence in Chapter 2.8 and my observations in Chapter 4 concerning the function influence can acquire, as a kind of transmission belt between factual social power and normative power, are accepted, then, it seems, the messy state diagnosed at the beginning of this book has not disappeared: it has merely been transformed – it has, so to speak, been dumped by the inhabitants of the conceptual realm into the frontyard of their theoretical neighbours.

In December 1998, the *New York Review of Books* carried an article with the graphic title 'Democracy for Sale', a review of a recently published book with the equally significant title *The Buying of the Congress: How Special Interests Have Stolen Your Right to Life, Liberty, & the Pursuit of Happiness* (Lewis et al. 1998). Concerning the realities of modern democracy, the reviewer comes to the following conclusion:

„In the end, we are talking about a system involving huge numbers of citizens [...] who have interests and demands that representatives may or may not take into account. In the conflicts between workers and employers, corporations and small businessmen, the employed and the retired, producers and consumers, politicians will respond to those voices they hear most clearly, which means those who have gotten access to them. It is inevitable that in this struggle, the richest among us will have the greatest influence over political power." (Nelson 1998, 10)

This short quote contains *en miniature* the main ingredients of the problem I am pointing at. The picture as such is anything but new, it is only too well known. And without explicitly asserting it, the citation also implies that the state of affairs it describes is not necessarily compatible with an ideal conception of representative democracy.

This seems almost automatically to give rise to questions such as the following: What consequences does the ubiquity, inevitability and, often, intractibility of influence processes have for normative democratic theory, and specifically for the possibility of the moral justification of liberal, representative democratic systems? What does it imply for the ascription of *responsibility* for political decisions, actions, and their consequences to the different agents involved? And what consequences are to be drawn from all this for the design of political institutions?

Formulated more bluntly, the basic question is: *Can* liberal representative democracy work? The average citizen of, say, an EU member state may think that this is a 'typically politological' (read: irrelevant, artificial) question to ask, in view of the overwhelming evidence that such systems, at least in their part of the world, *are* working – if only more or less perfectly. For a political theorist, the answer cannot be all that evident. After all, as I insinuated at the end of the previous chapter, it could very well be the case that what is commonly known as 'liberal representative democracies' do not really deserve the name; in other words, it could be that what on the face of it *looks* like a liberal, representative, and democratic system actually *operates* in ways that violate one or the other fundamental condition of liberty, representation, or democracy as presupposed in the pertinent normative theories.

Just how difficult it is to think up even in purely theoretical terms (not to speak of how to implement in practice) a system of social institutions capable of systematically generating decisions for a society that will satisfy a set of minimal conditions of legitimacy, reasonableness and consistency has been known for a long time. The development, over the past few decades, of new analytical tools in the context of what has come to be known as the field of 'social choice' has greatly enhanced our awareness and understanding of these problems. They have rocked the foundations of liberal representative democracy, by raising doubts about the meaning of some of its core elements: for instance, about the meaning of majority decisions, by pointing out their inconsistencies and instability; or about the meaning of the idea of *Gemeinwohl* (somewhat inadequately translatable as 'public interest' or 'common good'), by exposing the problems involved in the very idea of aggregating individual data into one single 'social welfare function'. Meanwhile, these concerns have generated a huge specialized literature.[1]

What I have argued for in the preceding chapters with regard to influence further complicates these tasks. While the question about the conditions under which political *power* can be justified has traditionally occupied a prominent position in *normative political theory* – particularly in the normative theory of democracy –, political *influence* has been treated, if at all, only sporadically and unsystematically.[2] This seems to indicate a theoretical gap. Specifically with respect to the normative theory of representative democracy, the idea that there is such a gap could be dismissed only if one were to argue either

(1) that influence phenomena do not occur in representative democracy – and therefore can also not pose a theoretical problem, or

(2) that influence can be subsumed entirely under power – and therefore whatever is said about the justification of power also takes care of the justificaton of influence, or

(3) that, although influence phenomena do occur independently of power, they just never give rise to any justificatory problem – and therefore there is no theoretical need to treat the question.

1 A considerable part of this literature is, it must be admitted, of a somewhat esoteric nature, even within political science, due to its relatively high degree of formalization. A very clear and insightful account of the practical relevance of these questions, and the problems that need to be solved for answering them, has been given by Amartya Sen in his Nobel Prize lecture (Sen 1999).

2 The only exception I am aware of has been Berg 1965, a work which has not received much attention in scholarship.

(ad 1) The first possibility, that influence simply does not occur in representative democracies, is entirely counter-intuitive; although influence as I have tentatively defined it poses special problems as to the possibilities of its empirical verification, its interference practically in everything human beings think and do can hardly be denied.

In the context of a theoretical study, not much can be said about such empirical questions as what kind of influence processes must be expected and to what extent, or whether certain influence constellations will really be unavoidable in representative democracy and whether, if so, they will necessarily lead to *de facto* unequal chances of political participation. But some general, analytical considerations about *necessary* conditions of influence processes seem to be possible.

The strong empirical relation between wealth and political influence asserted in the opening quotation does not seem self-evidently plausible. After all, there is certainly no *necessary* connection between wealth and access to political decision-makers; and access of one agent to another – the audibility of the 'voice' and/or the visibility of the actions of the former for the latter – is certainly a necessary, though not yet a sufficient condition for influence of the former over the latter.

In view of the conceptual considerations presented above, another necessary condition is a corresponding (conscious or unconscious) 'disposition' on the part of the agent to be influenced. What dispositions will be more or less conducive to what kinds of influence processes is, again, an empirical matter which must be answered by psychologists. In any case, *influence* of *A* over *B* and *indifference* of *B* towards *A* are incompatible, if only for conceptual reasons.

If we consider only these two factors conditioning the chances of influence, what can we say about their expected distribution in a representative democracy, under the conditions of modern mass societies? Perhaps at least the following:

(a) Immediate, *personal access* to political decision-makers is naturally very restricted (to the small number of members of the respective private and professional environment plus a few other accidental or organized contacts). However, access (in the sense of 'audibility' or 'visibility') can today be gained in a number of ways (indirectly: e. g., through the media; publicly: e. g., through demonstrations). Thus, while *physical access* is always limited, it is not necessarily exclusive; and, above all, there are, at least in principle, a number of ways and means to actively seek such *physical access*.[3]

(b) This does not, however, apply to the second factor mentioned above, namely the factor of: the necessary receptiveness of the person to be influenced, i. e., so to speak, to *mental access*. The possibilities of changing an attitude of indifference in another agent, in order to pass the 'threshold' necessary for a chance of influence are very limited. This seems to be the point where 'mere' influence relations sharply differ from power relations:

[3] The great difficulties, even for well-organized groups with a massive following, of gaining any perceptible degree of political 'influence', and its dependency, in the last instance, on close *personal* contacts with *individual* decision-makers, is clearly shown, e. g., in a case study recently presented by Ulrich Willems, of the development policy pursued by the organization of the protestant church in Germany; cf. Willems 1998, esp. ch. 5.2, on „lobbying political decision-makers“.

* If *A* has *personal* significance for *B* (something *A* himself can do very little about), then influence seems possible.[4]

* If *A* has *no personal* significance for *B*, then if he is to have any significance at all, it can only be of an impersonal, 'objective' type, where what *A* does, or could do, matters to *B* not because of *who A* is, but because of *where, in what position* he is.[5] But such an objective significance that 'makes a difference' for B seems to be able to arise only from a position of *power.*

Thus, the disposition presupposed for the possibility of influence – in contrast to physical access – is, indeed, 'exclusive': it exists only for those agents who stand either in a *personal* or in a *power* relationship to the agent to be influenced. *All others are basically excluded from it.*

Of course, this does not yet guarantee to all those who in this sense do have access to, and the attention of, another agent that they will actually be able to exercise influence intentionally and successfully. But those among them whose possibilities of *influence* derive, in the last instance, from a position of *power* can, if they think it necessary, simply play out this trump. For this group, therefore, the power relationship (with its implicit 'guarantee of success') will always be decisive.

With respect to the other group, whose members have potential influence because of their *personal* significance for the decision-maker, the following conjecture can be formulated: As the strength of the personal relationship and the personal significance for the decision-maker increase, the probability that there will in fact be a flow of influence also increases.

(ad 2) The second view, that influence is nothing but a particular subclass of power, I have tried to contest in Chapter 2; in any case, the assertion that the concept of influence is fully contained in that of power would presuppose at least an analysis, however brief, of the two concepts, and such an analysis is usually lacking in the theories in question. So in this respect at least, there is a theoretical gap.

(ad 3) And finally, likewise, the third contention, that influence generally does not require considerations of justification, is certainly not self-evident; its truth needs to be established by argument. Therefore, as long as such arguments are missing, there is even more of a gap in the theories in question in this respect too.

Hence, the need for further research activities concerning phenomena of political influence cannot reasonably be denied on any of the three accounts: either it must be shown that there really is no theoretical gap in that respect, or the existing gap(s) must be filled.

The direction into which reflections on the level of the normative theory of democracy will have to go, seems clear: in contrast to power, *influence*, according to the proposed definition, can probably not be regarded, in any interesting sense, as a matter

[4] E. g., when *B* has an attitude towards *A* that could be expressed in the statement „What *A* says is important to me because it comes from *A* (not from somebody else)".

[5] E. g., because he belongs to an organization representing a great number of voters, or to a company which pays a high amount of local taxes, or ...

of constraints on *freedom*.[6] This may be one of the reasons why the topic has so rarely been regarded as normatively relevant. However, at least *three other issues* come to mind where political influence processes may become problematic for the justification of a political system:

The first refers to another fundamental value, namely *equality*. While political equality is undoubtedly one of the fundamental conditions of the justifiability of a political system, the question, of course, is: 'Equality of what?' Hence, from that perspective, the specific question in the present context would be whether a case can really be made – as is sometimes stipulated without further explanations – for 'equality of influence', and what exactly this could mean.

The second issue, which is the one I have formulated a few reflections about in the final part of the previous chapter, is intimately linked to the first and, at the same time, refers us back to the question of freedom, but now in an *indirect* way: it concerns that large field of questions implied by the insight that *influence* on power-holders can be employed as a way of acquiring and exercising *power*.

The third issue, as mentioned repeatedly throughout this work, is that of *responsibility*. It too concerns, above all, the exercise of *power through influence*. To the extent that the exercise of power, in the last instance, has an impact on *action*, it seems that at least a co-responsibility of the agent exercising the power for the subsequent actions by the subject of that power is implied. On the other hand, if influence is conceived as operating on *beliefs*, and beliefs are, not implausibly, thought to be a matter of exclusive responsibility of their respective holder, exercises of influence do not seem to be able to produce a relocation of responsibility. The exercise of power through influence, thus, seems to lead to a kind of paradox: Such phenomena have *two* correct descriptions – one in terms of power, the other in terms of influence, and one can apparently conveniently choose the ascription of responsibility one prefers, simply by opting for one or the other description.

The mess is still there. It needs to be taken care of.

[6] However, before a final word on this can be said, a more detailed analysis of a number of questions concerning the proposed concept of influence is necessary. At the very least, something will have to be said about such conceptual distinctions as between freedom and autonomy (cf., e. g., Christman 1987, 1988), the 'internal' vs. the 'external' point of view (Hart 1994), and first-order in contrast to second-order preferences and volitions (G. Dworkin 1970, 1988; Frankfurt 1971; cf. for a discussion of their views Kristjánsson 1996, which first directed my attention to the relevance of the work of Dworkin and Frankfurt for the present topic).

REFERENCES

AARNIO, Aulis 1987: *The Rational as Reasonable*, Dordrecht: Kluwer.

ABELL, Peter 1977: The Many Faces of Power and Liberty: Revealed Preference, Autonomy, and Teleological Explanation, *Sociology* 11:1 (Jan.) 3–24.

AKERLOF, George 1984: *An Economic Theorist's Book of Tales*, Cambridge: Cambridge University Press.

ALBERT, Max 2003: The Voting Power Approach. Measurement without Theory, *European Union Politics* 4:3, 351–366.

ALCHOURRÓN, Carlos E. 1969: Logic of Norms and Logic of Normative Propositions, *Logique et Analyse* 12:47, 242–268.

ALCHOURRÓN, Carlos and Eugenio BULYGIN 1971: *Normative Systems*, Vienna and New York: Springer.

ALMOND, Gabriel A. (with Stephen Genco) 1990: Clouds, Clocks, and the Study of Politics, in: id., *A Discipline Divided*, Newbury Park et al.: Sage, 32–65 [first in: *World Politics* 29:4 (1977)].

– and Sidney VERBA 1989: *The Civic Culture* (1963), Newbury Park, Calif. et al.: Sage.

ANALYSE & KRITIK 21:1, August 1999: *Praktische Vernunft und Verstehen*, eds. M. Baurmann and A. Leist, Opladen: Westdeutscher Verlag.

ARNIM, Hans Herbert von 1993: *Demokratie ohne Volk. Plädoyer gegen Staatsversagen, Machtmißbrauch und Politikverdrossenheit*, Munich: Knaur.

ATIENZA, Manuel and Juan RUIZ MANERO 1994: Sulle regole che conferiscono poteri, in: P. Comanducci and R. Guastini (eds.), *Analisi e diritto 1994. Ricerche di giurisprudenza analitica*, Torino: Giappichelli, 55–84.

– / – 1995: Adversus Pompeyanos. A proposito di alcune critiche alla nostra concezione delle regole che conferiscono poteri, in: Comanducci/Guastini (eds.) 1995, 237–252.

– / – 1997: *A Theory of Legal Sentences*, transl. by R. Zimmerling, Dordrecht: Kluwer.

AYER, Alfred Jules 1946: *Language, Truth and Logic* (1936), 2nd ed. London: Victor Gollancz.

BACHRACH, Peter and Morton S. BARATZ 1962: Two Faces of Power, *American Political Science Review* 56, 947–952 [reprinted in: Scott 1994/II, 85–94].

BACHRACH, Peter and Morton S. BARATZ 1963: Decisions and Nondecisions: An Analytical Framework, *American Political Science Review* 57, 632–642 [reprinted in: Scott 1994/II, 95–110].

– / – 1970: *Power and Poverty. Theory and Practice*, New York: Oxford University Press [German transl: *Macht und Armut. Eine theoretisch-empirische Untersuchung*, with an introd. by C. Offe, Frankfurt a. M.: Suhrkamp 1977].

– / – 1975: Power and Its Two Faces Revisited: A Reply to Geoffrey Debnam, *American Political Science Review* 69, 900–904 [reprinted in: Scott 1994/II, 196–203].

BALDWIN, David A. 1971: The Power of Positive Sanctions, *World Politics* 24, 19–38.

– 1978: Power and Social Exchange, *American Political Science Review* 72, 1229–1242.

– 1980: Interdependence and power: a conceptual analysis, *International Organization* 34:4 (Autumn) 471–506.

BALL, Terence 1992: New Faces of Power, in: Wartenberg (ed.) 1992, 14–31 [shortened and revised version of ch. 4 of: id., *Transforming Political Discourse*, Oxford: Blackwell 1988].

– 1993: Power, in: R. E. Goodin and Ph. Pettit (eds.), *A Companion to Contemporary Political Philosophy*, Oxford: Blackwell 1993, 548–557.

BALZER, Wolfgang 1992: Game Theory and Power Theory: A Critical Comparison, in: Wartenberg (ed.) 1992, 56–78.

BANFIELD, Edward C. 1961: *Political Influence. A New Theory of Urban Politics*, New York: Free Press.

BARDHAN, Pranab K. 1991: On the Concept of Power in Economics, *Economics and Politics* 3:3 (Nov. 1991), 265–277.

BARRY, Brian 1970: *Sociologists, Economists and Democracy*, London: Collier-Macmillan.

– 1991: *Democracy and Power. Essays in Political Theory* I, Oxford: Clarendon.

– 1991a, Power: An economic analysis, in: id. 1991, 222–269 [first published in: id. (ed.) 1975, 67–101].

– 1991b, Is it better to be powerful or lucky?, in: id. 1991, 270–302 [first published in: *Political Studies* 28 (1980), 183–194 and 338–352].

– 1991c, The obscurities of power, in: id. 1991, 303–306 [first published in: *Government and Opposition* 10 (1975), 250–254].

– 1991d, The uses of 'power', in: id. 1991, 307–321 [first published in: *Government and Opposition* 23 (1988) 340–353].

– (ed.) 1975: *Power and Political Theory. Some European Perspectives*, London et al.: John Wiley.

BARRY, Norman P. 1989: *An Introduction to Modern Political Theory*. Second Edition (1st ed. 1981, 4th ed. 2000), Houndmills and London: Macmillan.

BARTLETT, Randall 1989: *Economics and Power: An Inquiry into Human Relations and Markets*, Cambridge: Cambridge University Press.

BAUMANN, Peter 1993: *Macht und Motivation*, Opladen: Leske + Budrich.

BAURMANN, Michael 1999: *Legal Authority as a Social Fact*, paper presented at the III Roland Seminar, Kangasala (Finland), May 27-29, 1999 (mimeo).

– 2002: *The Market of Virtue. Morality and Commitment in Liberal Society*, The Hague: Kluwer.

BECKER, Gary S. 1983: A Theory of Competition Among Pressure Groups for Political Influence, *Quarterly Journal of Economics* XCVIII:3 (August), 371–400.

BELL, Roderick, David V. EDWARDS, and R. Harrison WAGNER (eds.) 1969: *Political Power. A Reader in Theory and Research*, New York: Free Press and London: Collier-Macmillan.

BENN, Stanley I. 1988: *A Theory of Freedom*, Cambridge: Cambridge University Press.

BERG, Elias 1965: *Democracy and the Majority Principle*, Stockholm: Universitetsförlaget.

BERLIN, Isaiah 1969: Introduction, in: id., *Four Essays on Liberty*, Oxford and New York: Oxford University Press, ix–lxiii.

– 1980: Does Political Theory Still Exist?, in: id., *Concepts and Categories. Philosophical Essays*, ed. H. Hardy, Oxford et al.: Oxford University Press, 143–172 [orig.: La théorie politique existe-t-elle?, in: *Revue Française de Science Politique* 11 (1961) 309–337].

BERNHOLZ, Peter and Friedrich BREYER 1994: *Grundlagen der Politischen Ökonomie*, vol. 2: *Ökonomische Theorie der Politik*, 3rd ed., Tübingen: J. C. B. Mohr.

BIKHCHANDANI, Sushil, David HIRSHLEIFER and Ivo WELCH 1992: A Theory of Fads, Fashion, Custom, and Cultural Change as Informational Cascades, *Journal of Political Economy* 100:5, 992–1026.

– 1998: Learning from the Behavior of Others: Conformity, Fads, and Informational Cascades, *Journal of Economic Perspectives* 12:3 (Summer) 151–170.

BIRNBAUM, Pierre 1975: Power Divorced from its Sources: a Critique of the Exchange Theory of Power, in: B. Barry (ed.) 1975, 15–31.

BLALOCK, Hubert M, Jr. 1989: *Power and Conflict*, Newbury Park et al.: Sage.

BLAU, Peter M. 1964: *Exchange and Power in Social Life*, New York: Wiley.

BLOCH, Michael, Bryan HEADING and Philip LAWRENCE 1979: Power in Social Theory: A non-Relative View, in: S. C. Brown (ed.), *Philosophical Disputes in the Social*

Sciences, Brighton, Sussex: Harvester and Atlantic Highlands, N. J.: Humanities, 243–260.

– 1985: El Poder y el Derecho, in: id. and Michelangelo Bovero, *Origen y Fundamentos del Poder Político*, transl. by J. F. Santillana, Mexico City: Grijalbo, 19–36 [orig.: *Il potere e il diritto*, 1981].

BOBBIO, Norberto 1998: Kelsen and Legal Power, in: S. L. Paulson and B. Litschewski Paulson (eds.) 1998, 435–449 [orig.: Kelsen e il potere giuridico, 1982].

BOESCHE, Roger 1998: Thinking about Freedom, *Political Theory* 26:6 (Dec.), 855–873.

BÖHRET, Carl 1985: Zum Stand und zur Orientierung der Politikwissenschaft in der Bundesrepublik Deutschland, in: H.-H. Hartwich (ed.), *Policy-Forschung in der Bundesrepublik Deutschland. Ihr Selbstverständnis und ihr Verhältnis zu den Grundfragen der Politikwissenschaft*, Opladen: Westdeutscher Verlag, 216–330.

BOOCKMANN, Bernhard 1998: Agenda Control by Interest Groups in EU Social Policy, *Journal of Theoretical Politics* 10:2 (April) 215–236.

BOULDING, Kenneth E. 1989: *Three Faces of Power*, Newbury Park et al.: Sage.

BOVERO, Michelangelo 1985: Lugares Clásicos y Perspectivas Contemporáneas Sobre Política y Poder, in: Norberto Bobbio and Michelangelo Bovero, *Origen y Fundamentos del Poder Político*, transl. by J. F. Santillana, Mexico City: Grijalbo, 37–64 [orig.: Luoghi classici e prospettive contemporanee su politica e potere, 1982].

BOWLES, Samuel and Herbert GINTIS 1992: Power and Wealth in a Competitive Capitalist Economy, *Philosophy & Public Affairs* 21:4 (Fall), 324–353.

– / – 1999: Power in competitive exchange, in: S. Bowles, M. Franzini and U. Pagano (eds.): *The Politics and Economics of Power*, London and New York: Routledge, 13–30.

BRADSHAW, Alan 1976: A Critique of Steven Lukes' *Power: A Radical View*, *Sociology* 10, 121–128 [reprinted in: Scott 1994/II, 269–277].

BRAMS, Steven J. 1969a: The Structure of Influence Relationships in the International System, in: J. N. Rosenau (ed.): *International Politics and Foreign Policy*, New York: Free Press, 583–599.

– 1969b: Measuring the Concentration of Power in Political Systems, in: Bell/Edwards/Wagner (eds.) 1969, 346–359.

– 1975: Voting Power, in: id., *Game Theory and Politics*, New York: The Free Press and London: Collier-Macmillan.

BULYGIN, Eugenio 1982: Norms, normative propositions, and legal statements, in: G. Fløistad (ed.), *Contemporary Philosophy. A New Survey*, Vol. 3, The Hague, Boston and London: Martinus Nijhoff, 127–152.

– 1992: On norms of competence, *Law and Philosophy* 11, 201–216.

BUNGE, Mario 1998: *Social Science under Debate: A Philosophical Perspective*, Toronto: University of Toronto Press.

CAMPBELL, Tom D. 1997: Legal Positivism and Political Power, in: A. Vincent (ed.), *Political Theory. Tradition and Diversity*, Cambridge et al.: Cambridge University Press, 172–192.

CAPORASO, James A. and David P. LEVINE 1992: *Theories of Political Economy*, Cambridge: Cambridge University Press.

CARACCIOLO, Ricardo 1995: Due tipi di potere normativo, in: Comanducci/Guastini (eds.) 1995, 199–218.

CARE, Norman S. 1973: On Fixing Social Concepts, *Ethics* 84:1, 10–21.

CARNAP, Rudolf 1936/37: Testability and Meaning, *Philosophy of Science* III, 419–471, and IV, 2–40 [reprinted by the Graduate Philosophy Club, Yale University 1950; New Haven, Conn.: Whitlock 1954].

– 1956: The Methodological Character of Theoretical Concepts, in: H. Feigl and M. Scriven (eds.), *Minnesota Studies in the Philosophy of Science*, Vol. I, Minneapolis, Minn.: University of Minnesota Press, 38–76.

– 1960: *Meaning and Necessity. A Study in Semantics and Modal Logic*, Chicago, Ill.: University of Chicago Press.

CARRIÓ, Genaro R. 1990: *Notas sobre derecho y lenguaje*, 4th ed. Buenos Aires: Abeledo-Perrot.

CARTER, Ian 1996: The Concept of Freedom, Part I: Background, methodology, and the 'negative-positive' debate, *Humane Studies Review* 10:3 (Fall 1996) [http://osfl.gmu.edu/~ihs/ hsrfall96.htm].

– 1997: The Concept of Freedom, Part II: Classical liberalism and contemporary debates, *Humane Studies Review* 10:4 (Winter 1996-1997) [http://mason.gmu.edu/~ihs/hsr/w96hsr. htm].

– 1999: *A Measure of Freedom*, Oxford: Oxford University Press.

CARTWRIGHT, Dorwin 1959: A Field Theoretical Conception of Power, in: Cartwright (ed.) 1959, 183–220.

– 1969: Influence, Leadership, Control, in: Bell/ Edwards/Wagner (eds.) 1969, 123–165 [first published in: J. March (ed.), *Handbook of Organizations*, 1965].

– (ed.) 1959: *Studies in Social Power*, Ann Arbor: University of Michigan Press.

CARTWRIGHT, Dorwin and Alvin ZANDER (eds.) 1960: *Group Dynamics: Research and Theory*, 2nd ed. Evanston, Ill. and Elmsford, N. Y.: Row, Peterson.

CASSINELLI, C. W. 1966: *Free Activities and Interpersonal Relations*, The Hague: Martinus Nijhoff.

CHAIT, Jonathan 2002/3: Special K, *The New Republic* nos. 4589/4590 (Dec. 30, 2002 & Jan. 6, 2003), 16–19.

CHRISTMAN, John 1987: Autonomy: A Defense of the Split-Level Self, *Southern Journal of Philosophy* XXV, 281–293.

– 1988: Constructing the Inner Citadel: Recent Work on the Concept of Autonomy, *Ethics* 99:1 (Oct.), 109–124.

– 1998: Book Review of Pettit, Philip. Republicanism: A Theory of Freedom and Government, *Ethics* 109:1 (Oct.) 202–206.

CIALDINI, Robert B. 1984: *Influence. How & Why People Agree to Things*, New York, N. Y.: William Morrow [currently latest edition: *Influence: Science and Practice*, 4th ed. Needham Heights, MA: Allyn & Bacon 2001].

– 2001: The Science of Persuasion, *Scientific American* 284:2 (Feb.) 62–67.

CLARK, Terry N. 1967: The Concept of Power, *Southwestern Social Science Quarterly* 48, 271 ff.

CLARKE, Barry 1979: Essentially Contested Concepts, *British Journal of Political Science* 9, 122–126.

CLEGG, Stewart R. 1989: *Frameworks of Power*, London et al.: Sage.

COHEN, Joshua 1997: The Arc of the Moral Universe, *Philosophy & Public Affairs* 26:2 (Spring) 91–134.

COLEMAN, James S. 1990: *Foundations of Social Theory*, Cambridge, Mass. and London: Belknap.

COMANDUCCI, Paolo and Riccardo GUASTINI (eds.) 1995: *Analisi e diritto 1995. Ricerche di giurisprudenza analitica*, Torino: Giappichelli.

CONNOLLY, William E. 1983: *The Terms of Political Discourse*, 2nd ed. Oxford: Martin Robertson [1st ed.: Lexington, Mass.: D. C. Heath 1974].

– 1983a: Essentially Contested Concepts in Politics, in: id. 1983, 9–44.

– 1983b: Power and Responsibility, in: id. 1983, 85–137.

COPI, Irving M. 1982: *Introduction to Logic* (1953), 6th ed. New York and London: Collier-Macmillan.

COPI, Irving M. and Carl COHEN 1998: *Introduction to Logic*, 10th ed. Upper Saddle River, N. J.: Prentice Hall.

D'AGOSTINO, Fred 1992: Art. 'Social sciences, epistemology of', in: *A Companion to Epistemology*, eds. J. Dancy and E. Sosa, Oxford and Malden, Mass.: Blackwell, 479–483.

DAHL, Robert A. 1957: The Concept of Power, *Behavioral Science* 2, 201–215 [reprinted in: Bell/Edwards/Wagner (eds.) 1969, 79–93].

– 1968: Power, in: *IESS*, vol. 12, New York: Macmillan, 405–415 [reprinted as: Power as the Control of Behavior, in: Lukes (ed.). 1986, 37–58].

– 1970: *Modern Political Analysis* (1963), 2nd ed. Englewood Cliffs, N. J.: Prentice Hall [German transl.: *Die Politische Analyse*, Munich: List 1973].

DAO, James and Eric SCHMITT 2002: Pentagon Readies Efforts to Sway Sentiment Abroad, *The New York Times on the Web*, Feb. 19, 2002 [www.nytimes.com].

DASGUPTA, Partha 1993: *An Inquiry into Well-Being and Destitution*, Oxford: Oxford University Press.

DE JASAY, Anthony 1998: *The State* (1985), Indianapolis, Ind.: Liberty Fund.

DEBNAM, Geoffrey 1975: Nondecisions and Power: The Two Faces of Bachrach and Baratz, *American Political Science Review* 69, 889–899 [reprinted in: Scott 1994/II, 177–195].

DIGESER, Peter 1992: The Fourth Face of Power, *Journal of Politics* 54:4, 977–1007.

DOWDING, Keith M. 1990: *Ability and Ableness: Morriss on Power and Counteractuals*, Government Department Working Papers, 10, Uxbridge: Brunel University.

– 1991: *Rational Choice and Political Power*, Aldershot and Brookfield, Vt.: Edward Elgar.

– 1996: *Power*, Buckingham: Open University.

DUNLEAVY, Patrick and Brendan O'LEARY 1987: *Theories of the State. The Politics of Liberal Democracy*. Houndmills: Macmillan.

DUNN, John 1993: *Western political theory in the face of the future*, Cambridge: Cambridge University Press.

DWORKIN, Gerald 1970: Acting Freely, *Nous* 4 (Nov.), 367–383.

– 1988: *The Theory and Practice of Autonomy*, Cambridge: Cambridge University Press.

– 1988a: Is more choice better than less?, in: id. (1988), 62–81 [first published in: *Midwest Studies in Philosophy* 7 (1982) 47–61].

– 1988b: Behavior control and design, in: id. (1988), 150–160 [first published in: *Social Research* 52 (Autumn 1985) 543–554].

– 1988c: The serpent beguiled me and I did eat: entrapment and the creation of crime, in: id. (1988), 130–149 [first published in: *Law and Philosophy* 4 (May 1985) 17–39].

DWORKIN, Ronald 2002: Political Equality, in: id., *Sovereign Virtue*, Cambridge, Mass. and London: Harvard University Press, 184–210 [first published in: *University of San Francisco Law Review* (1987)].

EAVEY, Cheryl L. and Gary J. MILLER 1995: Subcommittee Agenda Control, *Journal of Theoretical Politics* 7:2 (April), 125–156.

ESSLER, Wilhelm K. 1970: *Wissenschaftstheorie*, Bd. I: *Definition und Reduktion*, Freiburg/München: Alber.

ETZIONI, Amitai 1968: *The active society – a theory of societal and political processes*, London: Macmillan und New York: Free Press.

– 1987: *Capital Corruption. The New Attack on American Democracy*, New Brunswick, N. J., and Oxford: Transaction Books

– 1993: Power as a societal force, in: Olson/Marger (eds.) 1993, 18–28 [= excerpts from: id., *The Active Society*, pp. 314–323 and 357–361].

FABER, Karl-Georg, Karl-Heinz ILTING and Christian MEIER 1982: Art. 'Macht, Gewalt', in: O. Brunner, W. Conze and R. Koselleck (eds.): *Geschichtliche Grundbegriffe. Historisches Lexikon zur politisch-sozialen Sprache in Deutschland*, vol. 3, Stuttgart: Klett, 817–935.

FELSENTHAL, Dan S. and Moshé MACHOVER 1998: *The Measurement of Voting Power: Theory and Practice*, Problems and Paradoxes, Cheltenham: Edward Elgar.

– / – 2001: Myths and Meanings of Voting Power: Comments on a Symposium, *Journal of Theoretical Politics* 13:1 (Jan.) 81–97.

FERRER BELTRÁN, Jordi 1995: Sul carattere delle norme di competenza, in: Comanducci/Guastini (eds.) 1995, 253–268.

FISCHER, John M. 1999: Recent work on moral responsibility, *Ethics* 110:1 (Oct.) 93–139.

FISCHER, John M. and Mark RAVIZZA (eds.) 1993: *Perspectives on Moral Responsibility*, Ithaca, N. Y.: Cornell University Press.

FOUCAULT, Michel 1978: *Dispositive der Macht*, Berlin: Merve.

– 1994: The Subject and Power, in: Scott (ed.) 1994, vol. I, 218–233 [reprinted from: H. Douglas and P. Rabinow (eds.), *Michel Foucault*, 1982, Afterword, 208–226].

FRANKFURT, Harry 1971: Freedom of the Will and the Concept of a Person, *Journal of Philosophy* 68:1 (Jan.), 5–20.

FRENCH, John R. P., Jr. 1960: A Formal Theory of Social Power, in: Cartwright/Zander (eds.) 1960, 727–744 [first published in: *Psychological Review* 63 (1956), 181–194].

FRENCH, John R. P., Jr. and Bertram RAVEN 1959: The Bases of Social Power, in: Cartwright (ed.) 1959, 150–167 [reprinted in: Cartwright/Zander (eds.) 1960, 607–623].

FRENCH, John R. P., Jr. and Richard SNYDER 1959: Leadership and Interpersonal Power, in: Cartwright (ed.) 1959, 118–149.

FREY, Frederick W. 1971: On Issues and Nonissues in the Study of Power, *American Political Science Review* 65, 1081–1101 [reprinted in Scott 1994/II, 141–172].

FRIEDKIN, Noah E. 1998: *A Structural Theory of Social Influence*, Cambridge: Cambridge University Press.

GAIS, Thomas 1996: *Improper Influence. Campaign Finance Law, Political Interest Groups, and the Problem of Equality*, Ann Arbor: University of Michigan Press.

GALBRAITH, John K. 1984: *The Anatomy of Power*, London: Hamish Hamilton.

– 1998: *Letters to Kennedy*, ed. J. Goodman, Cambridge, Mass., and London: Harvard University Press.

GALLIE, W. B. 1956: Essentially Contested Concepts, *Proceedings of the Aristotelian Society*, New Series, Vol. 56, 167–198.

GARZÓN VALDÉS, Ernesto 1965: Über das Verhältnis zwischen dem rechtlichen Sollen und dem Sein, in: id. (ed.), *Lateinamerikanische Studien zur Rechtsphilosophie*, *ARSP* Beiheft 41, N. F. 4, 291–321.

– 1981: Acerca de las limitaciones legales al soberano legal, *Sistema* (Madrid) 43-44 (Sept.), 43–56 [German transl.: Die gesetzliche Begrenzung des staatlichen Souveräns, *ARSP* LXVIII (1982) 4, 431–484].

– 1987: Allgemeine positive Pflichten und ihre Begründung, in: E. Bulygin and E. Garzón Valdés. (eds.), *Argentinische Rechtstheorie und Rechtsphilosophie heute*, Berlin: Duncker & Humblot, 167–188 [orig.: Los deberes positivos generales y su fundamentación, *DOXA* (Alicante) 3 (1986) 17–33].

– 1988: *Die Stabilität politischer Systeme*, Freiburg and Munich: Karl Alber.

– 1989: Representación y democracia, *DOXA* (Alicante) 6, 143–163.

– 1990: On Justifying Legal Paternalism, *Ratio Juris* 3:1 bis (March), 173–184.

– 1991: Interventionismus und Paternalismus, *Rechtstheorie* 22:2, 145–164 [orig.: Intervencionismo y paternalismo, *Revista Latinoamericana de Filosofía* XVI (March 1990) 1, 3–24].

– 1997: Über Verantwortungssätze, in: id. et al. (eds.), *Normative Systems in Legal and Moral Theory.* Festschrift *for Carlos E. Alchourrón and Eugenio Bulygin*, Berlin: Duncker & Humblot, 111–140 [orig.: El enunciado de responsabilidad, *DOXA* (Alicante) 19 (1996)].

– 1998: Two models of legal validity: Hans Kelsen and Francisco Suárez in: S. L. Paulson and B. Litschewski Paulson (eds.) 1998, 263–271.

– 1999: Algunas reflexiones sobre la ignorancia, *Isonomía* (Mexico City) 11 (Oct.) 129–148.

GAUTHIER, David 1986: *Morals by Agreement*, Oxford: Oxford University Press.

GAVENTA, John 1982: *Power and Powerlessness: Quiescence and Rebellion in an Appalachian Valley*, Urbana and Chicago, Ill.: University of Illinois Press.

GILLESPIE, Judith A. 1982: Some Basic Puzzles in Political Inquiry. Introduction to: id. and Dina A. Zinnes, *Missing Elements in Political Inquiry. Logic and Levels of Analysis*, Beverly Hills et al.: Sage, 11–34.

GOLDHAMER, Herbert and Edward A. SHILS 1939: Types of Power and Status, *American Journal of Sociology* 45, 171–182 [reprinted in Scott 1994/I, 101–111].

GOLDMAN, Alvin I 1986: Toward a Theory of Social Power, in: Lukes 1986, 156–202 [first published in: *Philosophical Studies* 23:4 (1972) 221–268].

GONZÁLEZ LAGIER, Daniel 2003: *The Paradoxes of Action. Human Action, Law and Philosophy*, Dordrecht: Kluwer Academic Publishers.

GOODIN, Robert E. 1988: *Reasons for Welfare. The Political Theory of the Welfare State*, Princeton: Princeton University Press.

GOODMAN, Nelson 1955: *Facts, Fiction and Forecast*, London.

GRAY, John 1977: On the contestability of social and political concepts, *Political Theory* 5, 333–348.

GREVE, Werner 1998: 'Menschliche Handlung' – Erkenntnis und Interesse, *Ethik und Sozialwissenschaften* 9:1, 37–39.

GUNNELL, John G. 1998: *The Orders of Discourse: Philosophy, Social Science, and Politics*, Lanham, Md.: Rowman & Littlefield.

HABERMAS, Jürgen 1988: *Theorie des kommunikativen Handelns*, vol. 2, Frankfurt/M.: Suhrkamp.

– 1997: *Between Facts and Norms. Contributions to a Discourse Theory of Law and Democracy*, transl. by W. Rehg, Cambridge: Polity Press [orig.: *Faktizität und Geltung. Beiträge zur Diskurstheorie des Rechts und des demokratischen Rechtsstaats*, Frankfurt a. M.: Suhrkamp 1992].

HANSON, Russell L. 1989: Democracy, in: T. Ball et al. (eds.), *Political Innovation and Conceptual Change*, Cambridge et al.: Cambridge University Press, 68–89.

HARDIN, Russell 1996: Russell's Power, *Philosophy of the Social Sciences* 26:3 (Sept.) 322–347.

HARE, Richard M. 1981: *Moral Thinking. Its Levels, Method, and Point*, Oxford: Clarendon.

HARSANYI, John 1962a: Measurement of Social Power, Opportunity Costs and the Theory of Two-Person Bargaining Games, *Behavioural Scientist* 7:1 (1962) 67–80 [reprinted in: id., *Essays on Ethics, Social Behaviour and Scientific Explanation*, Dordrecht: Reidel 1976, 162–184].

– 1962b: Measurement of Social Power in *n*-Person Reciprocal Power Situations, *Behavioural Scientist* 7:1 (1962) 81–91 [reprinted in: id., *Essays on Ethics, Social Behaviour and Scientific Explanation*, Dordrecht: Reidel 1976, 185–203].

HART, H. L. A. 1994: *The Concept of Law* (1961), 2nd ed. Oxford: Clarendon.

– 1998: *Punishment and Responsibility* (1968), Oxford: Clarendon.

HEIDER, Fritz 1958: *The Psychology of Interpersonal Relations*, New York: Wiley.

HEIL, John 1992: Art. 'Disposition', in: J. Dancy and E. Sosa (eds.), *A Companion to Epistemology*, Oxford: Blackwell, 108.

HEMPEL, Carl G. 1974: *Grundzüge der Begriffsbildung in der empirischen Wissenschaft*, Düsseldorf: Bertelsmann Universitätsverlag [orig.: Fundamentals of Concept Formation in Empirical Science, in: *International Encyclopaedia of Unified Science*, Vol. II, No. 7, Chicago and London: University of Chicago Press 1952].

HERMANN, Emanuel 1896: *Das Geheimniss der Macht. Originalstudien*, Berlin: Allgemeiner Verein für Deutsche Litteratur.

HIRSHLEIFER, David 1993: The Blind Leading the Blind: Social Influence, Fads, and Informational Cascades, eScholarship Repositories, University of California, Los Angeles [http://repositories.cdlib.org/anderson/fin/24-93].

HIRSHLEIFER, Jack 1991: The Paradox of Power, *Economics and Politics* 3:3 (Nov.) 177–200.

HOBBES, Thomas 1651: *Leviathan*, ed. C. B. Macpherson, Harmondsworth: Penguin 1985.

– 1668: *Behemoth or The Long Parliament*, ed. F. Tönnies (reprint of the 1889 edition), Chicago, Ill. and London: University of Chicago Press 1990.

HOFFMANN-LANGE, Ursula 1992: *Eliten, Macht und Konflikt in der Bundesrepublik*, Opladen: Leske + Budrich.

HOLLER, Manfred J. 1998: Two Stories, One Power Index, *Journal of Theoretical Politics* 10:2 (April) 179–190.

– (ed.) 1981: *Power, Voting, and Voting Power*, Würzburg: Physica.

– (ed.) 1991: *Political Entry*, Special Issue of the *Journal of Theoretical Politics* 3:2 (April).

HOLMES, Stephen 1988: Gag rules or the politics of omission, in: J. Elster and R. Slagstad (eds.), *Constitutionalism and Democracy*, Cambridge: Cambridge University Press, 19–58.

HONNETH, Axel 1991: *The Critique of Power. Reflective Stages in a Critical Social Theory*, Cambridge, Mass.: MIT Press [orig.: *Kritik der Macht. Reflexionsstufen einer kritischen Gesellschaftstheorie*, Frankfurt/M.: Suhrkamp 1986].

HÖSLE, Vittorio 1995: Macht und Moral, *Ethik und Sozialwissenschaften* 6:3, 379–387.

HOSPERS, John 1990: *An Introduction to Philosophical Analysis* (1956), 3rd ed. London: Routledge.

HRADIL, Stefan 1980: *Die Erforschung der Macht. Eine Übersicht über die empirische Ermittlung von Machtverteilungen durch die Sozialwissenschaften*, Stuttgart et al.: Kohlhammer.

HUGHES, Barry B. 1978: *The Domestic Context of American Foreign Policy*, San Francisco: W. H. Freeman.

VON HUMBOLDT, Wilhelm 1993: *The Limits of State Action* (1791-92?), ed. J. W. Burrow, Indianapolis, Ind.: Liberty Fund [reprint of the 1969 Cambridge University Press edition; orig.: *Ideen zu einem Versuch, die Grenzen der Wirksamkeit des Staates zu bestimmen*, Stuttgart: Reclam 1995].

HURLEY, Susan L. 1989: *Natural Reasons. Personality and Polity*, Oxford: Oxford University Press.

ISAAC, Jeffrey C. 1992: Beyond the Three Faces of Power: A Realist Critique, in: Wartenberg (ed.) 1992, 32–55 [first published in: *Polity* 20:1 (Fall 1987) 4–30].

JONES, Andrew J. I. and Marek SERGOT 1997: A Formal Characterisation of Institutionalised Power, in: E. Garzón Valdés et al. (eds.), *Normative Systems in Legal and Moral Theory.* Festschrift *for Carlos E. Alchourrón and Eugenio Bulygin*, Berlin: Duncker & Humblot, 349–367.

JOSEPH, Sarah 1988: *Political Theory and Power*, Leiden et al.: E. J. Brill.

JUDT, Tony 2000: The White House & the World, *The New York Review of Books* XLVII:20 (Dec. 21), 98–99.

KANT, Immanuel 1784: Idee zu einer allgemeinen Geschichte in weltbürgerlicher Absicht, AA VIII, 15–32.

KATZ, Alfred 1992: *Staatsrecht: Grundkurs im öffentlichen Recht*, 11th ed. Heidelberg: Müller.

KATZ, Elihu and Paul F. LAZARSFELD 1955: *Personal Influence. The Part Played by People in the Flow of Mass Communications*, Glencoe: Free Press.

KELSEN, Hans 1949: *General Theory of Law and State*, Cambridge, Mass.: Harvard University Press.

– 1960: *Reine Rechtslehre*, 2nd ed. Vienna: Deuticke.

KEOHANE, Robert O. and Joseph S. NYE, Jr. 1977: *Power and Interdependence. World Politics in Transition*, Boston: Little, Brown.

– / – 1987: 'Power and Interdependence' revisited, *International Organization* 41:4 (Autumn) 725–753.

KERBO, Harold R. and John A. MCKINSTRY 1995: *Who Rules Japan? The Inner Circles of Economic and Political Power*, Westport, Conn. and London: Praeger.

KERSTING, Wolfgang 1991: Drei Theorien der Macht, *Analyse & Kritik* 13:2 (Dec.) 134–154.

KLIEMT, Hartmut 1981: A Philosophical View of Power, in: Holler (ed.) 1981, 52–64.

KNIGHT, Frank H. 1939: Bertrand Russell on Power, *Ethics* 49 (April) 253–285.

KOHLER-KOCH, Beate 1996: Die Gestaltungsmacht organisierter Interessen, in: M. Jachtenfuchs and B. Kohler-Koch (eds.), *Europäische Integration*, Opladen: Leske + Budrich, 193–222.

KOLLER, Peter 1991: Facetten der Macht, *Analyse & Kritik* 13:2 (Dec.) 107–133.

KOSCHNICK, Wolfgang J. 1992/1993: *Standardwörterbuch für die Sozialwissenschaften, Bd. 2: Deutsch-Englisch / Standard Dictionary of the Social Sciences, Vol. 2: German-English*, Munich et al.: K. G. Saur.

KRAMER, Matthew, Nigel SIMMONDS and Hillel STEINER 1998: *A Debate Over Rights*, Oxford: Oxford University Press.

KRISTJÁNSSON, Kristján 1990: *Freedom as a moral concept*, Ph. D. Diss., University of St. Andrews [published as KRISTJÁNSSON 1996].

– 1992a: For a *Concept* of Negative Liberty – but which *Conception*?, *Journal of Applied Philosophy* 9:2, 221–231.

– 1992b: Freedom, Offers, and Obstacles, *American Philosophical Quarterly* 29, 63–70.

– 1992c: Social Freedom and the Test of Moral Responsibility, *Ethics* 103:1 (Oct.) 104–116.

– 1992d: What is Wrong with Positive Liberty?, *Social Theory and Practice* 18:3 (Fall) 289–310.

– 1992e: 'Constraining Freedom' and 'Exercising Power Over', *International Journal of Moral and Social Studies* 7, 127–138.

– 1993: Moral Concepts: Normativity without Relativity, presented at the 10th Inter-Nordic Philosophical Symposium, Finland (unpublished).

– 1995: Social Concepts: Normativity without Relativity, *Res Publica* 1, 71–89.

– 1996: *Social Freedom*, Oxford: Oxford University Press.

– 1998a: Is There Something Wrong With 'Free Action'?, *Journal of Theoretical Politics* 10:3 (July) 259–273.

– 1998b: Reply to Pettit and Norman, *Journal of Theoretical Politics* 10:3 (July) 291–298.

KÜNSKEN, Rainer 1976: *Eine Untersuchung über Machtbeziehungen mit Hilfe der Spieltheorie*, Ph. D. Diss., Fachbereich Informatik, TU Berlin.

KURAN, Timur 1987: Preference Falsification, Policy Continuity and Collective Conservatism, *Economic Journal* 97 (Sept.) 642–665.

KURAN, Timur 1995: *Private Truths, Public Lies. The Social Consequences of Preference Falsification*, Cambridge, Mass., and London: Harvard University Press.

LAL, Deepak 1998: *Unintended Consequences*, Cambridge, Mass. and London: MIT Press.

LA TORRE, Massimo 1998: *Derecho, Poder y Dominio*, transl. from the Italian by F. Gargallo, Mexico City: Fontamara.

LAPORTA, Francisco J. 1996: Poder y derecho, in: E. Garzón Valdés and F. J. Laporta (eds.), *Enciclopedia Iberoamericana de Filosofía*, Vol. 11: *El derecho y la justicia*, Madrid: Trotta, 441–453.

LARRAÑAGA, Pablo 2000: *El concepto de responsabilidad*, Mexico City: Fontamara.

LASSWELL, Harold D. 1936: *Politics: Who Gets What, When, How*, New York: McGraw-Hill.

LASSWELL, Harold D. and Abraham KAPLAN 1950: *Power and Society. A Framework for Political Inquiry*, New Haven, Conn.: Yale University Press.

LAUMANN, Edward O. and David KNOKE 1987: *The Organizational State. Social Choice in National Policy Domains*, Madison: University of Wisconsin Press.

LEE-CHAI, Annette Y. and John A. BARGH (eds.) 2001: *The Use and Abuse of Power*, Philadelphia, Penn.: Psychology Press.

LENSKI, Gerhard 1986: Power and Privilege, in: Steven Lukes (ed.) 1986, 243–252.

LEWIN, K. 1951: *Field theory in social science*, New York: Harper.

LEWIS, Sir George Cornewall 1898: *Remarks on the Use and Abuse of Some Political Terms*, Oxford: Clarendon.

LIVELY, Jack 1975: The Limits of Exchange Theory, in: B. Barry (ed.) 1975, 1–13.

LOCKE, John 1690: The Epistle to the Reader, in: id., *An Essay Concerning Human Understanding*, ed. A. C. Fraser (1894), reprinted in 2 vols., New York: Dover 1959, vol. I.

LUCAS, J. R. 1993: *Responsibility*, Oxford: Clarendon.

LUHMANN, Niklas 1975: *Macht*, Stuttgart: Enke.

– 2000: *Die Politik der Gesellschaft*, ed. A. Kieserling, Frankfurt/M.: Suhrkamp.

LUKES, Steven 1974: *Power. A Radical View*, Houndmills and London: Macmillan [quoted from the 15th reprint 1991; also reprinted in: Scott 1994/II, 233–268].

– 1979: On the Relativity of Power, in: S. C. Brown (ed.), *Philosophical Disputes in the Social Sciences*, Brighton, Sussex: Harvester, and Atlantic Highlands, N. J.: Humanities Press, 261–274.

– 1986a: Introduction, in: id. (ed.) 1986, 1–18.

– 1991: Power and Authority (1979), in: id., *Moral Conflict and Politics*, Oxford: Clarendon, 83–139.

– (ed.) 1986: *Power*, Oxford: Blackwell.

MCCONNELL, Terrance 2000: *Inalienable Rights*, Oxford: Oxford University Press.

MACINTYRE, Alasdair 1973: The Essential Contestability of Some Social Concepts, *Ethics* 84:1, 1–9.

MACKIE, John L. 1990: *Ethics. Inventing Right and Wrong* (1977), Harmondsworth: Penguin.

MCLACHLAN, Hugh V. 1981: Is 'Power' an Evaluative Concept?, *British Journal of Sociology* 32, 392–410 [reprinted in: Scott 1994/II, 308–324].

MANN, Michael 1986: *The Sources of Social Power*, Vol. I: *A History of Power from the Beginning to A. D. 1760*. Cambridge: Cambridge University Press.

– 1993: *The Sources of Social Power*, Vol. II: *The Rise of Classes and Nation-States, 1760-1914*. Cambridge: Cambridge University Press.

MARCH, James G. 1957: Measurement Concepts in the Theory of Influence, *Journal of Politics* 19, 202–226.

MARGALIT, Avishai 1981: Open Texture, in: id (ed.), *Meaning and Use*, Amsterdam: D. Reidel, 141–152.

– 1996: *The Decent Society*, Cambridge, Mass. and London: Harvard University Press.

MASON, Andrew 1990: On Explaining Political Disagreement: the Notion of an Essentially Contested Concept, *Inquiry* 33, 81–98.

– 1993: The notion of an essentially contested concept, in: id., *Explaining political disagreement*, Cambridge: Cambridge University Press, ch. 2.

MEIER, Kurt 1979: *Interesse, Macht und Einfluß. Entwicklung eines begrifflichen Bezugsrahmens und Interpretation einer historischen Epoche*. Meisenheim a. Glan: Hain.

MENDONCA, Daniel 1995: *Exploraciones Normativas. Hacia una Teoría General de las Normas*, Mexico City: Fontamara.

MENDONCA, Daniel, José Juan MORESO and Pablo NAVARRO 1995: Intorno alle norme di competenza, in: Comanducci/Guastini (eds.) 1995, 219–236.

MILL, John Stuart 1992: *Utilitarianism* (1863), in: id., 'On Liberty' and 'Utilitarianism', London: Everyman's Library, 113–172.

MILLER, David 1983: Constraints on Freedom, *Ethics* 94:1 (Oct.) 66–86.

– 1985: Reply to Oppenheim, *Ethics* 95:2 (Jan.) 310–314.

MILLS, Claudia 1998: Choice and Circumstance, *Ethics* 109:1 (Oct.) 154–165.

MOKKEN, R. J. and F. N. STOKMAN 1975: Power and Influence as Political Phenomena, in: B. Barry (ed.) 1975, 33–54.

MORESO, José Juan 1998: *Indeterminacy and Constitutional Interpretation*, transl. by R. Zimmerling, Dordrecht: Kluwer.

MORGENSTERN, Oskar 1973: Spieltheorie als allgemeine Theorie des Machtkonflikts, in: H. K. Schneider and Ch. Watrin (eds.), *Macht und ökonomisches Gesetz. Verhandlungen auf der Tagung des Vereins für Socialpolitik, Gesellschaft für Wirtschafts- und Sozialwissenschaften, in Bonn 1972*, Schriften des Vereins für Socialpolitik, N. F. Bd. 74/I and 74/II, 2 vols. Duncker & Humblot: Berlin, vol. I, 385–402.

MORRISS, Peter 1972: Power in New Haven: a Reassessment of 'Who Governs?', *British Journal of Political Science* 2, 457–465 [reprinted in: Scott 1994, vol. III, 34–42].

– 1987: *Power: A Philosophical Analysis*, Manchester: Manchester University Press.

MOSCOVICI, Serge 1979: *Sozialer Wandel durch Minoritäten*, transl. by A. Hechler, Munich et al.: Urban und Schwarzenberg [orig.: *Social Influence and Social Change*, London: Academic Press 1976].

– 1985: Social Influence and Conformity, in: *Handbook of Social Psychology*, Vol. 2, eds. G. Lindzey and E. Aronson, New York: Random House, 347–412.

MUMFORD, Stephen 1998: *Dispositions*, Oxford: Clarendon.

MÜNCH, R. 1976: *Legitimität und politische Macht*, Opladen: Westdeutscher Verlag.

MURPHY, Jeffrie G. 1994: *Kant: The Philosophy of Right*, Macon, GA.: Mercer University Press [originally published: London and Basingstoke: Macmillan 1970].

MUTZ, Diana C. 1998: *Impersonal Influence. How Perceptions of Mass Collectives Affect Political Attitudes*, Cambridge: Cambridge University Press.

NAGEL, Jack H. 1975: *The Descriptive Analysis of Power*, New Haven, Conn. and London: Yale University Press.

NELSON, Lars-Erik 1998: Democracy for Sale, *New York Review of Books* Vol. XLV, No. 19 (Dec. 3) 8–10.

NORMAN, Wayne J. 1991: Taking 'Free Action' Too Seriously, *Ethics* 101:3 (April) 505–520.

NORTH, Douglass C. 1986: A Neoclassical Theory of the State, in: J. Elster (ed.), *Rational Choice*, Oxford: Basil Blackwell, 248–260.

– 1990: *Institutions, Institutional Change and Economic Performance*, Cambridge: Cambridge University Press.

– 1993: *Economic Performance Through Time, Prize Lecture in Economic Science in memory of Alfred Nobel*, Dec. 9, 1993 (typescript).

NOZICK, Robert 1997: Coercion, in: id., *Socratic Puzzles*, Cambridge, Mass. and London: Harvard University Press, 15–44 and 333–345 [first published in: Sidney Morgenbesser et al. (eds.), *Philosophy, Science, and Method*, New York: St. Martin's Press 1969, 440–472].

OAKESHOTT, Michael J. 1991: Talking Politics (1975), in: id., *'Rationalism in politics' and other essays*, 2nd ed. Indianapolis, Ind.: Liberty Fund, 438–461.

OLSEN, Marvin E. and Martin N. MARGER (eds.) 1993: *Power in Modern Societies*, Boulder, Col., et al.: Westview.

OLSON, Mancur 1982: *The Rise and Decline of Nations*, New Haven: Yale University Press.

– 2000: *Power and Prosperity. Outgrowing Communist and Capitalist Dictatorships*, New York: Basic Books.

O'NEILL, Onora 1991: Which are the offers *you* can't refuse?, in: R. G. Frey and Ch. W. Morris (eds.), *Violence, Terrorism, and Justice*, Cambridge: Cambridge University Press, 170–195 [revised version in: id., *Bounds of Justice*, Cambridge: Cambridge University Press 2000, 81–96].

– 1996: *Towards Justice and Virtue. A Constructive Account of Practical Reasoning*, Cambridge: Cambridge University Press.

OPPENHEIM, Felix E. 1981: *Political Concepts. A Reconstruction*, Oxford: Basil Blackwell.

– 1985: 'Constraints on Freedom' as a descriptive concept, *Ethics* 95:2 (Jan.) 305–309.

– 1995: Social freedom and its parameters, *Journal of Theoretical Politics* 7:4 (Oct.) 403–420.

PARSONS, Talcott 1963: On the Concept of Political Power, *Proceedings of the American Philosophical Society* 107, 232–262 [reprinted in: id., *Sociological Theory and Modern Society*, New York: Free Press and London: Collier-Macmillan 1967, 297–354; and as: Power and the Social System, in: Lukes (ed.) 1986, 94–143].

– 1967: On the Concept of Influence, in: id., *Sociological Theory and Modern Society*, New York: Free Press and London: Collier-Macmillan, 355–382 [first published in: *Public Opinion Quarterly* (Spring 1963)].

PAUL, Thazha Varkey 1994: *Asymmetric Conflicts: War Initiation by Weaker Powers*, Cambridge: Cambridge University Press.

PAULSON, Stanley L. 1988: An Empowerment Theory of Legal Norms, *Ratio Juris* 1:1 (March) 58–72.

– 1990: Toward a Periodization of the Pure Theory of Law, in: L. Gianformaggio (ed.), *Hans Kelsen's Legal Theory: A Diachronic Point of View*, Torino: Giappichelli, 11–47.

PAULSON, Stanley L. and Bonnie LITSCHEWSKI PAULSON (eds.) 1998: *Normativity and Norms. Critical Perspectives on Kelsenian Themes*, Oxford: Oxford University Press.

PETTIT, Philip 1987: Towards a social democratic theory of the state, *Political Studies* 35, 537–551.

– 1989: The Freedom of the City: A Republican Ideal, in: A. Hamlin and id. (eds.), *The Good Polity. Normative Analysis of the State*, Oxford: Basil Blackwell, 141–168.

– 1996: Freedom as Antipower, *Ethics* 106:3 (April 1996) 576–604.

– 1997: *Republicanism. A Theory of Freedom and Government*, Oxford: Clarendon.

– 1998: Comment on Kristjánsson: Actions, Persons and Freedom as Nondomination, *Journal of Theoretical Politics* 10:3 (July) 275–283.

– 2001: *A Theory of Freedom. From the Psychology to the Politics of Agency*, Oxford: Oxford University Press.

– 2003: Agency-Freedom and Option-Freedom, *Journal of Theoretical Politics* 15:4 (Oct.) 387–403.

PHILLIPS, Anne 1995: *The Politics of Presence*, Oxford: Clarendon.

PIERSON, Paul 2000: Increasing Returns, Path Dependence, and the Study of Politics, *American Political Science Review* 94:2 (June) 251–267.

PITKIN, Hanna Fenichel 1988: Are Freedom and Liberty Twins?, *Political Theory* 16:4 (Nov.) 523–552.

PÖRN, Ingmar 1970: *The Logic of Power*, Oxford: Basil Blackwell.

PRZEWORSKI, Adam et al. 1995: *Sustainable Democracy*, Cambridge: Cambridge University Press.

RAVEN, Bertram H. 1965: Social Influence and Power, in: I. D. Steiner and M. Fishbein (eds.), *Current Studies in Social Psychology*, New York: Holt, Rinehart, Winston, 371–382.

– 1990: Political applications of the psychology of interpersonal influence and social power, *Political Psychology* 11, 493–520.

– 1992: A power/interaction model of interpersonal influence: French and Raven thirty years later, *Journal of Social Behaviour and Personality* 7, 217–244.

– 1993: The bases of power: Origins and recent developments, *Journal of Social Issues* 49, 227–251.

– 1999: Influence, power, religion, and the mechanisms of social control, *Journal of Social Issues* 55, 159–186.

RAVEN, Bertram H., Joseph SCHWARZWALD and Meni KOSLOWSKY 1998: Conceptualizing and measuring a power/interaction model of interpersonal influence, *Journal of Applied Social Psychology* 28, 307–322.

RAWLS, John 1971: *A Theory of Justice*, Harvard, Mass.: Harvard University Press.

RAZ, Joseph 1990a: Authority and Justification, in: id. (ed.), *Authority*, Oxford: Basil Blackwell, 115–141 [first published in: *Philosophy & Public Affairs* 14:1 (Winter 1985) 3–29].

– 1990b: *Practical Reason and Norms* (1975), 2nd ed. Princeton, N. J.: Princeton University Press.

READ, James H. 1995: „Our complicated system": James Madison on Power and Liberty, *Political Theory* 23:3 (Aug.) 452–475.

REDONDO, María Cristina 1999: *Reasons for Action and the Law*, transl. by R. Zimmerling, Dordrecht: Kluwer.

REICH, Robert B. 1997: *Locked in the Cabinet*, New York: Knopf.

RIKER, William H. 1986: *The Art of Political Manipulation*, New Haven and London: Yale University Press.

RIPSTEIN, Arthur 2004: Authority and Coercion, *Philosophy & Public Affairs* 32:1 (Winter), 2–35.

ROBINSON, Richard 1962: *Definition* (1954), Oxford: Clarendon.

RORTY, Amelie Oksenberg 1992: Power and Powers: A Dialogue Between Buff and Rebuff, in: Wartenberg (ed.) 1992, 1–13.

ROSS, Alf 1958: *On Law and Justice*, London: Stevens & Sons.

– 1971: 'He could have acted otherwise', in: A. J. Merkl (ed.), *Festschrift für Hans Kelsen zum 90. Geburtstag*, Vienna: Deuticke, 242–261.

– 1975: On Guilt, *Responsibility and Punishment*, Berkeley, Calif.: University of California Press.

ROTHGEB, John M., Jr. 1992: *Defining Power. Influence and Force in the Contemporary International System*, New York: St. Martin's Press.

RÖTTGERS, Kurt 1990: *Spuren der Macht. Begriffsgeschichte und Systematik*, Freiburg/Munich: Karl Alber.

RUBEN, David-Hillel 1990: *Explaining Explanation*, London: Routledge.

RUITER, Dick W. P. 1993: *Institutional Legal Facts. Legal Powers and their Effects*, Dordrecht: Kluwer.

– 1994: Economic and Legal Institutionalism: What Can They Learn From Each Other?, *Constitutional Political Economy* 5:1 (Winter), 99–115.

RUSSELL, Bertrand 1938: *Power. A New Social Analysis*, reprint London et al.: Unwin 1988 [German transl.: *Macht: Eine sozialkritische Studie*, Zürich: Europa-Verlag 1947].

– 1986: The Forms of Power, in: Lukes (ed.). 1986, 19–27 [from: Russell 1938, ch. 3].

SALAMON, Lester M. and John J. SIEGFRIED 1977: Economic Power and Political Influence: The Impact of Industry Structure on Public Policy, *APSR* 71, 1026–1043.

SCHÄFER, Ingeborg Eleonore 1994: *Bürokratische Macht und demokratische Gesellschaft*, Opladen: Leske + Budrich.

SCHAUER, Frederick 1991: *Playing by the Rules. A Philosophical Examination of Rule-Based Decision-Making in Law and in Life*, Oxford: Clarendon.

SCHÜTT-WETSCHKY, Eberhard 1990: Praxisorientierte Politikwissenschaft. Kritik der empirisch-analytischen und behavioralistischen sowie der traditionellen normativen Position, in: P. Haungs (ed.), *Wissenschaft, Theorie und Philosophie der Politik: Konzepte und Probleme*, Baden-Baden: Nomos 1990, 19–62.

SCOTT, John (ed.) 1994: *Power*, 3 vols., London und New York: Routledge.

SEN, Amartya 1985: Well-Being, Agency and Freedom: The Dewey Lectures 1984, *Journal of Philosophy* 82:4 (April) 169–221.

– 1988: *The Standard of Living*. The Tanner Lectures, Clare Hall, Cambridge, 1985, ed. G. Hawthorn, Cambridge et al.: Cambridge University Press.

– 1999: The Possibility of Social Choice, *American Economic Review* 89:3 (June) 349–378.

SIMON, Herbert A. 1953: Notes on the Observation and Measurement of Power, *Journal of Politics* 15, 500–516 [reprinted in: Bell/Edwards/Wagner (eds.) 1969, 69–78].

– 1957: *Models of Man*, New York: Wiley.

SMITH, Richard A. 1993: Agreement, Defection, and Interest-Group Influence in the U. S. Congress, in: W. H. Riker (ed.), *Agenda Formation*, Ann Arbor: University of Michigan Press, 183–207.

SOROKIN, Pitirim A. and Walter A. LUNDEN 1959: *Power and Morality: Who Shall Guard the Guardians*, Boston: P. Sargent.

STEGMÜLLER, Wolfgang 1983: *Probleme und Resultate der Wissenschaftstheorie und Analytischen Philosophie, Band I: Erklärung – Begründung – Kausalität*, Studienausgabe, Teil A, 2nd ed. Berlin et al.: Springer.

STEINER, Hillel 1974/75: Individual Liberty, *Proceedings of the Aristotelian Society* 75, 33–50.

STOLTE, John F. and Richard M. EMERSON 1977: Structural Inequality: Position and Power in Network Structures, in: R. L. Hamblin and J. A. Kunkel (eds.), *Behav-*

ioral Theory in Sociology. Essays in Honor of George C. Homans, New Brunswick, N. J.: Transaction Books, 117–138.

STOPPINO, Mario 1990: Art. Potere, in: N. Bobbio, N. Matteucci, G. Pasquino (eds.), *Dizionario di Politica*, Torino: TEA, 838–847.

SULLIVAN, Michael P. 1990: *Power in Contemporary International Politics*, Columbia, S. C.: University of South Carolina Press.

SUSKIND, Ron 2004: *The Price of Loyalty. George W. Bush, the White House, and the Education of Paul O'Neill*, New York et al.: Simon & Schuster.

SWANTON, Christine 1985: On the 'Essential Contestedness' of Political Concepts, *Ethics* 95:4 (July) 811–827.

– 1992: *Freedom. A Coherence Theory*, Indianapolis, Ind. and Cambridge: Hackett.

SYMPOSIUM on: Power Indices and the European Union, with contributions by Geoffrey Garrett/George Tsebelis, Jan-Erik Lane/Sven Berg, Manfred Holler/Mika Widgrén, and Bernard Steunenberg/Dieter Schmidtchen/Christian Koboldt, *Journal of Theoretical Politics* 11:3 (July 1999).

TABUCCHI, Antonio 1995: *Sostiene Pereira. Una declaración*, Barcelona: Anagrama.

THIBAUT, J. W. and H. H. KELLEY 1959: *The social psychology of groups*, New York: Wiley.

THOMAS, K. 1978: Power and Autonomy: Further Comments on the Many Faces of Power, *Sociology* 12:2 (May) 332–335.

TOOBY, J. and L. COSMIDES 1990: The Past Explains the Present – Emotional Adaptations and the Structure of Ancestral Environments, *Ethology and Sociobiology* 11, 375–424.

TOULMIN, Stephen 1992: *Cosmopolis: the hidden agenda of modernity*, Chicago, Ill.: University of Chicago Press.

TRENCHARD, John and Thomas GORDON 1995: *Cato's Letters, or Essays on Liberty, Civil and Religious, and Other Important Subjects (1720-23)*, edited and annotated by R. Hamowy, 2 vols., Indianapolis, Ind.: Liberty Fund.

UNIACKE, Suzanne 1994: *Permissible Killing. The Self-Defence Justification of Homicide*, Cambridge: Cambridge University Press.

VANBERG, Viktor 1982: *Markt und Organisation. Individualistische Sozialtheorie und das Problem korporativen Handelns*, Tübingen: J. C. B. Mohr (Paul Siebeck).

VANDEVEER, Donald 1986: *Paternalistic Intervention*, Princeton, N. J.: Princeton University Press.

VERBA, Sidney et al. 1987: *Elites and the Idea of Equality. A Comparison of Japan, Sweden, and the United States*, Cambridge, Mass., and London: Harvard University Press.

WAGNER, R. Harrison 1988: Economic interdependence, bargaining power, and political influence, *International Organization* 42:3 (Summer) 460–483.

WAISMANN, Friedrich 1951: Verifiability, in: A. G. N. Flew (ed.), *Logic and Language: First Series*, Oxford: Basil Blackwell, 117–144.

WARD, Hugh 2004: Pressure Politics. A Game-Theoretical Investigation of Lobbying and the Measurement of Power, *Journal of Theoretical Politics* 16:1 (January), 31–52.

WARTENBERG, Thomas E. (ed.) 1992: *Rethinking Power*, Albany, N. Y.: State University of New York Press.

WEBER, Max 1922: *Wirtschaft und Gesellschaft* (*Grundriß der Sozialökonomik*, vol. III), Tübingen: J. C. B. Mohr (Paul Siebeck).

– 1947: *The Theory of Social and Economic Organization*, ed. T. Parsons, transl. by A. M. Henderson and T. Parsons, New York: Oxford University Press.

– 1978: *Economy and Society*, transl. by G. Roth and C. Wittich, 4th ed. (1st ed. 1956) Berkeley: University of California Press.

WEISS, Ulrich 1995, Macht, in: *Lexikon der Politik*, vol. 1: *Politische Theorien*, eds. D. Nohlen and R.-O. Schulze, Munich: Beck, 305–315.

– 1998, Macht, in: *Lexikon der Politik*, vol. 7: *Politische Begriffe*, eds. D. Nohlen, R.-O. Schulze, S. S. Schüttemeyer, Munich: Beck, 359–361.

WEST, Darrell M. 2000: Checkbook Democracy. How Money Corrupts Political Campaigns, Boston, Mass: Northeastern University Press.

WILDAVSKY, Aaron 1994: Why self-interest means less outside of a social context. Cultural contributions to a theory of rational choices, *Journal of Theoretical Politics* 6:2 (April) 131–159.

WILLEMS, Ulrich 1998: *Entwicklung, Interesse und Moral. Die Entwicklungspolitik der Evangelischen Kirche in Deutschland*, Opladen: Leske + Budrich.

WILLIAMS, Bernard 1993: Possibility, Freedom and Power, in: id., *Shame and Necessity*, Berkeley et al.: University of California Press, 130–167.

WOLFERS, Arnold 1962: *Discord and Collaboration. Essays on International Politics*, Baltimore: Johns Hopkins University Press.

WOLFINGER, Raymond E. 1971: Nondecisions and the Study of Local Politics, *American Political Science Review* 65, 1063–1080 [reprinted in: Scott 1994/II, 111–140].

WOLIN, Sheldon S. 1993: Democracy, Difference, and Re-Cognition, *Political Theory* 21:3 (Aug.) 464–483.

VON WRIGHT, Georg Henrik 1957: *The Logical Problem of Induction*, 2nd, rev. ed. Oxford: Basil Blackwell.

– 1963: *Norm and Action. A Logical Enquiry*, London: Routledge & Kegan Paul, and New York: Humanities Press.

– 1984: *Erklären und Verstehen*, 2nd ed. Königstein/Ts.: Athenäum [orig.: *Explanation and Understanding*, Ithaca, N. Y.: Cornell 1971].

– 1998: Of Human Freedom, in: id., *In the Shadow of Descartes. Essays in the Philosophy of Mind*, Dordrecht et al.: Kluwer, 1–44.

WRONG, Dennis H. 1988: *Power. Its Forms, Bases, and Uses* (1979), 2nd ed., with a new preface, Oxford: Basil Blackwell.

YOUNG, Garry 1996: Committee Gatekeeping and Proposal Power Under Single and Multiple Referral, *Journal of Theoretical Politics* 8:1 (Jan.) 65–78.

ZAGARE, Frank C. 1987: *The Dynamics of Deterrence*, Chicago and London: University of Chicago Press.

ZELGER, Josef 1971: *Zur komparativen und metrischen Explikation des Begriffes 'Macht'*, Ph. D. Diss. Innsbruck.

– 1972: 17 Vorschriften zur Vermeidung der ärgsten Verwirrungen beim Gebrauch des Wortes 'Macht', *Conceptus* 6, 51 ff.

– 1975: *Konzepte zur Messung der Macht*, Berlin: Duncker & Humblot 1975.

ZIMMERLING, Ruth 1991: *Externe Einflüsse auf die Integration von Staaten. Zur politikwissenschaftlichen Theorie regionaler Zusammenschlüsse*, Freiburg and Munich: Karl Alber.

– 1995: Nichts als Fragen. Kritik zu Vittorio Hösle, Macht und Moral, *Ethik und Sozialwissenschaften* 6:3, 424–427.

– 1997: Die Analyse Internationaler Regime in ihrem dritten Jahrzehnt. Einige wohlwollend-kritische Bemerkungen (mimeo).

– 1998: Some remarks on the relationship between legal and social power', *Associations* (Berlin) 2:2, 189–210.

– 2000: Power and freedom. A comment on the conception of Felix Oppenheim', in: W. Krawietz et al. (eds.), *The Reasonable as Rational? On Legal Argumentation and Justification.* Festschrift *for Aulis Aarnio*, Berlin: Duncker & Humblot, 441–460.

INDEX OF NAMES

Law and Philosophy Library

1. E. Bulygin, J.-L. Gardies and I. Niiniluoto (eds.): *Man, Law and Modern Forms of Life*. With an Introduction by M.D. Bayles. 1985 ISBN 90-277-1869-5
2. W. Sadurski: *Giving Desert Its Due*. Social Justice and Legal Theory. 1985 ISBN 90-277-1941-1
3. N. MacCormick and O. Weinberger: *An Institutional Theory of Law*. New Approaches to Legal Positivism. 1986 ISBN 90-277-2079-7
4. A. Aarnio: *The Rational as Reasonable*. A Treatise on Legal Justification. 1987 ISBN 90-277-2276-5
5. M.D. Bayles: *Principles of Law*. A Normative Analysis. 1987 ISBN 90-277-2412-1; Pb: 90-277-2413-X
6. A. Soeteman: *Logic in Law*. Remarks on Logic and Rationality in Normative Reasoning, Especially in Law. 1989 ISBN 0-7923-0042-4
7. C.T. Sistare: *Responsibility and Criminal Liability*. 1989 ISBN 0-7923-0396-2
8. A. Peczenik: *On Law and Reason*. 1989 ISBN 0-7923-0444-6
9. W. Sadurski: *Moral Pluralism and Legal Neutrality*. 1990 ISBN 0-7923-0565-5
10. M.D. Bayles: *Procedural Justice*. Allocating to Individuals. 1990 ISBN 0-7923-0567-1
11. P. Nerhot (ed.): *Law, Interpretation and Reality*. Essays in Epistemology, Hermeneutics and Jurisprudence. 1990 ISBN 0-7923-0593-0
12. A.W. Norrie: *Law, Ideology and Punishment*. Retrieval and Critique of the Liberal Ideal of Criminal Justice. 1991 ISBN 0-7923-1013-6
13. P. Nerhot (ed.): *Legal Knowledge and Analogy*. Fragments of Legal Epistemology, Hermeneutics and Linguistics. 1991 ISBN 0-7923-1065-9
14. O. Weinberger: *Law, Institution and Legal Politics*. Fundamental Problems of Legal Theory and Social Philosophy. 1991 ISBN 0-7923-1143-4
15. J. Wróblewski: *The Judicial Application of Law*. Edited by Z. Bańkowski and N. MacCormick. 1992 ISBN 0-7923-1569-3
16. T. Wilhelmsson: *Critical Studies in Private Law*. A Treatise on Need-Rational Principles in Modern Law. 1992 ISBN 0-7923-1659-2
17. M.D. Bayles: *Hart's Legal Philosophy*. An Examination. 1992 ISBN 0-7923-1981-8
18. D.W.P. Ruiter: *Institutional Legal Facts*. Legal Powers and their Effects. 1993 ISBN 0-7923-2441-2
19. J. Schonsheck: *On Criminalization*. An Essay in the Philosophy of the Criminal Law. 1994 ISBN 0-7923-2663-6
20. R.P. Malloy and J. Evensky (eds.): *Adam Smith and the Philosophy of Law and Economics*. 1994 ISBN 0-7923-2796-9
21. Z. Bańkowski, I. White and U. Hahn (eds.): *Informatics and the Foundations of Legal Reasoning*. 1995 ISBN 0-7923-3455-8
22. E. Lagerspetz: *The Opposite Mirrors*. An Essay on the Conventionalist Theory of Institutions. 1995 ISBN 0-7923-3325-X

Law and Philosophy Library

23. M. van Hees: *Rights and Decisions.* Formal Models of Law and Liberalism. 1995
ISBN 0-7923-3754-9
24. B. Anderson: *"Discovery" in Legal Decision-Making.* 1996 ISBN 0-7923-3981-9
25. S. Urbina: *Reason, Democracy, Society.* A Study on the Basis of Legal Thinking. 1996
ISBN 0-7923-4262-3
26. E. Attwooll: *The Tapestry of the Law.* Scotland, Legal Culture and Legal Theory. 1997
ISBN 0-7923-4310-7
27. J.C. Hage: *Reasoning with Rules.* An Essay on Legal Reasoning and Its Underlying Logic. 1997 ISBN 0-7923-4325-5
28. R.A. Hillman: *The Richness of Contract Law.* An Analysis and Critique of Contemporary Theories of Contract Law. 1997 ISBN 0-7923-4336-0; 0-7923-5063-4 (Pb)
29. C. Wellman: *An Approach to Rights.* Studies in the Philosophy of Law and Morals. 1997
ISBN 0-7923-4467-7
30. B. van Roermund: *Law, Narrative and Reality.* An Essay in Intercepting Politics. 1997
ISBN 0-7923-4621-1
31. I. Ward: *Kantianism, Postmodernism and Critical Legal Thought.* 1997
ISBN 0-7923-4745-5
32. H. Prakken: *Logical Tools for Modelling Legal Argument.* A Study of Defeasible Reasoning in Law. 1997 ISBN 0-7923-4776-5
33. T. May: *Autonomy, Authority and Moral Responsibility.* 1998 ISBN 0-7923-4851-6
34. M. Atienza and J.R. Manero: *A Theory of Legal Sentences.* 1998 ISBN 0-7923-4856-7
35. E.A. Christodoulidis: *Law and Reflexive Politics.* 1998 ISBN 0-7923-4954-7
36. L.M.M. Royakkers: *Extending Deontic Logic for the Formalisation of Legal Rules.* 1998
ISBN 0-7923-4982-2
37. J.J. Moreso: *Legal Indeterminacy and Constitutional Interpretation.* 1998
ISBN 0-7923-5156-8
38. W. Sadurski: *Freedom of Speech and Its Limits.* 1999 ISBN 0-7923-5523-7
39. J. Wolenski (ed.): *Kazimierz Opalek Selected Papers in Legal Philosophy.* 1999
ISBN 0-7923-5732-9
40. H.P. Visser 't Hooft: *Justice to Future Generations and the Environment.* 1999
ISBN 0-7923-5756-6
41. L.J. Wintgens (ed.): *The Law in Philosophical Perspectives.* My Philosophy of Law. 1999
ISBN 0-7923-5796-5
42. A.R. Lodder: *DiaLaw.* On Legal Justification and Dialogical Models of Argumentation. 1999
ISBN 0-7923-5830-9
43. C. Redondo: *Reasons for Action and the Law.* 1999 ISBN 0-7923-5912-7
44. M. Friedman, L. May, K. Parsons and J. Stiff (eds.): *Rights and Reason.* Essays in Honor of Carl Wellman. 2000 ISBN 0-7923-6198-9
45. G.C. Christie: *The Notion of an Ideal Audience in Legal Argument.* 2000 ISBN 0-7923-6283-7

Law and Philosophy Library

46. R.S. Summers: *Essays in Legal Theory*. 2000 ISBN 0-7923-6367-1
47. M. van Hees: *Legal Reductionism and Freedom*. 2000 ISBN 0-7923-6491-0
48. R. Gargarella: *The Scepter of Reason*. Public Discussion and Political Radicalism in the Origins of Constitutionalism. 2000 ISBN 0-7923-6508-9
49. M. Iglesias Vila: *Facing Judicial Discretion*. Legal Knowledge and Right Answers Revisited. 2001 ISBN 0-7923-6778-2
50. M. Kiikeri: *Comparative Legal Reasoning and European Law*. 2001 ISBN 0-7923-6884-3
51. A.J. Menéndez: *Justifying Taxes*. Some Elements for a General Theory of Democratic Tax Law. 2001 ISBN 0-7923-7052-X
52. W.E. Conklin: *The Invisible Origins of Legal Positivism*. A Re-Reading of a Tradition. 2001 ISBN 0-7923-7101-1
53. Z. Bańkowski: *Living Lawfully*. Love in Law and Law in Love. 2001 ISBN 0-7923-7180-1
54. A.N. Shytov: *Conscience and Love in Making Judicial Decisions*. 2001 ISBN 1-4020-0168-1
55. D.W.P. Ruiter: *Legal Institutions*. 2001 ISBN 1-4020-0186-X
56. D.G. Lagier: *The Paradoxes of Action*. (Human Action, Law and Philosophy). 2003 ISBN 1-4020-1661-1

Volumes 56–63 were published by Kluwer Law International.

---

57. G. den Hartogh: *Mutual Expectations*. A Conventionalist Theory of Law. 2002 ISBN 90-411-1796-2
58. W.L. Robison (ed.): *The Legal Essays of Michael Bayles*. 2002 ISBN 90-411-1835-7
59. U. Bindreiter: *Why Grundnorm?* A Treatise on the Implications of Kelsen's Doctrine. 2002 ISBN 90-411-1867-5
60. S. Urbina: *Legal Method and the Rule of Law*. 2002 ISBN 90-411-1870-5
61. M. Baurmann: *The Market of Virtue*. Morality and Commitment in a Liberal Society. 2002 ISBN 90-411-1874-8
62. G. Zanetti: *Political Friendship and the Good Life*. Two Liberal Arguments against Perfectionism. 2002 ISBN 90-411-1881-0
63. W. Sadurski (ed.): *Constitutional Justice, East and West*. 2002 ISBN 90-411-1883-7
64. S. Taekema: *The Concept of Ideals in Legal Theory*. 2003 ISBN 90-411-1971-X
65. J. Raitio: *The Principle of Legal Certainty in EC Law*. 2003 ISBN 1-4020-1217-9
66. E. Santoro: *Individual Autonomy, Freedom and Rights*. 2003 ISBN 1-4020-1404-X
67. D. González Lagier: *The Paradoxes of Action*. (Human Action, Law and Philosophy). 2003 ISBN Hb-1-4020-1661-1
68. R. Zimmerling: *Influence and Power*. Variations on a Messy Theme. 2005 ISBN Hb-1-4020-2986-1

Law and Philosophy Library

69. A. Stranieri and J. Zeleznikow (eds.): *Knowledge Discovery from Legal Databases.* 2005
ISBN 1-4020-3036-3

SPRINGER – DORDRECHT / BOSTON / NEW YORK

Kolibri 360 GmbH
Ferdinand-Jühlke-Straße 7
99095 Erfurt, Deutschland
produktsicherheit@kolibri360.de